J.L. VIVES

DE INSTITUTIONE
FEMINAE CHRISTIANAE

LIBER SECUNDUS
&
LIBER TERTIUS

SELECTED WORKS OF J.L. VIVES

GENERAL EDITOR

C. MATHEEUSSEN

EDITORIAL COMMITTEE

C. Matheeussen, President, Brussels
M. de Schepper, Brussels
C. Fantazzi, Windsor, Canada
E. George, Lubbock, Texas
J. IJsewijn, Louvain

VOLUME VII

J.L. VIVES

DE INSTITUTIONE
FEMINAE CHRISTIANAE

LIBER SECUNDUS
&
LIBER TERTIUS

J. L. VIVES

DE INSTITUTIONE FEMINAE CHRISTIANAE

LIBER SECUNDUS & LIBER TERTIUS

Introduction, Critical Edition, Translation and Notes

EDITED BY

C. FANTAZZI and C. MATHEEUSSEN

TRANSLATED BY

C. FANTAZZI

BRILL
LEIDEN · BOSTON · KÖLN
1998

This book has been published with the financial support from the Ministerie van de Vlaamse Gemeenschap.

This book is published on acid-free paper.

Library of Congress Cataloging-in-Publication Data

Vives, Juan Luis, 1492–1540.
 [De institutione feminae Christianae. English & Latin]
 De institutione feminae Christianae / J.L. Vives ; introduction
critical edition, translation, and notes ; edited by C. Matheeussen,
C. Fantazzi ; translated by C. Fantazzi.
  <v. 1 > ; 25 cm. — (Selected works of J.L. Vives, ISSN
0921–0717 ; v. 6-< >)
 Includes bibliographical references and indexes.
 ISBN 9004106596 (bk. 1 : alk. paper)
  1. Women—Early works to 1800. 2. Women—Education—Early works
to 1800. 3. Virginity—Early works to 1800.   I. Matheeussen,
Constant. II. Fantazzi, Charles. III. Title. IV. Series:
Vives, Juan Luis, 1492–1540. Selections, English & Latin. 1987 ;
v. 6, etc.
B785.V62E5   1987 vol. 6, etc.
[HQ1201]
196'.1 s
[305.4]—DC20   96–9824
                                                      r98

Die Deutsche Bibliothek - CIP-Einheitsaufnahme

Vives, Juan Luis:
[Selected works]
Selected works of J. L. Vives / general ed. C. Matheeussen. – Leiden
; Boston ; Köln ; Brill
Vol. 7. Vives, Juan Luis: De institutione feminae Christianae
Liber secundus & tertius. – 1996

Vives, Juan Luis:
De institutione feminae Christianae : introduction, critical edition,
translation and notes / J. L. Vives. Ed. by C. Fantazzi and C.
Matheeussen. Transl. by C. Fantazzi. Leiden ; Boston ; Köln ; Brill
 (Selected works of J. L. Vives / Juan Luis Vives ; ...)
 Liber secundus & liber tertius 1998
 (Selected works of J. L. Vives / Juan Luis Vives ; Vol. 7)
 ISBN 90–04–11090–9

ISSN 0921-0717
ISBN 90 04 11090 9

PRINTED IN THE NETHERLANDS

CONTENTS

INTRODUCTION[1]

In the second and third books, Vives continued his assiduous work of re-
vision, as he had done in the first one, more by way of addition than sub-
traction, following his usual penchant for amplification. He decided, however, to excise altogether the first introductory chapter, 'De coniugio,' which
upon further reflection he may have found to be too theoretical, in contrast
with his professed intention to write a practical güide.[2] In the course of this
chapter Vives speaks of marriage in glowing terms, calling it 'a most sacred
thing' instituted in paradise. But at the end of his brief eulogy he retracts his
words, leaving it to others to sing the praises of matrimony and returning
to his more humble mode of instruction.[3]

Some of the changes introduced into the revised version seem to stem from
suggestions made in an epistolary exchange between Vives and Erasmus
with regard to the *De institutione*. In a letter of 6 August 1526 (Allen, Ep.
1732, 29–39) Vives reports an opinion to Erasmus concerning the reception
of the *Colloquies*. Among other things he mentions that the *Confabulatio pia*,
staged as a conversation among school boys, seemed rather incongruous to
some of his friends since the young participants discourse upon a serious
subject with a wisdom well beyond their years. Vives avows that he tried
to give some explanation of this lapse but that he really was not convinced
of its propriety himself. Susceptible as he was to such criticism, Erasmus
responded almost a year later (Allen, Ep. 1830, 29 May 1527) that he
was quite disappointed that Vives with his oratorical prowess could not
silence such petty criticism. He then proceeds to give in turn his frank
evaluation of Vives' pronouncements on marriage in the *De institutione*.
First he chides him for his extemporaneous style of writing and lack of
flexibility in his approach to the reader. He then accuses him of being too
hard on women, adding ironically that he hopes he is more gentle with
his own wife. Vives' graphic description of the syphilitic condition of his

---

[1] The introduction to this volume will be brief inasmuch as the genesis, sources and scope
of the entire work as well as the history of the text were discussed in the introduction to Vol. I,
pp. ix–xxvii. The reader is referred to these pages for further information. It is also recom-
mended that the notes to the English translation be read in conjunction with the *apparatus
fontium*.

[2] 'They [i.e., other writers] gave very few precepts or rules of life, thinking it preferable
to exhort their readers to the best conduct and to point the way to the highest examples
rather than give instruction about more lowly matters.' Vol. I, p. 3.

[3] Although Vives removed the introductory chapter from the revised edition, we have
decided to print it in an appendix, with translation and notes, for its intrinsic interest.

father-in-law[4] also draws his criticism, and lastly he thinks that Vives writes too much about his own family.

In his response (Allen, Ep. 1847, 20 July 1527), after some innocuous persiflage Vives launches into a vehement defense of his treatise. He says in part: 'You say that I treat women rather harshly. Do you say this, the one who restored Jerome to us? What is more uncontrollable than a woman? If you relax the reins even a little, there will be no limit or restraint. But Cato will defend me and the *lex Oppia* in that same speech:[5] I did not mention those things by way of example or to exaggerate but because I think that is the way they should live; and doubtless they will if they keep these two things in mind: that they are Christians and that each of them forms one person with her husband. On scabies how much more can be found in Jerome, and with much more explicitness! ... You say that I take delight in mentioning my family, but who does not? Does not Seneca? and Quintilian? and Pliny? Tacitus even dedicated a sizeable volume to the life of his father-in-law. I mention my family three times in all, I think, my mother twice and my mother-in-law once. But I do not refer to her as my mother-in-law nor was she at that time. In her case I was motivated by truth, and in my estimation it was a story worth recording, no less than other stories that have been handed down by other writers. In the case of my mother I am justified by filial piety, and I related her story with restraint, fearing to excite envy and keeping in mind that by nature men are more willing to hear blame than praise.'

When he revised the work many years later Vives, rather than relenting, showed himself even more intransigent. He reinforced his arguments with long quotations from such notoriously misogynistic writers as John Chrysostom and Tertullian. He added a vituperative passage (§§8–9) in the form of a stern reproach addressed to a supposed adulterous woman, whom he harangues on the evil consequences of her actions. There are several additional passages in which he exalts the inherent superiority of the male sex over the weakness and instability of women. Although in his reply to Erasmus he protested that personal references to his family were permissible, it seems that he took Erasmus' admonitions to heart. In the chapter on concord between spouses Vives had given his own parents as models and recounted a few anecdotes about their perfectly harmonious existence together, which

---

[4] In the March 1529 edition of the *Colloquies* Erasmus added '"Αγαμος γάμος sive coniugium impar' (A Marriage in Name Only), a dialogue about the forced marriage of a young bride to an old man afflicted with syphilis. Unlike Vives, who includes the story as an example of perfect wifely devotion, Erasmus in his colloquy delivers a scathing attack on such unions.

[5] The reference is to the speech of Marcus Porcius Cato (Livy, 34, 2–7) in opposition to the repeal of the sumptuary law, *lex Oppia*, passed in 215 B.C.

had almost become proverbial, as he says. In that same passage he expresses his confidence that his mother is already reaping her eternal reward for her upright life and states that he did not wish to talk further of her in a book written for another purpose since it was his intention to write a separate book about her. All this is suppressed in the 1538 edition. He does not mention his father by name and the epithet *sanctissima* used of his mother is omitted. As for writing a book about her, Vives now states simply that 'there will be another occasion to speak of her in detail.'

It is quite remarkable, one might even say disingenuous, that in his letter to Vives Erasmus gives no intimation that he had already published his own treatise on marriage, the *Christiani matrimonii institutio*, dedicated to the same Queen Catherine, in August 1526. In the dedicatory letter to the Queen, dated 15 July 1526 (Allen, Ep. 1727) he confesses that he had promised William Mountjoy, the Queen's chamberlain, more than two years ago, that he would write something on this subject. In corroboration of this we have a previous letter of his from October, 1525 (Allen, Ep. 1624) to Thomas Lupset, to whom he confides that he was prevailed upon by a person of high rank (Mountjoy) to write on the preservation of marriage. Erasmus says that Vives had already done so in his 'Virgin, Wife and Widow' (a rather uncomplimentary manner of referring to the work) and wonders why the Queen is looking for something more. One is led to believe that the Queen was dissatisfied with the treatise written by her compatriot. It is strange, too, that Thomas More, who had himself begun a translation of the *De institutione* and then commissioned it to his servant, William Hyrde, makes no mention of the work.

Erasmus' *Christiani matrimonii institutio* is a thorough-going, detailed examination of the institution of marriage in all its aspects. The book displays a remarkable familiarity with both Roman marriage law and the dictates of the *Decretum* on the subject, together with the voluminous commentaries of the medieval schoolmen. The treatise almost turns into a legal disquisition in the lengthy exposition of the eighteen impediments to marriage. In general Eramus' tone is more lenient and liberal than Vives' strict precepts. He regards the sexual aspect of marriage as an essential element, and not merely a concession to human frailty. He stresses, too, the importance of companionship in the married state.

On widows Vives fills his short treatment with classical examples and traditions, patristic canons and Scriptural quotations in his usual manner. On the subject of remarriage he reluctantly allows it in extreme cases, but not without first prefixing his remarks with a highly rhetorical passage from Jerome's letter to Furia, telling of the manifold disadvantages of a second marriage. Vives once again chooses the harsher doctrines of Jerome over other Church Fathers, in this case Ambrose, whose tract on widows is much milder and more tolerant. He does quote from the rather liberal teachings

of Paul in 1 Timothy, 5, 3–16 but without comment. It must be said that he gives some good practical advice on how widows should conduct themselves. Curiously, Vives' treatment of this estate of a woman's life is less pietistic and more lively than Erasmus' contribution to the subject, the *De vidua christiana* (*On the Christian Widow*), CWE 66, pp. 178–257.

ABBREVIATIONS USED IN THE INTRODUCTION AND NOTES

1. Ancient Latin authors and works are cited according to the *Thesaurus Linguae Latinae*; for Greek authors the abbreviations of *Der Kleine Pauly* are used.

2. Specific editions of classical and humanist authors:

Chadwick = *The Sentences of Sextus* ed. Henry Chadwick, Cambridge, 1959.

Erasm. ad. LB II = Erasmus, *Opera omnia*, ed. Clericus, Lugduni Batavorum, P. van der Aa, 1703–1706, vol. II, *Adagia*.

Nauck = *Tragicorum graecorum fragmenta*, ed. Augustus Nauck. Supplementum adiecit Bruno Snell, Hildesheim, 1964.

Orellius = *Opuscula graecorum veterum sententiosa et moralia*, ed. Io. Conradus Orellius, Leipzig, 1819, vol. I.

PG = *Patrologiae cursus completus. Series graeca*, ed. J.P. Migne, Paris, 1857–1866.

PL = *Patrologiae cursus completus. Series latina*, ed. J.P. Migne, Paris, 1841–1864.

Ross = *Aristotelis fragmenta selecta*, ed. W.D. Ross, Oxford, 1955.

Stob. = *Ioannis Stobaei Florilegium*, ed. Augustus Meinike, Leipzig, 1856.

3. Secondary sources:

Allen = *Opus epistolarum Des. Erasmi Roterodami*, eds. P.S. Allen, H.M. Allen, and H.W. Garrod, Oxford 1906–47, 11 vols.

CWE = Collected Works of Erasmus, Toronto, 1969–

OLD = *Oxford Latin Dictionary*, Oxford, 1983.

SIGLA

H = Vives, *De institutione foeminae Christianae*, Antverpiae, apud Michaelem Hillenium Hoochstratanum, 1524.

W = Vives, *De institutione foeminae Christianae*, Basileae, per Robertum Winter, 1538.

W² = Vives, *De officio mariti, De institutione foeminae Christianae, De ingenuorum adolescentum ac puellarum institutione*, Basileae, in officina Roberti Winter, 1540.

B = Vives, *Opera*, Basileae, in aedibus Nic. Episcopii, 1555.

V = Vives, *Opera omnia*, cura Gregorii Maiansii edita, Valentiae Edetanorum, 1782–1790.

Γ = lectiones communes in **WW²BV**.

J. L. VIVES

DE INSTITUTIONE
FEMINAE CHRISTIANAE

LIBER SECUNDUS

IOANNIS LODOVICI VIVIS VALENTINI
DE INSTITUTIONE FEMINAE CHRISTIANAE

LIBER SECUNDUS
QUI EST DE NUPTIS

CAP. I. QUID COGITARE DEBEAT QUAE NUBIT

1. Feminae cum nubit origo connubiorum in mentem revocanda est et leges illius animo ac cogitatione crebro revolvendae; et sic ipsa se parare debet ut tanto mysterio intellecto prius, postmodum satisfaciat. Princeps et Conditor immensi huius operis Deus, postea quam hominem marem in orbem terrarum invexisset, non existimavit congruum esse illum relinqui solum. Itaque sociam illi adiunxit animantem animo ac forma simillimam, quacum versari, sociare sermones, commode ac suaviter degere aetatem posset, postremo esset sobolis procreatio, si liberet. Etenim coniugium non tam ad prolem sufficiendam institutum est quam ad communionem quandam vitae et indissociabilem societatem. Nec maritus nomen est libidinis, sed coniunctionis ad vitae universas actiones. Feminam Deus ad marem deduxit, quod aliud non est quam Deum ipsum nuptiis auctorem conciliatoremque praefuisse. Ideo Christus in Evangelio coniunctos a Deo nominat. Vir ilico ut feminam generis sui conspicatus est, unice illam amare coepit dixitque: 'Hoc nunc os ex ossibus meis et caro ex carne mea. Haec vocabitur virago, quia de viro sumpta est. Propter hanc relinquet homo patrem et matrem et adhaerebit uxori suae, et erunt duo in carnem unam.' Cum in carnem unam dicitur, una caro est intelligenda. Porro caro hominem significat utrumque ex Hebraei sermonis proprietate. Itaque qui prius duo erant homines, conglutinati matrimonio fiunt unus. Hoc est coniugii mysterium

---

1. (illum relinqui solum) *Vulg. gen. 2, 18* // (Christus ... nominat) *Vulg. Matth. 19, 6* // (Hoc ... unam) *Vulg. gen. 2, 23–24* //

1 LODOVICI **H** LUDOVICI **Γ** VALENTINI **HW²** *deest in* **WBV** // **4** QUI ... NUPTIS **H** *deest in* **Γ** // **5** CAP. I. *etc. Caput primum libri secundi aliud invenitur in* **HV**, *quibus in editionibus caput primum nostrae editionis itaque est caput secundum; in hac nostra editione secuti sumus* **WW²B**, *quae non habent illud caput quod invenitur primum in* **HV**; *quod autem caput invenitur in fine huius nostrae editionis (Appendix I).* // **8** postmodum **Γ** postea **H** // **10** existimavit **Γ** putavit **H** // **11** simillimam **Γ** simillimis **H** // **12** commode ac **Γ** *deest in* **H** // **13** postremo **Γ** postremum **H** // **16** ad vitae universas actiones **Γ** affinitatisque **H** // **17** deduxit **Γ** duxit **H** // **23** est intelligenda **Γ** intelligenda est **H**

JUAN LUIS VIVES
ON THE EDUCATION OF THE CHRISTIAN WOMAN

BOOK TWO
WHICH TREATS OF MARRIED WOMEN

CHAPTER 1. WHAT THOUGHTS SHOULD OCCUPY THE MIND
OF A WOMAN WHEN SHE MARRIES

1. When a woman marries she must call to mind the origins of marriage
and frequently go back over its laws in thought and meditation; and she
must so prepare herself that, having first understood this great mystery, she
may fulfill its obligations later. God, the originator and founder of this great
institution, after bringing man into the world, thought it was not fitting
to leave him alone. So he joined to him a living partner, like to him in
mind and body, with whom he could associate, converse and spend his life
suitably and agreeably and finally, provide for the procreation of offspring,
if he so desired. For marriage was instituted not so much for the production
of offspring as for community of life and indissoluble companionship. The
name of 'husband' does not signify the gratification of lust, but a mutual
association in all the activities of life. God brought woman to man, which
means that God himself was the chief author and mediator of marriage.
Therefore Christ in the Gospel refers to them as joined by God. As soon as
man looked upon the female of the species, he began to love her above all
else and said: 'This is now bone of my bone and flesh of my flesh. She shall
be called woman because out of man was she taken. Because of her, man will
leave father and mother and will cleave to his wife and they shall be two in one
flesh.' When he says 'one flesh' it means literally one flesh. Moreover, flesh
means mankind, both male and female, according to the proper meaning of
the Hebrew tongue. Therefore those who were previously two human beings
become one, joined together in matrimony. This is the marvelous mystery

---

1. woman: The Latin word used for 'woman' in the Vulgate in this context is *virago*,
which is from the same root as *vir*, 'man'. This similarity is also present in the original
Hebrew words: *ish and isha*.

   Hebrew tongue: The Hebrew word *basar*, meaning flesh, can also be used generically
to denote the whole human race, male and female.

admirandum: sic copulare coniuges et commiscere ut unum faciat ex duobus; quod et praestitit in Christo et Ecclesia, sicut docet apostolus Paulus.
Hoc nulla vis valeret efficere nisi divina. Necesse est sanctissimam rem esse,
cui sic peculiariter adest Deus.

5   **2.** Quapropter non ad choreas se venire femina aut ad lusus aut ad convivia arbitretur cum huc accedet. Altius ipsi cogitandum est: Deus est auspex, Ecclesia pronuba. Qua de causa, quod tantis auctoribus coniunctum est
et fixum, non sinit Christus a quoquam mortali vel refigi vel dissolvi atque ex
uno duo fieri qui ex duobus facti sunt unum, dicens in Evangelio suo: 'Quod
10   Deus coniunxit, homo ne separet.' Quod si separari nefas est, et nodus ille
non est humanis manibus resolvendus quem constrinxit Deus nec alius debet temptare aperire quod clausum est clave David quam solus habet Agnus
ille immaculatus.

       3. Iam nunc initio sic te, honesta, para, femina, uti eo modo tibi coniun-
15   gas amore quem coniunxit sacramento Deus, ut colligatio facilis tibi ac levis
fiat. Nec solutum aut laxatum optes vinculum, ne te ac comparem tuum in
molestiam inextricabilem perpetuamque miseriam convolvas. Nam magna
pars huiusce rei in tua manu sita est, ut vel pudicitia et modestia et moris
gestione commodo utaris marito et feliciter agatis, aut rursum vitiis animi
20   corporisque duro atque aspero molestiamque et tormentum tibi ac illi fabriceris, ne morte quidem finiendum. Eris quidem perpetuo in pistrino ancilla,
laborabis, trahes molam, plorabis, afflictabis te, exsecraberis diem quo illi
toro iuncta es, exsecraberis illum quo es nata et parentes et consanguineos
et quotquot eiusmodi matrimonio suam operam commodarunt, si maritum
25   tuis vitiis offensum in tui odium impuleris. At vero vives iucundis in aedibus domina, laetaberis, exsultabis, bene precaberis diei quo nupsisti et iis
qui te illi iunxerunt, si tuis virtutibus, modestia, commoditate amabilem te
illi praestiteris. Prudens enim ait Mimus: 'Bona mulier ad virum parendo
imperat.' Plinius Iunior cum uxore uteretur ex animi sententia, vicissim se
30   illi tractabilem ac suavem praeberet, Hispullae, uxoris suae amitae, gratias

---

1. (quod ... Paulus) *Vulg. Eph. 5, 31–32*
       2. (Quod ... separet) *Vulg. Matth. 19, 6; Marc. 10, 9* // (clave David) *Vulg. apoc. 3, 7* //
(Agnus ... immaculatus) *Vulg. apoc. 5, 9; I Pet. 1, 19*
       3. (Bona ... imperat) *Publil. B 108* //

5 Quapropter Γ Itaque **H** // **6** accedet Γ veniet **H** // **7–8** coniunctum est et fixum Γ fixum
et coniunctum est **H** // **8–9** atque ... unum Γ *deest in* **H** // **11** resolvendus Γ solvendus **H**
// **12** est Γ esset **H** // **16** aut laxatum optes vinculum Γ nodum velis **H** // **17** perpetuamque miseriam convolvas Γ conicias perpetuamque miseriam **H** // **19** agatis Γ agas **H**
/ rursum Γ *deest in* **H** // **20** molestiamque ... fabriceris Γ cruciatumque tibi pares **H** //
21 perpetuo **W²BV** perpetua **WH** // **25** impuleris Γ adduxeris **H** / vives Γ eris **H** // **26**
nupsisti Γ nupta es **H** // **27** virtutibus, modestia, commoditate Γ virtutibus et modestia **H**
// **28** Prudens Γ Sapiens **H** // **30** tractabilem Γ mitem **H**

of marriage, that it so joins and unites the two spouses that the two become one, which was true also of Christ and the Church, as the Apostle Paul teaches. No power could bring this about except it were divine. Of necessity this must be a very holy thing since God is present in it in such a special manner.

2. Therefore a woman should not think that she is on her way to dances, amusements and banqueting when she approaches the marriage ceremony, but must think of higher things. God is the sponsor, the Church is the matron of honor. Therefore Christ does not allow that what has been joined and ratified before such witnesses should be undone and dissolved by any mortal, and that those who from two have become one should not become two from being one. For he says in the Gospel: 'What God has joined together, let no man put asunder.' Now if it is a crime to separate them, and if the knot that God has tied cannot be loosed by human hands, then no other should try to open what has been closed with the key of David, which only the immaculate lamb holds in his possession.

3. Right now, from the beginning, good woman, prepare to join to yourself in love the one whom God has joined to you in the sacrament in such a way that the joining may become easy and light for you. Do not wish that the bond be dissolved or loosened, lest you involve yourself and your companion in inextricable trouble and unending misery, for a great part of this lies in your hands. By your chastity, modesty and obedience you can enjoy the pleasant companionship of your husband and you will live happily together or, on the other hand, by your vices of mind and body, you will render him harsh and bitter and create torture and exasperation for you and for him that will not even end with death. You will be a maidservant in eternal drudgery; you will work, pull the millstone, cry, be afflicted, curse the day you were joined to him in the marriage bed, and the day on which you were born, your parents and relatives and whoever else had a hand in arranging such a marriage, if by your vices you offend your husband and inspire his hatred. But you will be mistress of a happy household, you will be happy, exultant, and will bless the day you were married and those who joined you to him if by your virtues, modesty, and compliance you render yourself lovable to him. The wise writer of mimes said 'The good woman by obeying rules her husband.' Pliny the Younger, who had the wife whom he desired and showed himself in turn to be a pliable and agreeable husband, thanked Hispulla, his wife's aunt, in his own name

---

2. sponsor ... matron of honor: Vives uses words from the Roman marriage ceremony: *auspex*, a functionary who originally took the auspices, and *pronuba*, a married woman who conducted the bride to the bridal chamber.

et suo et uxoris agit nomine: 'Ego,' inquit, 'quod illam mihi, illa quod me
sibi dederis, quasi invicem elegeris.'

4. Super haec omnia caput illud connubialium legum primum et haud
scio an solum: 'Erunt duo in hominem unum' cardo est coniugii, vinculum
sanctissimae societatis. In hunc velut scopum si cogitata, dicta, facta mulier
direxerit, rectissime atque integerrime connubii sanctitatem ut tueatur et
conservet optimeque ac beatissime vivat necesse est. Hoc obversari semper
debet animo castae mulieris et probae. Huic legi ut satisfaciat eamque ut
operibus suis exprimat et repraesentet dies ac noctes meditabitur, non ignara nullam ei virtutem defuturam quae legem hanc servarit, ut putet se
unum esse cum marito et ita vivat ut plane unum esse et videatur et sit;
contra, nullam adfuturam ei quae non fuerit.

5. Simillimum hoc est praecepto illi quod se unicum suis tradere saepissime Christus testatus est, ut se mutuo diligerent. Sapientissimus artifex affectuum humanorum non ignorabat quaecumque societas hoc glutine coiret,
ei nullis aliis legibus, edictis, statutis, pactis, conventis opus fore; omnia in
placidissima tranquillitate et concordia futura; nullas rixas, nullas lites, nullas querimonias suborituras. Neque enim aut invidet quis aut irascitur aut
iniuriam facit aut litem movet aut negotium facessit aut anteferri se cupit ei
quem amat, non aliter de illo cogitat ac de se ipso nec minus ei bene cupit
quam sibi, cum et omnia illius sua et vicissim sua omnia illius esse ducat, se
quoque alterum esse illum et hunc esse alterum se. O divini sermonis ado-
randae vires! Plane verbum fecit Dominus abbreviatum; quod ut sapientiam
divinam contineret sic humanam omnem longe antecederet. Tria tantum
verba dixit et quaecumque longissimis orationibus mortales non tam expli-
cant quam explicare balbutie ac infantia sua conantur et laborant, expressit.
Nullam fero aliam coniugiis legem, sola haec sufficit, sola haec quaecumque
vel humanum excogitare ingenium vel mortalis eloqui posset facundia comprehendit. Credat femina non mihi, sed primo nostri generis parenti, Adae,
immo vero pareat Christo iubenti in Evangelio suo ut sint duo in hominem
unum et dicenti: 'Quod Deus coniunxit ...' Nam quae ita vivit ut se ac
maritum rem prorsus unam esse arbitretur, haec absolvit numeros omnes
sanctae uxoris. Liberati eramus scribendi labore ac cura hoc uno Dei praecepto, si tam alte in mentes mulierum penetrasset, ut intelligere id facile, ut

3. (Ego ... elegeris) *Plin. epist. 4, 19*
4. (Erunt ... unum) *Vulg. Matth. 19, 5*
5. (ut ... diligerent) *Vulg. Ioh. 13, 34; 15, 17* // (Quod ... coniunxit) *Vulg. Matth. 19, 6*

5 cogitata **Γ** cogitat **H** // 6–7 tueatur et conservet **Γ** servet **H** // 13–22 Simillimum ...
hunc esse alterum se **Γ** *deest in* **H** // 23–24 Plane ... antecederet **Γ** *deest in* **H** // 26 balbutie
... conantur et **Γ** *deest in* **H** // 30 suo **Γ** Matthei **H** // 31–32 dicenti ... haec **Γ** *deest in* **H**
// 33 scribendi labore ac cura **Γ** labore scribendi **H** // 34 id **Γ** *deest in* **H**

and in that of his wife: 'I, because you gave her to me, and she, because you gave me to her, as if you chose us for each other.'

4. Above all these considerations this is the first and perhaps only law of marriage: 'They shall be two in one flesh.' This is the hinge of marriage, the bond of a most sacred fellowship. If a woman will direct her thoughts, words and deeds to this goal, then it follows of necessity that she will guard and protect the holiness of marriage with honor and integrity and will live an excellent and happy life. This a chaste and honourable woman must always keep before her mind. To fulfill this law and express and manifest it in her works will be her one thought night and day, conscious that no virtue will be lacking to the one who considers herself to be one with her husband and so lives that she both plainly appears to be and is in truth one with him. On the contrary, she who does not do this will be entirely without virtue.

5. This precept is very similar to that which Christ often declared was the only one he left to his disciples, that they should love one another. That most wise artificer of human emotions was not unaware that whatever alliance was fastened together with this glue would not have need of any other laws, edicts, statutes, pacts or agreements. All would proceed in the greatest tranquility and harmony; there would be no quarrels or litigations or complaints. For no one is envious or becomes angry or does harm or causes trouble or brings a lawsuit or wishes to be preferred to the one he loves. She will think of that person as she would of herself and will wish no less good for him than she wishes for herself, since she will consider everything that is his as being hers as well, and that he is her alter ego as she is his. O what force in the divine word, worthy of our total adoration! Obviously the Lord used very concise language, which was instilled with divine wisdom far surpassing all human wisdom. He spoke only three words and gave expression to what mortals cannot explain in the longest speeches but merely labor and try to explain in their infantile stammerings. I propose no other law of marriage; this alone suffices, this alone contains all that human ingenuity can devise or mortal eloquence express. Let women not rely on my word, but believe the first parent of our race, Adam, or rather, let them hearken to the words of Christ in the Gospel, who commands that they be two in one person and says 'What God has joined together ... '" For she who lives in such a way as to be convinced that she and her husband are one in every respect fulfills to perfection all the duties of a holy wife. We would have been spared the labor and care of writing by this one precept of God if it had penetrated so deeply into the minds of women that they would be able and willing to understand it readily, uphold it and put it into practice.

continere atque exsequi possent et vellent. Sed quo haereat fixius radicesque firmiores ducat, multis evolutum et tractatum modis, variis effictum formis ponendum sub oculos docendumque erit quo capi ac teneri queat facilius. Meminerit tamen prudens mulier quaecumque dixerimus illud unum documentum esse, velut hominem eundem saepius mutato cultu.

6. Nuptiarum die (quandoquidem initium hoc est novae vitae, cuius eventus sunt incerti) nihil opus est saltationibus et choreis et strepitu illo compotationum et immoderatae ac proiectae laetitiae, ne contingat quod Sapiens ait: 'Risus dolore miscebitur, et extrema gaudii luctus occupat.' A votis est potius et comprecationibus auspicandum ut is praebeat laetos successus in cuius sunt manu. Cum longum aliquod iter, varium, incertum ineundum est, nemo auloedum accersit et ad saltandum amicos convocat, sed Dei opem implorat, ut bene ac feliciter eveniat quod aggreditur. Quanto id sollicitius et pio magis animo faciendum est die nuptiarum, qui est utrique coniugum vel ad felicitatem vel ad calamitatem natalis! Mira dictu res quam pervertit hominum sensus diabolus, pessimi cuiusque exempli suasor atque instigator, ut quae divinitus sunt nobis tributa contra venenum antidota, iis ipsis tantum nos admisceamus veneni ut plane fiant exitialia, et unde speranda erat salus inde nascatur pernicies! Profitemur in baptismo renuntiare pompis Satanae; nos baptismo ingentem pompam adiunximus. Permissae sunt nuptiae in remedium libidinis, nos effecimus ut nihil esset eis libidinosius. Graviter Chrysostomus conqueritur quod ipso statim nuptiali die tenerae puellae animus tot undique flagitiorum machinis impetatur. Satis nobiscum ageretur praeclare si in tanta tempestate perturbationum rectum tenere possemus clavum mentis nostrae, nedum ut illis afflati atque impulsi ventis salvi veniamus in portum.

CAP. II.   DUO MAXIMA IN MULIERE CONIUGATA

7. Inter coniugatae feminae virtutes duas praestare illam oportet maximas et praeter ceteras eminentes. Quae solae si adsint, coniugia possunt firma, stabilia, perpetua, facilia, levia, dulcia, beata reddere; sin alterutra absit, infirma, gravia, inamabilia, intolerabilia, miserrima. Hae sunt pudicitia et

---

6. (Risus ... occupat) *Vulg. prov. 14, 13* // (Chrysostomus ... impetatur) *Ioh. Chrys. in gen. cap. 29 hom. 56, PG 54, 486–487*

1 possent et vellent Γ possent **H** / radicesque Γ et radices **H** // 2 evolutum Γ volutum **H** // 3 capi ac teneri queat facilius Γ capi melius tenerique possit **H** // **4–5** documentum Γ praeceptum **H** // **6–26** Nuptiarum ... veniamus in portum Γ *deest in* **H** // **28–29** Inter ... eminentes Γ Inter ceteras coniugatae feminae virtutes duas adesse oportet maximas et praestantissimas **H** // **29** sin alterutra Γ si alterum **H**

But in order that it adhere more strongly and have deeper roots I must place it before your eyes developed and elaborated in many ways and given various forms and taught in such a way that it will be more easily grasped and retained. Let the prudent woman remember, however, that whatever we say does not deviate from that one teaching, just as a person remains the same no matter how often he changes his clothes.

6. On the day of the wedding (since this is the beginning of a new life, whose outcome remains uncertain) there is no need of leaping about, round dances, and all that hubbub of drinking and uncontrolled and prolonged gaiety, lest the wise man's words be verified: 'Laughter will be mixed with sadness and grief occupies the last moments of mirth.' Rather they should begin with prayers and supplications that he in whose hands they are may grant them a happy outcome. When it is necessary to set out on a long, varied and uncertain journey, one does not send for a fluteplayer and invite his friends to a dance, but he implores the help of God so that what he is undertaking may turn out well and prosperously. With how much more solicitude and more pious spirit must this be done on the wedding day, which is the birthday of both spouses either for happiness or misfortune! Strange to say how the devil, counsellor and instigator of the worst possible examples, perverts men's senses so that to those antidotes which God has given us against poison we mix in so much poison that they become lethal, and from that source whence salvation was hoped for destruction arises. We profess in baptism to renounce the pomps of Satan and we have added immense pomp to baptism. Marriage was permitted as a remedy for lust and we have made of the wedding day an occasion for unbridled lust. St. John Chrysostom bitterly complains that immediately on the wedding day itself the mind of the young girl is assailed on all sides by the machinations of vice. We would behave well enough if in this storm of perturbations we could keep the rudder of our mind on a straight course, not to say arrive safely in port after being buffeted by these winds.

CHAPTER 2. TWO POINTS OF GREATEST IMPORTANCE
FOR THE MARRIED WOMAN

7. Among the virtues proper to a married woman two must be regarded as the most important, surpassing all others. If these two are present, they can render marriages strong, stable, lasting, easy, light, pleasant, happy. If either of them is absent, they become weak, burdensome, unloving, intolerable and full of misery. These two are chastity and great love for one's

amor in virum summus. Prius illud paterna domo debet afferre, posterius
ingrediens mariti limen sumere ut relictis parentibus, consanguineis, necessariis omnibus, in viro se cuncta illa reperturam non dubitet. In utroque imaginem referet Ecclesiae, quae et castissima est et sinceram fidem tenacissime
5   servat sponso suo Christo, tot intrinsecus petita procis, baptizatis haereticis,
tot extrinsecus oppugnata gentilibus, Agarenis, Iudaeis, numquam tamen
vel minima labe infecta est et in Christo suo omnia sibi bona posita esse et
ducit et sentit. Castitas in marita debet esse maior etiam quam in caelibe;
nam si nunc eam inquinas et violas (quod avertat Deus), vide quam multis
10   uno scelere facis iniuriam, quot irritas adversum te vindices. Laedis primum
duos quibus nihil neque maius neque melius neque carius tibi esse convenit:
Deum, quo auctore estis coniuncti et per cuius numen puritatem tori iurasti;
tum Deo proximum maritum, cui uni dicasti te, in quo omnes omnium caritates et pietates violaris; nam tu es ei quod Eva Adae: filia, soror, socia,
15   uxor.

   8. Adde his alterum te esse itaque perinde est ac si tibi manum intulisses.
Dissolveris maximam omnium coniunctionem, ruperis sanctissimum rerum
humanarum vinculum: fidem, quam multi etiam armatis hostibus datam,
cum certa sui pernicie servaverunt. Tu marito violaris et ei pectori quod
20   carius tibi tuo ipsius esse debuerat. Polluis mundissimam Ecclesiam, quae
in te coniungenda manus suas accommodavit. Dirimis civilem societatem;
violas leges et patriam; caedis amarissimo flagello patrem; verberas matrem,
sorores, fratres, propinquos, affines, necessarios. Es exemplo tuis aequali-
bus ad scelus; inuris notam aeternam generi tuo; et, mater dementissima ac
25   crudelissima, filios tuos in eam adducis necessitatem ut nec de matre audire possint sine pudore nec de patre sine dubitatione. Quocirca et periu-
rio te devincis et sacrilegio, nam per sacramentum et votum corpora vestra
Deo sunt dicata. Tum praeter decus sanguinis transfers hereditates a domi-
nis ad alienos; adducis in periculum fratres ut inceste misceantur sororibus.
30   Quomodo plus peccant aut taetriore facinore se contaminant qui patriam

---

3 cuncta illa reperturam non dubitet Γ omnia inventuram credat **H** // 4 referet **H** refert Γ
/ et sinceram fidem Γ fidemque **H** // 6 Agarenis Γ *deest in* **H** // 7 vel minima labe infecta
Γ corrupta **H** // 8 et ducit et sentit Γ ducit **H** / marita Γ coniugata **H** // 9–10 quam ...
iniuriam Γ quot simul uno flagitio offendis ac laedis **H** // 10 vindices. Laedis Γ vindices.
Tam multi sunt et graves ut inter quosdam delectus vix haberi possit; congeram tibi illos sine
ordine et ante oculos ponam. Laedis **H** // 14 violaris Γ incesta violasti **H** // 16 Adde his
Γ Quid dicam **H** // 16 itaque ... intulisses Γ Quid dicam alterum te esse in quo etiam
desperata mulier perinde est ac si tibi manum intulisses, si te praefocasses aut iugulasses **H**
// 17 Dissolveris Γ Dissolvisti **H** / ruperis Γ rupisti perfida **H** // 19 violaris Γ rupisti **H**
// 22 et patriam Γ et laedis patriam **H** / matrem Γ tristem matrem **H** // 24–25 et, mater
... adducis necessitatem Γ crudelissima mater, adducis filios tuos in eam necessitatem **H** //
26–29 Quocirca ... sororibus Γ *deest in* **H** // 30 taetriore Γmaiore **H**

husband. The first she brings with her from her father's house, the second she assumes when she crosses the threshold of her husband's house, so that after leaving behind parents, relatives and friends, she has no doubt that she will find them all again in her husband. In each of these virtues she reflects the image of the Church, which is both most chaste and tenaciously preserves unshaken faith in its spouse Christ. Though harassed internally by suitors, which is to say, baptized heretics, and attacked externally by pagans, Moors and Jews, it has never been contaminated by the least stain and it believes and senses that all its good is found in its spouse, Christ. Chastity must be greater in a married woman than in an unmarried one, for if you pollute and violate it now (which may God forbid!), see the harm you do to many and how many avengers you incite against you by one wicked deed. In the first place you harm two persons, than whom none should be greater, better or dearer to you: God, by whose authority you were joined and by whose divinity you swore to the purity of the marriage-bed; and after him your husband, next to God, to whom you dedicated yourself and to him alone, in whom you violate all loves and loyalties; for you are to him what Eve was to Adam– daughter, sister, companion and wife.

8. Add to this the fact that he is another self; and so it is as if you laid hands on yourself. You will have dissolved the greatest of bonds, broken the holiest association that exists in human affairs: trust, which many have given even to an armed enemy and kept it although it meant their own certain destruction. You will have broken faith with your husband and that breast which should have been dearer to you than your very self. You contaminate the immaculate Church, which sanctified your union. You destroy civil society; you violate the laws of your country; you lash your father with a bitter scourge; you beat your mother, sisters, brothers, near ones, your kinsmen by marriage, your close friends. You are an example of wicked behavior to your peers; you sear an indelible brand into your family and like a crazed and cruel mother you reduce your children to the point of not being able to hear about their mother without shame or about their father without doubt. You subject yourself to perjury and sacrilege since your bodies are dedicated to God by sacrament and vow. Then besides the defilement brought upon your family you transfer the heredity from its right owner to strangers. You drag your brothers into the danger of having incestual relations with their sisters. What greater sin do they commit or what fouler contamination

evertunt, qui leges et iustitiam tollunt, qui parentes iugulant, qui sacra et profana contemerant ac polluunt?

9. Quos deos quosve homines putas tibi propitios esse posse? Te cives, te leges, te iura humana, te patria, parentes, cognati, liberi, te maritus damnant
5 et puniunt. In te Deus laesam abs te et conculcatam maiestatem suam atrocissime ulciscetur. Et ne sis ignara, mulier: pudicitiam et castitatem habes tu quidem, sed creditam iam et apud fidem tuam depositam commendatamque a viro; quo iniquius est te dare quod alienum est, domino invito, ut ad cetera flagitia furtum etiam adiungas. Lacaena quaedam marita iuveni rem foedam
10 roganti: 'Darem,' inquit, 'si meum peteres; nam quod petis patris erat dum essem virgo, nunc mariti postquam nupsi.' Facete illa quidem et argute, sed ad bonas mulieres commonefaciendas prudenter. Nec minus illa in Insubria commode, quae cum Marfidium maritum suum tenerrime diligeret et amator rem ab ea turpem contenderet idque per vitam et salutem Marfidii:
15 'Atqui Marfidius,' inquit illa, 'mallet centies mori quam id semel a me committi. Quod vero per salutem illius a me requiris ab ipso eodem petito.'

10. Apostolus Paulus Ecclesiam Dei docens inquit: 'Mulier non habet potestatem sui corporis, sed vir.' Quod dictum usque adeo rem omnem turpem taetramque arcere a muliere modo non perditissimis vitae rationibus
20 par est, ut etiam Augustinus ne votum quidem aut institutum continentiae probet in coniugata, nisi probarit vir. Reprehendit Celantiam optimam matrem familias sive Hieronymus sive quis alius qui ad eam scripsit, vir haud dubie doctus et sanctus, quod votum in se suscepisset continentiae perpetuae, marito inconsulto. Ne ad bonum quidem continentiae ius habet in cor-
25 pus suum femina; cogitet quisque ad impudicitiae malum quantum habeat. Vituperatur continentia inscio marito, quid fiet adulterio, invito marito? Audi quibus verbis utitur: 'Sed illud quoque didici, quod me non mediocriter angit ac stimulat, te videlicet tantum hoc bonum continentiae absque consensu et pacto viri servare coepisse, cum hoc apostolica omnino interdicat
30 auctoritas, quae in hac dumtaxat causa non modo uxorem viro, sed etiam

---

9. (Darem ... nupsi) *Plut. mor. 242B*
10. (Mulier ... vir) *Vulg. I Cor. 7, 4* // (Augustinus ... vir) *Aug. bono coniug. 6, PL 40, 377* // (Sed ... duorum) *Hier. epist. 148, 28, PL 22, 1217* //

2 contemerant Γ contemnunt **H** // **7** apud ... depositam Γ *deest in* **H** // **8–9** ut ... adiungas Γ *deest in* **H** // **9** Lacaena quaedam marita Γ Hinc Lacaena illa coniugata **H** // **11** postquam nupsi Γ *deest in* **H** // **12–16** Nec ... petito Γ *deest in* **H** // **19** modo non perditissimis vitae rationibus Γ non perditissima **H** // **20** votum ... continentiae Γ perpetuam quidem continentiam **H** // **22** quis alius **W²BV** quis est alius **HW** // **23** doctus et Γ *deest in* **H** // **23–24** quod votum ... perpetuae Γ quod continentiae perpetuae votum suscepisset **H** // **25** habeat Γ habet **H** // **26** adulterio **HWW²B** adulterium **V** // **27** quod me **HW** *Hier.* quod **W²BV**

do they contract who overthrow their country, do away with laws and justice, slit their parents' throats, defile and adulterate both the sacred and the profane?

9. What gods or what men do you think can be well-disposed towards you? You are condemned and punished by your fellow citizens, the laws, human rights, your country, your parents, your relatives, your children, your husband. God will exact terrible vengeance for the wrong done to his majesty, which you have crushed underfoot. And do not mistake the fact, woman, that modesty and chastity have been entrusted to you, given into your custody and commended to you by your husband. For which reason it is more unjust that you give away what belongs to another without the consent of the owner, so that you add to your other crimes also the crime of theft. A Lacedemonian married woman gave this answer to a young man who asked a base thing of her: 'I would give it if what you asked were mine to give, but what you ask belonged to my father, while I was a young girl, and now belongs to my husband after I was married.' That was a shrewd and clever answer but it was also wise advice for good women. No less apt was the answer of the Insubrian woman, who loved her husband Marfidius tenderly, and when a would-be lover asked a disgraceful thing of her by the life and health of Marfidius, she said: 'But Marfidius would prefer to die a hundred times rather than that I submit once to what you ask of me by his health. Go ask it of him.'

10. The Apostle Paul teaching the Church of God said: 'A woman does not have power over her own body but the husband does.' According to this statement it is right to keep every shameful and lowly thing away from a woman, unless she is completely depraved, to the extent that Augustine even forbids the vow or practice of continence in a married woman unless her husband approves it. In the letter to Celantia, Jerome, or whoever wrote it, undoubtedly a learned and holy man, reprehends her, an exemplary matron, because she had taken a vow of perpetual continence without consulting her husband. A woman does not have the right over her own body even when it comes to the virtue of continence. How much right do you think she has when it is a question of the vice of unchastity? Continence is censured when it is practiced without the knowledge of the husband. What shall we say of adultery entered into against the will of the husband? Listen to the words he employs: 'I have learned also to my great consternation and distress that you have begun to practice this good proposal of continence without the consent and agreement of your husband, although the authority of the Apostle prohibits this categorically, which in this case not only subjects the wife to the husband but also the husband

10. whoever wrote it: The letter is also attributed to Paulinus of Nola. The style does not seem to be that of Jerome.

virum uxoris subiecit potestati. "Uxor," inquit, "sui corporis potestatem non habet, sed vir." Similiter autem: "Vir potestatem non habet sui corporis, sed mulier." Tu vero, quasi oblita foederis nuptialis pactique huius et iuris immemor, inconsulto vovisti Domino castitatem. Sed periculose promittitur
5   quod in alterius potestate est, et, nescio quam sit grata Deo donatio, si unus offerat rem duorum.' Ad hunc modum ille. Quae est concors sacrorum omnium scriptorum sententia. Quod si ille ob rem sanctam, quod iuris ipsius non erat, tam acriter honestissimam matronam obiurgat, quibus usus esset verbis in nefaria, de re foedissima insectanda?

10   **11.** Et ut intelligas quantum et Deus et homines crimen esse adulterium censeant, Christus in Evangelio suo, cum retinendas omnino uxores edixisset nec ullam permisisset divertendi ansam, unicum adulterium excepit. Ferenda igitur temulenta, iracunda, luxuriosa, iners, gulosa, mendax, vaga, valetudinaria, iurgatrix, maledica, fatua, insana; solam licet adulteram eicere.
15 Gravia quidem et reliqua vitia, sed tolerari tamen possunt. At fidem toro non servasse intolerabile est. Homerus inter exsecrationes et diras in viros illam praecipuam ponit: 'Eorum uxores aliis viris misceantur.' Iobus quoque, si insidiatus sit ad ostium amici sui, hoc sibi imprecatur: 'Scortum,' inquit, 'alterius sit uxor mea et super illam incurventur alii.' Videlicet quod id
20 cum matrimonii natura totaque ratione pugnat, quae in mutuo amore sita est. Quo momento alium virum quam legitimum mulier in cor admittit, eodem iis intemperiis ac mariti metu concutitur, ut nihil oderit illo capitalius; numquam occurrit quin expavescat atque exhorreat, tamquam si a Furiis exagitetur ardentibus facibus, ut est in fabulis.

25   **12.** Sunt et alia duo bona quibus connubium donavit natura: proles et res familiaris. Haec quoque polluit ac corrumpit adulterium, quippe sobolem, ut dicebam modo, incertam facit; rem domesticam pessundat. Negligit enim domum mulier adulterio alienata et immemor sui nec fortunas diligere potest eius cuius odit vitam ac ne liberos quidem. Iam quid non concedat
30 ei mulier cui se et pudicitiam suam, hoc est, maxima sua bona, prostituit? Scilicet pecuniam negabit aut regnum aut filiorum mortem, cui non negavit

---

10. (Uxor ... mulier) *Vulg. I Cor. 7, 4*
11. (Christus ... excepit) *Vulg. Matth. 19, 9* // (temulenta ... insana) *Isid. ecc. off. 2, 19, 1, PL 83, 737* // (Eorum ... misceantur) *Hom. Od. 11, 427–428* // (Scortum ... alii) *Vulg. Iob 31, 10*
12. (ut dicebam modo) *inst. fem. Christ. 2, 8* //

6–7 Quae ... sententia Γ *deest in* H // **7** Quod si ille Γ Qui si H // **8** usus esset Γ uteretur H // **12** excepit **HWW²B** excipit **V** // **13** iracunda Γ iracunda, malis moribus **H** / iners Γ *deest in* **H** / mendax Γ *deest in* **H** // **14** valetudinaria Γ *deest in* **H** / fatua, insana Γ *deest in* **H** / eicere Γ repudiare **H** // **15** Gravia Γ Aspera **H** / tolerari tamen **W²BV** tolerari **HW** // **17** praecipuam Γ vel praecipuam **H** / Iobus Γ Iob **H** // **19**–p.16,12 Videlicet ... abiecit Γ *deest in* **H**

to the wife. "The wife," he said, "has no power over her body, but the husband does," and similarly "The husband has no power over his body, but the wife does." But you, oblivious, as it were, of the marriage contract and unmindful of the compact and of the rights entailed, inadvisedly vowed your chastity to God. But it is dangerous to promise what is in the power of another and I do not know how it can be a pleasing gift to God if one offers that which belongs to two.' Such are his words, and this is the unanimous opinion of all the sacred writers. But if he upbraids a respectable matron so harshly for a holy resolution, since it was not in her power, what words would he use to rebuke a wicked woman involved in a disgraceful act?

11. And that you may understand how great an offense adultery is considered to be by God and men, when Christ proclaimed in the Gospel that wives should be kept at all costs and allowed no possibility for divorce, he made the sole exception of adultery. Therefore one must tolerate a wife who is drunk, hot-tempered, extravagant, lazy, gluttonous, lying, fickle, of fragile health, quarrelsome, slanderous, foolish, insane; only the adulteress can be cast out. The other vices are serious, but they can be tolerated; not to keep faith to the marriage-bed, however, cannot be tolerated. Homer among the curses and bad omens that may befall a man says, 'To have a wife who has carnal relations with other men is the worst of all.' Job also says that if he were to lie in wait for a woman at his friend's door, he would call down this imprecation upon his head 'May my wife be the harlot of another man, and may others kneel on top of her.' All of which shows that this vice is totally opposed to the nature of marriage, which is based on mutual love. From the moment a woman admits another man other than her legitimate husband into her heart, she is immediately stricken by those intemperate desires and by fear of her husband so that she hates no one more implacably than him; he can never be present to her without her becoming terrified and shuddering with fear as if she were being hounded by the Furies with their burning torches, as it is recounted in fables.

12. There are two other blessings that nature bestowed upon marriage: offspring and family possessions. These too are defiled and contaminated by adultery, since it creates doubt about the offspring, as I said a little earlier, and it ruins the domestic economy. For a woman who has been estranged by adultery neglects the home and, unmindful of herself, she cannot have any love for the fortunes of the one whose life she hates and not even for her children. What will a woman not grant to the man to whom she has prostituted herself and her chastity, that is, her most precious possessions? No doubt she will deny money or power or the death of her children to the man to whom she did not deny herself and to whom she betrayed her conscience? When Livia, the sister of Germanicus, had surrendered her chastity

semetipsam, cui conscientiam suam prodidit! Livia, Germanici soror, tradita
semel Seiano pudicitia, homini plus aetate media, ignobili, impuro, abnuere
illi non sustinuit Drusi mariti sui, filii Tiberii Caesaris, heredis tanti imperii, iuvenis formosissimi, generosissimi, animosissimi, ad haec liberorum
quos ex eo susceperat, necem, spreta regni certissima spe, excussa pietate
filiorum, non reverita Antoniam matrem et Augustam aviam, gravissimas
saeculi sui matronas, immemor nobilissimi sanguinis, tum patris fratrisque
quos humanum genus de probitate pro diis venerabatur, paratis sub sagacis-
simo et saevissimo socero tormentis, sub quibus et Liviae ipsi et Seiano et
eorum amicis omnibus anima erat (ut evenit) per mille atrocissimas neces
exigenda.

13. Nimirum nihil sibi reservat mulier quae pudicitiam abiecit. Quod
non Christianae tantum sanctae feminae intellexerunt, sed etiam barbarae;
ex quibus fuerunt nonnullae quae pollutae indignas se vita iudicaverunt, ut
Lucretia Collatini uxor, cuius factum ob admirabilem pudicitiae amorem
merito nobilissimum est. Aliae, quae ne castitatis naufragium facerent, se
peremerunt. Captis Athenis a Lysandro, Lacedaemoniorum Rege, imposi-
tisque triginta viris qui civitatem regerent, cum adeo superbe insolenterque
sese gererent ut etiam tyranni appellarentur illuderentque multarum pudicitiae, Nicerati uxor, ne et ipsa eorum libidini servire cogeretur, voluntaria morte se subtraxit. Quid singulas referam? Teutonicorum coniuges
post proelium ad Aquas Sextias, quo C. Marius infinitam eorum multitudinem delevit, Marium oraverunt ut sacris Vestae virginibus dono mitte-
rentur, se non minus quam illas virilis concubitus expertes victuras. Id cum
a ferreo illo C. Marii animo non impetrassent, nocte insequenti laqueis se
omnes praefocarunt.

14. Bello quod Phocensibus cum Thessalis fuit cum Thessali Phocensium
fines cum ingenti exercitu ingressi essent, Daiphantus, summus Phocensium
magistratus, ad populum tulit ut magna et valida coacta manu obviam hostibus prodiretur, pueros vero et senes et coniuges reliquamque imbellem
turbam in secretiorem aliquem locum includerent, magna eodem lignorum
et stipularum congesta vi, ut si victi essent, illi se statim subiecto igne

---

12. (Livia ... exigenda) *Tac. ann. 4, 3*
13. (Captis ... subtraxit) *Hier. adv. Iovin. 1, 44, PL 23, 286* // (Teutonicorum ...
praefocarunt) *Val. Max. 6, 1, 3*
14. (Bello ... redierunt) *Plut. mor. 244B–D* //

---

12 Quod Γ Haec nimirum **H** // **13** etiam barbarae Γ et Gentiles **H** // **14** nonnullae Γ
aliae **H** // **18–19** adeo ... appellarentur Γ superbissime et insolentissime se gererent **H** //
21 subtraxit Γ subduxit **H** // **25** ferreo Γ duro **H** / laqueis Γ laqueo **H** // **26** praefocarunt
Γ suspenderunt **H** // **28** ingenti Γ incredibili **H** // **29** et valida Γ *deest in* **H** // **32** congesta
Γ ingesta **H** / statim Γ *deest in* **H**

to Sejanus, a man well past the prime of life, of low birth and vile character, she could not deny to him the death of her husband, Drusus, son of Tiberius Caesar, heir to a vast empire, a youth of exceptional beauty, nobility and courage. She sacrificed too the children she had from him, spurning the most certain prospects of rule, casting away her children's devotion to her, showing no respect for her mother Antonia or her grandmother Augusta, both of them revered matrons of their time, unmindful of her noble blood, her father and brother, whom the human race venerated as gods for their moral rectitude. In the end torments were made ready under the direction of her shrewd and cruel father-in-law, by which the lives of Livia herself and Sejanus and all their friends would be exacted of them, as indeed it happened, in all manner of violent deaths.

13. Evidently, a woman who has thrown away her chastity makes no provision for her future. Not only holy Christian women were aware of this, but pagan women as well, among whom there were some who when they suffered defilement deemed themselves unworthy of living, like Lucretia, the wife of Collatinus, whose deed, done out of her laudable love of chastity, is justly famous. Others likewise took their lives to preserve their chastity. When Athens was captured by Lysander, king of Sparta, and thirty men were set over the city as rulers, who conducted themselves so haughtily and insolently that they earned the name of tyrants, and made sport of the chastity of many women, the wife of Niceratus committed suicide so that she would not be forced to satisfy their lust. Must I recount single instances? The wives of the Teutones, who after the defeat at Aquae Sextiae at the hands of Caius Marius were slaughtered in great numbers, begged Marius that they be given as a gift to the sacred Vestal Virgins since like them they would live without any carnal relations with men. When the hard-hearted Marius denied their prayers they all hanged themselves on the following night.

14. In the war between the Phocians and the Thessalians, when the Thessalians invaded the land of the Phocians with a huge army, Daiphantus, the chief magistrate among the Phocians, proposed to the people that they gather together in a strong contingent and go out to meet the enemy, but that children, old men, women and all others who could not bear arms should be confined in a hidden place. There they piled up a great supply of wood and straw so that if they were defeated those stationed there would

13. Lysander: After Athens' defeat in the Peloponnesian War Lysander appointed thirty men to run the government. They lasted for only one year, from the spring of 404 B.C. to May, 403 B.C.

Teutones: A Germanic tribe who had migrated to southern France, annihilated by the army of Gaius Marius at Aquae Sextiae (the modern Aix-en-Provence) in 102 B.C.

14. Thessalians: A people from the north of Greece who were always on bad terms with the Phocians and attempted several times to gain control of Delphi, which was in the territory of Phocis. The incident here referred to took place some time before the Persian Wars.

concremarent. Cum frequens populus hoc decerneret, surrexit grandior quidam natu qui sententiam feminarum super ea re sciscitandam censuit. Si
consentirent, ita fieret; sin quid secus, iniquum esset id statuere illis invitis.
Interrogatae sunt mulieres; quae universae, consilio inter se capto, approbare se Daiphanti legem responderunt, quin etiam agere illi gratias maximas
qui optime et civitati prospexisset et saluti suae. Ergo in secretiorem quen-
dam locum ea mente abductae sunt. Phocenses tamen, ut tanta feminarum
pudicitia merebatur, superiores domum e bello redierunt. Damo, Pythagorae filia, rogata quando esset mulier a viro pura: 'A suo,' inquit, 'ilico, ab
alieno numquam.' Et haec quidem praestabant barbarae in tenebris quibus
omnia obscura erant et incerta et quae tantum connubii mysterium ignora-
bant; quo magis erubescendum est Christianis, sanguine Domini redemptis,
baptismo ablutis, doctrina eruditis, luce illustratis!

CAP. III. QUOMODO SE ERGA MARITUM HABEBIT

15. Rem variam admodum et explicatu difficilem de officio uxoris in virum
unico verbo (sicuti paulo antea memoravi) comprehendit Dominus. Recor-
detur mulier quod dudum diximus, unum esse hominem cum marito atque
ea de causa non aliter amet eum ac se ipsam. Docui modo, sed iterandum
est saepe; nam haec est summa virtutum omnium coniugatae mulieris. Hoc
significat, hoc praecipit coniugium: debere mulierem existimare maritum
sibi esse omnia omnibusque caris nominibus unum succedere: patri, matri,
fratribus, sororibus; quod Adam fuit Evae, quod sibi Hectorem esse ait apud
Homerum probissima Andromache:

> Tu mihi, tu solus pater es materque verenda,
> Tu dulcis frater, tu gratus ad omnia coniunx.

Quod si amicitia ex duobus animis unum reddit, quanto id a coniugio verius efficaciusque praestari convenit, quod unum reliquas omnes amicitias

---

14. (Damo ... numquam) *Diog. Laert. 8, 43*
15. (sicuti ... memoravi) *inst. fem. Christ. 2, 4* // (Tu ... coniunx) *Hom. Il. 6, 429–430* //

1 concremarent Γ comburerent H // 3 esset V esse **HWW²B** // 5 quin Γ *deest in* H //
6 Ergo Γ Ita H // 7 ea mente Γ eo fine H // 7–8 ut tanta ... redierunt Γ superiores
redierunt haud dubie meritis mulierum adeo pudicarum H // 8–10 Damo ... numquam
Γ *deest in* H // 10 praestabant barbarae Γ agebant Gentiles H // 15 Rem variam ... virum
Γ Longa res et explicatu difficilis, si singula velim persequi de officio uxoris in virum mira
dictu res H // 16 sicuti ... memoravi Γ *deest in* H / comprehendit Dominus Γ Dominus
comprehendit H // 17 dudum Γ ante H / unum Γ *deest in* H / marito Γ viro H // 17–18
atque ea de causa Γ et proinde H // 18 ipsam H ipsa Γ / Docui modo, sed iterandum
Γ Dixi ante, sed dicendum H // 19 virtutum omnium coniugatae mulieris Γ coniugatae
mulieris virtus H // 23 probissima Γ casta H // 27 unum Γ *deest in* H / amicitias Γ amicitias ac necessitudines H

set it afire and burn themselves to death. When the assembled multitude gave their approval to this plan, an elderly man stood up and expressed the opinion that the women should be consulted in this matter. If they agreed, then it would be done, but if they thought otherwise, it would be unjust to make this decision against their will. The question was put to the women, who, after deliberating among themselves answered that they approved the measure of Daiphantus and indeed were most grateful to him for having provided both for the best interests of the city and for their safety. Therefore they were led off to a more secret place for that purpose. But the Phocians, as this heroic chastity of their wives deserved, returned home from the war victorious. When Damo, the daughter of Pythagoras, was asked when a woman remained undefiled by sexual contact with a man, she answered, 'With my husband instantly, with another never'. Such examples were given by pagan women in the darkness of their ignorance, to whom everything was obscure and uncertain and who knew nothing of the great mystery of marriage. Wherefore Christian women should be all the more ashamed, since they have been redeemed by the blood of the Lord, cleansed by baptism, instructed by the Gospel and illumined by the light divine.

CHAPTER 3.   HOW SHE SHOULD BEHAVE TOWARD HER HUSBAND

15. The married duties of a wife to her husband, difficult to set out in words, were summarized, as I mentioned previously, in one word by Our Lord. Let a woman remember what I said, that she is one person with her husband and for that reason should love him no less than herself. I have said this before, but it must be repeated often, for it is the epitome of all the virtues of a married woman. This is the meaning and lesson of matrimony, that a woman should think that her husband is everything to her and that this one name substitutes for all the other names dear to her–father, mother, brothers, sisters. This is what Adam was to Eve, what the virtuous Andromache said Hector was to her in the passage in Homer:

> Father and mother are you to me,
> Brother and well-beloved spouse.

If friendship between two souls renders them one, how much more truly and effectively must this result from marriage, which far surpasses all other

longissime antecellit? Idcirco non unum modo vel animum vel corpus ex
duobus facere dicitur, sed unum prorsus hominem. Quare quod vir de
muliere dixit: 'Propter hanc relinquet homo patrem et matrem et adhaerebit
uxori suae,' hoc feminam dicere ac sentire etiam maiore de causa et ra-
5   tione convenit, quoniam, etsi ex duobus factus sit unus, mulier tamen filia
est viri et imbecillior eoque defensione illius eget. Et marito deserta, sola,
nuda, obnoxia iniuriae est; marito comes, ubicumque sit, patriam, domum,
lares, parentes, necessarios, opes secum habet; cuius rei exempla sunt permulta.
10   **16.** Hypsicratea, Mithridatis Regis Ponti uxor, quae virili cultu maritum
profligatum fugientemque quocumque per solitudines latebras quaereret secuta est, ibi regnum, ibi opes et patriam sese inventuram duxit ubicumque
esset maritus. Quod profecto maximum dolorum lenimentum et tantorum
malorum solacium Mithridati fuit. Flaccilla Novium Priscum et Egnatia Ma-
15   ximilla Glitionem Gallum; utraque maritum in exilium comitata est, ingentium opum iactura, quod Urbe et Italia decessissent. Sed viros sibi suos universa illa quae in patria reliquerant superare ac copiosissime repraesentare
arbitrabantur, ideo maxima gloria apud omnes fuere. Non minore Turia,
quae Q. Lucretium maritum a triumviris proscriptum inter cameram et tec-
20   tum cubiculi, una conscia ancilla, ab imminenti exitio non sine magno suo
periculo tutum praestitit. Et Sulpicia, Lentuli uxor, quae cum a Tullia matre diligentissime custodiretur ne virum a triumviris proscriptum sequeretur,
famulari veste sumpta, cum duabus ancillis et totidem servis ad eum clandes-
tina fuga pervenit nec recusavit se ipsa proscribere, ut ei fides sua in coniuge
25   proscripto constaret.
          17. Fuerunt multae quae maluerint ipsae subire discrimen quam viros
suos. Uxor Fernandi Gonzalii, Castellae Comitis, cum Rex Germanicae Le-
gionis, quae urbs est in Hispania Asturiensi, maritum in custodia teneret,
ipsa velut visendi gratia ad carcerem venit viroque persuasit ut cultu secum

---

15. (Propter ... suae) *Vulg. gen. 2, 4*
16. (Hypsicratea ... fuit) *Val. Max. 4, 6, ext. 2* // (Flaccilla ... fuere) *Tac. ann. 15, 71* //
(Turia ... praestitit) *Val. Max. 6, 7, 2* // (Sulpicia ... constaret) *Val. Max. 6, 7, 3*

---

1 unum Γ virum **H** // **4–5** maiore ... convenit Γ maiore ratione oportet **H** // **6** eoque
defensione illius Γ itaque eius defensione **H** // **8** secum Γ *deest in* **H** // **8–9** exempla sunt
permulta Γ exemplum est **H** // **11** fugientemque Γ et fugientem **H** // **12** sese inventuram
duxit Γ esse rata **H** // **13** esset Γ *deest in* **H** // **14** Novium **H** Nonium Γ // **16** decesissent Γ
decederent **H** // **17** reliquerant Γ relinquerent **H** // **17–18** ac copiosissime repraesentare
Γ *deest in* **H** // **18** ideo Γ idcirco **H**

friendships? Therefore it is said that wedlock does not make just one mind or one body of two, but one person in every respect. Wherefore, what the man said of the woman: 'For her sake a man shall leave father and mother and cleave to his wife', should be said with all the more reason by the woman since, even if one is created out of two, the woman is still the daughter of the man and weaker, and for that reason needs his protection. And when she is bereft of her husband she is alone, naked, exposed to harm. As the companion of her husband, wherever he is, there she has a country, home, hearth, parents, close friends and wealth. Examples of this abound.

16. Hypsicratea, wife of Mithridates, king of Pontus, followed her husband in male disguise when he was defeated and put to flight, wherever he sought refuge, even in the most remote solitude. She considered that wherever her husband was, there she would find her kingdom, her riches and her country, which was of the greatest comfort and solace to Mithridates in his many misfortunes. Flaccilla followed her husband Novius Priscus into exile and Egnatia Maximilla followed Glitio Gallus with a loss of great wealth because they had to leave Rome and Italy. But they were persuaded that their husbands surpassed and more than compensated for everything they had left behind in their native country. For this reason they acquired great glory in the eyes of all. No less glory accrued to Turia who hid her husband, who had been proscribed by the triumvirs, between the ceiling and the roof of her bedroom, with the complicity of a handmaid, thus saving him from imminent death at great peril to her own life. And Sulpicia, wife of Lentulus, who was diligently guarded by her mother Tullia so that she would not follow her husband, who had been proscribed by the triumvirs, put on the guise of a servant and with two female and male servants reached him after a clandestine flight, not hesitating to exile herself in order to demonstrate her fidelity to an exiled spouse.

17. There were many women who preferred to endure danger themselves rather than that their husbands should do so. When Fernán González, Count of Castille, was being held in custody by the king of León, a city in the Asturias, his wife came to the prison pretending to pay him a visit, and

16. Mithridates: Mithridates VI Eupator Dionysus (120–63 B.C.), greatest of the Hellenistic kings of that name, ruler of Pontus in Asia Minor, a formidable enemy of Rome in the 1st cent. B.C. The story of Hypsicratea is a favorite one in the lives of famous women, including those written by Boccaccio and Christine de Pisan.

Flaccilla: Novius Priscus was a friend of Seneca and was probably exiled for that reason. Egnatia Maximilla was mistress of a great fortune, which was confiscated when her husband was exiled. The pair returned to Rome after the death of Nero.

17. Fernán González: (c.915–970), a legendary figure who secured the independence of Castille from León and fought against the Moors. *El poema de Fernán González*, composed c.1260, recounts his exploits. The story of his rescue by Doña Sancha is told in *La leyenda de Fernán González*, ed. Evaristo Correa Calderón (Madrid, 1964) p. 267.

commutato se subduceret ac ipsam ibi relinqueret in casum periculi; quod et fecit. Rex admiratus mulieris pietatem, precatus tales sibi suisque liberis coniuges, illam marito remisit. Ex eadem gente illa quae Roberto Britanniae Regi nupta, cum maritus in expeditione adversum Syrios plagam in brachio accepisset luculentam gladio venenato rediissetque in patriam nec sanitati reddi posset nisi pus illud virulentum alicuius ore exsugeretur, Rexque, certissimum illi parari exitium intelligens quicumque id muneris obiisset, neminem eiusmodi discrimini obicere sustineret, ipsa noctu solutis vulneris fasciis, primum inscio marito, post etiam connivente, exsugens et paulatim exspuens, venenum omne elicuit plagamque medicis praebuit facillime curandam. O quam doleo, si qua est fides, non tenere me tantae matronae nomen, dignissimae quae eloquentissimis encomiis celebraretur! Nec tacitum tamen est. Nam in actis Hispaniae legitur, ni fallor, quae Rodericus Toletanus Archiepiscopus conscripsit, unde ego aliquando in libros meos cum honestissima mentione transferam.

18. Tyrrheni cum frequentes ex insula sua Lacedaemonem migrassent venissentque Lacedaemoniis in suspicionem tamquam res novas molirentur, omnes custodiae publicae traditi et capitali supplicio addicti sunt. Uxores eorum, impetrato a custodibus ad viros ingressu tantum salutandi et consolandi gratia, vestes cum viris permutarunt. Hi vero capite obvoluto, ut illarum mos erat, carcere elapsi sunt eo loci feminis relictis; quas mox cum liberis omnibusque bonis recuperavere, iniecto Lacedaemoniis terrore, quod Taygetam montem ceu arcem occuparant. Huius tam praeclari facinoris Valerius Maximus et Plutarchus meminerunt. Cum Acastus, Peliae filius, sorores suas ad mortem expeteret quod illae patrem suum occidissent, tametsi imprudentes (nam revocare ad vigorem iuventae voluerant), Alcestis una illarum apud Admetum virum erat. Hunc Acastus cepit et necaturum

---

18. (Tyrrheni ... occuparant) *Val. Max. 4, 6, ext. 3; Plut. mor. 247B–C* // (Acastus ... servaret) *Hier. adv. Iovin. 1, 45, PL 23, 275; Val. Max. 4, 6, 1*

1 se subduceret ac ipsam Γ fugeret ac se H // **2** mulieris pietatem Γ caritatem uxoris H // **3** Ex **HWW**[2] Et **BV** / Roberto Γ cuidam H // **6** virulentum alicuius ore exsugeretur Γ et virus exsugeretur H // **7** exitium intelligens Γ periculum videns H // **9–10** exsugens et paulatim exspuens Γ sugens paulatim et exspuens H // **13** ni fallor Γ *deest in* H // **17–18** tamquam res novas molirentur Γ res novas moliri H // **21** elapsi sunt Γ exierunt H / mox Γ deinde H // **22** recuperavere Γ recepere H / Lacedaemoniis Γ Lacedaemonibus H // **23** quod Γ cum H / occuparant Γ occupassent H // **23–24** Huius ... meminerunt Γ Sic Plutarchus. Idem Valerius Maximus quantum ad factum mulierum attinet H // **24–p.24,3** Cum ... servaret Γ Admetus, Thessaliae Rex, cum eo morbo laboraret ad cuius curam vita alterius esset impendenda, solam Alcestin uxorem invenit, quae libens mortem pro salute viri obiret H

persuaded her husband to change clothes with her and make his escape, and to leave her to face the danger, which he did. The King in admiration of the woman's loyalty and praying for wives like her for himself and his children, sent her back to her husband. Of that same calibre was the wife of Robert, King of England. Her husband in an expedition against the Syrians had sustained a grievous wound in his arm from a poisoned sword and after returning to his native land was not able to have it cured unless someone would suck out the poisonous pus. The King, knowing that anyone who would undertake this task would meet certain death, would not allow anyone to expose himself to such danger. At night his wife undid the bandaging of the wound and at first without her husband's knowledge and then with his permission sucked out the poison and spat it out little by little until she had drawn it all out and rendered the wound easily curable for the physicians. How sorry I am (if this story is to be believed) not to know the name of such a noble matron, worthy to be celebrated with the most eloquent of encomiums! Yet her name has not remained in silence for it is contained, if I am not mistaken, in the chronicles of Spain written by Rodrigo, Archbishop of Toledo, and I shall introduce it into my own writings one day with honorable recognition.

18. When the Etruscans migrated in great numbers to Sparta from their island and aroused suspicion in the Spartans that they were plotting a political uprising, they were all delivered into public custody and condemned to capital punishment. Their wives, obtaining permission from the guards to visit their husbands to greet and console them, changed clothes with them. The men with their heads veiled, as was the custom among Etruscan women, escaped from the prison and left their wives in their place. They later recovered them together with their children and possessions, striking fear into the Spartans since they occupied Mt. Taygetus, making it their citadel. This outstanding deed is recounted by Valerius Maximus and Plutarch. When Acastus, the son of Pelias, wished to put his sisters to death since they had killed their father, albeit unintentionally, for they wanted to restore him to the vigor of youth, one of them, Alcestis, was with her husband, Admetus. Acastus took him captive and threatened to kill him unless he delivered over

---

17. Robert: This may be Robert Curthouse (1054–1134), eldest son of William the Conqueror, who became Duke of Normandy, but failed in his attempt to gain the English crown. He was a heroic warrior during the First Crusade and participated in the siege of Antioch. Many legends survive concerning him, of which this may be one.

Rodrigo: Rodrigo Jiménez de Rada, made Archbishop of Toledo in 1208, died 1247. He wrote a *Historia de rebus Hispaniae* (ed. Juan Fernández Valverde, Turnhout, 1987), translated into Spanish at an early date as *Historia gótica*. The story here related is not to be found in his extant works.

18. wives: In Herodotus' account of this incident (4, 145) the women are Spartans, wives of descendants of the heroes of the *Argo*.

se illum est minatus ni uxorem traderet; ille vero constanter pernegare, cumque non procul abesset quin occideretur, Alcestis ultro est ad mortem profecta ut virum servaret.

19. Fuere quae mortuis maritis superesse non sustinuerunt. Laodamia, ubi nuntium accepisset Protesilaum virum ad Troiam ab Hectore interfectum esse, ipsa se occidit. Paulina, Senecae coniunx, cum marito mori voluit et scissae sunt illi venae; sed a Nerone inhibita est retentaque in vita et obligata brachia pressusque sanguis vel invitae vel ignarae, vixit paucis annis post, ore ac membris ita pallentibus ut ostentui esset corporisque habitu apertissime coniugalem pietatem testante. Demotionis, Areopagitarum Principis, filia virgo, audito Leosthenis sponsi interitu, se ipsa interfecit, affirmans tametsi intacta esset, tamen cum illi toto animo denupsisset, adulteram se fore cuicumque alteri coniungeretur. Vetustissimi scriptores Halcyonem referunt Ceyce marito non passam esse supervivere, ergo in mare se dedisse praecipitem. Addunt fabulae, quae saepenumero vitam nostram instituunt, versos in Halcyones aves, sic caras Thetidi ut quoties nidificent, maxima sit in mari et caelo tranquillitas, idque statis quotannis diebus contingere, qui ea de causa Halcyonii vocentur. Hoc a diis tribui pietati uxoris in coniugem. Iidem perhibent Andromedam Cepheo genitam translatam a Pallade inter sidera, quod maritum Perseum patriae ac parentibus praetulisset. Evadne, funus Capanei coniugis celebrans, in rogum se coniecit, ne vel morte ipsa a carissimo socio separaretur.

20. Caecina Paetus uxorem habuit Arriam. Is cum in armis fuisset, quae mota Scriboniano in Illyrio erant contra Claudium Caesarem, Romam est pertractus. Arria milites oravit ut se ministram darent marito pro famulis quos viro consulari erant relicturi. Quod cum non impetrasset, conducta piscatoria cymbula, magnam navem secuta est Romaeque paucis diebus post mariti supplicium se ipsa interemit, cum superesset ei filia Thraseae nupta,

19. (Laodamia ... occidit) *Hier. adv. Iovin. 1, 45, PL 23, 275* // (Paulina ... testante) *Tac. ann. 15, 63–64* // (Demotionis ... coniungeretur) *Hier. adv. Iovin. 1, 41, PL 23, 271* // (Halcyonem ... coniugem) *Ov. met. 11, 674–748* // (Andromedam ... praetulisset) *Hyg. astr. 2, 11* // (Evadne ... separaretur) *Ov. ars 3, 21*
20. (Caecina ... interemit) *Plin. epist. 3, 16* // (cum ... viro) *Tac. ann. 16, 34* //

7–8 obligata bracchia pressusque Γ dum obligantur brachia et premitur H // **10** apertissime Γ liquido H sustinuisse testante Γ indicaret H // **14** non passam esse supervivere Γ superstitem esse non sustinuisse H // **16** caras Thetidi Γ Thetidi caras H // **19–20** Iidem ... praetulisset Γ *deest in* H // **21–22** ne ... separaretur Γ maritumque comitata est H // **28** supplicium Γ mortem H

his wife. He persisted in refusing almost to the point of being killed when Alcestis freely offered herself to die in order to save her husband's life.

19. There were those who chose not to survive their husband's death. When Laodamia heard the news that her husband Protesilaus had been killed before the walls of Troy by Hector, she killed herself. Paulina, the wife of Seneca, wished to die with her husband and she opened her veins, but she was restrained by Nero and kept alive; her arms were bound up and the blood was staunched either against her will or without her knowing it. She lived a few years longer, her countenance and limbs so pale that the condition of her body gave clear evidence of her conjugal fidelity. When the unmarried daughter of Demotion, prince of the Areopagus, heard of the death of her promised spouse, Leosthenes, she killed herself, declaring that even if she were still a virgin, she was spiritually married to him, and would be committing adultery with whomever else she married. Ancient writers tell the story of Halcyon, who did not allow herself to survive her husband, Ceyx, but plunged headlong into the sea. The fables, which often provide teachings on how to live, add that they were turned into birds called halcyons, who are so endeared to Thetis that whenever they build their nests there is the greatest calm at sea and in the heavens. This occurs on fixed days every year, which for that reason are called the halcyon days. This was the gods' tribute to a wife's fidelity to her husband. The same writers tell us that Andromeda, daughter of Cepheus, was transported by Pallas Athena to the stars, because she had preferred her husband Perseus to her country and her parents. Evadne, assisting at the funeral rites of her husband Capaneus, threw herself upon the pyre so that she would not be separated even in death from her dear spouse.

20. Caecina Paetus had a wife named Arria. When he joined a mutinous rebellion led by Scribonianus in Illyria against the Emperor Claudius, he was brought back a prisoner to Rome. Arria begged the soldiers that they let her minister to her husband's needs instead of the servants that were assigned to him because of his consular rank. When she failed to obtain this request, she hired a small fishing smack, followed the sailing vessel and arriving in Rome a few days after her husband's execution, took her own life, although her daughter was still living, married to Thrasea, a respected and learned

---

19. Laodamia: According to one version of the myth the gods granted to Laodamia that her husband return to the upper world for three hours. After this she died together with him and accompanied him to the underworld.

Leosthenes: Commander of the combined Greek army in the Lamian war, died in the siege of Lamia, 322 B.C.

Capaneus: One of the seven Argive chieftains in the expedition against Thebes. Zeus struck him with a thunderbolt for his blasphemy and impiety.

20. Thrasea: Later on, when Thrasea was also condemned for treason, Arria Minor did not follow her mother's example, but chose to live for the sake of her daughter.

gravissimo temporum illorum et sapientissimo viro. Porcia, Catonis filia, M. Bruti uxor, victo et perempto marito, mori statuit. Ferrum est ablatum, ipsa se prunis ardentibus in os ingestis suffocavit. Panthea, Susii Principis uxor, viro fidem captiva servavit et pro eius salute, universis effusis opibus, oc-
5 cisum quoque in bello voluntaria morte prosecuta est. Iulia, Caesaris dictatoris filia, cum Pompeii Magni mariti sui vestis cruenta domum e campo referretur, suspicata saucium esse virum, exanimis paene concidit. Qua consternatione animi eicere partum immaturum coacta interiit. Postrema eiusdem Pompeii uxor, Cornelia, turpe dicit esse occiso marito posse vel solo
10 dolore non mori. Artemisia, Lydorum Regina, ut litteris traditum est, Mausoli coniugis defuncti cineres potioni aspersos bibisse prae immodico amore fertur, sepulcrum eius viva fieri cupiens.

21. Cammae facinus egregium praetermittendum non est. Id ego totidem Latine referam verbis quot Graece Plutarchus neque enim possem
15 melius. 'Erat,' inquit, 'in Galatia Sinatus et Sinorix, tetrarcharum illius regionis potentissimi et coniuncti sanguine. Sinatus uxorem habebat Cammam nomine, forma quidem et venustate insigni, sed virtute cum primis admiranda. Non enim erat tantum moderata et mariti amans, sed prudens et magnanima, tum etiam propter commoditatem benevolentiamque sub-
20 ditis cara. Accedebat his omnibus claritudo quod Dianae sacerdos esset, quam deam Galatae in praecipua habent veneratione ac cultu, in cuius sacris et pompis Camma sese magnifice admodum gerebat. Huius ergo amore Sinorix captus, cum adducere in suam sententiam nec hortatibus nec vi posset, foedo atque indignissimo facinore Sinatum per dolum interfecit. Nec ita
25 multo post de connubio allocutus est Cammam, versantem in templo circa rem sacram, ferentem mariti necem non lamentabiliter neque abiecte, sed iram prementem in corde, observantem occasionem qua Sinorigis scelus ulcisceretur. Ille autem suppliciter admodum precabatur orationemque adhibebat non omnino indecentem, quod cum ceteris rebus omnibus Sinato
30 esset praestantior, tum quod necem illius non ulla alia de causa nec flagitio suscepisset quam Cammae impulsus amoris impotentia. Mulier autem initio non iracunde abnuebat, deinde paulatim visa est remolliri ac flecti, nam familiares et necessarii ut Sinorigis gratiam captarent, hominis potentissimi, in eandem voluntatem incumbebant suadendo, tundendo et quodammodo

---

20. (Porcia ... suffocavit) *Val. Max. 4, 6, ext. 1; Plut. Brut. 53, 4* // (Panthea ... prosecuta est) *Xen. Kyr. 6, 4, 3; 7, 3, 14; Hier. adv. Iovin. 1, 45, PL 23, 275* // (Iulia ... interiit) *Val. Max. 4, 6, 4* // (Postrema ... mori) *Plut. Pomp. 74, 3* // (Artemisia ... cupiens) *Val. Max. 4, 6, ext. 1*
21. (Erat ... emisit) *Plut. mor. 257F–258C*

1 temporum illorum **Γ** sui saeculi **H** // 5 prosecuta **Γ** secuta **H** // 10 ut ... est **Γ** *deest in* **H** // 13–p.28,21 Cammae ... negligunt **Γ** *deest in* **H**

man of those times. Porcia, the daughter of Cato, wife of Marcus Brutus, was determined to die after her husband had been defeated and killed. They took every weapon away from her, but she put burning coals in her mouth and died of suffocation. Panthea, wife of the King of Susa, kept faith to her husband while he was imprisoned and expending all her resources for his safety, took her own life when he was killed in war. Julia, the daughter of Caesar the dictator, on seeing the bloody garments of her husband, Pompey the Great, brought home from the battlefield, suspecting that her husband was wounded, fell half-dead to the ground. In her state of shock she gave birth prematurely and died. Cornelia, the last wife of that same Pompey, said it was a disgrace not to be able to die of grief alone when one's husband was killed. Artemisia, Queen of the Lydians, as it has been recorded, out of her boundless love, drank the ashes of her dead husband, Mausolus, diluted in a potion, wishing to be his living sepulchre.

21. The extraordinary deed of Camma must not be passed over in silence. I shall reproduce the story in Latin literally from Plutarch's Greek, for I could not improve on his version:

> In Galatia there were two men named Sinatus and Sinorix, the most powerful of the tetrarchs in that region, related by ties of blood. Sinatus had a wife named Camma of exceptional beauty and charm but especially renowned for her exemplary virtue. She was not only modest and devoted to her husband but judicious and generous, and because of her pleasant manner and benevolence was beloved by her subjects. In addition to all these qualities was her fame as a priestess of Diana, a goddess whom the Galatians hold in special reverence and veneration. In her festivities and solemnities Camma stood out for the magnificence of her attire. Sinorix was smitten with love for her, but unable to win her over by persuasion or by force, he slew Sinatus in a foul and treacherous manner. Not long afterwards he spoke to Camma of marriage as she performed her sacred duties in the temple, bearing up with the killing of her husband not in a mournful or abject way, but repressing the anger in her heart and awaiting the opportunity to avenge the crime of Sinorix. He humbly entreated her and resorted to supplications that seemed not altogether inappropriate, protesting that he was superior to Sinatus in material possessions and would never have committed this atrocious murder if he had not been driven to it by his uncontrollable love for Camma. The woman at first refused his advances, without showing anger, then little by little seemed to weaken and give way, for her friends and relatives gave support to his desires, persuading her, dinning it into her ears and almost coercing her since they were eager to gain favor with Sinorix.

Panthea, wife of the King of Susa: Xenophon in his prose romance, the *Cyropaedia*, relates that when her husband, Abradatas, King of Susa, was killed in battle, she sought out his dead body and committed suicide upon it.

Mausolus: King of Caria. At his death in 353 B.C. his wife, Artemisia, had a huge tomb built, the so-called Mausoleum, numbered among the seven wonders of the ancient world.

cogendo illam. Tandem ea cessit accersitque illum ad se in templum, ut consensus et approbatio mutua pactaque connubialia sub teste ac iudice dea celebrarentur; illumque templum ingressum comiter exceptum ad aram deduxit, ubi praelibavit ei ex phiala, cuius ipsa partem hausit prior, alteram partem ei ebibendam porrexit. Inerat autem mulsum veneno temperatum. Ut vero conspicata est eum exhausisse, sustulit clamorem et ante deam provoluta genibus, "Testor te," inquit, "sanctum numen et venerabile, quod huius diei ac temporis causa sustinui Sinato marito meo supervivere, medii huius temporis nullum alium capiens usum ex vita praeter spem solam ultionis; quam ubi sum assecuta, descendo ad virum meum. Tibi vero, mortalium omnium scelestissime atque impiissime, ministri tui sepulcrum parent pro nuptiis et lecto geniali." Haec ubi Sinorix audivit, sentiens iam venenum serpere per vitalia corpusque universum concitare, raedam conscendit ut sese agitaret et commoveret valide, sed iam impos sui in lecticam translatus exspiravit ad vesperum. Camma vero, cum adhuc vitam nocte tota protulisset, postquam mortuum esse illum cognovit, libens laetaque animam emisit.' Sic Plutarchus.

22. Propter has sexus universus feminarum bene audit et iuvat uxores ducere et filias tollere atque in spem bonam educare, sicut e contrario prorsus cum in eas solum intuemur quae femineae virtutis officium vel spernunt vel negligunt. Haec maxima proposui ut saltem mediocria non praestare pudori sit. Quo intolerabilior est illarum inhumana impietas quae perferre valent maritis vel ignominias vel damna vel quid aliud adversi accidere pecuniae causa, cum sit ipsis in arca satis aeris quo eximere eiusmodi calamitatibus viros possent. Etiam si nihil esset, ferre non deberent. O animum quavis fera immaniorem! Et tu sanguinem, tu corpus tuum, te ipsam in marito perpeti potes sic affligi! Nimirum civiles mores legesque quae id tolerant maiorem habuerunt pecuniae rationem quam pietatis ac fidei. Sed haec, ut alia inter nos permulta, relicta ex gentilitate tenacius Christianis adhaeserunt quam lex Christi permittebat; in qua, non dico ab uxore propter virum, sed a Christiano propter Christianum quamlibet ignotum quicquid in arcis conditur vestium et metallorum, quicquid possidemus opum profundendum est. Quocirca sciat mulier quae non etiam ob levissima mariti incommoda vitanda universum semel patrimonium effundit, nec Christianae nec probae nec uxoris nomine dignam esse. Certissimum est signum pudicitiae maritum toto (quod dicitur) pectore amare.

---

22 inhumana Γ crudelis H // 24–25 eiusmodi calamitatibus Γ talibus incommodis H // 25 Etiam ... deberent Γ *deest in* H // 26 quavis Γ omni H // 27 perpeti potes sic affligi Γ sic afflictam potes perpeti H // 32 conditur Γ est H // 32–33 possidemus Γ *deest in* H // 34 incommoda vitanda Γ vitanda incommoda H // 34–35 effundit Γ elargit H // 35–p.30,18 Certissimum ... supervixit Γ *deest in* H

Finally she yielded and summoned him to the temple so that their mutual consent and approval and marriage agreement could be formalized before the goddess as witness and judge. When he entered the temple she received him cordially, led him to the altar and offered him to drink from a cup from which she had already drunk, presenting the rest for him to drink. It contained a drink made from honey and wine mixed with poison. When she saw him quaff the drink, she uttered a loud cry and throwing herself on her knees before the goddess, said: "I invoke you as my witness, holy and venerable deity, that for the sake of this day and this moment I have lived on to survive my husband, making use of this interim period of life for no other reason than the hope of revenge, and now that I have attained it, I descend to my husband. As for you, most wicked and impious of men, let your servants prepare your tomb rather than the nuptial bed." When Sinorix heard this, feeling the poison creep through his vital parts and his whole body shaking, climbed into a chariot so that he could find strength to move his limbs, but already powerless he was placed on a litter and expired as evening drew nigh. Camma prolonged her life through the night and after she learned that he was dead gladly and happily gave up her spirit.

22. Because of women like these the whole female sex has a good reputation and it is a pleasure to marry wives, have daughters and educate them with good hopes, just as we are affected in an entirely opposite way when we observe only those women who either spurn or neglect the duties of female virtue. I have proposed these heroic examples in order to shame those women who do not exhibit at least ordinary acts of virtue. How much more intolerable is the inhuman lack of loyalty of those women who can allow ignominy, harm or any adversity to befall their husbands for the sake of money, although they have enough coin in their coffers to free their husbands from such calamities. Even if they did not have the money, they should not endure it. O soul more ruthless than a wild beast! You can suffer your own blood, your own body, you yourself to be afflicted in this way in the person of your husband! Obviously public customs and the laws which tolerate them gave greater importance to money than to trust and loyalty. But these things and many others that are still among us, the legacy of paganism, have clung more tenaciously to Christians than the law of Christ permitted, according to which not only a wife for her husband, but a Christian for any other Christian, even one unknown to him, should give freely whatever clothes, metals and other possessions are hoarded away in family chests. In this regard a woman who would not spend her entire substance to free her husband from the least discomfort should account herself unworthy of the name of Christian, upright woman or wife. The most sure sign of chastity is to love one's husband with one's whole heart, as the saying goes.

Tanta fuit Agrippina, Germanici uxor, opinione castitatis propter amorem coniugis, ut Tiberius Caesar, cum eam eiusque filios ob odium criminaretur quo illos praetextu aliquo perderet, Neroni, Agrippinae filio, impudicitia obiecta est. Hoc in mulierem cum alia dixisset atrocia ne fingere quidem est ausus.

23. Refertur et a maritis ea gratia ut uxores a quibus amari se compertum habent, ipsi quoque ardentissime redament. Sic Ulysses Circem et Calypso deas sprevisse traditur propter mortalem Penelopem et ad eam per decennale naufragium, per tot aerumnas et discrimina contendisse ac pervenisse. Hector quod Andromachen sciret in se uno sitas omnes habere caritates, ita illam redamavit ut excidium Troiae non tam parentum aut fratrum causa dolere se dixerit quantum uxoris. Non disputo an haec sint fabulae. Certe ad imaginem humanae vitae ab ingeniosissimo vate sunt conficta. Sed in rebus gestis illud a Cicerone, Valerio Maximo, Plinio et aliis refertur Tiberium Gracchum optione proposita utrius vitam servari mallet, suam an Corneliae uxoris cui unice erat carus, cum alterutri omnino existimaret fato defungendum, mori se quam Corneliam maluit. Felix uxor, quae talem virum habuit! Infelix, quae supervixit!

24. Neque vero sic amandus est maritus quemadmodum amicum amamus aut fratrem geminum, ut solum sit amor; plurimum cultus ac reverentiae admistum oportet, plurimum oboedientiae atque obsequii. Non modo mores maiorum atque instituta, sed leges omnes humanae ac divinae, ipsa etiam rerum natura clamat mulierem debere esse subditam viro ac ei parere. In omni animalium genere feminae suis maribus obtemperant, illos assectantur, illis blandiuntur, ab illis castigari se ac verberari patienter ferunt. Et natura docuit fieri id oportere ac decere. Quae natura, uti Aristoteles in libris de Animalibus perhibet, omnium animantium feminis minus nervorum roborisque quam masculis dedit et carnem molliorem et delicatiorem pilum. Tum partes quas ad se tuendum tribuit—ut dentes, cornua, calcaria et cetera id genus—plurimis feminis negavit; quarum viris attribuit, ut cervis et apris. Si quibus autem femellis concessit, eas ipsas partes potiores fecit in maribus, sicut cornua in tauris firmiora quam in vaccis. Quis omnibus

22. (Tanta ... est ausus) *Tac. ann. 5, 3*
23. (Hector ... uxoris) *Hom. Il. 6, 450–454* // (Tiberium Gracchum ... maluit) *Cic. div. 1, 18, 36; Val. Max. 4, 6, 1; Plin. nat. 7, 172*
24. (Aristoteles ... vaccis) *Aristot. hist. an. 5, 11 (538b)*

19 amandus est maritus quemadmodum **Γ** amari velim maritum ut **H** // **20** solum **Γ** solus **H** // **22** atque instituta **Γ** *deest in* **H** // **26** Et natura **Γ** naturaque **H** / id **Γ** *deest in* **H** / Quae **Γ** *deest in* **H** // **28** quam masculis dedit **Γ** dederit quam masculis **H** / delicatiorem pilum **Γ** pilum delicatiorem **H** // **29** ad se tuendum **Γ** velut arma **H** // **30** attribuit **Γ** dedit **H** // **31** autem femellis concessit **Γ** tribuit feminis **H** // **32** firmiora **Γ** robustiora **H** / in **Γ** *deest in* **H**

So renowned was the chastity of Agrippina, wife of Germanicus, for love of her husband that when Tiberius Caesar out of hatred tried to incriminate her and her sons to cause their ruin by whatever pretext, he trumped up the charge of unchastity against her son Nero. He did not dare to make this accusation against her, although he had accused her of other gross offenses.

23. Husbands show gratitude to their wives by whom they know they are loved by loving them in return. Thus it is told that Ulysses spurned the goddesses Circe and Calypso for the love of Penelope, a mere mortal, and wandering the seas for ten years he held course for home and arrived there after many perils and hardships. Hector so loved Andromache in return for her steadfast and undivided love for him that he said that his grief for the fall of Troy was not for the sake of parents or brothers, but for his wife. I am not going to debate whether these are fables or not. What is certain is that they were fashioned by a poet of great genius after the model of human life. But to turn to actual historical occurrences Cicero, Valerius Maximus, Pliny and others relate that when Tiberius Gracchus was asked whose life he would prefer to save, his own or that of his wife Cornelia, whom he fondly loved, aware that one or the other would have to be victims of fate, he preferred to die himself rather than that his wife die. O happy wife, who had such a husband! Unhappy that she survived him!

24. A husband is not to be loved as we love a friend or a twin brother, where only love is required. A great amount of respect and veneration, obedience and compliance must be included. Not only the traditions and institutions of our ancestors, but all laws, human and divine, and nature itself proclaim that a woman must be subject to a man and obey him. In all races of animals the female obeys and follows the male; she fawns upon him and allows herself to be beaten and punished by him, and nature has taught that this is the way things should be. This same nature, as Aristotle demonstrates in his books on *The History of Animals*, has given less muscles and strength to females than to males and a softer flesh and more delicate hair. Likewise it denied many female animals those parts that are more suitable for defense, such as teeth, horns, spurs and the like, as with deer and boar. If it did concede such weapons to the female, it gave stronger ones to the male, as the horns of a bull are stronger than those of a cow. In all of this nature in her

sapientissima natura nos edocuit ad marem spectare propugnationem, ad feminam vero sequi marem suum et sub eius tutela delitescere illique praebere se ipsam morigeram, ut tutius et commodius vivat.

25. Sed nos a beluarum actibus, quibus tamen pudefimus ni antecellamus virtute, ad rationem humanam ascendamus. Quae mulier eo insolentiae atque arrogantiae venerit ut audiens esse nolit dicto mariti, si cogitet illum sibi pro patre, pro matre, pro consanguineis esse omnibus, illi se uni amorem omnem pietatemque reliquorum universorum debere? Haec non cogitat ea mulier demens, quaecumque coniugi non obsequitur, nisi forte nec patri, matri et consanguineis obsequi institerit. Nam si his oboediat, et marito eam oboedire necesse est; in quo iure omni, more, statuto, praecepto naturali, humano, divino cuncta sunt ei posita et collocata. Non est apud homines honoratior mulier quae sibi supra maritum honorem arrogat, sed stultior et magis ridicula. Adde etiam omnibus invisa atque exsecrabilis, tamquam quae sancitas a natura leges conetur invertere, non secus ac miles imperare suo imperatori si postulet aut luna soli praeesse aut bracchium capiti. In coniugio enim, ut in homine, vir est pro animo, mulier pro corpore; illum imperare, hoc servire oportet, si victurus est homo.

26. Declaravit hoc eadem ipsa natura, quae marem finxit gubernationi aptiorem quam feminam; quippe magnis in rebus et in discrimine feminam ita frangit et confundit pavor ut nec ratione uti possit nec iudicio, ut est affectus ille impotentissimus quique omnem consilii usum semel eripiat. Vir animosus est nec tantopere metu concutitur quin facile dispiciat quidnam expediat rebus praesentibus. Ad haec, ut in femina crebriores exsurgunt perturbationes, iudicium est semper affectu aliquo commotum ac proinde minus sibi constat, iactatum tempestatibus affectionum in diversa raptantium, ideo plerumque invalidum atque inefficax. Sapientissime Paulus, ut cetera: 'Caput,' inquit, 'viri Christus; caput mulieris vir.' Truncus est vir et plane mortuus cuius caput non est Christus. Demens et temeraria est mulier cui vir non praeest. Hic iam divina iussa ingredior; quae apud saniores mentes plus legibus, plus humanis omnibus rationibus; plus naturae ipsius voce valere ac posse ius fasque est, quippe natura saepe inflectitur ac depravatur. Deus integerrimus semper idemque ac sui similis persistit et conditor est naturae Deus; quo potior et mentibus nostris venerabilior esse debet fideique certioris.

---

26. (Caput ... vir) *Vulg. I Cor. 11, 3*

1 nos edocuit Γ nobis declaravit **H** // **4–5** antecellamus Γ superemus **H** // **8** universorum Γ *deest in* **H** // **8–9** Haec non cogitat ... obsequitur Γ Haec mulier non cogitat demens quae coniugi morem non gerit **H** // **10** obsequi institerit Γ parituram se dixerit **H** // **11** eam oboedire Γ oboediat **H** // **12** cuncta ... collocata Γ sunt omnia **H** // **14–15** invisa ... invertere Γ exsecranda ceu quae datas a natura leges invertat **H** // **16** postulet Γ cupiat **H** // **19–27** Declaravit ... inefficax Γ *deest in* **H** // **27–28** Sapientissimus Paulus ... vir Γ Vel, ut Paulus dicit: 'Caput mulieris est vir' **H** // **28–30** Truncus ... praeest Γ *deest in* **H** // **31** rationibus **H** *deest in* Γ // **32–34** quippe ... certioris Γ *deest in* **H**

great wisdom has instructed us that the male has the role of defender and the female follows the male and takes refuge under his protection and shows herself obedient to him in order to live more safely and comfortably.

25. But from the actions of beasts, which put us to shame if we do not excel them, let us pass to human reason. What woman has reached that point of arrogance and presumption that she is unwilling to hearken to her husband's word, if she reflects that he takes the place of father, mother and all her kin, that she owes all her love to him alone and all the loyalty due to all others? The mad woman who does not obey her husband does not think of this, unless perhaps she began by not obeying her father, mother and nearest of kin. For if she obeys them, then she must obey her husband, in whose authority everything has been placed by every law, custom, statute, and natural precept, human and divine. A woman does not achieve more honor in the eyes of men by arrogating more honor to herself than is given to her husband, but she becomes more foolish and ridiculous. By the same token, she becomes hated and abominable to all as if she were attempting to invert the laws sanctioned by nature, like a soldier demanding the right to give orders to a general, as if the moon were superior to the sun or the arm to the head. In marriage as in human nature the man stands for the mind, the woman for the body. He must command, she must serve, if man is to live.

26. Nature herself has declared this by making the man more fit for governing than the woman. In great affairs and in moments of crisis the woman is so shaken and confused by fear that she cannot use her reason or judgement since that emotion is uncontrollable and deprives us of all use of discretion. A man is courageous and is not so shaken by fear as not to perceive clearly what is fitting to be done in present circumstances. Moreover, since more frequent perturbations arise in women, her judgement is always influenced by some emotion and it is less consistent, tossed about by the storms of passion that pull it in various directions, so that often it is impotent and ineffectual. With great wisdom, as in other matters, Paul said 'The head of man is Christ, the head of woman is man.' The man who does not have Christ as his head is truncated and completely dead. The woman not subject to a man is reckless and raging. Here I am entering into the divine commandments, which among men of good sense are duly and rightfully more efficacious than all laws, all human reasoning, and the voice of nature itself, since nature is often twisted and perverted. God is always unchanged, always identical and like unto himself, and God is the creator of nature, wherefore in our minds also he should be more powerful, more worthy of respect and firmer trust.

27. Auctor ergo universitatis mundi huius, mundo novo adhuc et rudi, cum generi humano poneret leges, feminae sic statuit: 'Sub viri potestate eris et ipse dominabitur tibi.' In quibus verbis illud est animadversione dignum, quod non solum viro ius et dominium traditur in feminam, sed usus quoque
5 possessionis. Apostolus Paulus, magister Christianae, hoc est divinae sapientiae, mulierem dominari viro non permittit, sed subditam illi esse, idque non uno in loco. Petri, apostolorum Principis, hoc est edictum: 'Mulieres sint subditae viris suis, sicut et sanctae mulieres, sperantes in domino. Sic Sara obediebat Abrahae, dominum eum vocans.' Hieronymus ad hunc modum
10 Celantiae praecipit: 'Servetur in primis viro auctoritas sua totaque a te discat domus quantum illi honoris debeat. Tu illum dominum obsequio tuo, tu magnum illum tua humilitate demonstra, tanto ipsa honoratior futura quanto illum amplius honoraveris. "Caput enim," ut ait Apostolus, "mulieris est vir." Nec aliunde magis reliquum corpus ornatur quam ex capitis digni-
15 tate.' Haec ille.

28. Insipientes feminae non considerant, cum omnis ad se honor ex maritis demanet, se fore inhonoras, si viros habeant quibus praeesse mulieres possint. Ita honorem dum captant amittunt: nam illud statim perdunt unde maximus ad mulieres redit honos, honoratis esse viris coniunctas. Nihil
20 genus, nihil opes, nihil fortuna proderunt; honore carebis, si caruerit vir. At quis honorem poterit habere ei viro cui videat imperare feminam? Contra vero, nihil oberit ignobilitas, nihil paupertas, nihil faciei nulla gratia. Honoraberis si honestetur maritus. Ita nec Orestillam adiuvit vel forma vel genus vel divitiae quo minus contemptui et odio esset scelerati Catilinae
25 coniunx. Nec Saloniae tenuitas nocuit quin cara et admiranda esset populo Romano Censorii Catonis uxor. Sed ut melius parere possis marito et omnia ex eius animi sententia perficere, pernoscendi sunt prius illius mores et consideranda vel fortunae vel naturae condicio. In his multa sunt maritorum genera; omnes quidem amandi, colendi, reverendi omnes, obsequen-
30 dum omnibus, sed non omnes similiter tractandi, ut linea (quod dicunt) alba in lapide albo. Et in maritis puto equidem illud debere usui accommodari

---

27. (Sub ... tibi) *Vulg. gen. 3, 16* // (Apostolus Paulus ... esse) *Vulg. Eph. 5, 22; Col. 3, 18* // (Mulieres ... domino) *Vulg. I Pet. 3, 5–6* // (Servetur ... dignitate) *Hier. epist. 148, 26, PL 22, 1216*
28. (Ita ... coniunx) *Sall. Catil. 15, 2* // (Saloniae ... uxor) *Plut. Cat. 24, 2–3* // (linea ... albo) *Gell. praef. 11* //

1 ergo Γ *deest in* **H** / huius Γ huius Deus **H** // **2** poneret Γ ferret **H** // **3–5** In ... possessionis Γ *deest in* **H** // **6** mulierem dominari viro non Γ mulierem non dominari viro **H** // **9** ad hunc modum Γ ita **H** // **15** ille Γ illae **H** // **16** considerant Γ vident **H** // **18** honorem dum Γ dum honorem **H** // **19** honoratis esse viris coniunctas Γ honorati viri uxores esse **H** // **21** ei Γ *deest in* **H** / imperare feminam Γ feminam imperare **H** // **23** honestetur Γ honoretur **H** // **27** perficere Γ agere **H** / illius Γ mariti **H**

27. The author of this whole fabric of the universe, when the world was still new and inexperienced and he was establishing laws for the human race, said to the woman: 'You shall be under the power of the man, and he shall have dominion over you.' In these words it is worthy of note that not only is man given right and dominion over the woman, but also use and possession. The Apostle Paul, teacher of Christian, that is, divine wisdom, does not permit the woman to have mastery over the man but to be subject to him, and he says this in more than one place. This is the pronouncement of Peter, Prince of the Apostles: 'Let women be subject to their husbands, as were the holy women, hoping in the Lord.' So Sarah obeyed Abraham, calling him lord. Jerome gives these instructions to Celantia: 'First and foremost his authority must be safeguarded, and let the whole household learn from you how much honor is due him. Show him to be master by your obedience, and show him to be great by your humility. You will be so much the more honored as you honor him more. For, as the Apostle said, 'The head of the woman is man' and the rest of the body cannot receive more distinction than from the dignity of the head.

28. Foolish women do not consider that since all honor derives from their husbands they will be without honor if they have husbands whom women can command. Thus while they seek honor, they lose it, since they immediately lose that which gives greatest honor to women, namely, to be wedded to husbands who are honored. Race, wealth, fortune will be of no avail; you will be without honor if your husband is without it. But who can have respect for a man who he sees is ruled by a woman? On the contrary, lowness of birth will be no obstacle, nor will poverty or unbecoming appearance. You will be honored if your husband is given honor. Neither beauty, lineage or riches saved Orestilla from being an object of contempt and hatred as the wife of the wicked Catiline. The penury of Salonia did not prevent her from being loved and admired by the people of Rome as wife of Cato the Censor. But that you may better obey your husband and accomplish everything to his liking you must first be thoroughly acquainted with his character and consider the circumstances of his nature and fortune. In these respects there are many kinds of husbands. All husbands must be loved, respected and revered, all must be obeyed but not all are to be treated in the same way like a white line on a white stone, as the saying goes. I think what Terence said of human life, taking his cue from Plato, can be well adapted

---

28. Catiline: According to the historian Sallust Catiline had his son of a previous marriage killed at Orestilla's wish so that he could marry her.

quod de vita humana dicit ex Platone Terentius: 'Vita,' inquit, 'hominum
perinde est ac si ludas tesseris, ut si quod iactu opus non est evenit, id arte ut
corrigas.' Sic in maritis: si is contigerit ex sententia, gaudendum; honorandus, amandus, sequendus est; sin parum optabilis, arte, si queas, vel emen-
5 dandus vel certe minus reddendus incommodus.

29. Aut igitur maritus erit fortunatus aut infortunatus. Fortunatos nunc
voco quibus aliqua bona contigerunt vel vitae vel corporis vel animi; infor-
tunatos quibus ex aliqua illarum trium partium mala. Fortunati facile uxoribus satisfaciunt, de infortunatis consulendum. Quamquam initio omnium
10 admonendae sunt ne amorem in mariti fortuna potius collocent quam in
marito ipso, alioqui minus firmiter amabunt ac lentius; et si fortuna, ut est
fluxa fere atque inconstans, discesserit, auferet simul secum et amorem. Ne
ament pulchros propter formam, ne divites propter pecuniam, ne magistratus ob dignitatem; aliter enim aegros, pauperes, privatos oderint. Si nacta es
15 doctum virum, haurienda ab eo sancta praecepta; si bonum, proponendus
in exemplum quod aemulere. Quod si sit infortunatus, illa debet in primis
animo occurrere Gnaei Pompeii, magni sine dubio et prudentis viri, ad Corneliam uxorem oratio, quam versibus Lucanus prosecutus est.

30. Victus enim a Caio Caesare Pompeius, cum Lesbum insulam peti-
20 isset ad recipiendam uxorem quam secum fuga abduceret, uxor maritum
conspicata victum in terram semianimis concidit, non tam dolens cecidisse
se quam illum. Pompeius sublatam e terra et sensibus redditam in hanc
sententiam est consolatus: 'Mea Cornelia, uxor, rerum omnium mihi carissima, miror te feminam isto genere natam, sic primo fortunae prostratam
25 ictu. Nunc tibi aperta est via ad immortalem gloriam. Nam materia laudis
in femineo sexu non est eloquentia, non respondere consulentibus de iure,
non bella gerere; unica tantum est, si maritum habeas miserum. Quem si
amaris, si colueris, si nihil miseria offensa, ita ut maritum decet tractaris, omnia te saecula cum ingente laude celebrabunt. Maiori tibi fuerit gloriae quod
30 victum Pompeium amasti quam quod principem populi Romani, ducem
senatus, imperatorem regum. Haec enim facile est cuilibet etiam stultae ac
improbae uxori diligere; amplecti vero miserum, id demum est optimae.
Quocirca hoc ipsum quod victus sum, debes diligere tamquam materiam

28. (ex Platone) *Plat. rep. 604C* // (Vita ... corrigas) *Ter. Ad. 739–741*
30. (mea Cornelia ... supersum) *Lucan. 8, 72–85*

2 evenit Γ evenerit **H** // 4 parum optabilis Γ malus **H** / queas Γ possis **H** // 7 vitae Γ
externa **H** // 9 initio Γ *deest in* **H** // 11 marito ipso Γ ipso marito **H** / ac Γ et **H** // 12 fere
Γ *deest in* **H** // 14 ob dignitatem Γ propter honorem **H** // 15 haurienda **H** hauriendum Γ /
proponendus ... aemulere Γ imitandus **H** // 21 concidit Γ decidit **H** // 23 est consolatus
Γ allocutus fertur **H** // 28–29 omnia ... celebrabunt Γ saecula de te omnia loquentur **H**
// 31 stultae ac Γ *deest in* **H** // 32 diligere Γ amare **H** // 33 debes diligere Γ diligere te
decet **H**

to husbands: 'The life of man is like a game of dice,' he said, 'if what comes out in the throw is not what you needed, correct it by skillful playing.' So with husbands, if you get the one you desired, you should be glad. He is to be honored, loved and followed. If he is not very desirable, you must correct him with skillfulness, if you can, or at least make him less troublesome.

29. Your husband will either be fortunate or unfortunate. By fortunate I mean those blessed with some good, either in their lives, in body or in mind; unfortunate are those who lack any of these three blessings. Fortunate men easily satisfy their wives. Concerning the unfortunate we must take thought. Yet at the beginning of all marriages women should be warned not to put their love in the fortune of the husband but rather in the husband himself. Otherwise their love would be less solid and less enduring and if fortune, which is fleeting and inconstant, were to depart, it would take love away with it at the same time. They should not love handsome men for their beauty, or rich men for their money, or magistrates for their rank, for when they become sick, poor and private citizens they will hate them. If it is your fortune to find a learned man, you should absorb holy precepts from him; if you find a good man you should take good examples from him to emulate. But if your husband is unfortunate, you should call to mind the speech of Gnaeus Pompey, a great and prudent man beyond all doubt, to his wife Cornelia, which Lucan expressed in verse.

30. When Pompey was defeated by Julius Caesar, he set out for the island of Lesbos to meet his wife, whom he was to take with him in his flight. When his wife saw her defeated husband, she fell in a swoon to the ground, not sorrowful that she had fallen, but that he had fallen low. Pompey raised her from the ground and when she had recovered her senses, consoled her in this way: 'My dear wife Cornelia, dearest to me of all things on earth, I marvel that a woman of your lineage should be so prostrated by the first blow of ill-fortune. Now the path to immortal glory is open to you. For the subject of praise in the female sex is not eloquence, nor answering questions about law, nor waging war, but only this, to have a husband who has suffered adversity. If you love and cherish him, if you are not resentful at his ill-fortune but treat him as a husband should be treated, all ages will celebrate your name with immense praise. It will be a greater glory for you to have loved the defeated Pompey than the leader of the Roman people, head of the Senate, and lord of kings. It is easy even for a stupid and dishonest wife to love such things, but to embrace one stricken by misfortune is the mark of an exceptional wife. Therefore you should love me for suffering defeat as

---

30. 'My dear wife Cornelia ... ': Vives' rendering is a free paraphrase of the passage from Lucan.

virtutis tuae; nam si quid tu me vivo defles et desideras, certe illud ipsum quod periit ostendis tibi fuisse carum, non me qui adhuc supersum.'

31. His atque aliis similibus verbis tunc ille utebatur aegram animi refovens. Quae proba matrona tamquam oraculum saepenumero in animo suo volvet, ne se afflictet quod maritus obtigerit infortunatus, ne hac illum de causa oderit, ne contempserit, quin potius si sit pauper, consolandus est unicas opes esse virtutem, adiuvandus honestis artibus, quas illi scias placituras et quas in te noti et necessarii probent quaeque sanctitatem bonae matronae deceant. Vide ne in tam perditam mentem ruas ut velis illum propter pecuniam indecoras artes exercere aut facinus aliquod foedum perpetrare aut ut tu vel delicatius vel affluentius alaris vel cultius ornere vel laxius habites; in summa, ut tibi optime et suavissime sit, illum labores et sudores magnos, etiam discrimina subire. Potius tibi ac melius est secundario tantum pane vesci et turbulentam potare aquam quam maritum cogere non dico vilibus se artibus et sordidis aut labori immodico dedere, verum cuivis exercitio ad quod ipse, invitus quidem, sed accedat tamen, ut morem tibi gerat et domesticas tuas rixas effugiat sitque aliqua domi pax.

32. Maritus sui iuris est et dominus uxoris, non uxor mariti; nec plus a marito contendere uxor debet quam quantum ipso volente libenteque videat se impetraturam. In quo peccant multae, quae maritos importunis suis vocibus flagitando, tundendo, denique odio ad illicitas artes et gravia vel facinora vel flagitia impellunt, ut quaestum faciant, suae gulae ac vanitati, suae superbiae consulentes, non maritis. Quid dicam esse molestas aliquas et inimicas virtutibus coniugum, si has esse rei familiari damnosas videant? Id eo est turpius quod cum femineus sexus tantam prae se ferat pietatem et natura videatur devotior sacris rebus quam virilis, obliviscitur sui et pietatem omnem abicit pecuniae gratia. Has mulieres Sanctae Litterae sub uxoribus Iobi et Tobiae coarguunt, quae insanissimae pietatem et magnas virtutes maritis calamitosis exprobrabant. In quo erant etiam impiae, nedum vecordes, quod non reputarent vel maiores esse opes quae virtutibus parantur vel situm in manu Domini locupletissimum felicissimumque uno momento facere quemcumque velit.

33. Quid opus est aliis tyrannis ad martyrium? Istae irreligiosae non secus persequuntur maritos ob religionem quam apostolos Nero, aut Christianos

---

3–4 aegram animi refovens Γ *deest in* **H** ∥ **8** quaeque Γ et quae **H** ∥ **10** artes exercere Γ exercere artes **H** / perpetrare Γ designare **H** ∥ **13** etiam discrimina Γ *deest in* **H** ∥ **14** turbulentam Γ caenosam **H** ∥ **16** invitus ... tamen Γ non invitus accedat tamen **H** ∥ **17** effugiat Γ vitet **H** / sitque ... pax Γ *deest in* **H** ∥ **20** multae Γ plurimae **H** ∥ **21** denique odio Γ *deest in* **H** ∥ **21–22** gravia ... flagitia Γ atrocia facinora **H** ∥ **24** coniugum Γ maritorum **H** ∥ **25** prae se ferat Γ praeferat **H** ∥ **28** insanissimae pietatem Γ stultissimae religionem **H** ∥ **29** vecordes Γ stultae **H** ∥ **30** reputarent Γ crederent **H** ∥ **33–34** Istae irreligiosae ... religionem Γ istae non secus persequuntur maritos ob religionem, ipsae irreligiosissimae **H**

an occasion to display your virtue, for if you long and mourn for anything while I am alive, you show that you love that which has perished, not me, who am still alive.'

31. These and similar words he used to comfort her sick spirit. A good woman will turn these words over in her mind as if they were an oracle, so that she will not be afflicted when her husband suffers misfortune, will not hate or despise him on that account. Rather, if he is poor, she must console him with the thought that virtue is the only true wealth; you must help him by exemplary behavior, which you know will please him, which will have the approval of friends and acquaintances and which befits the integrity of a good woman. See that you do not plunge into such a wretched state of mind that you would wish him to engage in some unseemly pursuits for the sake of money or commit some disgraceful action so that you may live more luxuriously and extravagantly, or dress more elegantly or live in a more comfortable house, in a word, to have him toil and sweat and even endure danger so that you may have a more pleasant life. It is preferable that you eat stale bread and drink turbid water rather than compel your husband to submit himself let us not say to occupations that are vile and sordid, or to excessive labor, but to any activity whatever that he undertakes against his will simply to please you, avoid domestic quarrels and have some peace at home.

32. The husband is his own master and lord over his wife, not the wife over her husband, and a wife should not ask more of her husband than she sees he will grant her gladly and willingly. Many wives do wrong in this regard who through their insistent demands, constant nagging and importunate behavior drive their husbands to unlawful pursuits and grave deeds, even crimes, to earn money, looking to their own gluttony and pride, not the interests of their husbands. What shall I say of those women who are annoyed and hostile towards the virtues of their spouses if they see that these are detrimental to the family economy? This is all the more disgraceful since although it is the female sex that exhibits more piety and is by nature more devout in sacred worship than the male, she forgets herself and casts off all piety for the sake of money. The Sacred Scriptures confute these women in the wives of Job and Tobias, who foolishly blamed their husbands' ill-fortune on their piety and great virtues. In so doing they were not only stupid but impious because they did not recognize that the riches that are acquired by virtue are of greater value and that it lies in the hands of the Lord to make anyone he wishes rich and prosperous in a single moment.

33. What need is there of other tyrants to obtain the crown of martyrdom? These irreligious women persecute their husbands for their faith in the same way the Apostles were persecuted by Nero and other Christians

---

32. Tobias: Sara, the wife of Tobias, is not so depicted in the *Book of Tobias*.

alios Domitianus vel Maximinus vel Decius vel Diocletianus. Equidem arbitror relictam fuisse solam uxorem Iobo, ut tristitiam viri plus urgeret et
maledica sua rabie pondus adderet tot modis presso. O exsecrabilis et impi-
entissima mulier! Sanctitatem vitae marito tamquam crimen obicis? Hoc ne
5   diaboli quidem facere auderent. Evertit diabolus fortunas omnes Iobi, familiam occidione perdidit, filios absumpsit, ipsum ulceribus et sanie induit,
numquam opprobravit quod in pristina animi simplicitate permaneret. Opprobravit mulier, ut ostenderet diabolo se esse confidentiorem. Insulet sane
coniunx quantum volet, hoc non aliter coniugi gaudendum est quam apos-
10   tolis, quod digni essent habiti ut contumeliam paterentur propter nomen
Domini Iesu.

    34. Tu vero, filia, tantum aberit ut comparem tuum a probitate abdu-
cas, ut etiam certissimo universae rei familiaris dispendio, imitata tot sanctas
Christianas, ad innocentiam et pietatem et recordationem divinae bonitatis
15   ac potentiae adhorteris et contingat tibi quod Paulus inquit: 'Sanctificatur
vir infidelis per mulierem fidelem.' Sic amplae facultates, sic ingentes opes
quaeruntur. Recole verbum Domini neminem esse qui sua gratia aliquid in
hoc aevo neglexerit qui non multo plura et in altero et in hoc etiam con-
sequatur. Primum divitiae illae certae ac solidae sunt quae nullis obnoxiae
20   casibus custodiuntur: non internis, ut aerugini in metallis, tineae in vestibus;
non externis, ut furibus, ut praedonibus, ut violento ac iniquo principi aut
iudici rapaci. Tum de hac vita experimentis se id didicisse Psalmista profitetur longoque aetatis usu numquam se vidisse iustum derelictum aut semen
eius quaerens panem. Sed Domini in Evangelio habemus syngrapham, qua
25   iubemur optime de benignitate ipsius sperare, scire caelestem Patrem quibus ad victum egeamus; illum omnia haec suppeditaturum nobis, postquam
quaesierimus regnum suum et iustitiam eius.

    35. Si deformis est maritus, amandus animus cui nupsisti. Si aeger, ibi de-
mum praestanda est vera uxor: consolandus, confovendus, curandus, haben-
30   dus non minus carus et in deliciis quam si esset maxime sanus et valens magnamque morbi illius partem in te derivabis. Sic fiet ut ille minus doleat, cum

---

    33. (uxorem Iobo ... presso) *Vulg. Iob 2, 9* // (apostolis ... Iesu) *Vulg. act. 5, 4, 1*
    34. (Sanctificatur ... fidelem) *Vulg. I Cor. 7, 14* // (neminem ... consequatur) *Vulg. Luc.
18, 29–30* // (aerugini ... praedonibus) *Vulg. Matth. 6, 19–20* // (numquam ... panem)
Vulg. psalm. 36, 25

2 fuisse solam uxorem Iobo **Γ** Iob solam uxorem **H** // **3** tot modis **Γ** *deest in* **H** // **6** occidione perdidit **Γ** cecidit **H** // **9** coniunx quantum volet **Γ** quantum volet uxor **H** / non
aliter coniugi **Γ** marito non aliter **H** // **12** comparem **Γ** coniugem **H** // **13** universae **Γ**
deest in **H** // **14–15** et recordationem ... potentiae **Γ** *deest in* **H** // **17** sua **Γ** Christi ipsius **H** // **21–22** ut praedonibus ... rapaci **Γ** *deest in* **H** // **23** longoque **Γ** et longo **H** //
30 et in deliciis **Γ** *deest in* **H** // **30–31** magnamque ... derivabis **Γ** magnaque morbi illius
pars in te derivanda **H** // **31** Sic ... doleat **Γ** Sic illae minus dolebit **H**

by Domitian, Maximinus, Decius and Diocletian. I think Job's wife was the only possession left to him so that she could add to his misery and with her malicious tongue make his burden even greater. O detestable and impious woman! You reproach your husband for his holiness as if it were a crime! Not even devils would dare to do this. The devil destroyed all of Job's fortunes, slew all his servants, took away his children, covered him with sores and ulcerous discharges, but he never reproached him for persevering in his original purity of soul. His wife reproached him, showing that she was more shameless than the devil. Let his wife insult him as she will; her spouse will rejoice in this no less than the Apostles in that they were considered worthy of suffering indignity for the name of the Lord Jesus.

34. But you, good daughter, put it far from your mind ever to turn your spouse away from uprightness of life but rather even at the certain cost of losing all your family possessions, in imitation of countless holy women, exhort him to innocence, piety and mindfulness of divine goodness and power, so that the words of Paul may be verified in you: 'An unfaithful husband is sanctified by a faithful woman.' In this way great resources and immense wealth are obtained. Recall the word of the Lord that there is no one who neglects anything in this world for his sake who will not receive much more both in the next world and in this one as well. First of all, those riches are certain and lasting that are guarded without being exposed to the dangers of chance, whether from within, as rust in metals, moths in clothing, or from without, as thieves, robbers, a violent and unjust ruler, or a rapacious judge. In addition the Psalmist declares that after a long experience of life he learned that he had never seen a just man abandoned or his seed in search of bread. We have Our Lord's solemn promise in the Gospels, by which we are bidden to hope abundantly in his kindness, that our heavenly Father knows what things we need to live; that he will provide all of these things for us, when we have sought his kingdom and his justice.

35. If your husband is ugly, love his soul, which you have married. If he is sick, then you can show yourself a true wife. He must be consoled, tended, cared for and held no less dear and cherished than if he were healthy and strong, and in that way you will divert a great part of the illness to yourself. He will suffer less when he sees that he has someone to share his suffering.

sociam te aspiciet sui doloris. Non est bona coniunx quae coniuge maerente gaudet, aegrotante valet. Lecto affixa sis oportet, modo verbis dolorem
levans, modo fomentis leniens. Tu ipsa vulnera, tu ulcera, tu affectum tuis
manibus tracta, corpus tu tege, tu retege, tu exterge, tu potionem praebe,
5   tu urinam matella excipe. Ne haec abhorreas, nihil magis in illo fastidieris
quam in te ipsa. Ne reicias curam in famulas, quae rem segnius ac negligentius curant, quia non amant; et cum se non amari sentit aeger, ingravescit
corporis morbus ex animi aegritudine. Egone illas uxores et matronas et
sanctas (si diis placet) feminas ut appellem, quae in maritorum morbo tam
10   securae agunt ut eis satisfaciat cura quam circa illos gerunt famulae, ipsis
uxoribus ignaris? Nam quod video quasdam nec sua stata sacra nec convivia nec visitationes et congressus aequalium nec solita oblectamenta adduci ut intermittant, maritis morbo domi clausis, hoc iam non coniugum
esse officium dixeris, sed concubinarum aut etiam (ut aperta loquar) mere-
15   tricum, quae mercede conductae cum viris cubant. Cur enim me pudeat
merito nomine illas appellare quas non pudet id facere unde mereantur?
Quid, si tu nihil censes interesse aegrotetne maritus an vicinus, nisi quod
maritus est domi, vicinus foris? Impudentissima profecto es si postules ut te
uxorem vocem, cum quod uxoris est non praestes. An tu textricem vis te
20   haberi quae nec ordiri telam nec radium iacere nec telam pectine quatere
didicisti? Et quamquam virtus etiam nullis extrinsecus adiuta luminibus in
tenebris ipsis splendorem suum obtinet claraque et celebris est, tamen quantum in me erit non sinam hoc et praesentes et posteros ignorare quod ipse
vidi, quod alii pariter mecum quam plurimi sciunt.
25   **36.** Clara Cerventa, Bernardi Valdaurae coniunx, cum virgo tenerrima et
formosissima Brugas esset ad sponsum deducta iam plus quadraginta annos
natum, prima nuptiarum nocte crura eius fasciis involuta vidit deprehen-
ditque maritum sibi aegrum et valetudinarium obvenisse; nihil tamen illum
ob id aversata, non coepit eum odisse, cum praesertim nondum posset videri
30   amare. Incidit non multo post Valdaura in gravissimum morbum, de cuius
salute et vita medici omnes desperabant. Ipsa cum matre tanta cura et assiduitate circa lectum aegri versabatur ut sex totis hebdomadibus ambae nec

1 doloris **Γ** morbi **H** // **1–2** coniuge maerente **Γ** dolente coniuge **H** // **2** oportet **Γ** *deest
in* **H** // **3** levans **Γ** leva **H** / leniens **Γ** leni **H** // **4** praebe **Γ** da **H** // **5** urinam **Γ** lotium **H**
/ abhorreas **Γ** exhorreas **H** // **5–6** nihil ... ipsa **Γ** *deest in* **H** // **6–7** ac negligentius **Γ** *deest
in* **H** // **8** corporis ... aegritudine **Γ** morbus **H** / Egone **Γ** Ego **H** // **9** ut **Γ** *deest in* **H** //
12 et congressus aequalium **Γ** amicarum **H** // **14** esse officium dixeris **Γ** est **H** // **15** enim
Γ *deest in* **H** // **16** merito nomine illas appellare **Γ** nominare **H** / quas **Γ** quod illas **H** / id
... mereantur **Γ** sceleratas agere **H** // **17** Quid, si tu nihil censes **Γ** Si enim nihil putas **H**
// **20** haberi ... iacere **Γ** nominem si nec ordiri telam nec subtegmina ducere nec radium
iactare **H** // **21** extrinsecus **Γ** *deest in* **H** // **22** ipsis **Γ** *deest in* **H** // **25** Cerventa **Γ** *deest
in* **H** // **26** deducta **Γ** adducta **H** / quadraginta **Γ** quadraginta sex **H** // **28** obvenisse **Γ**
contigisse **H** // **31–32** assiduitate **Γ** sollicitudine **H**

She is not a good wife who is happy while her husband is sad or vaunts her health while her husband is ill. You should be constantly at his bedside, alleviating his pain with your words and soothing him with hot compresses. Treat his wounds and his sores yourself with your own hands and comfort his physical anguish. Dress him, undress him, dry him, give him to drink, bring him the bedpan. Do not shrink from these tasks any more than you would if it were for yourself. Do not pass these duties on to servants, who will execute them in a careless and slovenly manner because they do not love him, and when the sick person senses that he is not loved, his physical illness is aggravated by sickness of soul. Am I to call those women wives, matrons and holy women, (if you please!) who are so indifferent when their husbands are ill that they are content to have servants look after him, ignoring their wifely duties? When I see that some women do not discontinue their customary attendance at sacred functions, banquets, visits and meetings with their friends, and their usual amusements while their husbands are confined to the house through illness, you would not say they are fulfilling the role of wives, but of concubines, or, to speak more openly, of prostitutes, bought with a price, who share their bed with men. Why should I be ashamed to call them by that name when they are not ashamed to act in such a way as to merit it? What am I to say if you think there is no difference whether it is your husband who is sick or a neighbor, except that your husband is at home and your neighbor outside? You are really brazen if you demand to be called a wife when you do not show yourself to be a wife. Do you wish to be called a weaver when you never learned how to lay the warp, or throw the shuttle, or strike the web with the comb? And although virtue without the help of any external light shines in the dark of its own light and is bright and lustrous, yet as far as it lies in me, I shall not allow those of the present and of future ages to be ignorant of what I saw with my own eyes and what many others know besides me.

36. When Clara Cervent, the wife of Bernardo Valdaura, a young and beautiful girl from Bruges, was married to a husband more than forty years old, on the wedding night she saw that his legs were wrapped in bandages and discovered that she had married an infirm and sickly husband. Nevertheless, not put off by this she did not conceive hatred for him, in spite of the fact that it did not seem possible that she could feel any love for him. Not long afterwards, Valdaura fell victim to a very serious illness and the doctors despaired of his life. She and her mother stayed at his bedside for six weeks with such care and assiduity that they never took off their clothes

---

36. Clara Cervent: Clara Cervent and Bernard Valdaura were the parents of Vives' wife, Margaret Valdaura.

se exuerint nisi ut mutarent supparos, nec ulla nocte supra unam aut alteram
horam quieverint idque indutae, multis noctibus traductis insomnibus. Erat
radix morbi Indici, quem Gallicum hic vocant, saevi et contagiosi. Dissuade-
bant medici ne sic eum contrectaret, ne tam prope accederet. Idem consule-
5 bant necessarii. Tum aequales feminae in religionem adducebant non esse
tam anxia cura divexandum (ita enim loquebantur) hominem iam fatis debitum et magna mortis parte in corpus recepta; prospiciendum esse animae,
de corpore nihil cogitandum aliud quam ubi conderetur humo. Quibus vocibus adeo illa absterrita non est ut curarit quidem quae ad animum specta-
10 bant, sed ipsa culinae sorbitionibus quae remedium afferrent, ipsa pannis
subinde mutandis (nam soluta erat maiorem in modum alvus et aliis locis
pus taetrum dimanabat) esset intentissima, sursum deorsum toto die cur-
sitaret, animo corpusculum fulciens, laboribus impar ni tanta vis affectus
subveniret. Ita discrimen maximum Valdaura evasit, iurantibus medicis e
15 manibus Orci violentia coniugis ereptum esse. Alius facetius quam Christ-
ianius decrevisse dixit Deum Valdauram occidere, uxorem vero obstinasse
e manibus se illum non dimissuram.

37. Coepit ei, fluente quodam ardentissimo ex capite humore, arrodi interior narium caruncula. Medici pulvisculum dederunt, quo subinde res-
20 pergeretur ulcus tenui per fistulam aut calamum flatu; cumque nullus in-
veniretur qui non eum laborem recusaret, omnibus rem aversandam ex-
horrentibus, sola coniunx hoc praestitit. Scatentibus per genas ac mentum
papulis morbi, cum nullus rasor commode posset barbam eius radere nec
vellet, uxor forficulis octavo quoque die dexterrime attondebat. Collapsus
25 deinde in alium morbum longissimum septem fere annorum ipsa infatiga-
bili diligentia et cibum ei paravit, cum pedisequas haberet duas et filiam
grandescentem. Ipsa eadem tum foeda illivit ulcera tum et crura putidis-
sima undique sanie diffluentia contrectavit quotidie, turundas et malagmata
imposuit ac fasciis devinxit, ut muscum diceres eam contrectare, non rem
30 foetoris intolerabilis. Quin et anhelitum, quem nemo non etiam ad decem
passus aversabatur, ipsa suavissimum iurat fuisse et quidem serio mihi suc-
censuit, cum semel foetere dixissem. Aiebat enim sibi videri ceu fragrantiam
maturorum et dulcium malorum.

38. Atque hoc toto morbi tempore, cum essent quotidie magni faciendi
sumptus ad hominem tot morbis contusum alendum et curandum, in ea

2 quieverint Γ quierint **H** // 4 contrectaret Γ tangeret **H** // 6 tam … divexandum Γ af-
flictandum **H** / ita enim loquebantur Γ *deest in* **H** // 7 magna … recepta Γ a morte exhaus-
tum **H** // 12 pus taetrum dimanabat Γ pus demanabat **H** // 13–14 animo … subveniret
Γ *deest in* **H** // 20 aut calamum Γ *deest in* **H** // 21 aversandam Γ taetram **H** // 22 Scatentibus per genas ac mentum Γ Repletis genis ac mento **H** // 24 forficulis Γ forficibus **H**
/ Collapsus Γ Incurrit **H** // 26 pedisequas haberet duas Γ famulas tres haberet **H** // 27
grandescentem Γ grandisculam **H** // 28 diffluentia Γ scatentia **H** // 28–29 turundas …
fasciis Γ *deest in* **H** // 30 anhelitum Γ anhelitus **H** // 31 quidem Γ etiam **H**

except to change their underwear and never rested more than one or two hours and then fully clothed, and passed many sleepless nights. The cause of the illness was the Indian disease, which here we call the French pox, a violent and contagious illness. The doctors advised her not to touch him or go close to him. Her friends gave the same advice. Women of her own age considered it to be against religious principles to struggle so indefatigably to save the life of a man destined to die, as they said, and since death had gained control of so much of his body, thought should be given to his soul, and no concern taken for the body except providing for its burial. She was not deterred by these words but cared for both soul and body. She went in person to the kitchen to prepare the broth used for his cure, changed the bedding frequently, for he suffered from severe diarrhea and in other parts of his body repugnant suppurations were exuded. This she did running about all the day long, sustaining her frail body with her spirit, since her body was not equal to the task save that the force of love gave her strength. Thus Valdaura escaped a very grave crisis. The doctors swore that he had been snatched from the jaws of death by the forceful action of his wife. One person said, more jokingly than with a true Christian spirit, that God had decreed the death of Valdaura, but his wife had made up her mind that she would not let him go.

37. Then the soft fleshy tissue inside his nostrils began to become cankerous, caused by a burning humor that flowed down from his head. The doctors prescribed a powder which was to be sprinkled on the ulcer by gently blowing through a reed, and since no one could be found who did not recoil at this task in abhorrence, only his wife would perform this service. Then when pustules caused by the disease broke out on his cheeks and chin, since no barber could or would shave him, his wife cut them with scissors very skillfully every eight days. Then he sank into another protracted illness, which lasted almost seven years. Once again she attended to him with indefatigable care, prepared his food, although he had two maidservants and a grown daughter; she anointed his ugly sores, bandaged daily his foul-smelling legs dripping with purulent matter, applied powdered substances and poultices, and dressed his wounds as if she were handling musk instead of fetid sores. And his breath, which no one could tolerate even ten paces away, she swore was sweet-smelling. Once she became very angry with me when I said that it stank. She insisted that it reminded her of the fragrance of sweet, ripe apples.

38. And during all the time of this illness, when great expenses had to be assumed daily to nourish and cure a man afflicted with so many diseases,

domo ad quam multis iam annis nulla ex re quaestus aliquis redierat nec an-
nuos haberet proventus, ipsa se anulis, ipsa torquibus aureis, ipsa monilibus,
ipsa vestibus, ipsa abacum suum vasis argenteis libentissime spoliabat, ne
quid marito deesset, contenta quavis mensa, modo marito suppeteret quod
5   tam afflicto malis corpori conduceret. Sic ille vitam traxit uxoris cura ca-
daveroso corpore seu sepulcro verius decem annis a primo illo morbo. Quo
tempore ipsa duas ex eo proles suscepit, cum antea sex genuisset, viginti annis nupta, numquam contagiosissimo mariti morbo nec ulla omnino scabie
infecta non modo ipsa, sed nec ullus liberorum, corporibus omnium sanis-
10   simis atque mundissimis.

39. Ex quo liquidum fit quanta sit virtus, quanta sanctitas earum quae
vere ac toto pectore maritos (ut congruum est) amant; quemadmodum illis Deus praesentem quoque gratiam referat. Obiit tandem senex aegrotus, seu non obiit, sed abiit verius et exiit iugem cruciatum; tanto tamen
15   dolore Clarae ut qui illam norint fateantur numquam adolescentem maritum integro corpore, formosum, divitem, tantum reliquisse carissimae uxori desiderium, maerorem, luctum. Multi gratulatione citius putabant esse
opus quam consolatione. Quos illa propemodum exsecrabatur, optans ut
maritus qualis qualis erat fieri si posset sibi redderetur, etiam cum liberorum
20   omnium quos quinque habet iactura. Cumque sit integra aetate, numquam
statuit nubere, quod se alterum Bernardum Valdauram inventuram negat.
Praetereo pudicitiam cuius est exemplar, praetereo sanctitatem morum. De
pietate coniugis est sermo, quae numquam venit sola, semper reliquis omnibus comitata virtutibus. Quis hanc non perspiciat non corpori Bernardi
25   Valdaurae nupsisse, sed animo, aut non putasse corpus illius suum esse?
Quid quod viri sui praecepta et mandata omnia ita observat tanta reverentia
ac si adhuc viveret et ex eius praescripto multa agit, sic illum facere statuisse
aut mandasse dictitans. Talem uxorem, Euripides, si habuisses, tam lau-
dasses feminas quam eas vituperasti; talem si, Agamemnon, patria te multis
30   annis de Troia victa laetum spectasset triumphantem.

40. Tacenda haec non fuerunt, cum saepenumero minora memoriae man-
dentur ad maritas sui officii commonefaciendas. Plebeiarum sunt haec, inquit
illa nobilis. Primum non omnino ex faece plebis Clara Valdaura, et iuvenis et
formosissima et delicatissima et comitata famulabus quibus magnam curae
35   partem mandare poterat, si sustinuisset. Sed multae sunt nobilissimae quae
idem praestent, quas commemorare omnes non queo, nec praesentes modo,

---

1 quaestus aliquis Γ lucrum aliquod **H** // **3** libentissime Γ *deest in* **H** // **4** contenta Γ contenta erat **H** // **6** seu sepulcro verius Γ et potius sepulcro quam corpore **H** // **9** infecta
Γ attacta **H** // **13** referat Γ refert **H** // **13–14** aegrotus Γ aeger **H** // **17** desiderium Γ
luctum **H** // **19–20** etiam . . . iactura Γ *deest in* **H** // **23** venit sola Γ sola venit **H** // **24**
perspiciat Γ videat **H** // **26** sui Γ *deest in* **H** / et mandata omnia Γ *deest in* **H** // **28** mandasse
dictitans Γ iussisse dicens **H** // **31** saepenumero Γ *deest in* **H** // **32** maritas . . . commonefaciendas Γ commonefaciendas sui officii coniuges **H**

in that household where there had been no income and no crops for many years, she willingly despoiled herself of gold rings and necklaces, jewels and clothing, and emptied her cupboard of silver vessels so that her husband would lack nothing. She was content with any fare as long as there were sufficient provisions to care for the needs of her husband's body afflicted by such grave ills. So through his wife's care his life dragged on for ten years after his first illness in his cadaverous body, or more truly, a living tomb. During this time she bore him two children in addition to the six to whom she had already given birth since her marriage at the age of twenty, never becoming infected with her husband's contagious disease or any other scurvy, and her children also were endowed with healthy and clean bodies.

39. From this example it becomes clear how great is the virtue and holiness of those women who love their husbands with their whole heart, as is fitting, and how God rewards them in this life. At length the sick old man passed away or rather escaped from his unending torment. Clara was so stricken with grief that those who know her say that never has a young husband of sound body, handsome and rich, inspired such regret, mourning and grief in a loving spouse. Many thought there was more occasion for congratulations than consolation. She all but cursed them, expressing the wish that her husband might return, just as he was, if it were possible, even if she had to suffer the loss of the five children that remained to her. Although she was still of youthful age, she decided never to marry again because she said that she would never find another Bernardo Valdaura. I do not mention her chastity, of which she is an exemplar. I do not mention the sanctity of her life. I speak of her loyalty to her husband, which never comes alone, but always accompanied by all the other virtues. Who cannot perceive that she was married not to the body of Bernardo Valdaura, but to his soul, or that his body was her body? And what of the fact that she continues to observe the commands and wishes of her husband with such respect as if he were still alive and does many things according to his prescripts, saying that he had decided or ordered it? If you had had such a wife, Euripides, you would have praised women as much as you criticized them. If you, Agamemnon, had such a one, your country would have seen you living on happily for many years as the triumphant conqueror of Troy.

40. These things could not be passed over in silence when often lesser accomplishments are recorded to remind wives of their duties. 'But these are the actions of low-born women,' some noble lady will say. First of all, Clara Valdaura was not at all of lowly origin. She was young, very beautiful, refined and had many servants, to whom she could have assigned a great part of these duties if she had been willing. But there are many noble women who lend themselves to these same services, both of our own day

sed quae olim vixerunt. Nam magna ex parte vitia tantum superiorum ae-
tatum insequentia tempora usu retinent. An tu nobilior uxore Themistoclis,
Athenarum immo Graeciae principis, quae sola fere in adversa valetudine marito ministravit? Nobilior Stratonica, Deiotari Regis coniuge, quae viro seni,
5   maesto, valetudinario ipsa erat et coqua et medica et chirurga nihilque magis
eam urebat quam quod interdum difficilis et morosus senex parum sibi illam
diligentia satisfacere indicabat? Nobilior Regina illa Britanniae, quae vulnus
exsuxit mariti? Principes Romanae feminae non aliis manibus tractari sinebant
maritos aegros quam suis. An tu credis te Romanis etiam antestare nobili-
10   tate, in quos si quis genus potest referre nobilissimus existimatur? Sed quid
necesse est sanguine atque opibus nobiles referamus? Nobiles sunt virtute et
claris actibus illustres. Tu cum tua nobilitate iacebis obscura et ignobilis, istas
omnis aetas, omnis sexus noscet et celebrabit. I nunc et iacta tuam nobilitatem,
quam nec te viva nec mortua ullus cognoscet.
15   **41.** 'Pecuniam,' inquis, 'attuli, qua conducatur qui hoc agat.' Ergo pecuniae vir tuus nupsit non tibi et tu uxorem te esse censes solum quod tecum
cubitat vir? An in hoc uno situm esse coniugium arbitraris? Leges profecto
Dei et naturae violas. Nam si tuum corpus tractare te non pigeret aegre et
in pustulas ac ulcera oculos ac manus immittere, cur maritum aversaris sic
20   affectum, cum sitis duo in carne una, seu (ut dicam Latinius) homo unus, nisi
forsan hoc ad te dictum pertinere non putas? Ubi est deinde illa coniunx,
individua coniugis comes et socia, si cum te coniunctissimam esse oportuit discedis? Tu ergo nec fratri tecum genito nec patri nec matri qui te
genuerunt id officium praestares? Quod si hoc pudet confiteri, pudeat de
25   marito vel cogitare, qui apud te illis omnibus praeponendus est. Etsi ex istis sunt nonnullae quae etiam matres deserant aegrotas nec aliquem amant
praeter se, dignae vicissim quae a nullo amentur alio, ut nec amantur.
        42. Quoties vidimus mutam animantem feminam saniem et ulcera maris
sui lambere? Hoc boves, hoc canes, leones, ursi, bestiae tum cicures, tum
30   ferae. Mulier tangere non sustinet ac ne inspicere quidem? Vultis aperte

---

4. (Stratonica ... coniuge) *Plut. mor. 258D*

1 olim Γ praeteritis in annis **H** // **2** insequentia Γ nostra **H** // **9–10** etiam antestare nobilitate Γ quoque nobiliorem **H** // **10** potest referre Γ referre potest **H** // **11** necesse Γ
opus **H** // **12** actibus Γ actis **H** // **14** te **HWW²** *om.* **BV** // **16** tibi et tu Γ tibi, spurcissima
femina **H** / censes Γ putas **H** // **17** cubitat Γ cubet **H** / arbitraris? Γ arbitraris, taeterrima
mulier? **H** / profecto Γ *deest in* **H** // **18** violas Γ dissolvis **H** // **18–19** et in pustulas ...
immittere Γ et pustulas ac ulcera inspicere et tangere **H** // **19–20** maritum ... affectum Γ
cur pigeat mariti **H** // **20** dicam Latinius Γ Latinius dicam **H** // **22** et socia Γ *deest in* **H**
// **23** oportuit Γ oporteret **H** // **24** confiteri Γ concedere **H** // **25** cogitare Γ affirmare **H**
/ illis omnibus Γ omnibus illis **H** // **27** vicissim Γ etiam **H** // **28** saniem et Γ *deest in* **H** //
29 lambere Γ lambentem **H** // **29–30** tum cicures, tum ferae Γ et ferae et cicures faciunt **H**
// **30** sustinet Γ vult **H**

and from the past, all of whom I cannot enumerate. For the most part succeeding ages remember only the vices of those who lived before them. Are you nobler than the wife of Themistocles, leader of Athens or rather of all of Greece, who ministered to her husband unassisted when he was in poor health? Nobler than Stratonica, the wife of King Deiotarus, who when her husband was old, disillusioned and invalid, was cook, doctor and surgeon to him, and nothing gave her more grief than the fact that sometimes the difficult and cantankerous old man intimated that she did not give him sufficient attention? Are you nobler than that queen of England who sucked her husband's wounds? The leading Roman matrons did not allow their sick husbands to be touched by any other hands than their own. Do you think you surpass even the Romans in nobility, when any family that can trace its origins to them is regarded as one of great nobility? But why must we confine nobility to lineage and riches? They are noble who are illustrious in virtue and noble deeds. You with your nobility will lie obscure and ignoble while every age and every sex will know and celebrate the truly noble. Go, then, and vaunt your nobility, which no one will recognize, whether you are dead or alive.

41. You say, 'I have offered money to hire someone who will do this.' Therefore your husband wedded your money, not you. Do you think you are a wife merely because a man sleeps with you? Do you think marriage consists in this alone? You are clearly violating the laws of God and of nature, for if you do not feel revulsion in touching your own body and looking at and putting your hands on pustules and ulcers, why do you turn away from your husband in disgust when he is afflicted in this same way, since you are two in one flesh, or to use more precise Latin, one human being? Or perhaps you think this does not apply to you. Where is that spouse, indivisible companion and mate of her husband, if at the moment when you should be most united to him you take your leave? Would you not perform this service for a blood brother, a father or mother who brought you into the world? If you are ashamed to admit this, then you should likewise be ashamed even to think it with regard to your husband, whom you should prefer to all of these. Yet there are women like this who desert even their sick mothers and love no one but themselves, worthy in turn to be loved by no one else, as is the case.

42. How often have we seen the female among dumb creatures licking the gore and sores of her mate? This is done by cattle, dogs, lions, bears, beasts both tame and wild. Will a woman refuse to touch or even to look at

---

40. Stratonica: Since she had no children of her own, Stratonica prevailed upon her husband to have a child with a prisoner of war, and she treated this son in kingly fashion.

Deiotarus: King of Galatia in Asia Minor, friend of the Romans. A speech of Cicero in his defense is extant.

loquar? Haud paucae quae non tractant mariti tractant adulteri. Nam fuerunt quae in hoc sunt deprehensae. Ut sciatis non retrahi a natura, sed a
scelere; ut non videatur eas iniuria Iuvenalis sic incessere: 'Quae moechum
sequitur stomacho valet,' quae maritum delicatula et levissimarum quoque
5 offensiuncularum impatiens. Pergo vero dicere et alias infortunatorum species recensere, etsi omnes nec possum nec volo. Si incommodis sit moribus,
tolerandus nec improbitate cum eo contendendum, ne numquam sit finis
mali ac miseriae. Noli tu improbitate tua improbitatem illius retundere et
iracundia iracundiam coercere; id vero lacessere atque irritare morbum fu-
10 erit, non sanare. Ne speres te caenum caeno ablaturam vel incendium posse
restinguere oleo iniecto. Verte potius te ad illas quae maritis utuntur pluribus
vitiorum generibus aut certe maioribus, asperis atque intolerabilibus et ex
illarum fortunis solacium tuis sume. Non potes in eo amare quod habet vitia,
at ama quod multis nec minus difficilibus caret. Ne ad illas respicias quae
15 felicius videntur coniunctae. Quae ratio cogitationis universam vobis vitam
insuavem redderet, quamquam quid istis quoque domi lateat tu nescis. Sed
illas tamen contemplare quibus durior est vitae condicio.

43. Ceterum quo tempore tractabiliorem se maritus praebebit, comiter
est et blande admonendus, ut melius velit vivere. Si audierit, et tibi et illi
20 maximopere profueris; sin coeperit excandescere, noli contra niti et ex uno
insano duos facere, te atque illum. Tu functa es munere tuo, perfer; et erit
tibi non modo magnae apud mortales gloriae, sed merito apud Deum ingenti. Quod si forte eius vitio ac impotentia animi vapules, puta te a Domino
corripi et propter aliqua tua delicta id tibi accidere, quae illa via expiantur.
25 Beata es si modico vitae huius labore magnos alterius cruciatus redimis.
Quamquam rarae sunt bonae et prudentes uxores quae a viris quamlibet
sceleratis et insanis caedantur. Dolorem tuum domi devora nec in vicinia
vocifereris nec aliis de viro conquerare, ne quem videaris iudicem inter te
et illum statuere. Domestica mala domesticis parietibus ac limine cohibe,
30 ne se foras efferant, ne serpant latius. Sic moderatione tua commodiorem
reddes coniugem, quem alias querimoniis et futtilitate linguae exacerbares.

44. Sunt etiam nonnulli mariti fatui et mente capti; hos proba coniunx
tractabit arte nec exasperabit nec adimet honorem viri, sed persuasum prius

---

42. (Quae ... valet) *Iuv. 6, 100*

1 Haud ... adulteri Γ Quae non tractat mariti, tractat adulteri **H** // **2** sunt Γ sint **H** //
2–5 Ut sciatis ... impatiens Γ *deest in* **H** // **6** incommodis Γ malis **H** // **8–17** Noli ...
vitae condicio Γ *deest in* **H** // **18** Ceterum ... praebebit Γ Cum placatior erit **H** // **19** est
et blande Γ et suaviter **H** // **19** velit vivere Γ vivat **H** // **20** maximopere Γ *deest in* **H** //
20–21 et ex uno ... illum Γ *deest in* H // **21** perfer Γ patere **H** // **23** forte Γ *deest in* **H** //
24 delicta ... accidere Γ peccata id tibi contingere **H** // **25** modico ... labore Γ modica
in hac vita poena **H** // **26–27** a viris ... caedantur Γ a quamlibet sceleratis et insanis viris
caedantur **H** // **27–31** Dolorem ... exacerbares Γ *deest in* **H** // **32** fatui Γ stulti **H**

her husband's sores? Do you wish me to speak frankly? Not a few women who do not touch their husband's wounds touch those of an adulterer, for some have been caught doing this, making it clear that it was not nature that deterred them, but their own wickedness. Thus Juvenal does not seem unjust when he attacks them in this way:

A wife who's off with her lover has a strong stomach.

This same woman is very squeamish with her husband and cannot suffer the slightest annoyances. I could go on to enumerate other kinds of unfortunate husbands, although I cannot name them all nor do I wish to. If he is a man of disagreeable character, he must be tolerated and you must not vie with him in disagreeableness or there will be no end of ills and misery. Do not counter his insolence with insolence of your own or quell anger with anger. That would only stimulate and irritate his illness, not cure it. Do not hope that you can clean mud with mud or extinguish a fire by throwing oil on it. Turn your attention to those women who have husbands with more vices, or certainly greater ones, who are violent and intolerable, and from their misfortunes take consolation for your own. You cannot love him for his vices, but love him because he lacks many others that are no less troublesome. Do not look at those women who seem to be more happily married. This manner of thinking will render your whole life unpleasant, although you really do not know the secrets of their household. Look at those whose situation is more difficult.

43. When your husband shows himself more tractable, then admonish him politely and gently that he be willing to live a better life. If he listens to you, you will have been of great profit to both of you, but if he begins to flare up, do not struggle with him and make two madmen out of one, you and him. You have fulfilled your duty; persevere, and you will have great glory before men and immense merits in the eyes of God. But if through his proclivity to vice or lack of control he beats you, consider that you are being corrected by God, and that this is happening to you because of some of your sins, which are expiated in that way. Blessed are you if by a minor hardship in this life you can redeem great torment in the next. But good and prudent wives are rarely beaten by their husbands, no matter how wicked and insane they may be. Devour your grief at home, do not broadcast it in the neighborhood or complain to others about your husband so that it may not appear that you appoint a judge between him and you. Keep domestic problems within the walls and threshold of the house so that they will not be spread abroad. In that way you will render your husband more amenable when you would only further exacerbate him with your complaints and your useless tongue.

44. There are some husbands who are mentally feeble and deranged. A good wife will treat such a person tactfully and will not irritate him or be lacking in respect, but she will convince him that she will do everything in

omnia se ex animi eius sententia facturam et ut maxime illi expediet, facile prudentia reget, velut beluam mansuefactam. In hos mulier se habebit ut matres in similes filios, quae in maximam et vehementissimam miserationem ex miseria filiorum adducuntur et ex miseratione crescit caritas ita ut de-
5   biles, mutilos, stultos, deformes, valetudinarios plus saepe ament quam firmos, integros, prudentes, formosos, valentes. Nolo percurrere cetera infortunatorum genera; semel est de universis praecipiendum. Huic, qualiscumque est, nupsisti; hunc tibi Deus, hunc Ecclesia, hunc parentes dederunt virum, maritum, dominum. Ex tot virorum milibus haec est sors et pars tua. Fer-
10 endum est bono animo quod mutari non potest et amandus, colendus, honorandus, si non propter ipsum, certe propter eos a quibus tibi assignatus et commendatus est, propter fidem quam dedisti, sicut multi indignissimis prosunt ac benefaciunt, unam solum ob causam quod a carissimis commendatos habent. Multi quaedam agunt solum quod promiserunt, alio-
15 qui non facturi. Et danda est tibi opera ut quod vel nolens factura esses et facere videaris et facias libentissime. Sic enim leviora et iucundiora reddes tibi omnia, quae gravissima et molestissima essent invitae. Reputatio necessitatis fortiter docebit ferre, consuetudo facile, quae in durissimis etiam calamitatibus mollimentum invenit, 'cito in familiaritatem gravissima ad-
20 ducens,' uti Seneca inquit. Cogita te hoc debere viro, magnam tibi parari hoc modo apud Deum gratiam, magnum et honestissimum ad homines nomen.

45. Hic video posse a nonnullis dubitari quatenus sit marito obtemperandum. Quam quaestionem quoniam difficiliorem quarundam mulierum im-
25 probitas et contumacia reddidit, explicabo paulo fusius quod sit imperium viri in uxorem. Et in rebus quidem aut honestis aut quae nec vitiosae sunt ex se nec probae, nihil ambigi debet quin mariti iussa debeant esse uxori vice cuiusdam divinae legis. Maritus enim Deo succedit in terris et post divinam illam maiestatem ipse solus uxori refert omnes omnium caritates, cul-
30 tus, maiestates. Idcirco si quid est quod Deo velit uxor dare, non iussa a Deo, marito non permittente, dare nec debet nec licet. Quid est magis uxoris quam corpus, quam animus? At nec in corpus suum potestatem habere maritam feminam, testificatur Divus Paulus nec continentiam offerre potest

---

44. (Cito ... adducens) *Sen. dial. 9, 10, 2*
45. (Nec ... Deo) *Vulg. I Cor. 7, 4–5* //

2 velut beluam Γ ut feram **H** // **3** matres Γ mater **H** // **5** saepe Γ *deest in* **H** // **9** Ex tot ... pars tua Γ *deest in* **H** // **10** bono animo Γ *deest in* **H** // **11–12** assignatus et Γ *deest in* **H** // **12-13** indignissimis ... causam Γ plerosque amant amore indignos **H** // **15** facturi Γ acturi **H** // **16** et facias libentissime Γ libentissime et facias **H** // **16–17** reddes tibi Γ erunt **H** // **17–20** Reputatio ... Seneca inquit Γ *deest in* **H** // **20** Cogita Γ Cogitesque **H** // **23** nonnullis Γ quibusdam **H** // **23** obtemperandum Γ parendum **H** // **25** et contumacia Γ *deest in* **H** / fusius quod sit Γ pluribus **H** // **33** maritam Γ *deest in* **H**

accordance with his wishes and to his best advantage and will guide him gently like a tamed animal. A woman will comport herself with such men as mothers do towards children with similar defects, moved by their distress to great pity, and pity increases love so that they more often love weak, crippled, stupid, deformed, and sickly children than those that are strong, unimpaired, intelligent, beautiful and robust. I do not wish to run through other types of bad husbands but to give one general rule of conduct. Whatever his qualities, you married him. God, the Church and your parents gave him to you as your man, husband and master. Of the many thousands of men he is your lot and your portion. That which cannot be changed must be borne with equanimity, and he must be loved, respected and honored if not for his own sake, then for the sake of those by whom he was allotted and commended to you, because of the promise you gave, just as many persons do good to those totally unworthy of it for the sole reason that they have been commended to them by those whom they hold dear. Many do certain things merely because they promised it, otherwise they would not do them. And you must take care that what you do even against your will you both seem to do willingly and indeed actually succeed in so doing. Thus you make lighter and more pleasant a task that would be burdensome and painful if you were to do it unwillingly. Necessity will teach you to bear up with fortitude; habit, which finds solace even in the harshest calamities, will facilitate it, 'quickly making even the most painful things seem familiar,' as Seneca said. Think that you owe this to your husband and that in this way a great reward is stored up for you with God, and a great and honorable name among men.

45. At this point I see that some women can have doubts about how far they should obey their husbands. Since the unscrupulousness and wilful disobedience of some women has made this a vexed question, I shall give a rather lengthy explanation of the husband's authority over his wife. In matters having to do with virtue or that are neither good nor bad there can be no doubt that a wife must obey her husband's commands as if they were the law of God. The husband takes God's place on earth and after the divine majesty it is to him alone that a wife owes all her love, respect and obedience. Therefore if a wife should wish to give to God what is not commanded by God, she should not do so without her husband's permission. What can a woman consider more her own than her body and soul? But Paul bears witness that a married woman does not have power over her own body and cannot offer continence to God without her husband's knowledge, not to

Deo, non dico invito marito, sed nec inscio. Quocirca si cum maritus tuo egeat ministerio, tu velle te non dico saltare aut ire ad publicos ludos aut ad convivia aut deliciatum respondes (nam hoc plane scortorum est), sed orare, sed templa circumire, scias et ingratas tuas preces Deo futuras nec

5 te in templo Deum inventuram. Vult te Deus orare, sed negotiis coniugis liberam; vult sua templa invisere, sed cum nihil est quod domi maritus tui indigeat. Haec enim coniugalia sunt quae posuit Deus in officio coniugis. Accedere iubet ad aras suas, sed placato prius amico; quanto magis placato prius omnium mortalium amicissimo marito? Quid tu mihi sacra, quid tem-

10 pla visis, cum aliud vir tuus aut expresse iubet aut tacite poscit? Tu in templo quaeris Deum, cum comparem tuum a Deo tibi sociatum vel aegrum domi relinquas vel esurientem? Circa eius lectum sunt sacra omnia; ibi arae, ibi Deus ubi pax et concordia et caritas, inter eos praecipue qui his conglutinati rebus individui esse debent. Deum facile tibi amicum reddes, si hominem

15 reddideris. Non eget nostris ministeriis Deus; pietatem sibi uni et supremum cultum reservavit. Oboedientiam postulat, non sacrificium. Cetera prope hominibus hominum praecepit causa, ut inter se concorditer atque amice viverent. Hoc docet quod toties mutuam caritatem inculcat, quod eis quos in regnum suum admittit pro benevolentia in homines suam beatitudinem

20 rependere se profitetur. Quos reicit hoc nomine detestatur quod benefici in homines et benevoli non fuerint. Facile reconciliatur Deus si reconcilies hominem, nec ulla est expeditior via ad gratiam Dei quam per gratiam hominum.

46. Itaque magna se sacra facere putet mulier cum marito inservit; mag-

25 nas aedes sacras circumire cum mariti lectum. Quamquam sunt nonnullae quae quamlibet affectis maritis templa sua non relinquerent, haud aeque pietatis gratia quantum (ut equidem arbitror) vel consuetudinis vel oblectationis. De istis quid opus est disputemus? Illas vero quas ducit religio Paulus hunc in modum admonet: 'Virgo cogitat quae sunt Domini, quomodo Deo

30 placeat; mulier cogitat quae sunt viri, quomodo viro placeat.' Non tollit curam religionis in coniuge, sed ostendit minorem iam esse quod virgo tota sit Domini deque illo solo vacet ei cogitare; marita divisa inter Deum et virum, ut quam totam prius occupabat contemplatio vitae caelestis, ea nunc ad

---

45. (Accedere ... amico) *Vulg. Matth. 5, 23–24* // (Oboedientiam ... sacrificium) *Vulg. Matth. 9, 13*
   46. (Virgo ... placeat) *Vulg. I Cor. 7, 34* //

1 nec inscio Γ ne inscio quidem **H** // 2 tu velle te Γ tute velle **H** // 7 indigeat Γ egeat **H** / posuit ... coniugis Γ mavult Deus in coniuge **H** // 10 vir tuus Γ maritus **H** // 11 comparem ... sociatum Γ maritum **H** // 13–14 conglutinati rebus Γ rebus conglutinati **H** // 15 nostris Γ multis nostris **H** // 20 detestatur Γ exsecratur **H** // 24 facere Γ agere **H** // 26 haud Γ non **H** // 27 quantum **WW²B** ac **HV** / ut equidem arbitror Γ *deest in* **H** // 28–p.56,17 Illas vero ... in ea ipsa religione quam captat Γ *deest in* **H**

speak of acting without his consent. Therefore if your husband has need of
your service and you answer that you want to go, let us not say to a dance
or to a public entertainment or a banquet or some other pastime (for that
would obviously be more appropriate for harlots), but to pray and pay a
visit to the Church, know that your prayers will not be pleasing to God and
you will not find him in church. God wishes you to pray, but when you are
free of marital obligations; he wishes you to visit his temple but only when
your husband does not need you at home. These are the duties of marriage
that God placed upon a wife. He wishes you to approach his altar, but only
when you have reconciled yourself to your friend. How much more will he
require that you be reconciled with your husband, your greatest friend? Why
do you attend sacred functions and travel from church to church when your
husband expressly orders something else or tacitly demands it? Do you seek
God in church when you abandon your consort, to whom God joined you,
sick and hungry at home? Around his bed all things are sacred; there are the
altars, there is God, where peace and concord reign, especially between those
who are bound to each other by these vows to remain inseparable. It will be
easy for you to make God your friend if you make your husband your friend.
God has no need of our services; he reserved for himself piety and the highest
worship. He demands obedience, not sacrifice. Practically everything else
he prescribes for mankind is for their mutual benefit, that they may live in
harmony and friendship. That is why he so often inculcates mutual love and
declares that he admits into his kingdom and promises the reward of beatitude
to those who show kindness to their neighbor. He casts out and detests those
who were neither beneficent nor benevolent towards their neighbor. God will
easily be reconciled to you if you reconcile yourself with your neighbor. There
is no more accessible path to the favor of God than through the favor of men.

   46. So let a woman be convinced that she performs great acts of worship
when she serves her husband and goes the round of the great churches when
she stays by her husband's bed. And yet there are some women who would
not give up their visits to church no matter how gravely ill their husbands
might be, not so much for the sake of piety, in my opinion, as through habit
and personal satisfaction. Why should we discuss such women? As for those
who are motivated by religious devotion Paul gives this warning: 'The unmarried woman thinks of what pertains to the Lord, how she may please
God; the married woman thinks of what pertains to her husband and how
she may please her husband.' He does not take away the practice of religion from wives but he shows that it is now of less importance, because
an unmarried woman belongs totally to the Lord and has the time to think
only of him, whereas the married woman is divided between God and her
husband, and while previously she occupied herself exclusively with the contemplation of the heavenly life, now she must descend to the cares of this

---

46. great churches: Probably referring to the pilgrimage of the Roman basilicas.

curas vitae huius descenderit propter virum. Non quod ista ratio a Domino aliena sit, quam ipse idem constituit, sed altior erat altera et Domino propinquior. Placet quidem uxor Domino, sed per virum medium, quia marito studet satisfacere quem praefecit Dominus. Placet virgo et vidua sine viro
5 et quasi sine interprete. Distinctae sunt earum cogitationes, ut Marthae et Magdalenae distincta opera, non per contrarietatem, sed per gradum, ut excellentiora sint virginis quam maritae. Ergo pietatis in muliere maxima pars est cura et ministerium coniugis.

47. Neque vero existimet quis Apostolum cum ait: 'Mulier cogitat quae
10 sunt mariti,' quid fieri soleat, non quid debeat innuere. Neque enim Paulus in consuetudinem adducit res pravas nec fenestram illis aperit qua sese ingerant. Quid quod nec omnes virgines cogitant de Domino nec omnes uxores de maritis? Docet nos ergo quid oporteat et velit in utrisque fieri, ut quam prius in caelibatu cunctam esse in cogitatione de Domino par erat, ea nunc
15 de contemplatione illa detrahat quod impendat coniugali ministerio, alioqui nec Paulo magistro nec Christo Domino satisfactura et amissura religionem in ea ipsa religione quam captat. Idem Apostolus scribens ad Timotheum de mulieris officio illud posuit: 'Mulier in silentio discat, cum omni subiectione. Docere autem mulieri non permitto neque dominari viro, sed esse
20 in silentio.' Et ad Corinthios: 'Mulieres vestrae in Ecclesia ne loquantur; si quid vero dubitant, domi virum quaeque suum roget.' Quae mihi profecto lex eo videtur spectare ut discat mulier a marito et in rebus incertis sententiam illius sequatur et eadem credat quae ipse. Quod si erret, maritus solus in culpa est, uxore innoxia, nisi forte manifestiora sint quam quae ignorari
25 sine noxia non possint aut aliter doceant ii quibus fidem haberi etiam a marito convenit. Impia enim, ut maxime maritus imperet atque exigat, facienda non sunt, si scias esse talia; et unus agnoscendus viro superior, viro carior: Christus. Caput quidem mulieris vir, at viri caput Christus. Plurimae sanctae mulieres nostrae religionis etiam a maritis suis supplicio affectae sunt,
30 quod Christi praecepta contra voluntatem eorum sequerentur. Cavendum tamen ne temere et ex cuiuslibet sententia de pietate mariti statuas. Gravius est hoc quam ut cuiusvis iudicio credi debeat, quod esset in universo genere humano amplissima dissidiorum materia. Vetabat olim Apostolus ab impio marito uxorem discedere nisi ille sineret. Tantum est videlicet coniugii

---

46. (Marthae ... opera) *Vulg. Luc. 10, 42*
47. (Mulier ... mariti) *Vulg. I Cor. 7, 34* // (Mulier ... silentio) *Vulg. I Tim. 2, 11–12* // (Mulieres ... roget) *Vulg. I Cor. 14, 34–35* // (Caput ... Christus) *Vulg. I Cor. 11, 3* // (Vetabat ... sineret) *Vulg. I Cor. 7, 13*

17 Idem Apostolus Γ Apostolus Paulus **H** // **23** Quod si **H** Quod Γ // **24** forte Γ forsan **H** // **26** atque exigat Γ *deest in* **H** // **27** si scias esse talia Γ *deest in* **H** // **30–33** Cavendum ... dissidiorum materia Γ *deest in* **H** // **33** Vetabat olim Γ Tamen vetat **H** // **33–34** impio marito Γ impiis maritis **H** // **34** sineret Γ sinat **H**

life for her husband's sake. It is not that this way of life is alien to the Lord, since he instituted it, but the other is more lofty and closer to the Lord. The wife is pleasing to the Lord but through the intermediacy of her husband, because she is anxious to please her husband, whom God placed over her. The unmarried woman and the widow are pleasing to God without a man and without an intermediary, as it were. Their thoughts are different as the activities of Martha and Mary were different, not through opposition but in degree, as the thoughts of an unmarried woman are more elevated than those of a married woman. Therefore the greatest part of piety in a married woman is the care and ministry of her husband.

47. Let no one think that when the Apostle said 'The wife thinks of things that concern her husband,' he was implying that this was what a woman usually does rather than what she ought to do, for Paul does not induce us into bad habits nor does he leave an opening for them to rush in. What of the fact that not all unmarried women think of the Lord and not all wives think of their husbands? He teaches us what is fitting to be done in both states of life so that what befitted a woman in an unmarried state, namely, total absorption in the Lord, she should now convert to her marital duties. Otherwise she would not satisfy her master, St. Paul, or Christ the Lord, and in her very devotion she would lose the devotion that she is trying to attain. The same Apostle Paul writing to Timothy laid down this precept concerning the duties of a wife: 'Let a woman learn in silence, with all submissiveness. I do not allow a woman to teach or have authority over men, but to remain silent.' And to the Corinthians he wrote: 'Let your wives not speak in church; if they have any questions, let them ask their husbands at home.' This law clearly seems to me to mean that a wife should learn from her husband and in matters of doubt should follow his opinion and believe the same things he does. If the husband should err, he is solely to blame; the wife is innocent, unless his errors are so manifest that they could not be ignored without blame, or are contrary to the teachings of those in whom her husband should have put his faith. Acts of impiety should never be committed, no matter how much her husband orders and demands it of her, if you know them to be such. One person must be acknowledged as superior and dearer than your husband, and that is Christ. The head of the woman is man, but the head of the man is Christ. Many holy women of our religion have even suffered torture at the hands of their husbands in order to remain faithful to Christ's commandments against the will of their husbands. Nevertheless, care must be taken that you do not judge rashly or in accordance with another's opinion concerning the piety of your husband. This is too serious a matter for you to trust anyone else's opinion, one on which there are widespread differences of opinion among mankind. The Apostle forbade a wife to leave an impious husband, unless he allowed it. So strong is the bond of marriage

vinculum ut nec pietas dissolvat, Paulo auctore, nisi impietas permittat. Quid in utroque Christiano, utroque pio statuendum est? Quomodo in bonum virum affectam oportet esse uxorem?

48. Equidem praetermittere nec volo nec debeo de uxoris officio gravissima monita quae sunt in Oeconomicorum volumine posteriore quod Aristotelis nomine inscribitur. 'Existimare,' inquit, 'probam mulierem decet mores viri legem esse vitae suae, a Deo sibi impositam, per coniunctionem matrimonii atque consortii. Quos si quidem aequo tulerit animo, perfacile reget domum; sin contra, difficilius. Quapropter decet non solum in prosperis rebus secundaque fortuna unanimem se viro praestare et inservire velle, verum etiam in adversis. Si sit in rebus defectus vel corporis aegrotatio vel alienatio mentis, aequo ferat animo et obsequatur, nisi forte turpe aliquid sit et indignum. Ne si quid perturbatione animi vir deliquerit, memoriter servet, sed affectui ignorantiaeque adscribat. Nam quanto in his diligentius obsequetur, tanto illi maiorem gratiam habebit cum animi perturbatio erit sedata. Et si iubente eo id turpe non provenerit, melius recognoscet ad sanitatem reversus. Quapropter ab his cavere debet mulier, in aliis multo magis obtemperare quam si empta venisset in domum. Magno enim pretio empta fuit, societate vitae et procreationis liberorum, quibus nec maius nec sanctius quicquam inveniri potest. Praeterea si cum fortunato vixisset viro, non usque adeo virtus eius enituisset; nam est sane parum secundis rebus bene uti. Attamen adversas moderate perferre multo maius est existimandum; nam in magnis calamitatibus et iniuriis nihil abiecte facere excelsi est animi. Precandum est quidem ne quid tale accidat viro. Quod si quid accidat adversi, putare debet hinc optimam sibi laudem si recte gesserit perventuram, secum ipsa reputans quod nec Alcestis tantam sibi gloriam comparasset nec Penelope tot tantasque meruisset laudes, si cum fortunatis viris vixissent. Verum Admeti et Ulissis adversitates paraverunt illis memoriam sempiternam; in adversitatibus enim virorum suorum fidem ac iustitiam erga illos servantes gloriam non immerito sunt consecutae. Nam prosperitatis quidem facile est reperire participes, adversitatis vero nisi quae optimae sint mulieres participes esse renuunt. Ob quae omnia multo magis decet virum in honore habere nec illum contemnere.' Hactenus Aristotelis verba.

---

48. (Existimare ... contemnere) *Aristot. oec. 3, 1*

1 Paulo auctore Γ *deest in* H ∥ 2 statuendum Γ existimandum H ∥ 4–6 de uxoris officio ... inscribitur Γ Aristotelis de uxoris officio sanctissima praecepta quae sunt in eius oeconomico volumine posteriore H ∥ 8 tulerit Γ feret H ∥ 14 affectui Γ aegritudini H ∥ 15–16 animi ... sedata Γ ab aegritudine fuerit liberatus H ∥ 16 iubente eo id turpe non provenerit **B** iubente id turpe non provenerit **HWW²** iubenti aliquid turpe non paruerit **V** ∥ 19 societate vitae Γ societate magno pretio vitae H / procreationis Γ procreatione H ∥ 21 enituisset Γ illustrata esset H ∥ 23 excelsi Γ celsi H ∥ 24 quidem Γ igitur H ∥ 25–26 perventuram **HWW²B** proventuram **V**

that according to Paul, not even piety can dissolve it unless impiety permits it. What rules must be laid down when both are good and pious Christians? What attitude should a wife display towards a good husband?

48. I do not wish nor should I pass over in silence the grave recommendations concerning a wife's duties that are contained in the last book of the *Economics*, attributed to Aristotle:

> The virtuous woman should esteem that the customary mode of behavior of her husband is the law of her life, imposed by God through the bond of marriage and community of life. If she supports it with resignation, she will govern the house with great ease; if not, it will be more difficult. Therefore it behooves her to show herself of one mind with her husband not only in prosperity and good fortune but also in adversity. If there be some lack of material things or sickness of body or alienation of mind, she should bear it patiently and obey, unless it is something base and unworthy. And if her husband should commit some fault through some mental aberration, she should not retain it in her mind, but ascribe it to his emotional state or to ignorance. The more scrupulously she obeys him in these circumstances the more grateful he will be to her when his troubled mental state is calmed; and if the base thing be demanded of her does not turn out well, he will appreciate it the more when he returns to his senses. Therefore a woman should be cautious at such times but in other things she should show herself more obedient than if she had come into that house as a bought slave. Indeed she was bought at a great price—partnership in life and the procreation of children—which are the greatest and most sacred things that exist. Besides, if she lived with a successful husband, her virtue would not have stood out so clearly. It is a matter of little account to enjoy the fruits of prosperity. But it is considered a much greater thing to suffer adversity with patience. Not to be cast down in the midst of great calamities is the mark of a noble spirit. One must pray that no such misfortune will befall your husband, but if he does suffer the blows of fortune she should think that she will receive great praise if she acts courageously, reflecting within herself that neither Alcestis would have won such renown nor Penelope merited such praise if they had lived with husbands who enjoyed good fortune. Whereas the troubles of Admetus and Ulysses procured these women everlasting fame. By maintaining loyalty and justice towards their spouses in their adversities they not undeservedly attained undying glory. It is easy to find companions in prosperity but women refuse to be companions of misery, except those of exceptional mettle. For all these reasons it is better to hold one's husband in honor and not despise him.

CAP. IV. DE CONCORDIA CONIUGUM

49. Percensere concordiae bona et quemadmodum universa quae in mundo sunt atque adeo mundus ipse pace ac concordia consistat infinita res esset nec loci huius. De matrimonio est nobis sermo institutus. Dico maximam eius tranquillitatem ac perinde felicitatis partem esse concordiam, maximam tempestatem ac miseriae partem discordiam. Pythagorici inter magistri Pythagorae praecepta illa ex primis tenebant, ab ipsis saepenumero usurpata: 'Fugienda et abscindenda sunt prorsus languor a corpore, imperitia ab animo, luxuria a ventre, a civitate seditio, a domo discordia, et in universum a cunctis rebus intemperantia.' Ulysses apud Homerum Nausicaae, Alcinoi filiae, virum et domum optat et concordiam, quo nullum melius est in vita bonum aut magis expetendum. Nam cum concorditer vir atque uxor degunt, multos inimicis dolores afferunt, multa amicis gaudia et primum omnium sibi ipsis. Sic ille. Quam fortunatum coniugium putamus fuisse Albucii, qui cum Terentiana sua viginti quinque annos egit sine aliqua vel levi offensione? Quanto fortunatius Publii Rubrii Celeris, qui cum Ennia quattuor et quadraginta absque ulla querela? Oritur ex discordia dissensio, rixa, iurgium, pugna. Querulae sunt pleraeque feminae et difficiles cumque subinde levissimis de causis obiurgent maritos, res exit in maximas animorum offensiones. Nec aliquid est quod ita alienet virum ab uxore ut crebra rixa et uxoris lingua amarulenta, quam Salomon tecto in hieme perstillanti assimilat, quoniam utraque res virum domo expellit. Idem satius ait esse habitare in deserta terra quam cum uxore litigiosa et iracunda. Hoc beneficium conferunt in omnes quaedam intolerabiles, ut nulla ferenda videatur. Hinc Gai interpretatio 'Caelibes quasi caelites' et Graece, ἠίθεους quasi ἡμιθέους, hoc est, caelibes semidei. Tum dictum illud: 'Qui non litigat caelebs est,' ceu omnes coniugati litigent.

50. Eadem res quieta pleraque ingenia et rixarum inimica ab uxoribus ducendis absterruit. Multa etiam in opprobrium sexus propterea conscripta, immerito utique, et olim quaesita atque acriter exercita divortia; quae hodieque in Christiano populo desiderantur a plurimis, quod dicant se usuros

---

49. (Fugienda ... intemperantia) Γνῶμαι τῶν Πυθαγορείων *111a (Chadwick, p.93)* // (Ulysses ... ipsis) *Hom. Od. 6, 180–185* // (Salomon ... assimilat) *Vulg. prov. 19, 13* // (Satius ... iracunda) *Vulg. prov. 21, 9; 25, 24* // (Gai ... caelites) *Quint. inst. 1, 6, 36*

4 loci huius Γ oratio exitum inveniret H / matrimonio Γ coniugio H // **11** optat et concordiam Γ et concordiam optat H // **13–14** primum omnium Γ in primis H // **20** ut Γ ac H // **21–22** in hieme perstillanti assimilat Γ perstillanti in hieme comparat H // **22** expellit Γ pellit H // **24** conferunt in omnes Γ dant omnibus H // **25–26** et Graece ... semidei Γ *deest in* H // **28** et rixarum inimica Γ *deest in* H // **29** absterruit Γ avertit H // **30** immerito utique Γ *deest in* H // **30–31** quae hodieque Γ et nunc ea H // **31** plurimis Γ plerisque H

CHAPTER 4. ON CONCORD BETWEEN SPOUSES

49. To rehearse the blessings of concord and how everything in the universe and the universe itself consists of peace and concord would be an endless task, which has no place here. We have proposed to speak of marriage. I say that the greatest tranquility and a great part of happiness in marriage is concord, and the greatest disturbance and unhappiness comes from discord. The Pythagoreans often cited this saying of those handed down by their master, Pythagoras: 'Sloth must be avoided and banished from the body, ignorance from the mind, indulgence from the belly, sedition from the city, discord from the home and, in general, intemperance from all things.' In Homer Ulysses wishes for Nausicaa, daughter of Alcinoos, a husband and a home, and concord, which is the greatest and most sought after good in life. For when man and wife live together in concord, they cause great sorrow to their enemies, great joy to their friends and most of all to themselves.' How fortunate do we imagine the marriage of Albucius must have been, who lived with his wife Terentiana for twenty years without the slightest displeasure? How much more fortunate the marriage of Publius Rubrius Celer, who lived with his wife Ennia for forty-four years without a quarrel? From discord there arise dissension, wrangling, disputes, fighting. Most women are quarrelsome and difficult, and when they scold their husbands for the most trivial reasons, it ends up in hard feelings. There is nothing that so alienates a husband from his wife as frequent altercations and a wife's bitter tongue, which Solomon compares to a leaky roof in winter, since both things drive a man from his home. The same writer said that it was preferable to live in the desert than with a quarrelsome and irascible wife. A few insupportable women have conferred this benefit upon all women, so that no woman is thought to be tolerable. Whence came the interpretation of Gaius: 'Celibate is akin to celestial and in Greek ἠίθεοι is equal to ἡμίθεοι, that is, celibates are demi-gods.' A saying arose from this: 'He who is without a wife is without strife,' as if all married couples quarreled.

50. This very thing deterred many peaceable natures, alien to quarreling, from taking a wife. Many invectives have been written against the female sex on account of this, undeservedly, to be sure, and at one time divorces were sought and harshly carried out. Even today they are desired by many among the Christian people because they say that their wives would be more

---

49. Albucius: Probably C. Albucius Silus, a famous declaimer of the 1st cent. A.D., much admired by Seneca the Elder. Of his wife Terentiana nothing is known.

Gaius: Vives certainly believed this to be the famous Roman jurisconsult of the 2nd cent. AD, now best known for his *Institutes*, an elementary manual on Roman law. So did his contemporaries: Erasmus discusses the same etymology from a passage in Quintilian, where modern editions print 'Gavius' for 'Gaius.' Gavius Bassus was a grammarian of the time of Cicero (CWE 83, p.125 and n54).

commodis magis uxoribus si illae sciant se posse pelli ni morigerae sint et tractabiles. In quo mea sententia vel viri falluntur vel mulieres sunt stultissimae quae non reputant tanto obsequentiores debere se viris praebere, ut iucundius vivant cum iis, a quibus nulla ratione separari queant neu perpetuam necessitatem in miseriam vertant quam exuere numquam possint. Multum enim positum est in uxoris manu ut concordia sit domi. Nam viri animus minus est irritabilis nec in genere modo humano, sed in cunctis animantibus, sicut Aristoteles inquit: 'Mares, ut animosiores sunt et ferociores, ita simpliciores etiam minusque insidiosi, nempe generosioribus animis praediti; feminae contra, malitiosiores et suspicionibus atque insidiis magis intentae.' Quo fit ut infirmissimis quoque coniecturis pertrahantur et laedi se quamlibet levi ictu putent animi tenelli ideoque crebro expostulent virosque indignitate querelarum accendant. Sed facilior reconciliationi vir quam femina, sicut inter viros ut quisque maxime muliebri est pectore minimeque generoso, ita est iniuriae retinentissimus et pertinacissime vindictam expetit nec mediocriter se vindicasse contentus est. Erat Romae sacellum in Palatio deae cuiusdam, in quo, si quid domi inter coniuges inciderat iurgii, locuti quae volebant reconciliabantur. Dea haec Viriplaca nuncupata est, quae nomine suo admonebat non uxorem a viro placandam esse, sed virum ab uxore. Etiam in mariti culpa, nulla tua, abs te tamen, qui in illius es manu ac potestate, initium est captandum reconciliandae gratiae. Quanto magis si in te haereat culpa aliqua, summissione, blandimentis, paenitentia maritus est deliniendus! Et quamquam optima pars eorum quae diximus ad concordiam spectet, tamen propius huc quaedam afferemus.

51. Unum illud est ad concordiam praecipuum et efficacissimum: si amet virum uxor. Ea enim est amoris natura ut amorem eliciat. Nec mirentur quaedam se a maritis non amari cum ipsae affirment se amare illos. Videant ne non aeque ament, ut prae se ostentant. Ament vere et amabuntur: nam ficta, simulata, adumbrata, tum ipsa se aliquando tandem produnt, tum non easdem quas verae germanaeque res et expressae vires obtinent. Porro si ament se mutuo vir et uxor, idem volent, idem nolent, quae demum (ut inquit ille) firma amicitia est. Discordia et dissensio nulla esse inter eos

---

50. (Mares ... intentae) *Aristot. hist. an. 9, 1 (608b)* ∥ (Erat ... uxore) *Val. Max. 2, 1, 6*
51. (idem volent ... est) *Sall. Catil. 20, 4*

1 commodis magis Γ commodioribus **H** / morigerae sint Γ sint morigerae **H** ∥ 1–2 et tractabiles Γ *deest in* **H** ∥ 3 reputant Γ cogitant **H** / se viris praebere Γ viris esse **H** ∥ 4 neu Γ et **H** ∥ 5 numquam Γ non **H** ∥ 7 genere modo humano Γ genere humano modo **H** / cunctis Γ omnibus **H** ∥ 10 suspicionibus atque Γ *deest in* **H** ∥ 11 magis intentae Γ intentae magis **H** / infirmissimis ... pertrahantur Γ etiam leviculis suspicionibus ducantur **H** ∥ 11–12 et laedi ... tenelli Γ *deest in* **H** ∥ 20–23 Etiam ... deliniendus Γ *deest in* **H** ∥ 27 affirment Γ dicant **H** ∥ 28 prae se ostentant Γ dicunt **H** ∥ 29 tum ipsa Γ et ipsa **H** ∥ 29–30 tum non Γ et non **H**

agreeable if they knew that they could be driven out if they were not docile and tractable. In this matter, in my opinion, either men are deceived or women are very stupid not to see that they should show themselves more obedient to their husbands so that they may live more pleasantly with those from whom they can in no way be separated. Else they turn a permanent necessity into a misery which they can never throw off. Much depends on the woman to ensure concord in the home. For a man's character is less irritable than a woman's, not only among humans but in the whole animal world, as Aristotle said: 'Since males are more spirited and more fierce, they are also more simple and less cunning, endowed with a more noble spirit. Females, on the contrary, are more malicious and more inclined to suspicion and plotting. Therefore it comes about that they are influenced by the vaguest conjectures and their tender minds are hurt by the slightest blow and they frequently expostulate with their husbands and anger them by the importunity of their complaints. The male is quicker to be reconciled than the woman, and it is true also that among men those who have more feminine feelings and are less high-born retain the memory of offenses longer, seek revenge relentlessly and are not content with mere revenge.' There was in Rome a tiny shrine on the Palatine dedicated to a certain goddess, in which if there was some domestic quarrel between spouses, they said what they wished and were reconciled. This goddess was called Viriplaca, a name that signified that it was not the wife who had to be appeased by the man but the man by the wife. Even if the fault was your husband's and not yours, the initiative in winning back favor must be taken by you, since you are under his power and authority. How much more must your husband be mollified by submission, blandishments, and penitence if any of the fault resides with you. Although the most important part of what I have been saying has to do with concord, I shall add some further details.

51. The principal and most effective requirement to assure concord is that the wife love her husband. For it is the nature of love to elicit love in return. Certain women should not be astonished if they are not loved by their husbands even if they affirm that they love their husbands. Let them see if they love them as much as they claim. Let them love truly and they will be loved. Things that are feigned, simulated and counterfeited give themselves away eventually and do not have the same efficacy as genuine and clearly defined things. If husband and wife love each other mutually, they will want and not want the same things, which in the last analysis is staunch friendship, as the great authority wrote. There will be no discord or dissension among

---

50. Viriplaca: a Roman goddess who helped wives win back their husbands' favor after an estrangement.

poterit in quibus idem est cor, non diversa cupiens, eadem sententia, non diversa sentiens. Blanca, mater mea, cum in coniugio quindecim egisset annos, numquam a me visa est rixari cum patre aut in contrarium voluntatis illius tendere. Eadem illis erat omnino mens et affectus simillimi. Sed de 5 matre mea alius erit fusius dicendi locus commodior.

52. Porro quod nonnullae, cum imprudentius ament, ad infringendam concordiam impetu rapiuntur, aliquot praeceptiunculis promovenda est eorum prudentia et vehementia retardanda. Praecipuum est omnium, si continuerint animum, hoc est, affectum et perturbationem; quae imbecilles 10 feminarum animos maiore turbine et corripit et secum trahit, utpote quae minore robore possunt obsistere. Erit ergo in muliebri animo magna modestia et eam operibus exseret ac patefaciet. Iterum admonenda est, immo saepe, ne aliquid agat ut agere videatur. Nam id inefficax atque infirmum est. Sit qualis videri velit, eo facilius et certius et verius videbitur. Nec putet 15 se simulatione imponere oculis omnium posse. Non sunt homines stipites aut saxa qui rem fucatam fictamque discernere a vera et genuina nesciant. Adde quod ut spectantes fallant, non tamen rerum ipsam naturam fallent, quae non eandem energiam atque efficaciam rebus falsis adumbratisque indidit quam nativis et solidis. Experiantur hoc in se ipsis: reputent cum animis 20 suis num modestas putent eas quae modestiam imitantur cum non habeant, num redament eas quae se illas amare falso asseverant.

53. Proderit et illud nuptae exhibere consilium quod Lollio prudens poeta Horatius de amico, ut se amici moribus actibusque accommodet: ille venari si volet, ne tu poemata componas, sed excussis Camenis sequaris iu- 25 menta retibus onusta et canes. Fratres erant Amphion et Zethus ex Antiopa

---

52. (alius ... locus) *inst. fem. Christ. 2, 140*
53. (Ille ... canes) *Hor. epist. 1, 18, 39–40* //

---

3 rixari Γ litigare **H** // 3–4 aut in contrarium ... affectus simillimi Γ *deest in* **H** // 4 Sed de **WW²B** Duo solebat in ore frequentia habere ceu proverbia: cum vellet significare se aliquid credere, aiebat: 'Tamquam si dixisset Lodovicus Vives'; cum se velle: 'Tamquam si vellet Lodovicus Vives.' Eum ego Lodovicum Vivem patrem meum et alias saepe audivi dicentem et cum illud referret quidam seu Scipionis Africani Minoris seu Pomponii Attici (credo utriusque) quod numquam in gratiam rediisset cum matre nec se, quod difficilius esset, cum uxore; reliquis id verbum admiratis, cum paene in proverbium venisset concordia Vivis et Blancae, respondit: 'Ut Scipio cum matre, cuius gratiam numquam exierat, ideo nec rediit.' Sed de **HV** // 4–5 de matre mea Γ de sanctissima matre mea **H** // 5 alius erit ... commodior Γ quam ego nil dubito in caelis fructum integerrimae actae vitae iam percipere, non est in alieno copiosius loquendum opere, cum destinatus sit nobis de illius actis vitaque liber **H** // 6 imprudentius ament Γ ament imprudentius **H** // 7 promovenda Γ promonenda **H** // 8 Praecipuum est omnium Γ idque unica sola re **H** // 10 utpote quae Γ ut **H** // 12 exseret ac patefaciet Γ ostendet **H** // 14 eo ... verius Γ nam eo facilius, certius, melius **H** // 18 eandem ... efficaciam Γ idem robur easdem vires **H** // 18–19 indidit Γ dedit **H** // 19–20 reputent cum animis suis Γ videant **H** // 21 falso asseverant Γ profitentur et simulant quando non ament **H**

those who have one heart, which does not desire different things, and one mind, which does not think different things. I never saw my mother, Blanca, in fifteen years of marriage, fighting with my father or entertaining views contrary to his. They had one mind and identical feelings. But concerning my mother there will be another opportunity to speak of her in more detail.

52. Since some women love impetuously and are driven by impulse to destroy marital discord, I must exhort them to prudence by some little rules and calm their violent feelings. The most important thing is to control these impulses, that is, the passions and emotions which take hold of women's weak minds with greater violence and drag them along, since they offer less resistance. There must be great restraint in a woman's mind and she should manifest it in her actions. She must be continually warned not to act in a certain way only for the sake of appearance, for that is useless and ineffective. Let her be what she wishes to appear, and her appearance will be more natural, more authentic. She should not think that she can deceive everyone by her simulations. Men are not stumps or stones, who cannot distinguish the artificial and the feigned from the true and genuine. Furthermore, though they may deceive onlookers, they cannot deceive nature, which did not endow false and counterfeit things with the same energy and efficacy that it gave natural and real things. Let them make proof of it themselves, considering within themselves whether they think women to be modest who affect modesty, and whether they love in return those women who falsely claim to love them.

53. The counsel that the poet Horace gave to Lollius concerning a friend, that he should accommodate himself to his friend's character and activities, will be of use to the married woman. Horace advises: 'If he wants to go hunting, do not set about composing poems, but, dismissing the Muses, follow in the train of the pack animals laden down with nets and dogs.' Amphion and Zethus, sons of Antiope, were brothers, in fact, twins. The first was very

et quidem gemini: prior lyra doctissimus, Zethus rudis. Cumque parum
lyrae sonus placeret Zetho et videretur ea causa germanorum discindi gratia, Amphion lyram posuit. Sic uxor attemperet se mariti moribus ac studiis,
ne illa oderit aut aspernetur. Andromachen, Hectoris coniugem, memoriae
5   mandatum est ipsam suis manibus fenum et avenam Hectoris equis prae-
buisse, quod maritus illis delectaretur et in bellorum usum accuratissime ac
indulgenter aleret. Caecilius Plinius amasse uxorem se unice multis epistolis
suis declarat, inter quas est quaedam ad Hispullam, uxoris amitam, quae
illam educarat. His litteris tum agit illi gratias quod talem formarit puellam,
10   tum causam cur tantopere uxorem amet aperit, sic de illa scribens: 'Amat
me, quod castitatis indicium est. Accedit his studium litterarum quod ex mei
caritate concepit. Meos libellos habet, lectitat, ediscit etiam. Qua illa sollicitudine, cum videor acturus, quanto, cum egi, gaudio afficitur? Disponit
qui nuntient sibi quem assensum, quos clamores excitarim, quem eventum
15   iudicii tulerim. Eadem, si quando recito, in proximum discreta velo sedet
laudesque nostras avidissimis auribus excipit. Versus quidem meos cantat
formatque cithara, non artifice aliquo docente, sed amore, qui magister est
optimus.'
       54. Nuper cum Lutetiae Parisiorum essem convenissemque Gulielmum
20   Budaeum domi suae praeteriissetque per impluvium qua nos deambulaba-
mus uxor eius formosissima et quae (quantum ex facie et totius corporis
habitu plane heroino coniectare poteram) proba cum primis et prudens mihi
materfamilias visa est, ubi maritum ea qua decebat reverentia, me etiam
comiter atque honorifice salutasset, rogavi ex illo num esset eius coniunx?
25   'Haec est,' inquit, 'coniunx mea, quae mihi sic morem gerit ut non tractet
negligentius libros meos quam liberos, quod videat me studiosissimum.' In
quo haec mea sententia maiorem etiam laudem meretur quam Pliniana,
quod litteras nescit, cum illa sciret.
       55. Quanto haec prudentius et honestius quam quae viros ab studiis lit-
30   terarum, ab honestis artibus retrahunt, ad quaestum, ad lusus, ad voluptates
adhortantur ac propellunt, ut ipsae etiam in partem veniant vel lucri vel
lusus vel deliciarum, quoniam communicari secum posse studia desperant?
Stultae ignorant quanto solidior et verior est voluptas ex gloria, quod maritis fruantur sapientibus quam opulentis aut deliciosis. Tum quanto et com-
35   modius et iucundius cum sapientibus viris vitam degant quam cum stultis vel

---

53. (Andromachen ... aleret) *Hom. Il. 8, 185–190* // (Amat ... optimus) *Plin. epist. 4, 19*

6-7 ac indulgenter aleret Γ haberet **H** // **10** illa Γ uxore **H** // **19** Nuper cum Γ Cum
proxime **H** // **20** per impluvium Γ *deest in* **H** // **23** ubi Γ haec ubi **H** // **31** ac propellunt
Γ *deest in* **H** // **32** desperant Γ non putant **H** // **35** et iucundius Γ *deest in* **H**

gifted in playing the lyre, the other had no training at all. Since the sound of the lyre did not please Zethus and this seemed to be a source of discord between them, Amphion laid aside the lyre. So a wife should adapt herself to her husband's character and interests, and not hate or despise them. It is recorded that Andromache, the wife of Hector, fed Hector's horses hay and oats with her own hands because she saw what delight her husband took in them, and used every care in feeding them so that they would be good in battle. Plinius Caecilius declares in many of his letters that he loved his wife singularly, and among these letters there is one that he sent to his wife's aunt, Hispulla, who had brought her up. In this letter he not only thanks her for having moulded her character when she was a young girl, but also gives the reason why he loved her so much, in these words:

> She loves me, which is a sign of chastity. In addition to this she has an interest in literature, which she conceived out of affection for me. She has copies of my books, she reads them again and again and even learns them by heart. What concern she shows when I have to plead a case, how joyful she is when I have finished it. She posts people to report to her what approval and what applause I won and what was the outcome of the trial. Whenever I give a public recitation of my works, she sits nearby, her face discreetly veiled and listens to my praise with avid ears. She sings my verses and sets them to the cithara, not taught by any musician, but by love, which is the best of all teachers.

54. Recently, when I was in Paris and visited Guillaume Budé at his home, his wife passed through the vestibule where we were walking. She was a very beautiful woman and I was able to divine immediately from her countenance and her whole bearing, which was truly that of a heroine, that she was a woman of great virtue and a prudent mistress of the household. After she greeted her husband with due respect and me courteously and graciously, I asked him if that was his wife. 'This is my wife,' he said, 'who is so attentive to my wishes that she treats my books with no less care than my children, for she sees that I am very dedicated to my studies.' In this she merits even greater praise than the wife of Pliny, in my opinion, because she knows nothing of literature, while the other was well versed in it.

55. How much more prudent and honorable these women than those who hold their husbands back from the study of letters and from honorable pursuits and exhort and impel them to the acquisition of wealth, amusements and pleasures so that they too may partake of this material gain, entertainment and luxuries, since they have no hope of being able to share their interests in study. In their stupidity they do not recognize how much more true and substantial is the pleasure that comes from having wise rather than rich husbands or those given to fine living. Nor do they see how much more agreeable and pleasant it is to spend your life with wise men rather

---

54. Guillaume Budé: Vives met the famous humanist scholar while in Paris in 1519.

cum iis qui sapientiae frenos affectibus suis non iniecerunt, quos passim
excitatae in animo perturbationes cunctos abripiunt et transversos longissime
a recto et iusto evehunt. Nec solum non studia, sed nec fastidiet in marito
quicquam, non verbis, non oculis, non gestu, nulla denique significatione.
5 Omnia diliget, omnia admirabitur, omnia colet, omnia assentietur; habebit
quidvis dicenti fidem etiam si narret veri dissimilia et incredibilia. Omnes
illius vultus sumet, ridenti arridebit, maesto se praebebit maestam, servata
semper auctoritate matronalis integritatis ac virtutis, ut magis illa ex amico
proveniant animo quam adulatorio. Nec se marito ulla in re praeferet, illum
10 patrem, illum dominum, illum maiorem, potiorem, meliorem se et putabit et
prae se feret et profitebitur. Qui poterit constare amicitia et amor si dives ipsa
contemnas maritum pauperem, si formosa deformem, si nobilis ignobilem?

56. Satyricus inquit: 'Intolerabilius nihil est quam femina dives.' Idem
Divus Hieronymus in Iovinianum: 'Theophrastus quoque divitem uxorem
15 ferre tormentum esse ait.' Non credo, nisi addant malam aut insipientem.
Nam quae (malum!) dementia est non considerare quam levis res est pecunia, ut est ultimum ex iis quae solent hominibus spiritus tollere! Sed in multis
leves et inanes animi, tenui aura intumescunt. Fatua, num non coniugium
omnia reddit communia? Si amicitia fiunt omnia communia, quanto com-
20 muniora matrimonio non solum pecuniae, sed amici, propinqui, nihil non?
'Quod Romani,' sicut Plutarchus inquit, 'suis legibus declararunt, quibus
vetabatur inter coniuges dari aliquid aut accipi, ne quid distinctum et pro-
prium esse alterutrius videretur.' In optima re publica, ut docet Plato, meum
et tuum auferri decet. Quanto magis in optima domo, quae tum demum
25 optima et perfectissima est ac ea de causa felicissima, cum sub uno capite
non est nisi unum corpus! Nam si vel plura habeat capita vel corpora, monstrum est. Quid dicam? Nihil esse uxoris, viri omnia? Ut, iuxta Plutarchi
similitudinem, vinum dilutum, etiam si plus infusum sit aquae quam vini,
vinum tamen dicitur, ita quantolibet plus attulerit femina quam vir, huius
30 tamen redduntur omnia.

57. An non is cuncta possidet quae sunt feminae, qui feminam ipsam
possidet quique eius est dominus? Atqui audis a Deo et conditore omnium

---

56. (Intolerabilius ... dives) *Iuv. 6, 460* // (Theophrastus ... insipientem) *Hier. adv. Iovin.*
1, 47, PL 23, 288–289 // (amicitia ... communia) *Erasm. ad. LB II, 13F–14F* // (Quod ...
videretur) *Plut. mor. 143A* // (In optima ... auferre) *Plat. rep. 462C* // (vinum ... dicitur)
Plut. mor. 140F

2 abripiunt Γ rapiunt **H** // **2–3** longissime ... evehunt Γ impellunt **H** // **4** denique Γ
prorsus **H** // **5** diliget Γ amabit **H** // **6–9** Omnes ... adulatorio Γ *deest in* **H** // **16**
malum Γ *deest in* **H** // **17** spiritus Γ animos **H** // **18** Fatua, num non Γ Demens, annon **H**
// **27** Nihil ... omnia Γ Omnia esse non uxoris sed viri **H** // **30** redduntur Γ fiunt **H** //
32 Deo et conditore omnium Γ *deest in* **H**

than with ignorant fools, who have not set the bridle of wisdom upon their passions, who are driven hither and thither by the passions awakened in their minds and drawn far away from the path of justice and moral rectitude. A wife shall not only not show aversion to her husband's studies but to anything else by word, look, gesture or any outward manifestation. She will love all things in him, admire everything, show her respect and approval. She will put faith in his words even if he tells her things that seem improbable or incredible. She will take on his facial expressions, smile at him when he smiles, be sad when he is sad, maintaining always the dignity of virtue and integrity befitting a married woman, making it clear to her husband that her sympathy with his moods comes from a spirit of friendship not adulation. She will not prefer herself to her husband in anything. She will think of him as father, master, greater, more powerful and better than herself, and she will reveal this in her conduct and state it openly. How can friendship and love exist if being rich you despise your husband who is poor, or beautiful despise a husband who is ugly, or noble disdain one lowly born.

56. The satirist said,

Nothing is more intolerable than a rich woman.

Jerome said the same thing, writing against Jovinian: 'Theophrastus also said that it was a torment to suffer a rich wife.' I do not believe this is so, unless they add that she is also wicked or foolish. What madness is it not to recognize how vain a thing money is, since it is the least of those things that can elevate men's spirits? But many people have shallow and empty minds that become inflated at the slightest breeze. Silly woman, does marriage not render all things common? If all things are common between friends, how much more is that true of marriage, not only in matters concerning money, but friends, relatives, and everything else as well? 'The Romans,' as Plutarch said, 'stated this in their laws, by which it was forbidden that anything could be given or received between spouses, so that nothing would seem to be the private property of either one of them.' In the ideal republic, as Plato teaches, 'mine and yours must be eliminated.' How much more is this true of the ideal home, which is best and most perfect, and therefore happiest, when it has one body under one head. If it had several heads or several bodies, it would be a monster. Am I saying that nothing belongs to the wife, everything to the man? Just as, according to a simile of Plutarch, diluted wine, even if it contains more water than wine, is still called wine, so no matter how much more the woman brings to the marriage than the man, it all belongs to him.

57. Does not he who possesses the woman herself and who is her master possess everything that belongs to her? And what is more, you hear what

Domino: 'Sub viri potestate eris, et ipse dominabitur tui.' Idcirco nec de forma contemnendus est maritus. Habes tu formam in corpore tuo, mulier, at maritus et formam tuam et te possessione sua. Non disputo primum quam exiguum ac tenue sit hoc formae munus, ut constat opinionibus. Eadem aliis
5   speciosissima, aliis deformissima videntur. Quam fluxum et fragile, quantis casibus obnoxium, quam fugax! Una te febricula, unus naevus, unus pilus deformissimam posset ex speciosissima facere. Et hoc quiddam nescio quid tam leve, tam evanidum, mirum quantopere stulta et inania corda tume-faciat atque attollat, ut ventus utrem! Qua de causa poeta ille dixit: 'Se-
10 quitur superbia formam.' Sed in viris nemo requirit illam formae gratiam, in mulieribus decere putant. Et tamen legis a sapientissimo Rege dictum: 'Fallax gratia et vana est pulchritudo: mulier timens Deum, ipsa laudabitur.' Denique si eadem estis caro seu idem potius homo, tu et maritus, utique deformis esse nequit cui est pulchra uxor. Sed quorsum de pulchritudine
15 spectat iactatio, quasi nesciamus quamlibet speciosum corpus feminae nihil esse aliud quam sterquilinium candido et purpureo velo opertum? Si illud formosissimum Alcibiadis corpus introspici posset, dixit philosophus nescio quis, quam multa in eo apparerent taetra et abominanda!

    58. 'Nobilitas' (ut inquit ille) 'sola est atque unica virtus.' Taceo ut stulta
20 res sit haec quam nobilitatem appellamus, bello, crudelitate, latrociniis, fraudibus, spoliationibus parta et conservata; cuius opinio alitur a magno erroris magistro populo. Sed quantumvis nobilis, si ignobili nubas, ignobilior eo redderis. Non est uxor marito nobilior nec in humano genere continget quod in nullis animantibus; filii patrem sequuntur gentium omnium ritu,
25 nempe potiorem. Quod si tu nobilissima es, maritus tuus aut nobilissimus fit per te aut tu ignobilis per illum. Iure civili mariti dignitatem tribuunt feminis, non patres, ita ut clarissimae non appellentur quae clarissimis ortae patribus plebeis nupserunt. Declararunt hoc patriciae mulieres Romanae quae Verginiam patriciis ortam parentibus, quia plebeio denupserat, sacello pu-
30 dicitiae patriciae exegerunt, plebeiam esse dictitantes, non patriciam. Neque id ipsa infitiata est nec pudori se esse plebeiam duxit nec prae illorum patriciatu plebem suam contempsit nec erubuit vocari Verginia Lucii Volumnii.

---

57. (Sub ... tui) *Vulg. gen. 3, 16* // (Sequitur superbia formam) *Ov. fast. 1, 5, 419* // (Fallax ... laudabitur) *Vulg. prov. 31, 30* // (Si illud ... abominanda) *Boeth. cons. 3, 8; Aristot. protrep. fg. 10a (Ross, p.40)*
    58. (Nobilitas ... virtus) *Iuv. 8, 20* // (Verginiam ... Volumnii) *Liv. 10, 23, 3–5*

---

3 possessione sua Γ *deest in* **H** // **4** exiguum ac Γ *deest in* **H** / formae Γ *deest in* **H** / constat **H** constet Γ // **7–10** Et hoc ... formam Γ *deest in* **H** // **13** utique Γ *deest in* **H** // **14–18** Sed quorsum ... abominanda Γ Addat etiam, si quis volet, nec pulchra uxor cui deformis maritus **H** // **20–21** bello ... conservata Γ *deest in* **H** // **22** quantumvis Γ quamlibet **H** // **25** potiorem Γ meliorem **H** / Quod Γ Et **H** // **26** per te Γ *deest in* **H** / per illum Γ *deest in* **H** // **29** ortam parentibus Γ parentibus ortam **H** / denupserat Γ nupserat **H** // **30** dictitantes Γ dicentes **H** // **31** duxit Γ habuit **H** // **32** suam Γ *deest in* **H**

God, Lord of all creation, says: 'You will be under the power of a man, and he will have dominion over you.' Therefore a husband must not be derided for his physical form. You have beauty in your body, woman, but your husband has your beauty and you in his possession. I am not going to discuss how trivial and insubstantial is the gift of beauty and how it depends solely on men's opinions. The same woman appears very beautiful to some and very ugly to others. How uncertain and fragile, fraught with danger, how fleeting! One fever, a single wart or hair could turn you from a fine beauty into a sight hideous to behold. And yet this unstable and perishable thing can swell and exalt foolish and vain minds to an astonishing degree, as the wind inflates a wineskin. For that reason the poet said, 'Pride on beauty waits.' In men no one looks for that grace of form, but in women they think it to be appropriate. And yet you read the saying of the wise king: 'Charm is deceitful and beauty is vain; the woman who fears the Lord will be praised.' Finally, if you and your husband are the same flesh, or rather the same person, then he cannot possibly be ugly if he has a beautiful wife. But what is the purpose of all this vaunting of beauty, as if we did not know that the body of a woman, however beautiful, is nothing but a dung-heap, covered with a white and purple veil? If we could see into the beautiful body of Alcibiades, said a certain philosopher, how many foul and abominable things would appear!

58. 'The only true nobility is virtue,' according to the poet. I will hold my tongue concerning the stupid conception we have of nobility, acquired and preserved by war, cruelty, robbery, fraud and pillaging, an idea nurtured by the masses, that great teacher of error. No matter how noble you may be, if you marry a husband of lowly birth, you make yourself even lower than he. The wife is not nobler than the husband, nor will the human race be different in this respect than all other living things. Children trace their lineage to the father according to the practice of all nations, since he is regarded as having the stronger claim. If you are of the highest nobility, either your husband becomes noble through you or you lose your nobility through him. In civil law husbands, not parents confer nobility on women. Consequently, those who were born of noble parentage were no longer called noble if they married one of low degree. This was made clear when the patrician women of Rome expelled Verginia, a daughter of noble parents, from the shrine of patrician chastity, saying that by her marriage to a plebeian she was no longer a patrician but a plebian. She did not deny it nor did she consider it shameful to be a plebeian, nor did she spurn the plebeian class in comparison with the patrician, nor was she ashamed to be called Verginia, wife of Lucius Volumnius.

---

58. Verginia: Not to be confused with the famous Verginia, whom her father killed in public rather than surrender her to the lust of the decemvir, Appius Claudius.

59. Cornelia, Scipionis filia, cum in domum venisset, amplam illam quidem multisque claram honoribus, sed plebeiam tamen, et quae cum paterna comparanda non esset, ipsa ex Cornelia gente, Romae omnium facile principe et ex ea gente familia primaria Scipionum, filia Scipionis illius,
5 Africae domitoris, principis senatus, populi Romani et omnium gentium, filia Tertiae Aemiliae, ex Aemilio genere Romae et toto orbe illustrissimo, tanta maiorum omnium et paternorum et maternorum gloria, claritate, stemmatibus, maluit tamen semper Cornelia Gracchi nominari quam Scipionis, irata etiam plerisque qui, honoris ut putabant gratia, Scipio-
10 nis cognominabant.Marpessa, ut scriptores Graeci tradunt, Idam maritum, hominem mortalem, Apollini deo (ut credebant) immortali praetulit. Soror prioris Dionysii, tyranni Syracusii, Thesta, Philoxeno nupta, cum Philoxenus molitus quiddam adversus Dionysium e Sicilia profugisset, accersita a Dionysio fratre et castigata quod fugam mariti non sibi detexisset, 'Quid
15 tu,' inquit, 'tam degenerem me et abiectam putasti uxorem ut si de mariti scissem fuga, non illum fuissem secuta et ubivis gentium maluissem Philoxeni exulis uxor dici quam hic in patria Dionysii regis soror?' Hunc tam sanctum, tam generosum animum Syracusani admirati, post exactos tyrannos et vivam coluerunt et omnibus honorum generibus prosecuti sunt
20 mortuam.

60. Uxor Maximiliani Caesaris Maria, cum ei haec Gallia Belgica patris Caroli hereditate obvenisset Gallique Maximiliano simplicem et mansuetum animum parvifacerent, ad Mariam tamquam principem de rebus omnibus dicionis referrent, nihil illa pro potestate umquam statuit inconsulto viro, cuius voluntatem semper pro lege habuit; et poterat absque mala
25 viri gratia omnia administrare sola pro arbitrio, nihil non permittente Maximiliano et ex miti animo suo et uxori carissimae ac prudentissimae et indole illius. Ita Maria virum in maximam auctoritatem brevi adduxit, plurimum ei tribuendo dicioque audientior fuit principibus, geminata reverentia
30 et quasi utriusque maiestate ab altero fulta et sustentata. Non debet prudens mulier dotem suam existimare quam in domum mariti inferat pecuniam vel

---

59. (Maluit ... Scipionis) *Plut. Tib. Gracch. 8, 5* // (Marpessa ... praetulit) *Plut. mor. 315E–F; Hom. Il. 9, 557–560* // (Soror ... soror) *Plut. Dio 21*

2 claram honoribus Γ honoribus claram **H** / tamen Γ *deest in* **H** // **7–8** claritate, stemmatibus Γ *deest in* **H** // **8** maluit tamen Γ tamen maluit **H** / nominari Γ dici **H** // **9** irata Γ iratis **H** // **10** cognominabant Γ dicebant, non Gracchi **H** / Marpessa *Hom. Plut.* Marpissa Γ // **10–11** Marpessa ... praetulit Γ *deest in* **H** // **12** Thesta *Plut.* Thesia *omnes edd.* // **13** quiddam Γ quaedam **H** / profugisset Γ se subduxisset **H** // **15** degenerem Γ vilem **H** // **16** scissem Γ rescissem **H** // **18** generosum Γ magnum **H** / Syracusani Γ Syracusii **H** // **23** parvifacerent Γ contemnerent **H** // **27–28** indole Γ in bonis **H** // **28** brevi Γ *deest in* **H**

59. When Cornelia, daughter of Scipio, entered into a household that was eminent and distinguished for the holding of many high political offices, but plebeian nonetheless, and not to be compared to her paternal household, since she was of the Cornelian line, undeniably the leading family in all of Rome, and from the stock and pre-eminent family of the Scipio's, daughter of Scipio, the conqueror of Africa, prince of the Senate, of the Roman people, and of all peoples, daughter of Tertia Aemilia, of the Aemilian line, celebrated in Rome and in the whole world, with such glorious distinctions of race in all her ancestors, paternal and maternal, she still preferred to be called Cornelia, wife of Gracchus, rather than daughter of Scipio. She even became angry with some who, thinking to do her honor, called her by the name of Scipio. Marpessa, as Greek writers tell us, preferred her husband Idas, a mortal man, to Apollo, whom they considered an immortal god. Thesta, the sister of Dionysius I, tyrant of Syracuse, was married to Philoxenus. When he had set a plot in motion against Dionysius and was forced to flee from Sicily, Thesta was summoned by her brother and severely reproved for not having revealed the flight of her husband to him. She replied: 'Did you think me such a degenerate and base wife that if I knew of my husband's flight, I would not have followed him and would have preferred to be known in any part of the world as the wife of the exile Philoxenus rather than the sister of Dionysius, the king, here in my native country?' In admiration of this holy and noble spirit, the Syracusans, after the expulsion of the tyrants, honored her in her lifetime and rendered her the greatest honors upon her death.

60. Maria, wife of the emperor Maximilian, inherited this region of Flanders from her father Charles. The Flemish had little respect for the simple and meek character of Maximilian and referred all decisions concerning their governance to Maria, as if she were their leader, but she never decided anything that was within her power without consulting her husband, whose will she regarded as law. And she had the authority to administer everything according to her own wishes without incurring the ill will of her husband, since Maximilian refused nothing to his beloved and prudent wife owing both to his own mild disposition and her integral character. In this way Maria in a short time added much to his authority, enhancing his power, and that region became more obedient to its rulers, since respect for them was doubled, the sovereignty of the one supported and sustained by the other. The prudent woman should not think that the dowry she brings

59. Cornelia: Vives frequently cites Cornelia as a paragon of self-abnegation and devotion to her family. Plutarch tells us in his *Life of Cornelius Gracchus* that the Roman people erected a statue to her memory with the simple inscription 'Cornelia, Mother of the Gracchi'.

60. Maria: Duchess of Burgundy, daughter of Charles the Bold. Through his marriage to Maria in 1477 Maximilian became the ruler of the Burgundian Netherlands. Maria helped him to adapt to her country, but after her death in 1482 the people of Bruges rose up against Maximilian and even held him prisoner for a time (1488).

speciem vel claritudinem prosapiae, sed pudorem, pudicitiam, probitatem, oboedientiam virilis imperii, sedulam curam liberorum ac domus. Ampliter dotata venit quae sic est instructa; alioqui convicium adfert, non connubium mulier, quae fortunam habet qua insolescat, non habet qua regatur virtutem. Alcumenae apud Plautum haec sunt ad Amphitryonem verba:

> Non ego illam mihi dotem duco esse, quae dos dicitur,
> Sed pudicitiam et pudorem et sedatum cupidinem,
> Deum metum, parentum amorem et cognatum concordiam,
> Tibi morigera, atque ut munifica sim bonis, prosim probis.

61. Haec in animo. Nunc freni sunt linguae adhibendi, quos facile frenatus animus iniciet. Nam quod sunt impotenti lingua pleraeque feminarum, id ex impotentia proficiscitur animorum. Totas enim occupat ira et abripit nec quicquam illis sui iuris relinquit. Hinc in iurgando nec modus nec ratio ulla conviciorum, cum nullus sit rationi, nullus iudicio locus, omnia ignis accenderit et sua fecerit, nempe fomenta facile nactus in materia molli ac tenera et proinde ardori apta. Unde rabies effusissima tum affectus tum linguae, quam saepenumero miratus sum in probis; et in quibus nec pudicitiam nec pudorem nec sanctitatem nec alias magnas praeclarasque virtutes desiderarem coactus sum modestiam et temperationem irae linguaeque desiderare, non sine meo etiam pudore, cum tamen nihil ad me de toto iurgio pertineret, quod erat inter alienissimos; si quid modo quod Christianorum sit alienum esse Christiano potest. Quocirca ut difficillima ita pulcherrima praestantissimaque erit virtus feminae coercere linguam. Quod non erit operosum efficere si se habuerit in sua potestate, si se munierit et confirmarit, ne perturbationibus se tamquam tempestatibus auferendam permittat. Illud in primis, dum quieta est, dum sana, dum sobria et sui iuris saepe cogitet et obstinet animo, ne si in rixam cum marito incideret, probrum aliquod obiciat grave vel generis vel corporis vel animi vel vitae quo sciat illum male uri; nusquam quidem, sed minime omnium coram iis a quibus ipse id ignorari vehementer cupiat. Nam hac contumelia irritato difficilior erit deinceps reconciliatio; quin etiam reconciliatus, quoties ei maledicti illius in mentem venerit, non

---

60. (Non ego ... probis) *Plaut. Amph. 839–842*

6–9 Non ... probis Γ *deest in* **H** // 12 abripit Γ aufert **H** // 15 fomenta Γ incrementa **H** // 16 proinde Γ hinc **H** // 18–19 desiderarem Γ desiderabam **H** // 20 pertineret Γ spectaret **H** // 21–22 quod ... potest Γ est Christiano alienum quod Christianorum sit **H** // 22-23 praestantissimaque Γ *deest in* **H** // 23 coercere Γ cohibere **H** // 23-24 non erit operosum efficere Γ facile efficiet **H** // 24 si se munierit et confirmarit Γ *deest in* **H** / ne Γ nec **H** // 25 auferendam permittat Γ abripiendam permiserit **H** // 26 sobria et Γ *deest in* **H** / obstinet Γ destinet **H** // 27 probrum aliquod Γ maculam aliquam **H** / grave Γ insignem **H** // 28 quo sciat illum male uri Γ quam sciat illum male urere **H** // 28–30 nusquam ... cupiat Γ *deest in* **H** // 30 irritato Γ irritatus coniunx **H** / deinceps Γ *deest in* **H** // 31 maledicti Γ dicti **H**

with her into her husband's home consists of money, beauty, or splendor of lineage, but chastity, modesty, moral integrity, obedience to her husband's authority, diligent care of her children and of the house. She who is so endowed is richly dowered. Otherwise the woman who possesses wealth, which makes her overbearing, without virtue to guide her, brings wrangling, not wedlock in her train. These are the words of Alcmena to Amphitryon in Plautus:

> I think not that a dowry which is dowry called,
> But chastity and shame and curbed desire,
> Fear of the gods, the love of parents,
> Peace with kin; a wife compliant to your will,
> Generous to the good, helpful to the virtuous.

61. This for the mind. Now the bridle must be put on the tongue, which is easily done if the mind is bridled. The reason why many women have no control of their tongue is that their mind is uncontrolled. Anger takes hold of them, carries them away and renders them powerless over themselves. As a result, there is no limit to their quarreling and no logic in their abusiveness since there is no room for reason or judgement. The fire ignites and consumes everything, for it has found good kindling in a soft and yielding material ideal for burning. Then unrestrained rage of emotion and tongue bursts forth, which I have often marvelled at in good women. And in those in whom chastity or propriety or holiness or other excellent virtues were not lacking I was forced to find moderation and temperance lacking in their angry tongues. This made me quite ashamed even though their vituperations had nothing to do with me, but with people who were complete strangers to me, if what pertains to a Christian can be considered alien to any other Christian. Therefore, though it be very difficult, it is a beautiful and outstanding virtue in a woman to control the tongue. This will not involve too much effort if she will gain control over herself, fortify and strengthen herself so that she will not allow herself to be carried away by violent emotions. When she is at rest, sane and sober and in control of herself, let her often reflect and resolve in her mind that if she should get into an argument with her husband she should not hurl any grave insults against him concerning his family, body, mind or manner of life, which she knows will offend him greatly. This should never be done, but especially not in the presence of those who he strongly wishes not to know about it. Once he has been provoked by this insulting language it will be difficult for him to make reconciliation, and even if he does become reconciled, every time he remembers that humiliation, he will not be able to look at his wife with a favorable

aequis umquam oculis uxorem aspiciet. Iam apud Deum quanta offensa! Dominus in Evangelio Matthaei ait: 'Quisquis indignatus fratri suo in vocem affectionis proruperit "raca" (ceu quis dicat "at tu!"), reum fore concilio; quisquis "fatue," reum gehenna ignis.' Nunc ipsa reputato quid fiet tibi, qui maximum aliquod maledictum non in fratre modo, sed in patrem, in Dei (quantum ad te attinet) vicarium, in omnes consanguineos ieceris?

62. Iactum vero in te a marito cave ne memoriae adhaereat; patienter perferto et magnam apud eum iam sedatum gratiam ista tolerantia inieris indomitumque illius animum in bonum vertes uterisque posthac mitiore ac commodiore. Terentius, mores hominum fabulis suis exprimens, de puella pudica inquit:

> Haec uti liberali esse ingenio decet,
> Pudens, modesta, incommoda atque iniurias
> Viri omnes ferre et tegere contumelias

Has ob causas redditus est uxori mariti animus a qua erat alienatus. Hoc idem est sapientis apud Senecam tragicum nutricis consilium, quod illa Octaviae Neronis dabat: 'Vince obsequendo potius immitem virum.'

63. Estis quidem vos, feminae, tenero corpore, imbelli. Accedunt his quotidiani paene labores e sexu, menstruorum fastidia, molestiae uteri, pericula enitendi; plane estis condicione digna quam miserentur mariti. Videte ne importunitate vestra excutiatis ex maritorum animis misericordiam vobis debitam, ut miserabiles non sitis cum tamen miserae. Nec beneficium aliquod tuum exprobraveris marito; quae res etiam inter alienos odiosissima est et debitam gratiam pro beneficio amittit qui exprobrat, quippe excussit eam ex animo alterius. Adde quod si recte expenderis, beneficium non potest tuum exsistere in maritum aliquod, quippe cui tantum debes quantum patri, quantum ipsi tibi. Nec genus aut ingenium aut dotes suas modesta femina crebro commemorabit; quae res molesta est et fastidium solet vel marito amantissimo parere. Iuvenalis optare se dicit obscuram et ignobilem citius quam Corneliam Africani filiam, de cuius virtute multa commemoravimus, si animos illi faciat paterna claritas. Sic enim ait:

> Malo Venusinam quam te, Cornelia, mater
> Gracchorum, si cum magnis virtutibus affers

---

61. (Quisquis ... ignis) *Vulg. Matth. 5, 22*
62. (Haec ... contumelias) *Ter. Hec. 164–166* // (Vince ... virum) *Sen. Oct. 84–85*
63. (Malo ... migra) *Iuv. 6, 167–171*

2–3 indignatus ... at tu Γ dixerit fratri suo raca, id est, excerebrate **H** // **4** fiet tibi Γ tibi fiet **H** // **7** ne Γ *deest in* **H** // **8** gratiam ... inieris Γ inibis gratiam ista tolerantia **H** // **10** fabulis suis Γ poemate suo **H** // **16–20** Estis quidem ... tamen miserae Γ *deest in* **H** // **22** quippe Γ nam **H** // **24** exsistere Γ esse **H** // **25** ipsi **HWW²B** ipsa **V** // **26** molesta est et Γ *deest in* **H** // **27** optare Γ optaturum **H** // **28** commemoravimus Γ diximus **H**

eye. In the eyes of God too what displeasure it brings! The Lord said in the Gospel of Matthew: 'Whoever becomes angry with his brother and utters the expression "raca" (i.e., "Why you . . . !") will be liable to the council; and whoever says "You fool" will be liable to hell's fire.' Now consider what will happen to you if you utter a great injury not only against your brother, but your father, God's representative (as far as you are concerned), and all your relatives?

62. But if your husband insults you, do not let it remain in your memory. Bear up with it patiently and by this tolerance you will gain great favor with him when he has calmed down, and you will turn his furious temper to good thoughts and find him more docile and agreeable afterwards. Terence, who described human mores in his comedies, says of a chaste maiden:

> She, as befits a girl of decent birth,
> Modest and chaste, bears hurts and injuries
> From her spouse and hides his misdemeanors.

In this way a husband's affection is restored to his wife, from whom he had been estranged. This is the same advice given by the wise nurse in a play of Seneca to Octavia, wife of Nero, 'Vanquish rather a cruel spouse with obedience.'

63. Women, you possess a tender and defenseless body. In addition, you are burdened with almost daily troubles resulting from your sex, the annoyances of menstrual discharge, the discomforts of the womb, the dangers of childbirth, a condition that merits your husband's sympathy. See to it that you do not drive away the pity your husband owes you by your importunity, that your misery does not make you miserable. Do not bring up as a reproach against your husband some good deed you have done him. This is a hateful thing even among strangers, and he who throws his benefice in the teeth of another loses all gratitude for it, driving it from the other's mind. Besides, if you reflect on it, it is not possible to do a good deed for your husband since you owe him as much as you do your father and your own self. A modest woman will not make frequent reference to her lineage, her talent or her dowry. This is annoying and can arouse aversion even in the most loving husband. Juvenal says he would prefer to marry a humble woman of low birth rather than Cornelia, the daughter of Africanus, of whose virtue we have already said many things, if her father's fame should make her haughty:

> I prefer a Venusine to you, Cornelia,
> Mother of the Gracchi, if with your lofty virtues
> You bring great haughtiness and reckon

Grande supercilium et numeras in dote triumphos;
Tolle tuum precor Hannibalem victumque Syphacem
In castris et cum tota Carthagine migra.

64. Vir gravissimus Plutarchus praecipit initio coniugii vitandum omnem contentionis et rixae ansam, cum nondum satis cohaesit amor tenerque adhuc et fragilis quavis de causa dissolveretur haud secus quam vasa recenter ficta, quamlibet mediocri impulsu confringuntur. Nec iurgandum esse in lecto geniali. Nam ubi ponent animorum offensiones, si locum illum ad reconciliationem maxime idoneum rixis suis infestum et odiosum reddiderint ac velut medicinam corruperint qua illis animorum morbis subveniri oportebat? Sunt et minutiora quaepiam quibus vel confirmatur amor vel luxatur; quae uxor diligenter in viro animadvertet ut illius aptet ingenio ac voluntati. Aliqua pro exemplis subiciam unde reliqua intelligantur, velut quibusnam cibis, quomodo paratis, quomodo conditis delectetur, a quibus abhorreat; salsa amet an subfatua; calida an frigida; hoc genus carnium, piscium, potionis, an aliud quodpiam; qua hora, quibus mantilibus, quibus mappis, quadris, patinis, scutellis, cucumis, salino, poculis; quemadmodum poni sibi mensam gaudeat, quos adhiberi convivas, quales collocutiones; tum, quomodo sterni lectum, quibus culcitris, stragulis, opertoriis, linteis, pulvinis; hinc in sellis, in scamnis, in tota ratione victus, supellectilis ac instrumenti domestici, quae sunt muliebri curae iniuncta et delegata.

65. Sunt haec quidem per se, ut dicebam, parva, sed maximi interdum apud humanos animos momenti; qui non a magnitudine rerum commotiones accipiunt, sed a suis ipsorum aestimationibus. An non minutius est prunam cultello dissecari, linteum morderi, serram acui, suem grunnire et eiusmodi tenuia et levia quamplurima? At quam multi hisce rebus ita permoventur et exhorrescunt ut mallent vulnus accipere quam illa perferre, occulto sensu peculiaris cuiusdam naturae! Quanti fecit Isaac filii pulmentum ut hoc elicuerit ab eo benedictionem, maximam illo tempore hereditatem! Quis non audivit odium coniugum ex mora prandii, ex frigidiusculo iure, ex mantili sordido conceptum excessisse in dissidium et divortium atrocissimum? Haec est praeceptorum omnium summa: ut uxor, perspectis magna cura et iudicio mariti moribus, talem se erga illum praebeat qualem vellet famulam suam esse in se, si eisdem et uxor ipsa esset moribus praedita. Illud quoque addendum, crebras offensiunculas amorem, quamlibet radicatum et fixum, commovere primum, hinc nutantem iam facile subruere.

---

64. (initio ... confringuntur) *Plut. mor. 138E–F*
65. (Isaac ... benedictionem) *Vulg. gen. 27, 4*

---

6 haud secus quam Γ ut **H** // **7–8** iurgandum esse in lecto geniali Γ in thoro iurgandum esse **H** // **10** qua Γ quibus **H** // **11**–p.80,25 Sunt et minutiora ... atque industria incomparabili Γ *deest in* **H**

Triumphs as part of your trousseau.
Take away your Hannibal, I pray,
And Syphax vanquished in the camp.
Away with you and all of Carthage too!

64. That sage writer, Plutarch, warns that at the beginning of a marriage any occasion for contention and argument must be avoided, since love has not yet adhered, and tender and fragile as it is, could be dissolved on any pretext, as newly made vases break at the slightest touch. There should be no quarreling in the marriage bed. For where will they lay aside their resentments if they make the place best suited for reconciliation hateful and hostile because of their quarrels, and spoil the medicine, as it were, that should have served to cure these troubles? There are certain little things that can strengthen or weaken love, which the wife should notice in her husband so that she may adapt herself to his temperament and wishes. I shall give a few examples, which will suffice for the understanding of all the rest. Know what kind of foods he likes, how he likes them prepared and with what seasoning, and which ones he dislikes. Does he like his food highly seasoned or bland, hot or cold; this kind of meat, fish and drink, or some other; what hour does he prefer, what tablecloths and napkins, tables, trays, plates, bowls, kettles, salt cellars, cups; how does he like the table set, what guests does he prefer, what type of conversation? Then you must please him in the way you make the bed: the cushions, blankets, bedspread, sheets and pillows you should use. The same goes for chairs, benches, furnishing and all kinds of domestic appurtenances, which are entrusted and delegated to the woman.

65. These are little things in themselves, as I said, but of great importance to human beings, whose emotions are aroused not by the size of things but by their evaluation of them. Is it not a small thing to cut a plum with a knife, to rip linen, to sharpen a saw, to hear a pig grunt and similar insignificant things? Yet how many people are profoundly disturbed and shudder at these things so that they would more readily be wounded than tolerate these sounds, by some strange quirk of nature, peculiar to each individual. How much Isaac appreciated the porridge offered to him by his son so that this act won him his father's blessing, which was esteemed as the greatest inheritance in those days! Who has not heard of hatred between spouses arising from a late supper, or broth that was a bit cold, or a dirty tablecloth, which then developed into violent conflict and a bitter divorce? This is the essential rule to follow: a wife should observe her husband's ways carefully and discreetly and behave towards him as she would wish her servants to behave towards her if she had the same disposition. It must also be added that these repeated peccadillos first shake the foundations of love, though they be firmly fixed, and then when it begins to totter, undermine it altogether.

66. Olim haec fuit regum ars, ut res gratas et quae benevolentiam conciliarent ipsi obirent per se, velut munificentiam, largitiones, veniam; tristia
vero, amara, aspera per ministros, sicut exilia, spoliationes fortunarum,
supplicia capitalia. Sic ferunt fuisse in Sicilia feminam primariam memoria
5   patrum, quae sedulo animum adverteret quid famuli sui agerent gratum
domino idque ipsa deinde exsequebatur. Mandabat vero illis quae forent
subaspera et submolesta. Quo gravius castigandae sunt mihi uxores Belgicae,
quae maritis, cum levare volunt fessum animum et genio indulgere, segniter
maligneque quae sunt opus subministrantes, abigunt eos domo, tamquam
10 ex solitudine; illi vero in cervisiariam aut vinariam cauponam se recipiunt
nactique ibi ad rem omnem sodales commodos et rerum omnium paratam
copiam, facile in omne se vitiorum genus effundunt: ingluviem, ebrietatem,
aleationem, scortationem, desidiam. Relictis domi uxore et parvis liberis esurie confectis, ipsi censum universum usque ad tunicas et lectulos profundunt,
15 domum aversati ut specum aliquod in quo fera bestia incubet, nempe uxor
inimica. Nec desunt inter eas quae haec omnia non invitae perferant, modo
ne sit ipsis manus vel suppellectili vel operi culinario admovenda. Tanta
est in illarum pectoribus segnities ac socordia, interdum protervitas quoque
et pervicacia, qua malunt perire se quam si semel indignari coeperint vel
20 minimum de animis remittere in gratiam maritorum. Itaque ipsae in causa
sunt ut corrumpantur maritorum mores simul cum re familiari; videasque
hic plerosque caelibes frugi, maritos nequissimos ac perditissimos. At istae
adeo in rebus necessariis tardae ac desides dictu incredibile quam promptae
diligentesque sunt in vagando, discurrendo, garriendo, in se ipsis autem
25 comendis et ornandis sedulitate atque industria incomparabili.

CAP. V.   QUOMODO PRIVATIM SE CUM MARITO HABERE DEBET

67. Non fuerit alienum iam hic disserere quemadmodum se in privato et
remotis arbitris cum marito geret. Sciat ante omnia veteres illos, qui Iunoni,
nuptiarum praesidi ac tutrici, sacra faciebant, numquam immolata victima
30 fel reliquisse, sed illud exemptum hostiae post aram reicere consuevisse,
significantes nec iram nec amaritudinem aliquam inter coniuges incidere
oportere; iidem Veneri deae Mercurium adiungebant, quasi leporem et
suavitatem quandam in connubio; quippe debet uxor commoditate morum
et sermonis lepore ac blanditiis coniugem delinitum sibi copulare artiusque

---

67. (veteres ... oportere) *Plut. mor. 141E–F* // (iidem ... connubio) *Plut. mor. 141F*

27 fuerit Γ erit **H** // 30 exemptum hostiae Γ hostiae demptum **H** // 31 incidere Γ
esse **H** // 33 quippe debet Γ debet enim **H** / commoditate Γ lenitate **H** // 34 lepore
ac blanditiis Γ *deest in* **H** / coniugem Γ maritum **H**

66. Once it was the custom of kings to go about personally dispensing pleasant things and favors that would win them good will, such as acts of munificence, distribution of gifts and pardon; painful, hateful and harsh things were executed by their ministers, such as exile, confiscations, capital punishment. The story is told that within the memory of our fathers there was a prominent woman of Sicily who carefully observed what her servants did that found pleasure with their master and then she discharged those duties herself, leaving to them tasks that were ungrateful and annoying. In this regard I must severely castigate Flemish wives, who, when their husbands wish to relax their tired minds and indulge their fancy, perform their duties sluggishly and grudgingly and drive them out of the house, as if it were a desert. The husbands betake themselves to local beer or wine taverns and finding willing companions there for their entertainment and an abundance of everything, give themselves over to every kind of vice —gluttony, drunkenness, gambling, whoring and idleness. They leave their wives and small children at home starving and they squander all their substance, even to their tunics and wallets, avoiding their home as if it were a cave in which a wild beast lurked, to wit, their shrewish wife. Some of these wives are not unwilling to put up with this as long as they do not have to lay a hand on the furniture or the kitchen utensils. Such is their indolence and torpor, and at times their impudence and obstinacy that they would rather die, once they have taken offence, than show even the slightest forgiveness to their husbands. Thus they bring about the corruption of their husbands' morals together with the loss of their possessions. You will see that many men who were frugal when they were bachelors become wicked and profligate husbands. But these same women, who are so slow and lethargic in their domestic duties, are marvellously quick and diligent in roaming about, dallying and gossiping and show remarkable assiduity and alacrity in dressing and adorning themselves.

CHAPTER 5. HOW SHE WILL CONDUCT HERSELF IN PRIVATE WITH HER HUSBAND

67. It will not be inappropriate here to discuss how a wife should act with her husband in private, without other witnesses. She should know first of all that in ancient times those women who made sacrifice to Juno, the guardian and protectress of marriage, never left the gall-bladder behind after the sacrifice was completed but removed it from the victim and threw it behind the altar, signifying by this that neither anger nor bitterness should exist between spouses. They also coupled Mercury and Venus im marriage, that is, cleverness of language and the gratification of the senses, since a wife should unite herself to her husband and bind him to herself more closely day by day through the complaisance of her manner, the charm of her speech and

in dies devincire. Nihil enim est quod validius ad se attrahat et rapiat quam dulcedo morum ac orationis. Quid prodest mulieri ingenium et prudentia nisi adsit lenitas et mansuetudo erga virum? Nemo non malit cum cane suo conversari quam cum muliere importuna et feroci. Tenebit prudens mulier
5 fabulas et historias et narratiunculas ut iucundas ita etiam puras ac honestas, quibus fessum maritum aut aegrum reficiat ac recreet; tum praecepta sapientiae, quibus vel adhortetur ad virtutem vel retrahat a vitiis; aliqua etiam graviter dicta contra impetus assultusque utriusque fortunae, quibus virum seu elatum secundis rebus sensim demittat in planum, seu abiectum prostra-
10 tumque adversis erigat, utrimque autem ad mediocritatem reducat. Si qui in eo affectus tumultuantur et saeviunt, muliebribus, castis prudentibusque lenimentis tempestatem illam mitiget et sedet. Sic Placidia Theodosii filia Athaulphum, Gothorum Regem, maritum suum, Romanum nomen delere molientem a tam immani cogitatione dulcedine orationis ac morum suorum
15 leniorem commodioremque factum ad sanitatem humanitatemque revocavit.

68. Multa sunt hac de re a Divo Ioanne Chrysostomo in Ioannis Evangelium conscripta, quarum haec fere est summa: 'Grande momentum est mulier ad virum recte admonendum, et si qua invaserit animum illius tempestas, sedandum. Neque enim maritus vel patri aeque vel magistro aus-
20 cultabit ac coniugi probae. Habet voluptatem nescio quam, haud sane exiguam admonitio uxoria, quandoquidem ex ingenti benevolentia videtur nasci. Amat enim mulier hunc cui consulit nec aliter prospectum ei cuperet quam sibi ipsi multosque testimonii gratia possem adferre ex immitibus uxorum opera mansuefactos. Verum enimvero re est maritus admonen-
25 dus, non inani verborum strepitu. Id perficies si te non vitiosam animadverterit, non pretiose indutam nec superflua expetentem, sed contentam necessariis. Quod si verbis quidem philosophere, actionibus autem longe aliud praestes, ilicet nugas ille tuas aspernabitur et praecepta tua operibus tuis confutabit; exempli causa, cum aurum non quaeres, non gemmas, non pre-
30 tiosam vestem, sed pro his modestia ac caritate indueris et ab illo exiges, consulentem te feret. Nam si studendum est ut viro placeas, anima ornanda est, non corpus corrumpendum. Non enim aurum uxorem efficit perinde amabilem et desiderabilem ut modestia et pietas et affectus, quo vitam pro marito impenderes, si esset opus. Corporis cultus marito sumptuosus est et
35 gravis, animus vero ille gratus, sine sumptu.' Hactenus ex Chrysostomo.

---

68. (Grande ... sumptu) *Ioh. Chrys. in Ioh. hom. 61, 3, PG 59, 340–344*

1 validius **Γ** magis **H** / attrahat **Γ** trahat **H** // **2–4** Quid prodest ... et feroci **Γ** *deest in* **H** // **5** et narratiunculas **Γ** *deest in* **H** / etiam puras ac **Γ** *deest in* **H** // **8** graviter **Γ** grave **H** // **9** in planum **Γ** *deest in* **H** // **11** tumultuantur et **Γ** *deest in* **H** // **12** lenimentis **Γ** blanditiis **H** // **15** leniorem ... humanitatemque revocavit **Γ** delinitum mansuefactumque revocavit **H** // **16**–p.84,9 Multa sunt ... leniat tollatque **Γ** *deest in* **H**

her ingratiating behavior. There is nothing more efficacious in attracting someone to yourself than pleasantness of manners and conversation. What good is a woman's talent and intelligence unless it is accompanied by gentleness and mildness towards her husband? There is no one who would not prefer to converse with his dog rather than with an oppressive and surly wife. A prudent wife will have a store of fables, narratives and anecdotes that are both pleasant and edifying to restore and revive her tired or sick husband. She will also regale him with wise precepts that exhort to virtue and deter from vice. Likewise she will have on hand a selection of grave sayings against the attacks and assaults of both kinds of fortune, by which she will gradually bring her husband back to earth when he is too elated by prosperity or raise his spirits when he is cast down and prostrated by adversity, in both cases restoring him to equilibrium. If he is the victim of raging emotions she will calm the storm through womanly, chaste and prudent assuagements. That was the way Placidia, daughter of Theodosius, calmed her husband, Athaulf, king of the Goths, when he was set on obliterating the Roman name from the face of the earth. She turned him from his cruel resolve by the sweetness of her eloquence and her manner and brought him back to sanity and humane feelings.

68. There is much on this subject in St. John Chrysostom's writings on the Gospel of John, of which I give the following synopsis:

> It is of great importance for a wife to give good advice to her husband and to calm him when he is overcome by agitated emotions. A husband will not listen to his father or teacher as he does to a good wife. A wife's admonitions have a certain pleasure not to be ignored, since they seem to emanate from an unbounded good will. For a wife loves the man whom she is counselling and looks out for his prosperity no less than for her own. I could adduce many examples of this, of men tamed through their wives' help. A husband must be given advice by example and not by the empty sound of words. You will accomplish this if he sees you without defect, not dressed luxuriously, nor in quest of superfluities but content with what is necessary. But if you philosophize with words and show yourself quite different in action, he will scorn your idle talk and refute your preaching with your actions. To give an example: if you do not seek out gold, jewels and costly attire, but adorn yourself with modesty and charity, and require the same of him, he will abide by your counsel. If you are anxious to please a man, you must adorn your soul, not corrupt your body. Gold does not make a wife lovable and desirable, but modesty and piety and affection, which would lead you to give your life for your husband, if it were necessary. Care of the body is costly and burdensome to a husband, but the soul is pleasing to him and costs nothing.

67. Placidia: Galla Placidia, sister of the Emperor Honorius, was captured by the Goths in 410 AD and married to the Visigothic chieftain Athaulf in 414. In deference to his bride he wore Roman robes at the ceremony and allowed her to lead the procession. On his deathbed he asked his brother to give back Placidia and make peace with the Romans.

69. Observanda sunt porro admonendi tempora neque enim sunt omnia consentanea. Officium extra tempus molestia est. Sigillum molli cera imprimes et monita molli animo, scilicet cum pectus illius nulla perturbatione agitabitur, seorsum et semotis arbitris. Utere dexteritate ac suavitate
5 sermonis nec in consulendo sis immodica. Facias loquendi finem ante satietatem. Tum rationem adice quamobrem sic suadeas. Haec enim non aliter quam primae sagittae appositae efficient ut monitus tui altius in cor eius vibrentur. Sermonis conversionem in rem aliquam facies iucundam, quae totam superiorum verborum asperitatem, si qua fuit, leniat tollatque. Ipsa ad
10 eum de curis tuis omnibus et cogitatibus referto, modo non frivolis nec virili aure indignis. Illum unum habebis socium, confabulonem, consultorem, magistrum, dominum; in illius pectus depones cogitationes tuas et quicquid te angit in illo acquiesces. Faciunt haec ad amorem mutuum, faciunt ad concordiam, quoniam quidem illos amamus natura in quorum pectus curas
15 affectionesque nostras velut oneris partem derivamus quibusque plurimum fidimus. Vicissim nos illi amant qui se amari sentiunt et sibi tantopere fidi ut ad intimos etiam animi recessus admittantur nihilque sit illis in nostro corde tectum et occultum. Quam legem ne existiment feminae oportere sibi communem ac parem cum maritis esse; nolint ipsae omnia maritorum con-
20 silia scrutari. Molesta est plerumque illa curiositas et suspecta de garrulitate quaeque virorum animos quandoque exasperat. Habent quoque mariti nonnulla quae nolint uxoribus esse cognita, sibi unis reservant. Apud Homerum Iuno inquit Iovi: 'Ne tu mihi postmodum irascaris si te inscio ad profundi Oceani aedes abiero.' Iuppiter vero Iunoni: 'Noli mea omnia consilia rimari
25 neu te cognituram speres.'

70. Quamquam sapiens mulier quanta maxima poterit vigilantia et sagacitate illud odorabitur, num qua de se sinistra suspicio in animo mariti haereat, num semen irae et odii, num quae reliquiae, num vestigia. Si quid sit tale, navet sedulam operam ne sinat radices adolescere. Facile glis-
30 cunt haec levibus de causis et perniciosa fiunt. Evellet blanditer et satisfaciet marito; citius invalescunt et occidunt incogniti ac operti morbi quam qui se foras proferunt. Ne extorqueat, ne duriter attrectet, ne magis infigat

---

69. (Ne ... abiero) *Hom. Il. 14, 310–311* // (Noli ... speres) *Hom. Il. 1, 545–546*

---

10 tuis Γ suis H // **10–11** cogitatibus ... indignis Γ sollicitudinibus referet modo virilibus et haud stultis auribus non sint indignae H // **11** habebis Γ habebit H // **12–13** in illius pectus ... acquiesces Γ in illius sinum deponet cogitationes suas, in illo acquiescet H // **14** quidem Γ *deest in* H // **14–15** curas affectionesque nostras Γ nostra cogitata H // **17** etiam Γ *deest in* H // **18** corde Γ pectore H // **18–25** Quam legem ... cognituram speres Γ *deest in* H // **26–27** Quamquam ... odorabitur Γ Curabit etiam quanta poterit diligentia sapiens mulier ut callide scrutetur H // **29** navet sedulam Γ det maximam H // **29–30** gliscunt Γ haec increscunt H // **30** de Γ *deest in* H / perniciosa fiunt Γ fiunt perniciosa H // **32** foras Γ *deest in* H

69. The occasions for giving advice must be watched for; not all times are propitious. A friendly office performed at the wrong moment is an annoyance. You will imprint the seal on soft wax and impart counsel to a yielding spirit when his mind is not perturbed by some trouble, when he is alone without any witness. Use skillful and persuasive language and do not be exaggerated in your advice. Finish with your talking before producing satiety. Then give the reason why you are offering this advice. Like the first arrows that hit the target this explanation will make the words of admonition reverberate more deeply in his heart. Then you will turn the conversation to something more pleasant, which will mitigate and remove any previous harshness, if there was any. Tell him about all your cares and preoccupations, provided they are not frivolous and not unworthy of a man's hearing. Regard him as your sole associate, interlocutor, consultant, master and lord. Confide your thoughts to his bosom and if anything distresses you, find comfort in him. These things contribute to reciprocal love and harmony, since we are naturally inclined to love those into whose heart we can pass on our cares and emotions like an unburdening of part of our woes, and in whom we can most trust. In turn those love us who feel that they are loved and are so trusted that they are admitted into the inmost recesses of our heart, and that nothing remains secret or concealed to them. Women should not think, however, that this law applies equally to them and to their husbands. They should not wish to probe into all the designs of their husbands. This kind of curiosity is often troublesome and looked upon as garrulity, which sometimes irritates their husbands' feelings. Likewise husbands have some things which they do not wish to be known by their wives, and keep reserved for themselves. In Homer Juno says to Jupiter, 'Do not be wroth with me afterwards if I depart to the dwelling places of deep Ocean without your knowledge.' Jupiter replies, 'Do not pry into all my plans or hope to know them.'

70. And yet the discreet woman with utmost vigilance and instinctive sagacity will ferret out whether her husband harbors any suspicions against her or any seeds of anger or hatred, some remnant of distrust. If such exist, she will devote her energies to dispel them before they take root. These increase for the slightest reason and become fatal. She will rid his mind of these gently and make amends to her husband. Undetected and hidden diseases gain strength and kill more quickly than those that manifest themselves externally. Let her not wrench it out or handle it roughly lest she implant it

dum revellere conatur, demet potius sine doloris sensu, hoc est, sine ex-
postulatione, sine querelis. Nec putet sibi vel homines vel deos umquam
futuros propitios nisi placato marito. Dominus in Evangelio ait: 'Si offers
munus tuum et ad altare recordaris aliquid tibi offensiunculae cum fratre
5 tuo resedisse, posito ibi munere, e vestigio propera ut fratri reconcilieris, ita
demum oblaturus Deo quod instituisti.' Frustra Dei pacem imploras non
pacato amico, quanto magis coniuge irato? Videat etiam atque etiam ut
quaecumque in cubiculo et ad sacrosanctum genialem torum dicentur agen-
turve sacrosancta arcana existimet, maiore etiam premenda silentio quam
10 illa quondam Cereris Eleusinae seu, ut rectius et aptius dicam, quae in aurem dicuntur sacerdoti a confitente. Quae insania est efferre tam recondita,
tam reticenda?

71. Generosus et recte educatus populus Atheniensis bellum cum Philippo
Rege Macedoniae gerens, deprehensas illius ad Olympiadem uxorem lit-
15 teras resignare et legere non sustinuit, quod existimaret (id quod res habet)
arcana coniugum sacra esse nec fas evulgari aut ab alienis nosci. Ita obsignatas illas intactasque in Macedoniam ad Reginam transmiserunt. Digna
gens, quibus fidem et silentium coniuges omnes servarent! Quod si hoc illi fecerunt hosti armato, quanto congruentius est te idem marito facere? Porcia,
20 M. Bruti coniunx, ultroneo vulnere constantiam suam exploravit an reticere
magna secreta posset et, ubi vulnus se tacere et celare posse intellexit, tum
ex viro rogare est ausa quaenam animo tam anxius volveret consiliumque
Caesarianae necis commissum sibi a Bruto aeque tenaciter fideliterque ac
quivis conspiratorum tacuit. Nec studebit solum illi amica uti sit semper,
25 sed etiam ne alios ei inimicos faciat et in periculum coniciat susceptis si-
multatibus. Neque enim pro lenone utendum ipsi est marito ad iniurias si
quas putat illatas sibi ulciscendas, nisi periculum sit pudicitiae, quae est feminae res omnium pretiosissima. Sed neque huic tamen erit, si nolit et caveat.
Verba si quis parum honorifica dixerit aut id fecerit quod tenerum videa-
30 tur laesisse animum, non protinus est ad virum accurrendum et igneis verbis (qualia solet ira subministrare) accendendum illius pectus et armandae

---

70. (Si … instituisti) *Vulg. Matth. 5, 23–24*
71. (populus Atheniensis … transmiserunt) *Plut. mor. 799E* // (Porcia … tacuit) *Val.
Max. 3, 2, 15*

1 revellere conatur Γ hoc agit **H** // **4** ad altare Γ altari **H** // **5** ita Γ tum **H** // **10** quondam Γ *deest in* **H** // **10–11** seu … confitente Γ aut cuiusque alterius Dei Deaeve mysteria **H**
// **13** Generosus et recte educatus Γ Sapiens **H** // **15** existimaret **HWW²B** existimare **V**
// **16–17** obsignatas illas Γ integras **H** // **19** idem … facere Γ *deest in* **H** // **22** rogare est
ausa Γ ausa est quaerere **H** // **24** studebit solum Γ solum studebit **H** / amica uti sit semper
Γ semper amica esse **H** // **25** ei **HWW²** et **BV** // **27** illatas Γ factas **H** // **28** Sed neque
huic tamen Γ et huic non **H** // **29** id Γ *deest in* **H** // **31** armandae Γ armanda **H**

more deeply in her attempt to tear it out, but rather let her remove it without any sense of pain, that is, without protests and complaints. She should not think that either gods or men will be favorable to her if she does not appease her husband. The Lord says in the Gospel: 'If you are offering your gift at the altar and there remember that some grievance with your brother still remains, leave your gift there and hasten immediately to be reconciled to your brother and then come and offer the gift you intended.' In vain do you implore peace of God if you have not made peace with your friend. How much more so with an angry spouse? Let the wife see to it again and again that whatever is said or done in the bedroom and in the sacred marriage bed is to be considered an inviolable secret and must be guarded with greater silence than the secrets of Ceres at Eleusis, or to put it more aptly, than what is confided to the priest by the penitent. What madness it is to reveal such intimate and private matters!

71. When the noble and well-bred people of Athens were engaged in a war with Philip, King of Macedon, they apprehended letters of his to his wife Olympias but they refrained from opening them or reading them, considering that the secrets of spouses are sacred (as indeed they are), and they did not permit them to be divulged or known by others. Thus they sent them sealed and untouched to the Queen in Macedonia. They were a people worthy to have wives who would maintain silence and secrecy. If they did this to an armed enemy, how much more fitting that you should do the same for your husband? Porcia, the wife of Marcus Brutus, voluntarily tested her own constancy by inflicting a wound upon herself to see if she could keep important secrets, and when she was convinced that she could conceal her wound, she dared ask her husband what plans he was turning over in his troubled mind. The plot to murder Caesar that was confided to her by Brutus she guarded with as much tenacity as one of the conspirators. Nor shall a wife strive merely to be a friend to her husband always but also not to make enemies of others and expose her husband to dangers through personal feuds. She must not use her husband as a go-between to avenge wrongs she thinks have been done to her unless her chastity is at risk, which is a woman's most prized possession. But this will not occur if she does not wish it and if she uses caution. If someone has said something disrespectful to her or done something that has offended her delicate sensitivity, she should not go rushing off to her husband and stir up his anger with fiery words (which anger is wont to supply) and have him take up arms. A good woman will repress

70. Eleusis: A small town on the coast of Attica where the mysteries in honor of Demeter, or Ceres, were celebrated.

manus. Devorabit haec omnia proba mulier et existimabit se tutam undique ac munitam, salva et intacta pudicitia, qua polluta nihil superest purum. Erit in coniugali cubiculo ac lectulo maritali non modo pudicitia, sed etiam pudor, ut uxorem se meminerit, in qua Plutarchus summumamorem et sum-
5 mum pudorem coniunctos esse vult atque complexos.

72. Ferunt Persarum Regum legitimas uxores convivari quidem cum eis et genialiter agere consuevisse, cenis autem lascivioribus non admitti, sed psaltrias tantum et concubinas. Eum honorem coniugio deferebant. Nam ut Princeps ille solitus erat dicere: 'Uxor dignitatis nomen est, non voluptatis.'
10 Sic maritus coniunctionis, propinquitatis, unionis appellatio est, non libidinis, sicut est a nobis superius declaratum. Decet tamen viros nec immodicis se immergere voluptatibus nec cum aliis oblectare se quam cum propriis uxoribus. Sed hic viros non docemus qui locus ad eos potius spectaret, ne ipsi libidinum et lasciviae suis uxoribus magistri essent meminissentque senten-
15 tiolae illius Xysti Pythagorici: 'Adulter est in suam uxorem omnis impudicus amator ardentior.' Et parerent Apostolo Paulo praecipienti maritis: 'Ut uxores suas tamquam vasa generationis possideant in sanctificationem, non in cupiditates immoderatas atque illicitas, quod gentiles faciunt qui Deum ignorant.' Sponsus in Canticis canticorum sponsam sororem suam vocat, quo
20 puriorem denotet caritatem matrimonialem. Sed ad mulieres redeamus.

73. Ipsae pudicum et sanctum torum spurcis et libidinosis actibus ne coinquinent. 'Honorabile connubium sit inter vos omnes,' inquit idem Paulus, 'et torus immaculatus.' Casta illa Spartana rogata an accessisset umquam ad maritum, 'Minime vero,' inquit, 'sed maritus ad me.' Videlicet pudica fe-
25 mina mariti libidinem numquam irritarat nec venere usa erat, nisi ut coniugi obsecundaret. Zenobiam, Palmyrenorum Reginam, scribit Trebellius Pollio mulierem eruditissimam et regni administrandi prudentissimam ea castitate fuisse ut ne virum quidem suum nisi temptatis conceptionibus nosset.

---

72. (Persarum ... concubinas) *Plut. mor. 140B; 613A* ∥ (Uxor ... voluptatis) *Hist. Aug. 5, 11* ∥ (Adulter ... ardentior) *Sext. Pyth. 231 (chadwick, p. 39); Hier. adv. Iovin. 1, 49, PL 23, 281* ∥ (Ut ... ignorant) *Vulg. I Thess. 4, 4–5* ∥ (Sponsus ... vocat) *Vulg. cant. 4, 9; 4, 10; 4, 12 et passim*
73. (Honorabile ... immaculatus) *Vulg. Hebr. 13, 4* ∥ (Casta ... me) *Plut. mor. 242C* ∥ (Zenobiam ... liberis) *Hist. Aug. 13* ∥

---

3 ac lectulo maritali Γ *deest in* **H** ∥ **7–8** sed psaltrias tantum Γ tantum psaltrias acciri **H** ∥ **10** propinquitatis, unionis Γ affinitatisque **H** ∥ **12** immergere Γ dedere **H** ∥ **17–18** sanctificationem ... illicitas Γ sanctificatione non in cupiditatibus illicitis aut immoderatis **H** ∥ **19–20** quo ... matrimonialem Γ et faciat moderatiorem amorem **H** ∥ **27** regni administrandi Γ *deest in* **H** ∥ **28** nisi ... nosset Γ sciret nisi temptatis conceptionibus **H**

all this and consider herself safe and protected on all sides if her chastity is intact, without which nothing is pure. In the bedroom and the marriage bed there will be not only chastity but a sense of shame, so that she will remember she is a wife, in whom Plutarch wishes that the greatest love should be joined with the greatest modesty.

72. They say that the legitimate wives of the Persian kings feasted with them and behaved in a convivial manner, but that they were not admitted to the more lewd celebrations, which were reserved only for dancing-girls and concubines. They paid this homage to marriage. For as that prince was wont to say: 'Wife is the name of dignity, not of sensual pleasure.' So the title of husband is one of association, closeness and union, not of lust, as we have stated above. It is fitting that men do not immerse themselves in immoderate pleasures or divert themselves with other women than their wives. But we are not teaching men here what their role should be. Let them be on their guard that they do not become teachers of lust and lasciviousness to their wives and bear in mind the saying of Sextus the Pythagorean: 'Every unchaste and excessively impassioned lover is an adulterer with his wife.' They should also hearken to St. Paul's precepts: 'Let them possess their wives like vessels of generation unto holiness, not for immoderate and illicit cupidity as the Gentiles do, who do not know God.' The spouse in the Canticle of Canticles calls his spouse his sister to signify that marital love is purer. But let us return to women.

73. They must not contaminate the chaste and holy marriage bed by sordid and lustful acts. 'Let the marriage between you be honorable,' says St. Paul, 'and the marriage bed unspotted.' When the chaste Spartan woman was asked whether she had ever made the first advances to her husband, she answered, 'No, but my husband did to me.' This is to say that the chaste woman never roused her husband's desire or engaged in sex except to satisfy her husband. Trebellius Pollio writes that Zenobia, Queen of Palmyra, a very learned woman and wise in the governing of her kingdom, was of such chastity that she did not lie with her husband until after she had ascertained whether she was pregnant or not. After having sexual relations with

---

72. Sextus the Pythagorean: A collection of maxims, probably made in the 2nd cent. AD, was attributed to a certain Xystus in the Syriac translation or Sextus Pythagoreus according to Saint Jerome. The original collection was probably non-Christian, to which Christian accretions were made.

73. Trebellius Pollio: One of the writers of the so-called *Historia Augusta*, a collection of biographies of Roman emperors from 117 to 284.

Zenobia: Known also as Bath Zabbai; she was Queen of Palmyra, a buffer state between the Romans and the Parthians. She expanded her conquests from Arabia to Syria, Egypt and Asia Minor until she was finally defeated by the Emperor Aurelian in 272 AD. She was taken back to Rome in triumph but was allowed to live out her days comfortably as a Roman matron.

Nam ubi semel concubuisset, a viro abstinebat usque ad tempus menstrui. Si conceperat, omnino secubabat quoad peperisset; sin aliter, potestatem sui faciebat viro quaerendis liberis. Quis hanc credat non modo libidini, sed vel mediocri voluptati concubitum dedisse? Suspicienda et adoranda matrona
5 quae non plus muliebribus ad libidinem sollicitabatur quam pede aut manu! Digna quae vel sine concubitu pareret quem tantum in pariendi usum petebat vel sine dolore quae implebatur sine voluptate! Plus praestitit nostra Christiana Ethelfrida, Britannorum Regina, quae postquam semel peperisset, amplius viro suo congressa non est. Quanto magis illa Edeltrudis, Regina
10 itidem eius gentis, quae duobus ibi maritis nupta, utrumque ad perpetuam castitatem induxit. Fuerunt et alia coniugum paria quae concubitus prorsus expertia vixere, velut Henricus Bavarus, Romanorum Princeps, cum Sinegunda; Iulianus Martyr et Basilia; in urbe vero Alexandrina Chrysantus ac Daria, et Amos cum uxore sua; Malchus itidem Monachus, cuius vitam Hie-
15 ronymus rettulit, cum conserva illa sua.

74. Nimirum intellexerunt divini homines id quod a sapientissimis viris traditum est, corporis voluptatem indignam esse excellentia hac nostra quam per animi naturam possidemus. Idcirco eo magis ab unoquoque contemni et reici quo quisque largius de illa animi praestantia sortitus est Deo propin-
20 quior, non usurpari nec crebro ascisci nisi qui animus parum generosus, humilis, abiectus, multum sordidae ac despicatae naturae traxit, minimum altissimae illius. Uxores, exutae supparis induite pudorem et hoc naturae honestissimum amiculum semper retinete interdiu, noctu, cum alienis, cum viro, in luce, in obscuro. Numquam vos Deus, numquam angeli, numquam

---

73. (Malchus ... sua) *Hier. vita Malchi 6, PL 23, 56*

1 ubi Γ cum **H** ∥ **1–3** a viro ... quaerendis liberis Γ exspectatis menstruis, continebat se, si pregnans esset; sin minus, iterum potestatem quaerendis liberis dabat **H** ∥ **4** adoranda **H** adornanda Γ ∥ **12** expertia Γ expertes **H** ∥ **18** possidemus Γ habemus **H** ∥ **19–20** sortitus est Deo propinquior Γ accepit propinquiorque est Deo et reliquis mentibus divinis **H** ∥ **20** nec Γ et **H** / qui Γ quis **H** ∥ **21** sordidae ac despicatae Γ vilis **H** ∥ **24** obscuro Γ tenebris **H**

him she would abstain from her husband until the time of her menstruation. If she had conceived, she slept alone until she had brought forth, but if not, she gave her husband the opportunity to create children. Who would think that this woman derived any lustful or even moderate pleasure from the sexual act? Worthy of admiration and esteem is this matron who was no more moved to lust by her sexual organs than by her hand or foot. She was worthy to have children without sexual intercourse, which she desired only for the purpose of bearing children, or without pain since she was made pregnant without pleasure. Even more exemplary is our Christian Queen, Ethelfleda of England, who after her first child no longer lay with her husband. And Etheldreda, Queen of that same nation, went even further, for in her two marriages she induced both of her husbands to practice perpetual chastity. There were many other couples who lived entirely without carnal relations, like Henry of Bavaria, Roman emperor, with his wife Cynegunda; Julian Martyr with Basilia. In the city of Alexandria there were Chrysanthus and Daria; and there were Amos and his wife; Malchus the monk, also, with the woman who was his fellow-slave, whose life was recounted by Jerome.

74. These saintly persons understood all too well what has been handed down by wise men, that the pleasure of the body is not worthy of our preeminence as human beings, which we possess through the nature of the soul. Therefore the closer one is to God and the more he has received of that excellence of the mind, the more sensual pleasure is spurned and repudiated. Only the less noble, humble and lowly person, drawn to his baser and more loathsome nature, will make habitual use and exercise of sensual pleasure, and partake very little of that higher nature. Wives, put off your shawls and put on modesty and always hold on to this decorous mantle of nature, by day and by night, with strangers, with your husband, in the light and in the dark. May God and his angels and your own conscience never see you

73. Ethelfleda: Ethelfleda, or Aethelflaed (d. 918), was the daughter of Alfred the Great, king of Wessex. She married Aethelred, ruler of Mercia, in 886, and ruled in her husband's place long before his death.

Etheldreda: (d. 679) After a first short-lived marriage to a local ealderman, in which she remained a virgin, she was married again for political reasons to Egfrith, the young king of Northumbria. He agreed that she should remain a virgin as in her previous marriage. But twelve years later he wished their marital relationship to be normal. Etheldreda refused, became a nun and founded a double monastery at Ely.

Henry of Bavaria: Henry II, Duke of Bavaria (973–1024), Holy Roman Emperor, canonized by Pope Eugenius III in 1146.

Julian Martyr with Basilia: Saints Julian and Basilissa married but by mutual consent lived in perpetual chastity. She founded a convent and he was martyred under Diocletian. There is a very fanciful account of their lives in the *Acta Sanctorum* for January 9.

Chrysanthus and Daria: Chrysanthus, an Egyptian, and his Greek wife, Daria, lived together in virginal purity. They both openly professed Christianity and were put to death under the emperors Carinus and Numerianus in 282 AD.

conscientia vestra nudas pudoris tegumento conspiciat. Nihil fingi potest deformius aut turpius vobis sic renudatis. Gravis poeta Hesiodus ne nocte quidem mulieres interulam tunicam ponere vult quatenus noctes etiam deorum immortalium sunt. Rebecca, filia Bathuelis, cum ad Isaac duceretur cui erat nuptura cumque deambulantem offendisset in campo, rogavit quis ille esset. Ubi cognovit esse Isaac sponsum suum, continuo sese pallio operuit. Prudens virgo et probe instituta alias omnes edocuit primam ac praecipuam verecundiam marito deberi. Nam cui exhibenda est maior verecundia quam cui maxima reverentia?

CAP. VI.   DE ZELOTYPIA

75. Zelotypiam ex Stoicorum sententia Cicero finit: 'Aegritudinem ex hoc quod alter quoque potiatur eo quod quis concupivit.' Definitur etiam metum esse ne quis tecum habeat commune quod tuum unius velis esse. Quibuscumque explicetur verbis, perturbatio est certe truculentissima et plane tyrannus immitis atque impotentissimus, qui quamdiu in mariti animo regnat et saevit, desperanda est uxori concordia. Praestaret utrique mori quam alterum in zelotypiam incidere, sed virum praecipue. Qui cruciatus, quae tormenta aequari possunt, tum agitato intemperiis zelotypiae, tum ei de quo est ille metus? Hinc querimoniae, expostulationes, clamores, odium sui et alterius, perpetua mali suspicio, rixa, iurgium, pugna, caedes denique. Nam et legimus et fando audivimus occisas a plurimis coniuges suas sola zelotypia percitis. Quo affectu ferae quoque bestiae nonnullae graviter temptantur. Leaenam Aristoteles scribit a leone discerpi si adulteratam deprehenderit. Cycnum feminam multi viderunt confectam a masculo quod alterum marem secuta esset. Quocirca viribus est universis annitendum ne maritum eae Furiae invadant; si invaserint, ut liberetur. Hoc unica ratione assequetur mulier: si nihil vel dicat vel agat quod in suspicionem rapi a marito possit, tanto minus si natura sua sit suspicax.

---

74. (Hesiodus ... sunt) *Hes. erg. 729–730* // (Rebecca ... operuit) *Vulg. gen. 24, 64–65*
75. (aegritudinem ... concupivit) *Cic. Tusc. 4, 17–18* // (Aristoteles ... deprehenderit) *fons nobis ignotus*

1 nudas Γ nudam **H** // **1–2** deformius aut Γ *deest in* **H** // **2** renudatis Γ nudis **H** // **3** interulam tunicam Γ intimas tunicas **H** // **12** Definitur Γ Diffinitur **H** // **15** atque impotentissimus Γ *deest in* **H** // **17** virum praecipue Γ praecipue virum **H** // **20** caedes denique Γ etiam caedes **H** // **22** percitis Γ impulsis **H** // **22–23** nonnullae graviter temptantur Γ praecipites impelluntur **H** // **24** multi viderunt Γ ipse una cum multis vidi **H** // **25** Quocirca Γ Ideo **H** // **26** eae Furiae invadant Γ invadat **H** / si ... liberetur Γ vel si invaserit, ut relinquat et liberet **H** // **26–27** assequetur mulier Γ mulier assequetur **H** // **28** tanto ... suspicax Γ *deest in* **H**

divested of the veil of modesty. Nothing can be imagined more ugly or more foul than if you are divested of that cover. The grave poet Hesiod does not want women to take off their chemise even at night in as much as the nights also belong to the immortal gods. When Rebecca, the daughter of Bathuel, was brought to Isaac, whom she was to marry, and came upon him when he was walking in the field, she asked him who he was. When she learned that he was Isaac, her promised spouse, she immediately covered herself with her pallium. This wise and well brought up maiden taught all others that first and foremost deference is owed to one's husband. For to whom should we show greater deference than to the one to whom the greatest reverence is due?

CHAPTER 6.   ON JEALOUSY

75. Cicero defines jealousy after the opinion of the Stoics as 'A sickness that comes from the thought that another person may possess what one wished for oneself.' It is also defined as 'The fear that someone may share with you what you wish to be yours alone.' However it is defined, it is surely a ferocious vexation and a relentless and incontrollable tyranny, which as long as it reigns and rages in the mind of the husband, precludes any hope of concord in the marriage. It would be better for both of them to die than that either of them should fall victim to jealousy, especially the husband. What torment and torture can be compared to it, both for the one afflicted by the excesses of jealousy and the one who causes this fear? From this come complaints, protests, shouting, hatred of oneself and of the other person, unceasing suspicion, wrangling, altercation, fighting, even death. For we read and hear tell of many wives slain by their husbands for the sole motive of jealousy. Some wild beasts are also affected by this passion. Aristotle writes that the lion tears the lioness to pieces if he catches her in adultery. Many have seen the female swan killed by the male because she followed after another swan. Therefore every effort must be made to prevent the husband from being seized by these furies, and if he is seized by them, to free him from their power. The wife will succeed in this only in one way, viz., if she says or does nothing that may make her husband suspicious. She must give even less opportunity if he is suspicious by nature.

76. Bene Paulus, Hieronymus, Aristoteles et alii magni ac sapientes viri nec malum agendum nec quod mali habeat speciem. 'Grave hoc,' inquis, 'nam quis possit etiam suspiciones regere?' In multis modis: primum, si caste vixeris, et propemodum hac sola via expeditissima. Nam veritatis parens est
5 tempus; falsa tempus debilitat ac tollit, vera confirmat et corroborat. Si casta sis et maritum habeas zelotypum, spera facile ac brevi hanc illum animi per- turbationem positurum; sin impudica, pro certo scito non modo non dele- tum iri, sed invalituram in dies. In summa, si mariti zelum innocens per- fers, beata es; si nocens, misera. Amabis maritum et navabis operam ut ille
10 amari se sentiat, sed vide ne id simulate, nam eo magis et acerbius oderit quo viderit te simulare accuratius. Ficta enim non modo quo diriguntur non proficiunt, verum plerumque in contrarium.

77. Saepius admoneo feminas (et admonendae sunt saepissime plus quam viri) ne se fallant, existimantes nihil referre agasne aliquid an videaris agere.
15 Imperitae sunt et stultae, si figmentis et fucis suis rerum se naturam mu- taturas sperant. Neminem ostendat se amare mulier non aeque modo ac virum, sed nec alium quam virum. Si quos amet alios, mariti amet gratia aut ne diligat quidem quamlibet marito caros. Nam plerique, omnes viri facile patiuntur, gaudent etiam, ut cetera habeant cum uxore communia, amicos
20 communes non habere; quod et uxoribus usu venit de famulabus et feminis amicis suis. In publico gerat se maximo cum pudore, nec libenter seu ver- setur seu colloquatur cum alienis viris nec cum mulieribus quae de neglecta pudicitia male audiant; lenae vero nec conspectum sustineat. Litteras nullas vel det vel accipiat coniuge inscio. De alienis viris parcissime loquatur, neque
25 formam neque dotem aliquam corporis eorum laudet aut laudantem libens audiat, nec eos intente spectet nec illis praesentibus aliquid agat quod indi- cium possit cuiquam esse turpitudinis. Quem virum, quam mulierem nolet te maritus alloqui, eius omnino congressus et colloquia defugito, vel matris tuae si ita marito libeat. Quod si illum suspicacem esse noveris, nec apud
30 eum nec apud fratrem aut filium aut patrem aut propinquum pro viro ullo intercedes, nisi is forte consanguineus sit vel adeo affinis ut nulla in negotium possit incidere sinistra interpretatio. Alioqui enim alia potius re quapiam sus- picabitur adduci te quam benefaciendi aut commiserationis studio, ut sunt semper suspiciones in peiorem partem credulae. Pro multis simul viris tutius

---

76. (nec malum ... speciem) *Vulg. I Thess. 5, 22*

2 speciem Γ faciem **H** // 5 debilitat ac tollit Γ languescere et deficere cogit **H** / corroborat Γ roborat **H** / casta Γ bona **H** // 7 sin impudica Γ si mala **H** // 8 invalituram Γ adultum **H** // 9 navabis operam Γ laborabis **H** // 10 eo Γ *deest in* **H** // 11 te simulare accuratius Γ accuratius te simulare **H** // 16 mulier Γ *deest in* **H** // 17 amet alios Γ alios amat **H** / gratia Γ causa **H** // 18 ne ... caros Γ si non amat, mariti amicos saltem ne oderit **H** // **18–19** plerique ... patiuntur Γ multi sunt viri qui facile ferunt **H** // 21 gerat se Γ agat **H** / nec **HWW²** ne **BV** // 23 sustineat Γ ferat **H** // 27–p.96,2 Quem virum ... valebit Γ *deest in* **H**

76. Paul, Jerome, Aristotle and other great and wise writers say well that neither should evil be done nor that which has the appearance of evil. 'This is a difficult task,' you say,' for who can control suspicions?' You can, in many ways. First, if you live chastely, and this alone is the surest way. Time is the parent of truth. Time weakens and eliminates falsehood; it confirms and corroborates truth. If you are chaste and you have a jealous husband, hope that he will put away the disturbance of the mind in a short time. But if you are unchaste, know for certain that not only will it not be destroyed, but it will grow stronger with each passing day. In brief, if you are innocent and put up with a jealous husband, you are blessed; if guilty, you are wretched. You will love your husband and exert every effort to make him feel that he is loved, but make sure it is not feigned, for he will hate you the more bitterly as he sees your dissimulation more clearly. What is feigned not only does not achieve the desired effect but often has just the opposite result.

77. I warn women often, and they must be given this warning very often, more than men, not to be deceived into thinking that it does not matter whether you actually do something or seem to do something. They are inexperienced and stupid if they hope to change the way things are by resorting to their stratagems and pretences. Let the woman show that not only does she not love anyone as much as her husband but loves no one but her husband. If she loves anyone else, let it be for the sake of her husband, or let her not love them at all, however dear they are to her husband. Most, indeed one might say all men allow and even enjoy having other things in common with their wives, but not friends, and wives are the same with regard to their maidservants and female friends. In public she must comport herself with great modesty and should not take pleasure in associating or conversing with other women's husbands or with women who do not have a good reputation for their chastity. She should not even abide the sight of a loose woman. She should neither send nor receive letters without the knowledge of her husband. She should talk very sparingly of other women's husbands and should not praise their beauty or any of their physical endowments nor should she willingly listen to their being praised. She will not stare at them or do anything in their presence that could be construed as in the least improper. Avoid meeting or conversing with any man or woman your husband does not wish you to talk to, even if it be your mother, if that is his pleasure. If you know him to be of a suspicious nature, do not plead for any man's cause with him or with your brother or father or son or relative, unless he is a blood-relation or so closely related by marriage that it would not occasion any malicious interpretation. Otherwise your husband will suspect that you had other motives than the desire to do good or show compassion, for suspicions always tend to see the worse side of things. You will be on surer

poteris, ut pro civitate aut populo aut provincia; in quo iniqua interpretatio minus valebit.

78. Haec omnia dicenda fuerunt, quandoquidem non malum modo vitandum suademus, sed eius quoque imaginem ac similitudinem. Ceterum prava illa cogitatio eximenda est mulieribus quod caritatem maritorum et curam de ipsarum pudicitia zelotypiam esse nonnumquam interpretantur, cum tanti referat probas esse uxores. Sunt quae nisi solutissima in res omnes concedatur licentia, zelotypiam confestim arguant et ingenti temeritate atque impudentia marito apud loquacem famam civitatis invictissimam inurunt notam, unde ille et male audit immerito et a multis contemnitur atque irridetur. Sunt hae mulieres an viperae? Uxores an hostes? Non haec est Christiana disciplina, sed intemperantis cuiusdam stoliditatis ac brutae. Illud vero, risune magis an indignatione prosequendum sit nescias, quod nonnullae exeunt, manent, redeunt, colloquuntur, convivantur ubi, quamdiu, cum quibus volunt, agunt omnia pro animi sui libidine, maritis sinentibus, et inter haec omnia zelotypiae maritum insimulant.

79. Nunc de zelotypia feminae dicendum; qua quidem si tangatur, profecto non ita multa adhibuerim remedia ut sanem, modo ne sit nimia et violenta quaeque pacem domus turbet et marito sit gravis ac plane intoleranda. Nam si eiusmodi est, medicina succurrendum censeo. Ante omnia, ut mulieri veniat in mentem maritum dominum esse nec idem sibi licere quod illi; humanas leges non perinde a viro pudicitiam exigere ut a femina; liberiores esse viri quam feminae vitae totius rationes; viris curanda esse multa, feminis solam pudicitiam. Claudendae aures iis qui sinistrum quid de marito volunt deferre, ut sit nobis atque illis persuasum malam eos apud nos captare gratiam. Hermione, Cadmi Thebani uxor, cum a marito propter zelotypiam discessisset, lamentans queritur apud Euripidem malarum feminarum ingressu se perditam, quod illis obtrectatricibus aures fidemque adhibuisset. Mulier si ob paelicatum vel maritum deferre vel graviter cum eo rixari deliberet, faciat dictum illud cogitatione tractet, quod quidam cum fugitivum persequeretur isque in pistrinum se coniecisset, fertur dixisse: 'Ubi malim te videre?' scilicet 'quam eo loco in quem te coniecissem ipse

79. (Hermione ... adhibuisset) *Eur. Andr. 930* // (Ubi ... videre) *Plut. mor. 144A*

4 suademus **Γ** praecepimus **H** / imaginem ac similitudinem **Γ** speciem **H** // **4–16** Ceterum prava illa ... maritum insimulant **Γ** *deest in* **H** // **11** irridetur **WW²** invidetur **BV** // **17** qua quidem si tangatur **Γ** quam quidem si habuerit **H** // **18** sanem **Γ** eximam **H** // **19–20** gravis ac plane intoleranda **Γ** molesta **H** // **21** mulieri veniat in mentem **Γ** cogitet mulier **H** // **22–23** humanas ... rationes **Γ** pudicitiam non ita viro praestandam ut feminae, saltem humanis legibus. Nam divinis utrique ex aequo, liberiorem esse viri quam feminae vitam **H** // **23–24** curanda ... pudicitiam **Γ** curanda sunt multa, feminis sola pudicitia **H** // **25** ut sit ... persuasum **Γ** et censendum **H** // **29** deferre **Γ** narrare **H** // **31** fertur dixisse **Γ** dixit **H** // **32** loco **H** loci **Γ**

grounds to show favor to groups of men, as a city, a people, or a province, in which case a malicious interpretation will have less credibility.

78. All these things had to be said because I am trying to demonstrate that not only must evil be avoided, but any semblance or appearance of it. Women must rid themselves of the erroneous concept that the affection and solicitude for their chastity shown by their husbands is a form of jealousy, since a wife's good reputation is a matter of paramount importance. There are some women who if they are not granted the utmost liberty in everything accuse their husbands of jealousy and in their incredible impudence and temerity brand their husbands with an indelible stigma in the talk of the city, from which he will get a bad reputation and become the object of scorn and derision. Are these women or vipers? wives or enemies? This is not Christian conduct, but a mark of uncontrolled and irrational stupidity. You would not know whether to be amused or indignant by the fact that women of this sort come and go, stay home, return, engage in conversations and banquets wherever, whenever and with whom they wish, do everything they feel like doing, with their husband's consent, and then accuse him of jealousy.

79. Now I must say a word about female jealousy. If a woman suffers from this, I shall not suggest various remedies for her cure as long as it is not excessive and violent and does not upset the peace of the home and become an intolerable burden for her husband. If it is of that type, I think she must be given medical treatment. Above all, a woman should bear in mind that her husband is master of the household and not all things permitted to him are permitted to her, and human laws do not require the same chastity of the man as they do of the woman. In all aspects of life the man is freer than the woman. Men have to look after many things; women are responsible only for their chastity. They must close their ears to those who wish to convey some adverse comments about their husbands, making it clear to them that their gossip inspires our ill favor. Hermione, the wife of Cadmus, who left her husband because of her jealousy, laments in the play of Euripides that she met her ruin through the insinuations of evil women, because she had lent credence to these calumniators. If a woman decides to denounce her husband or engage in a serious quarrel with him on account of a concubine, let her call to mind the story about a certain man who was pursuing a fugitive slave, and when the slave took refuge in a mill, he said 'Where else would I rather find you?' that is to say, 'than in the place where I would have thrown you if I had caught you.' So she should reason

---

79. Hermione: She was not the daughter of Cadmus, as Vives mistakenly states (confusing her perhaps with Harmonia), but the only daughter of Helen and Menelaus. In the *Andromache* of Euripides, cited here, she is jealous of the attentions of her husband Neoptolemus to his slave-consort, Andromache, and plots to kill her. In a long digression she blames gossipy women for instigating her to this action. This line became proverbial.

si cepissem?' Sic ergo reputet: 'Ubi me aut quid potius agentem videre malit
paelex quam domo profugam et a geniali toro vel in gravi dissidio cum viro,
ut tum demum minima opera cunctam ad se mariti mentem allicefaciat,
quam ipsa a me importunitate mea averti et alienavi?' Ut taceam vulgi ser-
5　mones, quibus et se et maritum praebere fabulam honesta matrona, quibusvis a viro iniuriis et contumeliis affecta, non debet.

80. Memoriae a quibusdam traditum est puellas aliquas recens nuptas
cum maritos studio venandi foris quandoque pernoctantes suspicarentur
aliarum feminarum teneri consuetudine, illos esse in saltus prosecutas ibique
10　in tenebris a maritis iaculis confixas et a canibus dilaniatas cum esse ferae cre-
derentur. Nimis magnas dederunt poenas tam curiosae zelotypiae. Quanto
moderatius et prudentius Tertia Aemilia, prioris Africani coniunx! Quae
cum marito unam ex ancillulis suis placere sensisset, rem dissimulavit, ne
domitorem orbis ac populi sui principem incontinentiae damnare videre-
15　tur et sese impatientiae, quae iniuriam coniugis, maximi aetate sua viri,
ferre nequisset. Ac ne vulnus aliquod laesi animi aluisse in pectore cre-
deretur, marito mortuo ancillam illam, paelicem suam, honesto liberti sui
connubio prosecuta est, rata si quis nostrarum rerum apud vita functos
est sensus, et hoc quoque mariti manibus gratissimum futurum. Sapientis-
20　sima femina non ignorabat se uxorem, se dominam esse, quocumque vir
suus divertisset. Si mariti concubitus alteri invideret, hoc libidinis esse, non
amoris.

81. Quid quod maritum si suscenseas magis irritabis? Sin feras, citius
revocabis, praesertim ubi tuos faciles mores cum importuna paelicis inso-
25　lentia compararit? Sic Terentius, humanorum affectuum depictor, Pam-
philum a Bacchide concubina carissima ad invisam uxorem traductum
scribit in Hecyra, postquam et ipse Pamphilus sese et illam Bacchidem et
hanc quae domi erat cognovit, satis ad exemplum ambarum mores earum
existimans:

30　　　　Haec ita, uti liberali esse ingenio decet,
　　　　Pudens, modesta, incommoda atque iniurias
　　　　Viri omnes ferre et tegere contumelias;
　　　　Hic animus, partim uxoris misericordia
　　　　Devinctus, partim victus huiusce iniuriis,

---

80. (Tertia Aemilia ... prosecuta est) *Val. Max. 6, 7, 1*
81. (Haec ... nactus est) *Ter. Hec. 164–170*

---

2 domo ... toro Γ profugam a domo et geniali toro **H** // 3 minima ... allicefaciat Γ
facilius ad te totam mariti mentem alliciat **H** // 6 et contumeliis Γ *deest in* **H** // 9 aliarum
feminarum Γ alterius feminae **H** / prosecutas Γ secutas **H** // 10 dilaniatas Γ laniatas **H**
// 12 moderatius Γ civilius **H** // 13 ancillulis Γ ancillis **H** // 20–21 vir suus divertisset
Γ vir isset **H** // 34 devinctus **H** *Ter.* devictus Γ / huiusce Γ Bacchidis **H**

'Where would the concubine rather see me or what would she rather see me doing than fleeing from my home and the marriage bed in grave discord with my husband, so that then she can gain complete control of my husband with very little effort since I have estranged and alienated him by my unreasonableness?' I shall not mention popular gossip, to which a virtuous lady should not expose herself or her husband no matter what wrongs and indignities she may have suffered from him.

80. The story is recorded of certain young women, recently married, who suspected that their husbands, who sometimes spent the night hunting, were having amorous associations with other women. They followed them out into the woods and there in the darkness were transfixed by their husbands' javelins and torn to pieces by their dogs, since they thought they were wild animals. They paid a huge penalty for their prying jealousy. How much more moderation and prudence Aemilia Tertia, wife of Scipio Africanus the Elder, showed when she became aware that her husband was attracted to one of her maidservants. She pretended not to notice anything lest she seem to condemn the conqueror of the world and leader of his people for incontinence and herself for impatience in not being able to tolerate a wrong done to her by her husband, the greatest man of his time. And to show that she nourished no ill feelings for this affront, when her husband died, she rewarded this maidservant, her husband's concubine, with a legitimate marriage to one of her freedmen, thinking that if there is any feeling beyond the grave for what goes on in this life, her husband's shades would find pleasure in this. This wise woman was not unaware that she was wife and mistress of the household wherever her husband went. If she was envious of her husband's sleeping with another woman, that feeling was inspired by lust, not love.

81. Besides, if you become angry with your husband, you will irritate him the more, whereas if you put up with him, you will more quickly win him back, especially if he compares your pliant character to the obstinate insolence of a concubine. Terence, who portrays human emotions so well, writes in the *Hecyra* that Pamphilus was converted to his hated wife by his beloved concubine Bacchis after he came to know himself and Bacchis and the woman he had in his house. He compared the character of both of them in this way:

> She, as befits a girl of decent birth,
> Modest and chaste, bears hurts and injuries
> From her spouse and hides his misdemeanors.
> His heart, in part won over by his wife's compassion,
> In part worn down by the other's abuse,

Paulatim elapsus est Bacchidi atque huic transtulit
Amorem, postquam par ingenium nactus est.

Haec ille.

82. Non tacendum est nobilis illius matronae factum, quae cum maritum
haberet amore alienae uxoris captum itareque ad illam quotidie videret, inter virum et fratres illius insidiantes praesentissimo cum periculo maritum
aggressa: 'Tu,' inquit, 'mi vir, ab amore isto illicito divelli non potes, nec
ego abs te id contendo. Solum oro ne cum tanto vitae tuae discrimine ames.
Illa se velle sequi te ait, duc in arcem tuam. Ego ipsi hanc aedium partem
cedam instructissimam; in aliam migrabo ac dabo tibi fidem non aliter me
illam habituram quam si soror mihi esset germana. Si quid secus senseris,
tu me potius domo pellito, illam retineto.' Persuasit marito et nocte quadam
paelicem in arcem intulit vehementer trepidam ac metuentem uxorem ama-
toris; quae illam blandissime et humanissime exceptam in suis cubiculis collocavit nec aliter appellavit quam sororem visitque eam bis quotidie trac-
tarique iussit accuratius et delicatius quam semetipsam absque ulla vel in
verbis vel in factis odii significatione. 'Nunc,' inquit, 'marite, tutius amabis
et securius fruere.' Vir uno fere anno ad uxorem teneram, nobilem, castam
et paelice profecto formosiorem non accessit. Uxor quid in animo haberet
solus scit Deus. Quod homines iudicare poterant, non inique ferre videbatur, praesertim ubi maritum periculo subduxerat; multa in templo, multa
in precibus esse. Afflictam facile omnes intelligebant, indignantem aut con-
querentem nemo. Post annum maritus ad uxorem totus conversus amicam
coepit capitaliter odisse et ea pulsa tantum amorem ad uxorem transtulit ut
in ea se animum, vitam, spiritum suum situm esse praedicet nec sustinebit,
ut ait, superstes illi esse. Nominibus abstineo, quoniam omnes adhuc vivunt.

83. Et haec quidem dixi de iis quae certam habent zelotypiae causam.
Nam quae incertam importune ac intolerabiliter agunt et sibi ipsis et coniugibus certum cruciatum ob incertum admissum afferunt, quod faciunt
pleraeque immodice vel amantes vel indulgentes suis affectionibus vel quae
ipse sibi fingunt somnia et infirmas coniecturas pro magnis et compertis argumentis arripiunt. Iocatur cum aliqua maritus? Ne putet protinus amore
esse captum. Magna pars affectus est quid credas. Saepius enim ex opinionibus affectus quam ex rebus nascuntur. Ne traharis quibuslibet suspicionibus
quam ne perspectis quidem et exploratis moveri oportet.

---

1 elapsus est **H** elapsus **Γ** // **4** matronae **Γ** *deest in* **H** // **5** itareque **Γ** ireque **H** // **6** cum
Γ *deest in* **H** // **11** mihi esset germana **Γ** esset **H** // **12** pellito **Γ** expellito **H** // **15** visitque
Γ misit ad **H** // **16** semetipsam **Γ** se **H** // **17** marite **Γ** marito **H** // **19** paelice profecto **Γ**
certe concubina **H** // **24** transtulit **Γ** collocavit **H** // **26** adhuc **Γ** *deest in* **H** // **28–29** coniugibus **Γ** maritis **H** // **29** afferunt **Γ** afferre **H** // **30** suis affectionibus **Γ** affectibus suis **H**
// **32–33** amore esse captum **Γ** amare **H** // **35** perspectis **Γ** perspecta quidem et explorata
movere debent **H**

Slipped free of Bacchis and transferred his love
To the one in whom he found a kindred spirit.

82. Not to be passed over in silence is the deed of that noble matron who saw that her husband was snared in the toils of love by another married woman. He went to her house daily at great risk of his life since the woman's husband and her brothers were lying in wait for him. Going up to him, she said: 'My husband, you cannot tear yourself away from this illicit love and I do not demand this of you. I ask but one thing, that you do not engage in this love affair at so much peril to your own life. She says that she wishes to go with you; take her to your own guarded dwelling. I will give her the best furnished part of the house and I shall move to another part and I give you my word that I shall treat her no differently than I would my own sister. If you find that I act otherwise, you may drive me from the house and keep her.' She persuaded her husband and one night he brought her into his castle, though she was trembling and afraid of her lover's wife. But she welcomed her most warmly and most courteously, lodged her in her own bedroom, always called her by the name of sister, visited her twice a day and ordered that she be given more care and comfort than herself, without ever showing her any sign of hatred in word or in deed. 'Now,' she said, 'my dear husband, you will love and enjoy her more safely.' For almost a year the husband did not have sexual relations with his tender, noble and chaste wife, who was undeniably more beautiful than the concubine. Only God knows what the wife had in mind. As far as men were able to judge, she did not seem to take it badly, especially since she had delivered her husband from danger. She spent much time in church and in prayer. Everyone could easily see that she was afflicted, but none heard complain or show indignation. After a year the husband was reconciled completely to his wife and began to nurture a bitter hostility for his mistress. He expelled her and accorded such love to his wife that he proclaimed that his mind, life and spirit rested in her and that he would not be able to go on living if she died. I do not mention names because all parties are still living.

83. I have said all these things about persons who have a clear cause for jealousy. For there are those who have no sure reason yet act inappropriately and intolerably, procuring certain torment for themselves and their spouses for an uncertain offense. This is done by many women who love inordinately or indulge their passions to excess, or create fantasies for themselves or seize on weak conjectures as if they were proven facts. Is your husband exchanging pleasantries with someone? Do not immediately think that he is in love. A great part of your emotional state is based on what you believe. Feelings arise more from opinions than from facts. Do not be influenced by casual suspicions when you should not even be moved by tried and proven facts.

CAP. VII.   DE ORNAMENTIS

84. Et hoc, ut cetera, ad viri voluntatem moresque referendum est. Si malit tenuem cultum, hoc utendum; nam si ornatiorem ac splendidiorem quaeris, iam non adeo mariti oculis te componis atque alienis, quod non est probae.
5   Quid enim cum auro et argento mulieri, primum Christianae, deinde cuius maritus illis non delectatur? Tu iubente viro ad Christianum ornatum te non accommodas, quae etiam diabolicum debes induere si is velit? Ambrosius de fucis ad hunc modum scribit: 'Hinc illa nascuntur incentiva vitiorum ut quaesitis coloribus ora depingant, dum viris displicere formidant et
10   de adulterio vultus meditentur adulterium castitatis. Quanta haec amentia effigiem mutare naturae, picturam quaerere, et dum verentur maritale iudicium, prodere suum? Prior enim de se pronuntiat quae cupit mutare quod nata est. Ita dum alii studet placere, prior ipsa sibi displicet.' Ambrosius haec quae ipse sentit cum nihil super hoc uxori maritus diserte praecepit; nec
15   vir prudens praecipiet. Quod si fecerit aut illum id scias cupere, commode atque in tempore dissuade idque serio. Si nihil profeceris, dabis hoc quidem oculis et voluntati eius, sed dices cum sancta Esther, omni illa diaboli pompa compta et instructa: 'Tu scis, Domine, necessitatem meam; quod abominer signum superbiae et gloriae meae, quod est super caput meum
20   in diebus ostentationis meae, et detester illud quasi pannum menstruatae et non portem in die silentii mei.' Quod si liberum sit mulieri cum coniugata sit quibus velit indui ac ornari, cogitet iam non habere cur magnopere fastum et nitorem cultus exquirat et invenerit iam quod aliae per eiusmodi se retia dicunt quaerere.
25   **85.** Admonet Cyprianus Martyr nuptas 'ut videant ne nimium sibi per placendi studium de coniugum solacio blandiantur, ne dum eos in excusationem suam proferunt, in societatem criminosae consensionis asciscant.' Habent quid nos ante de ornamentis senserimus. Nunc magis decebit Petro auscultare et Paulo, qui cultum matronae Christianae simplicem para-
30   bilemque esse volunt, fulgentiorem sanctitate vitae quam auro vel gemmis.

---

84. (Hinc ... displicet) *Ambr. virg. 1, 6, 28, PL 16, 196C* // (Tu ... mei) *Vulg. Esth. 4, 16*
85. (ut ... asciscant) *Cypr. hab. virg. 8, PL 460* // (cultum ... gemmis) *Vulg. I Tim. 2, 9–10; I Pet. 3, 3–4* //

4 atque **Γ** quam **H** // **15–17** Quod si fecerit ... dabis hoc quidem **Γ** Quod si praecipiat aut velle illum scias, dabis hoc quidem **H** // **21–22** cum coniugata sit **Γ** *deest in* **H** // **23** exquirat et **Γ** exquirat cum coniugata sit **H** // **29–30** parabilemque **Γ** *deest in* **H** // **30** fulgentiorem **Γ** splendentiorem **H**

CHAPTER 7. ON ADORNMENTS

84. This like everything else should depend on the wishes and character of the husband. If he prefers simple adornment, that is what you should use. For if you seek more splendid adornment, you are decking yourself out not so much for your husband's eyes as for someone else, which is not the mark of a good woman. What does a woman who is first of all a Christian and moreover married to a husband who does not approve of such luxury have to do with gold and silver? Do you refuse to adapt yourself to Christian ideals of adornment at the bidding of your husband when you should even put on diabolical adornment if he so wished? Ambrose writes about cosmetics in this way:

> From this come provocations to vice that make them paint their faces with elaborate colors for fear of not pleasing their husbands and from adulteration of their visage they rehearse themselves for the adulteration of their chastity. What madness it is to change one's natural appearance and seek out artificial embellishment! While they are afraid of their husband's judgement, they betray their own, for she first pronounces judgement on herself when she wishes to change the face she was born with. So by trying to please others she first displeases herself.

This is the opinion of Ambrose when the husband has given no express command in this matter, and the prudent husband will not do so. But if he does or if you know that this is his wish, dissuade him politely at the right moment and in earnest. If you get nowhere, you will satisfy his wishes externally, but you will say with Esther, who was dressed and adorned with all the devil's pomp: 'Thou knowest my necessity, O Lord, that I loathe the symbol of my high position and my renown, which binds my brow when I appear at court. I loathe it like the menstrual cloth and will not wear it when I am alone in silence.' Even if a married woman has the liberty to choose her apparel and adornment as she wishes, let her reflect that she has no reason to seek out finery and fastidiousness of attire and has already caught what others say they are seeking with those nets.

85. Cyprian Martyr advises brides 'to take heed that they do not delude themselves into thinking that their desire to please themselves is to satisfy their husbands, lest while using them as an excuse, they make them accomplices to the crime.' I have already set out my own opinion on the subject of adornments. Now it is well to listen to Peter and Paul, who wish that the personal care of a Christian married woman be simple and easily obtainable, and that they stand out more for their sanctity of life than for gold and

---

85. Cyprian Martyr: Bishop of Carthage (249–258), martyred under the emperor Valerian. Vives quotes often from his treatise, *De habitu virginum* (On the Dress of Young Women), which prescribes a rather stern code of morals for unmarried young women.

Et nacta est iam honesta mulier alia veriora ornamenta, tum in pudicitia, ut Xystus inquit, tum in liberis honeste educatis, sicut dicebat Cornelia de Gracchis suis, tum in viri gloria. Philonis sapientiae sectatoris uxor, cum sine aurea corona processisset in publicum et aliae gestarent, rogata cur non et
5   ipsa ferret, uxori, respondit, satis ornatus esse viri virtutem et laudes. Quis non pluris faciebat Catonis non admodum divitis uxorem quam multorum publicanorum qui divitiis affluebant uxores? An non praestat Xanthippen Socratis pauperis coniugem fuisse quam Scopae vel cuiuslibet illius aevi opulenti? 'Ornamentum mulieris,' ait Democrates, 'sermonis atque ornatus par-
10 simonia.' Et ornatissima est quae optimum habet virum.

    86. Chrysostomus multis locis Lernam hanc feminei cultus ferro atque igni persequitur pestique renascenti toties, tam variae multa fomenta admovet; cuius sententiam quoniam fusa est, ut fere ubique, in pauca contraham et quidem non uno ex opere: 'Genus quoddam est idololatriae cultus
15 hic vestium, monilium et totius domestici ornamenti tam exquisitus tamque anxius ut pro idolis tibi sint aurum, gemmae ac vestitus. Nec aliter tractas ac revereris quam olim simulacra illa sua error antiquus. Quid quod marito et vilem uxorem ac contemnendam reddit et odiosam? Quos enim minoris aestimamus quam qui subinde nobis indigent? Quod si mulier saepenumero
20 maritum de ornatu interpellet, vilis illi profecto fuerit et suspicionem ei iniciet non se illum amare quod sit vir suus a Deo copulatus, sed quod procurator facultatum diligens et suppeditator vanitatis ac fomenti superbiae. Tum demum vere se intelliget maritus diligi, seposito respectu utilitatum, et sibi obtemperari tamquam maiori et vicario Dei, cum paucissima uxor requiret
25 et ea exigui pretii. Ita ille cognoscet non amari se propter necessitatem, sed propter caritatem a Deo iussam. Porro, cum auri pars maxima in uxoris ornamenta profusa est et in angustias res familiaris est contracta, quaenam esse potest coniugii voluptas? Fortasse hic mulieris apparatus inter matrimonii exordia gratus fuerit propter novitatem, paulatim vero gratiam illam
30 suam amittet cum novitate haud aliter quam consuetudo spectandi caelos et sidera, quibus nihil est speciosius, admirationem omnem consumpsit. Quod si illa iam maritus non curat, cui te tandem ornas? Foris vis placere et ab aliis laudari; atqui desiderium hoc mulieris est minime pudicae.

---

85. (in pudicitia ... Xystus) *Sext. Pyth. 235 (Chadwick, p.39* // (liberis honeste educandis) *Val. Max. 4, 4* // (Scopae) *Diog. Laert. 2, 25* // (ornamentum ... parsimonia) Δημοκράτους φιλοσόφου γνῶμαι χρυσαί *ed. Orellius, p.89*
    86. (Quod si ... a Deo iussam) *Ioh. Chrys. in. Ioh. hom. 61, 4, PG 59, 342* // (Porro ... pudicae) *Ioh. Chrys. in epist. ad Phil. hom. 10, PG 62, 260*

1 nacta est Γ habet **H** // **2–3** de Gracchis suis Γ Gracchi **H** // **7** affluebant uxores Γ diffluebant coniuges **H** // **9** Democrates **H** Demochares Γ // **11**–p.106,**27** Chrysostomus multis locis ... Haec ex sancto Ioanne Chrysostomo Γ *deest in* **H**

precious stones. The virtuous woman has found other truer adornments in chastity, as Sextus said, and in the proper raising of children, as Cornelia said of her sons, the Gracchi, and in the fame of her husband. The wife of Philo the philosopher went out in public without her gold crown when other women were wearing theirs, and was asked why she was not wearing it. She replied: 'Sufficient adornment for a wife is the virtue and glory of her husband.' Who did not have more esteem for the wife of Cato, who was not very wealthy, than for the wives of many tax collectors, who were inundated with riches? Is it not better to have been Xanthippe, wife of the poor Socrates, than wife of Scopas or any other rich man of the period? 'The adornment of a woman,' said Democrates, 'is sparseness of speech and of ornament.' And she who has an excellent husband is the most adorned.

86. Chrysostom in many passages persecutes with fire and sword this hydra of feminine adornments and suggests many remedies for this plague that renews itself continually and in so many different forms. I will compress his diffuse treatment, which is his usual manner, into a few words, drawing on several of his works:

> This cult of clothing, jewelry and household furnishing is a kind of idolatry. So recherche, so painstaking is it that gold, jewelry and clothing become idols to you. You treat them and revere them just as that ancient error revered its images. What would you think if I said that this vice renders you a vile and contemptible wife in the eyes of your husband? Whom do we esteem less than those who are frequently in need of us? If a woman often importunes her husband concerning her adornment, she will become contemptible in his eyes and will inspire the suspicion that she does not love him because he is her legitimate spouse joined to her by God, but because he is diligent in procuring her riches and abetting her vanity and pride. The husband will know that he is truly loved, when his wife makes little of material advantages and obeys him as her superior and as God's representative. When she demands very little and for things of little value, then he will know that she does not love him out of necessity but out of affection, as ordained by God. Indeed, when the greatest part of the husband's earnings are lavished on the wife's adornment, and the economic condition of the family are reduced to penury, what pleasure can there be in that marriage? Perhaps this female adornment was pleasing at the beginning of the marriage because of its novelty, but little by little it will lose its charm together with its novelty, just as the habitual contemplation of the heavens and the stars, the most beautiful spectacle that exists, loses its wonder. But if your husband is not interested in those things anymore, for whom do you adorn yourself? You wish to find external approval and to be praised by others, and that is the desire of a woman of little virtue.

Scopas: Of Crannon, a wealthy ruler who offered Socrates gifts and invited him to his court, which offers Socrates refused.

87. Quid quod modesta et modice culta plures laudatores invenit et meliores homines quam fastuosa illa cultusque sui ostentatrix? Temperatam probi et sapientes laudabunt, profusam luxuriosi et incontinentes iuvenes, quamquam nec hi tam laudabunt quam expetent, nam quantumcumque eorum libido lacessatur, improbabunt tamen luxum et incontinentiam mulieris. Dicet fortassis earum aliqua, "Quidnam ipsa commereor si alius de me male suspicatur?" Tu suspicioni huic per habitum, per incessum atque aspectum, per omnem denique corporis motum ansam praebes et fomenta sumministras. Nam si ea quae opum modo sunt indicia tanto studio Apostolus circumcidit (aurum scilicet, margaritas, et sumptuosa vestimenta), quanto magis ea quae tam anxie, tanta arte conquiruntur? Quod genus sunt: purpurisso vultus inficere, stibio oculos pingere, fracto gradu incedere, vocem formare molliorem, lascivum obtutum et qui libidinis iaculetur incendia, superfluam pallii ac tunicae iactationem, cingulum affabre confectum, stridentes crepidulas et cetera irritamenta lasciviae. Ista quippe a pudore sunt alienissima et dedecoris ac turpitudinis plena existimantur. Enimvero si haec Apostolus iis quae sub viro sunt, quae in deliciis vivunt, quaeque divitiis circumfluunt, interdicit, quid dicturum eum censemus de virginibus? Verum ut de cultu cum gentili nihil disputem (cedo) quid mihi respondebit Christiana pompa illa templum ingressa, ubi audit de sublimi loco praecipientes apostolos contraria? An huc venit ut illorum orationi factis suis repugnet et velut clamet, quantumcumque geminentur et inculcentur illorum verba, se tamen vel non audire vel pili non facere? Si quis paganus nostris interesset coetibus, cum illa dici ab apostolis Christi audiret, hanc vero apostolorum discipulam hoc facere conspiceret, numquid contineret risum et non potius discederet, velut inepta fabula offensus?' Haec ex sancto Ioanne Chrysostomo.

88. Ceterum ut non fastum et pompam et pretiosum in matrona cultum, ita nec sordes atque immunditiem probamus, modo ne in tenui ac vili vestitu emineat cura et studium ornatus. Sunt quas etiam rudis pannus ac crassus ob naturae venustatem deceat; sunt quae arte efficiunt, ut deceat. 'Dandum,' inquiunt, 'aliquid est loco, tempori, condicioni vitae et receptis moribus civitatis.' Dandum sane interdum nonnihil quando extorqueri aliud non potest, sed non multum ac multo minus etiam quam postulent. Aristoteles in Oeconomicis libris ex saeculari sapientia minore cultu apparatuque debere

---

87. (Quidnam ... virginibus) *Ioh. Chrys. in epist. ad I Tim. 2, 9 hom. 8, PG 62, 541* // (Verum ... offensus) *Ioh. Chrys. in psalm 48 hom., PG 55, 507*

28 fastum ... cultum **Γ** pretiosum cultum **H** // **29** sordes atque immunditiem **Γ** sordes in matrona **H** // **29–31** modo ... deceat **Γ** *deest in* **H** // **31–32** Dandum, inquiunt, aliquid **Γ** Dandum etiam nonnihil **H** // **32–33** condicioni vitae ... civitatis **Γ** *deest in* **H** // **33** Dandum ... potest **Γ** *deest in* **H** // **35** ex saeculari sapientia **Γ** *deest in* **H**

87. And is it not true that a modest woman of simple adornment finds more admirers and better men than an extravagant woman showing off her rich apparel? Men of wisdom and virtue will praise a woman of judicious taste while pleasure-loving and intemperate youths will praise the woman of lavish taste, although it is not so much a matter of admiration as desire. And yet, whatever the promptings of lust, they will still reproach the luxury and incontinence of a woman. One of them may say, 'What fault is it of mine if someone else has evil suspicions about me?' You give rise to this suspicion and fuel their passion in your style of dress, your walk, your appearance, every movement of your body. If the Apostle condemns so vehemently all signs of wealth, gold, pearls and sumptuous attire, how much more will he proscribe articles that are sought after so eagerly and with such wiles? I refer to such things as applying Tyrian purple pigment to the face, painting the eyes with antimony, walking affectedly, speaking in sweet tones, bestowing lascivious glances intended to enkindle the fires of lust, wearing the pallium and the tunic in a suggestive way, sporting an elaborately fashioned cincture, sandals that make noise and other incitements to lasciviousness. These things are totally opposed to chastity and are regarded as the essence of shame and indecency. If the Apostle forbids such things in those who are subject to a husband, live a pampered life and are overflowing with riches, what do we think he will say of unmarried women? While I do not wish to enter into discussion with pagan women in the matter of adornment, what will a Christian woman respond when she enters the church with such pomp and hears the apostles preaching the contrary from the pulpit? Does she come here to refute their words with her actions and to cry out, as it were, that no matter how often their words are repeated and inculcated into her she does not hear them and pays no heed to them? If a pagan assisted at one of our ceremonies and heard these words spoken by the apostles of Christ and then witnessed this follower of the apostles acting in this way, would he be able to contain his laughter and not prefer to walk out, offended by this useless farce?

This is all taken from Saint John Chrysostom.

88. For the rest, just as we do not approve excessive finery, pomp and precious apparel in a married woman, so we do not approve squalor and sloppiness or a careful and studied adornment in a simple and humble garment. There are some women on whom crude and coarse rags are becoming because of their natural attractiveness; there are others who know how to achieve this same effect by their clever ingenuity. 'One must allow for the place, time, manner of life and received custom of a city,' they say. Yes, some concessions must be made when nothing can be obtained otherwise, but not too much and much less than what is demanded. Aristotle in the *Economics*, books filled with traditional wisdom, is of the opinion that a woman

mulierem uti censet quam leges ac mores civitatis praescribant. 'Quippe quam considerare,' inquit, convenit quod nec vestimentorum nitor nec excellentia formae nec auri copia tantum valet ad mulieris laudem quantum modestia in rebus ac studium honeste vivendi et cum decore.' Est ergo plus
5 semper rationi tribuendum, plus sanctitati et pietati quam vanis iudiciis et pravis moribus per flagitiosos aliquos inductis atque a corruptis vulgi sensibus acceptis et confirmatis. Deberent sanctae aliquot matronae, velut conspiratione facta, in eiusmodi mores impetum facere, ut tenui ac parabili cultu et ipsae quod oporteret praestarent et aliis viam qua insistendum esset
10 indicarent. Quanto maior laus esset malum sustulisse morem quam secutam esse? Nec desperandum est posse tolli ab aliquibus, cum aliquae intulerint; nec ita deplorandum humanum ingenium ut accipere mala possit, bona non possit, praesertim cum rectus animi habitus huc propendeat. Quantum consensus malarum valuit in malum, tantum bonarum valeret in
15 bonum; inciperent modo honestate, modestia, pudicitia certare iisque vincere pulchrum ducerent, non ostentatione opum, quae leves animos in maximas aemulationes et certamina impingit.

89. Probitatem, patientiam, amorem atque obsequium mariti probant omnes et laudant, paucae invident aliis ad imitationem; ornatum vero,
20 vestes, torques, murenulas, monilia, inaures, anulos, vasa caelata omnes invident, omnes concupiscunt. O superbissima et stulta animalia, ficta ad vanitatem et ostentationem! Hinc contentiones tam accensis animis eousque progrediuntur ut, quemadmodum sapientissime Cato apud Livium inquit, 'Divites id habere velint quod nulla alia possit; pauperes, ne ob hoc ipsum
25 contemnantur, supra vires se extendant. Ita fit ut cum pudeat quod non oportet, iam quod oportet nihil pudeat.' Maritos ac liberos spoliant ut se vestiant; domi fames et egestas ut ipsae onustae auro et serico in publico incedant; maritos ad turpes quaestus, ad prava facinora suis querimoniis impellunt, ne vicina, ne consanguinea, ne affinis ditiorem se et ornatiorem
30 ostentet. Et haec gravia atque immodica tolerabilia essent si non etiam pudicitiam venderent, ut illinc pararent quod maritus dare vel nolit vel non possit.

---

88. (Quippe ... decore) *Aristot. oec. 3, 1* // (Divites ... pudeat) *Liv. 34, 4, 15–16*

3 copia Γ magnitudo **H** // **4** honeste vivendi et cum decore Γ honesteque decoreque vivendi **H** // **6** flagitiosos Γ sceleratos **H** // **7** sanctae Γ sanctissimae **H** // **9** praestarent Γ facerent **H** // **11–12** intulerint Γ attulerint **H** // **12–13** nec ita deplorandum ... propendeat Γ *deest in* **H** // **14** valeret Γ *deest in* **H** // **17** impingit Γ adducit **H** // **18-19** Probitatem ... imitationem Γ Paucae invident aliis probitatem, rarae patientiam et amorem viri **H** // **19** ornatum Γ pleraque **H** // **20–21** vasa ... concupiscunt Γ *deest in* **H** // **22** contentiones Γ certamen **H** // **26** iam Γ *deest in* **H** / nihil Γ non **H** // **28–29** querimoniis impellunt Γ querelis impellant **H** // **29–30** ditiorem ... ostentet Γ ditior est se et ornatior est ostentet **H** // **31–32** vel non possit Γ vel miser non possit **H**

should employ less adornment and display than the laws and customs of a
city prescribe. 'For she should consider,' he said, 'that neither elegance of
vesture nor excellence of beauty nor abundance of gold ensure a woman's
praise so much as modesty of possessions and the desire to live honorably
and with dignity.' Therefore more importance must always be given to reason, to holiness and to piety than to vain judgements and corrupt morals
introduced by men of infamous life and accepted and confirmed by the depraved sentiments of the crowd. A group of holy matrons should conspire
together to make an assault on these customs so that clothed in their humble ordinary apparel they may give an example of what is appropriate and
lead the way for others to follow. How much greater merit is there to get
rid of an evil custom rather than to follow it! And we should not give up
hope that a few women can eradicate what a few women have instituted.
Likewise we must not so despair of the human spirit as to think that it can
accept evil, but not good, especially since the natural condition of the mind
is to be inclined toward good. The consensus of good women should pre-
vail as much for good as the consensus of evil women has accomplished for
evil. They should begin to engage in the contest with integrity, modesty and
chastity and think it honorable to win victory by these virtues rather than
by ostentation of wealth, which drives frivolous minds to great rivalries and
contentions.

89. All women approve and commend honesty, patience, love and obedience to the husband; few envy others to the extent of imitating them,
but all without exception envy and covet adornment–clothing, necklaces,
brooches, jewels, earrings, rings, engraved vessels. O proud and foolish creatures, made for vanity and ostentation! Hence arise contentions which en-
flame the mind to the point that, as Cato wisely says in Livy's history: 'Rich
women wish to have what no other woman can have, and poor women
stretch themselves beyond their means in order not to be derided for their
poverty. It thus comes about that since they are ashamed of what they should
not be ashamed of, they will not be ashamed of what should shame them.'
They despoil their husbands and their children so that they may be clothed.
There is hunger and need at home so that they may parade in public clad
in gold and silk. They compel their husbands with their lamentations to ill-
gotten gains and lowly deeds so that no neighbor, blood-relation or relation
by marriage can show herself richer or better adorned. And these grave and
outrageous acts would be tolerable if they did not also sell their chastity to
acquire what their husbands would not or could not give them.

89. Cato: In 195 B.C. Cato the Elder gave a speech against the proposed repeal of the
Oppian Law, which had been passed in the critical time of the Second Punic War, imposing
severe restrictions on the expenses and luxuries of women. Despite Cato's efforts the law was
repealed.

90. His tantis malis succurrendum esset aut divitum matronarum consensu ac conspiratione, quae suo exemplo alias ad meliorem mentem revocarent, vel lege aliqua, tamquam frenis iniectis, qualis fuit vetus illa Oppia, quae mulierum sumptibus modum statuebat. Christianos contiona-
5 tores deceret non solum sanctos Christianae pietatis, sed gentilem hominem Pythagoram aemulari atque adeo in pulcherrimo certamine vincere, de quo Iustinus scribit in hunc modum: 'Docebat Pythagoras matronas pudicitiam et obsequia in viros; inter haec velut genitricem virtutum frugalitatem omnibus ingerebat consecutusque assiduitate disputationum erat ut matronae
10 auratas vestes ceteraque dignitatis suae ornamenta velut instrumenta luxuriae deponerent, vera ornamenta matronarum dicens pudicitiam, non vestes esse.' An non eandem sententiam apertius ac copiosius apud nostros invenient? Referti sunt eiusmodi consiliorum Cyprianus, Hieronymus, Chrysostomus, Ambrosius, Augustinus, Fulgentius.
15 **91.** Tertullianus vero sic adhortatur mulieres: 'Prodite vos iam medicamentis et ornamentis exstructae apostolorum, sumentes de simplictate candorem, de pudicitia ruborem, depictae oculos verecundia et spiritus taciturnitate, inserentes in aures sermonem Dei, annectentes cervicibus iugum Christi. Caput maritis subiicite et satis ornatae eritis. Manus lanis occu-
20 pate, pedes domi figite et plus quam in auro placebunt. Vestite vos serico probitatis, byssino sanctitatis, purpura pudicitae; taliter pigmentatae, Deum habebitis amatorem.' Sic Tertullianus. Quibus ego paucula quaedam adiiciam quae mihi ad eandem exhortationem videntur pertinere. Res omnes corporales incorporalium sunt signa; in spiritu est efficacia et veritas, in cor-
25 pore umbra atque imago. Caput viri est Deus, caput mulieris vir. An tu maius ornamentum aut praestabilius quaeris quam excellentiam et decus viri tui? Hoc tu caput si oboedientia texeris, elegantissimum caliendrum gestabis.
92. Virum non decet caput suum tegere, quoniam in mundo imago Dei est; mulierem decet, nempe viro subditam. Retegit ergo se quaecumque ma-
30 riti legem excussit. Si tibi auro et gemmis caput refulget, marito tuo repugnas. Si bysso et serico cooperiris soluta imperio virili, quid prodest inefficax signum sine re? Nudata capite ambulas et Apostoli praeceptum contemnis. Pyropus est ardor coniugalis caritatis; adamas sancti propositi firmitas, tenax atque invincibilis; eam enim esse lapidis illius naturam ferunt. Smarag-
35 dus exhilaratio in domino, de qua Apostolus dicit: 'Gaudete in Domino

---

90. (Docebat ... esse) *Iust. 29, 4, 8–11*
91. (Prodite ... amatorem) *Tert. cult. fem. 2, 13, PL 1, 1448B*
92. (Gaudete ... semper) *Vulg. Phil. 4, 4* //

---

5 deceret non solum ... sed gentilem hominem Γ deceret gentilem hominem **H** // **6** aemulari atque adeo Γ non aemulari modo sed **H** // **12**–p.112,**13** An non eandem ... gratiam amplissimam et aeternam Γ *deest in* **H**

90. Some remedy must be devised for these great evils, either through the agreement and conspiracy of rich matrons, who by their example could recall others to a better mentality, or by some law or restraint like the ancient Lex Oppia, which set a limit on female adornment. Christian preachers should emulate not only holy examples of Christian piety but the pagan Pythagoras and surpass him in this glorious struggle. Justinus wrote of him as follows, 'Pythagoras taught married women chastity and obedience to their husbands, and he inculcated frugality into them as the mother of these virtues, and by the assiduity of his preaching he brought it about that noble matrons put aside their gold vestments and other accoutrements of their high position as if they were instruments of luxury, saying that the true adornment of matrons was chastity, not fine raiment.' Will they not find this same sentiment expressed more clearly and more copiously in our own writers? Cyprian, Jerome, Chrysostom, Ambrose, Augustine, Fulgentius and Tertullian are full of this advice.

91. Tertullian exhorts women as follows: 'Go forth now adorned with the cosmetics and embellishments of the apostles, assuming the whiteness of simplicity, the red blush of chastity, your eyes painted with modesty and your spirit with silence, inserting in your ears the word of God, fastening to your necks the yoke of Christ. Bow your head to your husbands, and you will be sufficiently adorned. Occupy your hands with the working of wool, fix your feet at home and they will be more pleasing than if they were shod in gold. Dress yourselves in the silk of a good life, in the brocade of sanctity, in the purple of chastity. Painted in this way, you will have God as your lover.' I should like to add a few words to that, which seem to me to contain the same exhortation. All corporal things are signs of the incorporeal. In the spirit lie efficacy and truth, in the body shadow and vain appearance. The head of man is God; the head of woman is man. Do you seek a greater or more outstanding adornment than the excellence and honor of your husband? If you cover your head with obedience, you will be wearing a most elegant head-dress.

92. It is not fitting that a man cover his head since he is the image of God in the world. It does behoove a woman since she is subject to the man. Every woman who has shaken off the law of her husband uncovers her head. If your head gleams with gold and precious stones, you set yourself against your husband. If you are covered in silk and brocade, you are not subject to your husband's authority. What good is an ineffectual sign without the reality to which it corresponds? You walk about without a head-covering, and you repudiate the command of the Apostle. The ardor of conjugal love is a carbuncle. Firmness in a holy resolve, resistent and indestructible, is a diamond. These are said to be the qualities of that stone. An emerald represents exhilaration in the Lord, of which the Apostle says: 'Rejoice in the Lord always.' The ring is an adornment of the hands

semper.' Anulus ornamenta manuum in praeclaris operibus, de quibus Salomon: 'Operata est consilio manuum suarum.' Iugum illud Domini mite ac facile aureum est monile, gemmis distinctum. Zona est praecinctio illa lumborum, qua nos insistere iubet Dominus in exspectationem adventus sui.
Supparus pudor est et pudicitia, quibus universum feminae corpus contegitur. An vestitus est alius illustrior quam varietas illa virtutum, quibus ornatur sponsa filia Regis in Psalmo quadragesimo quarto, quae a dextris assistit sponsi sui in fimbriis et vestitu aureo variegato? Cuius gloria omnis introrsus se recipit, quo immittit oculos suos sponsus ille speciosus forma prae filiis hominum, in cuius labiis gratia est diffusa. Miserae, quid inanes umbras persequimini? Haec sunt certa et solida ornamenta, quae splendorem vobis et vivis et mortuis parient, quae decus conciliabunt ingens apud homines, apud Deum vero gratiam amplissimam et aeternam.

CAP. VIII.   DE PUBLICO

93. Nuptas decet rariores conspici in publico quam virgines. Nam quod hae videbantur quaerere, illae iam sunt adeptae. Ideo tota cura eo referenda est ut quod nactae sunt conservent atque illi uni studeant placere. Legislator Lacedaemonius nuptas velata facie prodire in publicum iussit, quod eas iam nec spectare alios nec ab aliis spectari conveniret quae domi haberent quem unum spectare et a quo uno spectari se deberent cupere. Quem morem Persae et prope populi omnes orientales tenuerunt, multi etiam Graecorum; sed non sic involuto capite, quomodo hoc tempore in quibusdam Europae civitatibus, ut ipsae incognitae atque invisae alios et videant et cognoscant. In quo subit admirari non tam mulierum delicias (delicias vero? immo in facie velo tenui operta densissimam impudentiam) quam stultitiam maritorum quanta sit haec flagitiis occasio non considerantium. 'Haud facient,' inquient. Utinam numquam fecissent, et alioqui non est fenestra licentiae peccandi aperienda. Sit ergo in mulieribus nuda velis facies, verecundia contecta et clausa. Velum illud priscum non perinde illuc pertinebat, ipsa uti ne a viris cerneretur ac ne cerneret viros. Fauna, Fauni Regis Aboriginum

---

92. (operata ... suarum) *Vulg. prov. 31, 13* // (Iugum ... facile) *Vulg. Matth. 11, 30* // (praecinctio illa lumborum) *Vulg. Luc. 12, 35* // (fimbriis ... variegato) *Vulg. psalm. 44, 14–15* // (labiis ... est) *Vulg. psalm. 44, 3*
93. (Legislator ... cupere) *Plut. mor. 232C* // (Fauna ... Faunum) *Macrob. Sat. 1, 12, 21–28* //

15 conspici Γ esse **H** // **16** sunt adeptae Γ habent **H** // **18** prodire ... iussit Γ cum prodirent in publicum esse iussit **H** // **20** se deberent cupere Γ deberent velle **H** // **23** civitatibus Γ populis **H** // **26** Haud Γ Non **H** // **28** peccandi Γ *deest in* **H** // **29** perinde illuc Γ adeo **H** // **30** ac Γ ut **H** / Fauna Γ Faunam **H**

in the performance of good works, of which Solomon said: 'She worked with the wisdom of her hands.' The easy and sweet yoke of the Lord is a gold necklace, set with precious stones. The cincture is that girding up of the loins that the Lord bids us to do as we press on in expectation of his coming. The shawl is modesty and chastity, with which the whole body of a woman is covered. Is there any garb more resplendent than the rich variety of virtues, with which the spouse, daughter of the king, is adorned in Psalm 44, who attends the spouse on his right side, dressed in many colored robes with gold fringes, whose glory is all turned within herself, where the gaze of her spouse is fixed, most beautiful among the sons of men, on whose lips grace is diffused? Unhappy women, why do you pursue vain shadows? These are true and substantial adornments that will bring you glory both in death and in life, that will win you great renown among men and abundant and eternal gratitude with God.

CHAPTER 8.   ON BEHAVIOR IN PUBLIC

93. Married women should be seen more rarely in public than unmarried women. For what the latter seem to be seeking the former have already obtained. Therefore all their attention should be directed to preserving what they have found and striving to please him alone. The Spartan legislator ordered that wives appear in public with their faces veiled, because it was fitting that they should neither look at others nor be looked at by others since they had at home one whom they should wish to look at and by whom they should wish to be looked at. This custom was observed by the Persians and practically all peoples of the East and many of the Greeks. But they should not go about with their heads covered, as they do nowadays in some European cities, in order to remain unknown and unseen, while they see and recognize others. In this custom one is tempted to admire not so much the elegant manner of these women (did I say elegant manner? I should say the gross impudence in a face covered with a thin veil), as the stupidity of their husbands, who do not see what an occasion for shameful acts this affords. 'They will not do anything,' their husbands will say. Would to God they had not! In any case a window must not be left open to the occasion of sin. Therefore let women's faces be free of veils, but veiled with modesty. The ancient custom of wearing a veil was not so much for the purpose of not being seen by men as not seeing men. Fauna, the wife of Faunus, King of the indigenous tribes of Italy, never laid eyes on any man save Faunus as

93. Fauna: Wife of the sylvan Italic deity, Faunus. She was often identified with the Bona Dea. According to Varro, an encyclopaedic writer on Roman antiquities, she never issued from the house and never saw men or was seen by them.

uxor, quamdiu vixit neminem umquam virum vidit praeter Faunum. Ideo
mortua nomine Bonae Deae culta est eiusque sacris non modo viris omnibus interdicebatur, sed nec imaginem licebat conspici masculi animalis.
Neque id dico quod clausas semper mulieres esse praecipiam aut opertas,
5   sed quod rariores in publico et minus inter viros; quo etiam nihil potest
gratius maritis contingere. Quam iucundum putamus fuisse Tigrani, apud
quem cum Cyrus Rex Persarum cenasset multusque post convivium esset
apud Tigranem de Cyri forma sermo (erat enim mirifice decora), rogavit
uxorem Tigranes ecquid esset ipsi visa Cyri facies, 'Non possum,' inquit illa,
10   'dicere nam, ita me dii bene ament, ut toto convivio numquam abs te ad
alium virum deflexerim oculos!'

94. Sancta matrona nec audiet libens viros alienos nec de eis deque eorum forma disseret. Quid ipsi cum pulchritudine aliorum cui omnes viros
aeque pulchros, omnes aeque deformes esse convenit praeter maritum? Is
15   unus ceteris pulchrior sit, ceteris venustior, ut matri suus unicus filiolus.
Sponso in Canticis canticorum feminarum omnium pulcherrima videtur
sua sponsa; vicissim huic ille viros universos forma et gratia vincit. Nec minus Duellio uxoris grata simplicitas. Dicam Hieronymi verbis: 'Duellius, qui
primus Romae navali certamine triumphavit, Biliam virginem duxit uxo-
20   rem, tantae pudicitiae ut illo quoque saeculo pro exemplo fuerit quo impudicitia monstrum erat, non vitium. Is iam senex et tremente corpore in
quodam iurgio audivit exprobrari sibi os foetidum et tristis se domum con-
tulit. Cumque uxori questus esset quare numquam se monuisset ut huic vitio mederetur, "Fecissem," inquit illa, "nisi putassem omnibus viris sic os
25   olere."' Laudanda in utroque pudica et nobilis femina: et si ignoravit vitium viri et si patienter tulit; et quod maritus infelicitatem corporis sui non
uxoris fastidio, sed maledicto sensit inimici. Idem Hieroni Syracusio Regi
ferunt contigisse. Nimirum hoc dicere non possent istae quae multos viros
ante connubium, multos in connubio deosculatae sunt.

30   **95.** In publico quantus sit servandus pudor ex hoc facile poterit col-
ligi quod et domi et in cubiculo et cum solo viro et de nocte servandum docuimus. Quid attinet morem illum barbaricum insectari quo apud

---

93. (Non possum ... oculos) *Xen. Kyr. 3, 1, 41*
94. (Sponso ... vincit) *Vulg. cant. 1, 7, 5–9* // (Duellius ... olere) *Hier. adv. Iovin. 1, 46,*
PL 23, 287 // (idem ... contigisse) *Plut. mor. 175C*
95. (docuimus) *inst. fem. Christ. 2, 67–74* //

1 uxor Γ uxorem **H** / neminem Γ nemo **H** / virum Γ vir **H** // **4** esse praecipiam Γ velim **H** // **6** maritis Γ viris **H** // **6–9** fuisse Tigrani, apud quem ... rogavit uxorem Γ fuisse
Tigrani Regi qui, cum Cyrum invitasset Regem Persarum et post convivium multus esset
apud Tigranem de Cyri forma sermo, rogavit uxorem **H** // **9** facies Γ forma **H** // **11** deflexerim Γ deflexi **H** // **29** connubium Γ connubio **H** / deosculatae Γ osculatae **H** // **32**
docuimus Γ volumus **H**

long as she lived. In death she was venerated under the name of the *Bona Dea*, and not only were all men excluded from her worship but not even the image of a male animal was allowed to be seen. I do not say this because I prescribe that women should always be cloistered and covered up, but that they should be seen rarely in public and even less among men, which will be greatly appreciated by their husbands. How pleasing it must have been to Tigranes, who had invited Cyrus, King of Persia, to a banquet, when in the ensuing discussion of Cyrus' beauty (for he was extremely handsome) he asked his wife what she thought of his countenance, and she answered: 'I cannot say, for as the gods love me, I never took my eyes off you during the whole banquet to look at any other man.'

94. A holy matron will not willingly listen to strange men or talk about them or their appearance. What importance do other men's beauty have to do with her, since she should regard all men, handsome or ugly, as the same to her except for her husband? He should be more beautiful, more attractive than all others, as an only son is to his mother. To the spouse in the Canticle of Canticles his bride is the fairest of all women, and reciprocally she thinks of him as surpassing all men in beauty and charm. No less pleasing to Duilius was the simplicity of his wife. I shall use Jerome's own words:

> Duilius, who was the first to have a triumph in Rome for a naval battle, married Bilia, a maiden of such chastity that she was an example to her age, when unchastity was regarded not as a vice, but as a thing of ill omen. When he was a palsied old man, he got into an argument and he was accused of having stinking breath. He went home sad and when he complained to his wife that she had never told him of this so that he could remedy this defect, she replied: 'I would have done so except that I thought all men's breath smelled that way.'

This chaste and noble woman is worthy of praise on both accounts: whether she was unaware of it or whether she bore it patiently, and because her husband discovered this physical defect not through his wife's disgust, but through the insult of an enemy. They say the same thing happened to Hiero, king of Syracuse. Certainly this could not be said by those women who have kissed many men before marriage and many while they were married.

95. How much modesty a woman should demonstrate in public can be deduced from what I have said about keeping secret what happens at home and in the bedroom alone with her husband at night. What is the good of my censuring that barbaric custom whereby among certain peoples husbands

---

94. Duilius: Gaius Duilius won a naval battle and destroyed the Carthaginian fleet off the town of Mylae in northeastern Sicily in 260 B.C.

quasdam gentes promiscue viri et uxores eisdem balneis lavant? Ne com-
memorandus is quidem est, ferinus potius quam humanus. Pauca mulier
audiet, praesertim viros loquentes; pauciora dicet. Si quid se vel auditu-
ram lascivum vel visuram putat, subducat quamprimum se. Declamator
quidam de saeculo sapienter de feminis sic loquitur: 'Ferat matrona oculos iacentes in terram et adversus officiosum salutatorem inhumana potius
quam verecunda sit; longe ante suam impudicitiam neget ore et vultu quam
verbo.' Hieron ille, cuius modo memini, Epicharmum poetam magna pecunia mulctavit quod praesente Regina indecorum quiddam recensuisset.
Augustus Caesar athletarum spectaculo, quod ii corpora nudare soliti erant,
feminas venire edicto vetuit. Non mirum; hic est Caesar qui leges tulit de
adulteriis et pudicitia. Propter eandem causam per dies Olympicorum cer-
taminum feminae omnes Olympia et Pisis excedebant, tum etiam ne in tanta
virorum frequentia versarentur.

96. Non ergo loquetur nisi quae obfuerit tacuisse; nec audiet aut certe
non attendet ea quae nihil ad probitatem morum attinent. Periculosa res
est carnis titillatio, quam semper nobiscum circumferimus, nec iudicio vel
rationi obtemperat. Annotavit Divus Augustinus quod Apostolus Paulus de
ceteris vitiis dixerit, 'Resistite'; de libidine autem, 'Fugite.' 'Nam reliquis,'
inquit 'vitiis Deo adiuvante debemus in praesenti resistere, libidinem vero
fugiendo superare. Contra libidinis impetum apprehende fugam si vis obtinere victoriam. Nec sit tibi verecundum fugere si castitatis palmam desideras
obtinere. Fugiendum est quoniam gravem castitas sortita est inimicum, cui
quotidie resistitur et semper timetur. Vere nimium miseranda et plangenda
condicio est ubi cito praeterit quod delectat et permanet sine fine quod cru-
ciat. Sub momento enim libidinis impetus transit et permanet sine termino
animae infelicis opprobrium.' Sic ille. Ubi sunt istae aulicae quibus morti est
solas esse aliquando sine turba iuvenum quibuscum dies et noctes fabulen-
tur? Quid respondebunt Augustino, immo Apostolo Christi? Aiunt se pure
ac sine ulla suspicione mali id agere. Mihi vero non fit credibile ac ne Sapienti quidem, qui interrogat: 'Quomodo quisquam continebit in sinu ignem
nec exuretur?' Sed fac illas absque ulla cogitatione obscenitatis versari. Certe
eiusdem quoque Sapientis sententia est periturum in periculo qui periculum
quaerit. Et ut illis, quod est sane perdifficile, nihil veniat in mentem mali,

---

95. (Ferat ... verbo) *Sen. contr. 2, 7, 3* // (Hieron ... recensuisset) *Plut. mor. 175C* //
(Augustus ... vetuit) *Suet. Aug. 44*

96. (Resistite ... opprobrium) *Caesar. Arlat.(!) serm. 41, 1, 8, Corpus Christianorum 108,
180–181* // (Quomodo ... exuretur) *Vulg. prov. 6, 27* // (periturum ... quaerit) *Vet. Lat.
Sirach 3, 27*

---

1 quasdam **Γ** nonnullas **H** // **4–8** Declamator ... verbo **Γ** *deest in* **H** // **8** Hieron ille **Γ**
Hieron **H** // **12–14** Propter ... versarentur **Γ** *deest in* **H** // **16**–p.118,2 Periculosa ... vel
periculo vel incitamento **Γ** *deest in* **H** // **27** morti **WW²** mori **BV**

and wives wash themselves promiscuously in the same public baths? Such a custom, more bestial than human, should not even be mentioned. I would have a woman hear few things, especially when men are speaking, and say even less. If she thinks she may hear or see something unseemly, let her withdraw immediately. A certain secular public speaker says wisely of women: 'A married woman should keep her eyes cast on the ground, and she should herself be more discourteous than demure towards those who greet her impolitely. She should rebuke his shamelessness first in her facial expression and then in word.' Hiero, whom I mentioned earlier, fined the poet Epicharmus a great sum of money because he had made reference to an indecorous story in the presence of the queen. Augustus Caesar forbade women by edict to attend athletic spectacles because the contestants were naked. This is not surprising, since the same emperor promulgated laws on adultery and chastity. For this same reason and also to avoid mixing with the great throngs of men who were present all women left Olympia and Pisa during the celebration of the Olympic games.

96. Therefore she will not speak save when it would be harmful to keep silent; she will not listen to or give heed to things that do not pertain to upright morals. The titillation of the flesh is a dangerous thing, which we always carry around with us, and it does not obey judgement or reason. Saint Augustine took note that the Apostle Paul in speaking of other vices said 'Resist,' but of lust he said, 'Flee.'

> For (says St. Augustine) we must resist the other vices on the spot with the help of God, but lust we must overcome by flight. Against the attacks of lust take flight if you wish to gain the victory. Do not be ashamed to flee, if you desire to obtain the palm of chastity. You must flee because chastity has inherited a formidable enemy, which it must resist and fear every day. Truly to be pitied and bewailed is the condition in which the pleasure passes quickly but the torment remains without end. The onslaught of lust passes in a moment but the dishonor of an unhappy soul lasts forever.

Where are those ladies of the court who find it is death to be alone without their entourage of young men to talk to day and night? What would they answer to Augustine or rather to the Apostle of Christ? They say they do this with purity of intention and without any suspicion of evil. This is not believable to me nor to the wise man who asks, 'How will anyone contain fire in his bosom without being burned?' But let us say that they carry on without any thought of obscene things. The same wise man says that he who seeks danger will perish in it. But if you assert that nothing evil will enter your mind, which is difficult to believe, can you say the same

---

95. Epicharmus: a Sicilian writer of comedy active during the first quarter of the 5th cent. B.C.

poteris tu idem praestare de viris quod de te ipsa? Delinquis ergo vel opere
vel periculo vel incitamento.

97. Sugillat Iuvenalis eas feminas quae sciunt

> Quid Seres, quid Thraces rerum gerant,
> quid toto agatur in orbe.

Cato in oratione de feminis omnino vult honestam matronam nescire quae
leges vel rogentur vel abrogentur in sua civitate, quid in foro, quid in cu-
ria tractetur. Hinc illud apud Graecos vulgare: 'Mulierum opera telae, non
contiones.' Aristoteles minus turpe ducit esse viro etiam quae in culina agan-
tur nosse quam mulieri quae extra domum. Idcirco eam prorsus vel loqui
de re publica vetat vel audire. Materteram suam scribit Seneca per sedecim
annos, quibus maritus suus Aegyptum rexit, numquam in publico conspec-
tam esse, neminem provincialium in domum suam admisisse, nihil ab ullo
viro petiisse, nihil a se peti passam. 'Itaque loquax,' inquit, 'et ingeniosa in
contumelias praefectorum provincia, in qua etiam vitaverunt quidam culpam, non effugerunt infamiam, velut unicum sanctitatis exemplum suspexit.
Et, quod illi difficillimum est cui periculosi sales placent, omnem verborum
licentiam continuit et hodie similem ipsi (quamvis numquam speret) semper optat. Multum erat si per sedecim annos illam provincia probasset, plus
est quod ignoravit.' Hactenus Senecae verba. Intelligebat profecto sapientissima femina congressus virorum aliquid nominis sui candori obfuturos,
delicatum et tenuem byssum non debere a multis contrectari. Numa, Ro-
manus Rex, sicut scriptum est a Plutarcho, tacere feminas et abstemias prorsus esse neque de necessariis rebus absente viro quicquam loqui assuefecit.
Fertur igitur cum mulier aliquando propriam in foro causam dixisset, sena-
tum consuluisse deos quidnam civitati id monstrum portenderet.

98. Novas nuptas amissa virginitate menses aliquot latere domi convenit.
Sic Elizabetha Zachariae, concepto foetu, aliquantisper latuit; haec quia
vetula cum viro cubuisset; illae quia virgines; utrasque pudere decet facti,
quamvis non illegitimi. Sunt quibus alienae dignitates spiritus sustollunt, ut
mariti, fratris, propinqui, affinis, etiam (si diis placet) amici aut vicini interdum leviter noti. Quantae stultitiae est sic agere ut alium sua virtus bonum

---

97. (Quid ... orbe) *Iuv. 6, 402–403* ∥ (Cato ... tractetur) *Liv. 24, 2, 10–11* ∥ (Aristoteles) *Aristot. oec. 3, 1* ∥ (Itaque ... ignoravit) *Sen. dial. 12, 19, 6–7* ∥ (Numa ... portenderet)
Plut. Numa 3, 5–6
98. (Elizabetha ... latuit) *Vulg. Luc. 1, 24–25* ∥

3 Sugillat Γ Vituperat **H** ∥ **4** rerum gerant Γ agant **H** ∥ **5** agatur Γ fiat **H** ∥ **8** tractetur
Γ geratur **H** / telae **HWW²** tela **BV** ∥ **13–14** ab ullo viro Γ a viro **H** ∥ **19** annos *Sen.*
dies *omnes edd.* ∥ **22** byssum Γ pannum **H** ∥ **22–30** Numa ... illegitimi Γ *deest in* **H** ∥
30 Sunt ... sustollunt Γ Sunt quaedam quibus animum faciunt alienae dignitates **H** ∥ **31**
aut vicini Γ *deest in* **H**

for the men as you do for yourself? You do wrong either in deed or in exposing yourself to danger or in instigation.

97. Juvenal castigates those women who know

> What the Chinese or the Thracians do,
> Or what goes on throughout the world.

In his oration on women Cato wishes that the virtuous woman know nothing at all about what laws are passed or abrogated in their city, what goes on in the forum or the senate-house. Hence the popular Greek saying 'Woman's work is the loom, not the assembly.' Aristotle thinks it is less unseemly for the man to know what is done in the kitchen than for the woman to know what takes place outside the home. Therefore he prohibits her from speaking or hearing about the conduct of the state. Seneca writes that his aunt was never seen in public for sixteen years while her husband was ruler of Egypt, never admitted into her house anyone from the provinces, never asked anything of any man and never suffered anything to be asked of her.

> And so that province, which was so given to gossip and so ingenious in slandering its prefects, in which even if one escaped blame he did not escape a bad name, looked up to her as a unique example of integrity. And, a difficult task for those who enjoy piquant wit, they curbed their freedom of speech and to this day they wish for another like her, although it is not to be hoped for. It would have been a great thing if that province had approved of her for sixteen years, but more marvellous is the fact that it never knew her.

Obviously this wise woman knew that contact with men would be detrimental to the integrity of her name, and that fine flaxen cloth should not be handled by many hands. Numa, King of Rome, as Plutarch tells us, accustomed women to be silent and completely abstemious and not to speak even of necessary matters in the absence of their husbands. It is related that when a woman once pleaded her case in the forum, the senate consulted the gods to ask what this prodigy portended.

98. It behooves newly-wed women to stay at home for several months after they have lost their virginity. Thus Elizabeth, wife of Zacharias, remained in the house for a little while after she had conceived. She did so because as an old woman she had lain with a man; newly-wed women because they were virgins. In both cases it behooved them to be ashamed of their deed, even though it was not illegitimate. There are some women who take on airs because of honors accruing to others, such as to their husband, brother, neighbor, relative or even, God forbid, a friend or a neighbor of slight acquaintance. What folly it is to act in such a way that another is made

---

97. Numa: Numa Pompilius, legendary second king of Rome, who is accredited with having established the religious institutions of Rome.

et honore dignum faciat, te aliena virtus malam et honore indignam! Nec
desunt quae sic propinquorum potentia abutantur ut non se modo, sed illos
ipsos potentes invisos reddant, ut uxor fratris Vitellii Imperatoris, quae ex
principatu leviri plus sumebat sibi quam Augusta ipsa. Hieronymi, Syracu-
5 sani Regis, impotens sororum dominatus impulit populum ad seditionem,
qua ille cum universa gente deletus est. Fuit nostra aetate nobili cuidam superbissima uxor. Is magnis opibus devolutus iure id passus iudicatus est quod
mariti potentia mulier arrogantissime ferociret. Thucydides ne laudari quidem sermonibus vulgi bonam mulierem permittit; tantum abest ut vitupe-
10 rari non abominetur; sed esse prorsus alienis incognitam minimumque de
illa famam loqui.

99. Non est argumentum pudicitiae nimis nosci feminam et celebrari et
cantari et publice quoque cognomine aliquo insignitam volitare per ora multorum, velut pulchram dici aut strabam aut paetam aut rufam aut clau-
15 dam aut obesam aut pallidam aut macilentam. Haec enim publice in proba
muliere ignorari oportet, quemadmodum superiore libro demonstravimus.
Sunt tamen quarum vitae ratio ita fert ut versari habeant in publico, velut
quae vendunt aut emunt. Nollem, fieri si posset, huiusmodi negotiis mulieres
admoveri, quamvis in hoc et regio spectatur et condicio vitae. Itaque si aliter
20 nequit, adhibeantur iis rebus vetulae aut mediam aetatem egressae coniugatae; sin vero necesse est omnino per puellas agi, dent operam ut sint comes
sine blanditiis et pudibundae sine arrogantia malintque aliquid iacturae in
mercibus facere quam in pudicitia. Hoc dico propter nonnullas quae nimis
blanditiis emptores alliciunt. 'At non matronarum,' inquit Plautus, 'par est
25 officium, sed meretricum, viris alienis subblandiri.' Quarum etiam dolos
brevi cognitos emptores vitant tamquam Sirenum cantus. Maiorem faciet

---

98. (uxor … Augusta ipsa) *Tac. hist. 2, 63* ⫽ (Hieronymi … deletus est) *Liv. 24, 4,
25–26* ⫽ (Thucydides … loqui) *Plut. mor. 242E*
99. (superiore libro demonstravimus) *inst. fem. Christ. 1, 94* ⫽ (At … subblandiri) *Plaut.
Cas. 586*

2–3 illos ipsos **HWW²** illos **BV** ⫽ **3** reddant Γ faciant **H** ⫽ **4** Augusta Γ imperatoris
uxor **H** / Hieronymi **WW²** Hieronis **HBV** ⫽ **6** gente Γ subole **H** / Fuit Γ Erat **H** ⫽ **7**
opibus Γ operibus **H** ⫽ **8** ferociret. Thucydides Γ Vultis admiscere vos publicis negotiis
et impetu vestrorum animorum existimastis vos populos et nationes administraturas; moli-
mini vobiscum transversas rapere civitates et impingitis in durum vobis scopulum, unde res
publicae licet afflictae et concussae enatant tamen. Vos peritis, non nostis modum ac mode-
rationem et, quod pessimum est, nosse vos creditis. Nulla re cedere expertissimis vultis, sed
trahere omnia affectu temptatis, non consilio. Arbitramini de nihilo esse quod sapientes sub-
moverint vos gubernaculis rerum publicarum, quod Paulus Apostolus vetet vos loqui in ecclesia, hoc est in conventu et consensu hominum, quod iussae sitis velare caput? Haec omnia
eo spectat ne civitas sit vobis curae. Abunde magna civitas vobis sit domus, publicum neque
noscatis neque vos noscat. Thucydides **H** ⫽ **9** permittit Γ vult **H** ⫽ **16** demonstravimus Γ
nobis est dictum **H** ⫽ **19** quamvis … vitae Γ *deest in* **H** ⫽ **21** omnino Γ *deest in* **H**

good and worthy of honor through his own virtue while you become wicked and unworthy of honor because of some one else's virtue. There are not lacking those who so abuse their relatives' prestige that they make them unpopular, like the wife of the brother of the Emperor Vitellius, who arrogated more power to herself from her brother-in-law's rule than did the Empress herself. The imperious domination of the sisters of Hieronymus, King of Syracuse, drove the people to rebellion, in which he and all his family were annihilated. There was a certain nobleman of our own time who had a most haughty wife, and when he was divested of his wealth, it was universally thought that he deserved it since his wife had so cruelly abused her husband's power. Thucydides does not even allow that a good woman be praised in the conversations of the crowd, much less criticized, but he wishes that she be completely unknown to strangers and not be the subject of rumor.

99. It is not a proof of chastity for a woman to be too well known, celebrated and sung of and to be on people's lips under some name they have given her, as to be called beautiful or squint-eyed, or red-haired, or lame, or obese, or pale, or skinny. These are characteristics that should not be publicly known in the case of a good woman, as we pointed out in the previous book. There are some women, however, whose manner of life requires that they have public dealings, such as those who buy and sell. I should prefer, if possible, that women did not engage in these affairs, but it depends on the country in which they live and their state of life. If it cannot be avoided, then let old women be employed or married women past middle age. But if it is absolutely necessary that young women be occupied in these activities, let them be courteous without flattery and modest without arrogance and sooner suffer a loss in their sales than in their chastity. I say this on account of some women who entice the buyer with too much coaxing. 'It is not the duty of matrons, but of prostitutes, to fawn on strange men,' said Plautus. Buyers are quick to learn their wiles and they avoid them like the Siren's

---

98. Emperor Vitellius: Tacitus partially attributes the increasing arrogance of the emperor to the political machinations of his sister-in-law Triaria, contrasting her behavior to the modesty of the emperor's wife, Galeria.

Hieronymus: Grandson of Hiero II, tyrant of Syracuse; succeeded him at his death in 216 B.C. He was left in the charge of guardians since he was only fifteen years old. It was his aunts rather than his sisters who exercised an evil influence over him.

quaestum verecunda quam nec mentituram nec imposturam de facie et
moribus emptores iudicabunt. Delectatur quandoque blanditiis et lusibus
locuples mercator, sed rarus est qui pecunia redimat. Et cum ad serium mer-
catus ventum est, nulla fides habetur lascivae. Quod si habetur aliquando a
5   iuvenibus affectu deceptis, aliter senibus et veteranis et ditibus usu venit, in
quibus affectus omnes vincit lucri cupiditas. Ceterum quomodo se cumque
hae res habeant, illud semper mulieris animo et cogitationi obversetur, certissimum et fixum unicum feminae thesaurum esse pudicitiam cum pudore.

100. Cum probam coniugem domi sic cluserim, intelligi satis potest quan-
10 tum illi concedam in bello gerendo et tractandis armis. Ne nominare quidem
haec illam volo, quae utinam et Christianis adimerentur viris. Iam evanuit
illa Iudith vidua, umbra tantum rerum futurarum, quae continentia et sanctitate sua Holofernis, hoc est diaboli, caput abscidit. Iam Debbora, quae iu-
dicavit Israelem, Evangelio Christi cessit, quamquam haec non tam bellicis
15 consiliis et artibus populum Dei bellantem adiuvit ut ieiuniis, precationibus,
vaticinio. De quis duabus feminis cum Divus Ambrosius in libro de Viduis
disseruisset ad Christianas conversus feminas inquit: 'Ecclesia autem non
armis saecularibus vincit adversarias potestates, sed armis spirtualibus, quae
sunt fortia Deo ad destruendas munitiones et altitudinem nequitiae spiritalis.
20 Arma Ecclesiae fides, arma Ecclesiae oratio est, quae adversarium vincit.'

101. Mulieris in publico neque vox neque verba neque gestus neque in-
cessus significationem aliquam praebebunt vel arrogantiae vel fastidii vel
deliciarum. Omnia erunt simplicia et recta, modestia et pudore temperata
atque condita. Matronas ubique decebit gravitas et severitas in sermone,
25 in vultu et cuncto gestu; erga viros autem iuniores et lascivos etiam feroci-
tas ac supercilium; maxime vero omnium adversus eas feminas quae non
sunt famae integrae ne blanditiis vel humanitate mores illarum videantur
approbare, sed vultu ipso quid de illis sentiant testentur. Livius scribit Hispalam, scortum Romae nobile, a Sulpicia accersitam prope exanimatam
30 fuisse quod tam gravem esset feminam conventura. Ita debent dignitatem
suam tueri matronae ut pudeat improbas vel illas aspicere. Neque vero existimet mulier, quia nupta est, iam quidvis sibi licere vel audire vel loqui.
Cum esset virgo, ignorantiae poterat habere excusationem si quid absque
rubore vel audiret obscenum vel loqueretur; nunc marita et virum experta
35 intemperantiae ac turpitudinis nota non caret si quid accidat tale.

---

100. (Ecclesia ... vincit) *Ambr. vid. 1, 49, PL 16, 262C*
101. (Hispalam ... conventura) *Liv. 39, 9, 11–14*

4–6 Quod si ... lucri cupiditas Γ *deest in* **H** // **7** hae res **H** res Γ // **7–8** certissimum
et fixum Γ *deest in* **H** // **9** cluserim Γ eluserim **H** // **16** cum Γ postquam **H** // **24–35**
Matronas ... si quid accidit tale Γ *deest in* **H** // **28–29** Hispalam *Liv.* Hispullam *omnes edd.*

song. A reserved woman will make greater profit since the buyers will judge from her face and her manner that she will not lie or deceive. A rich merchant takes pleasure sometimes in flattery and joking but rare is the person who pays money for it. And when it comes to serious bargaining, they will put no faith in a wanton woman. If it works sometimes with young clients who are deceived by their emotions, it does not succeed with old men, mature persons and the rich, in whom the desire for gain overrides all feelings. But no matter what the case, a woman should always have in mind that the most certain and stable treasure is chastity joined with modesty.

100. Seeing that I would have women confined to their homes, one may well imagine what I would allow her in waging war and the use of arms. I would ordain that she never mention these things by name, and would to God that they could be taken away from Christian men as well! The widow Judith is dead and gone, who was merely a figure of things to come, and who by her continence and holiness cut off the head of Holofernes, that is, the devil. Deborah, who was a judge of Israel, has made way for the Gospel of Christ, and yet even she did not so much help the people of God at war with war-like counsels and stratagems as with fasting, prayers and prophecy. When St. Ambrose spoke of these two women in his book *On Widows*, addressing himself to Christian women, he said: 'The Church does not conquer enemy powers with secular arms but with spiritual arms, which have strength from God to destroy fortifications and the heights of spiritual wickedness. The armor of the Church is faith; the armor of the Church is prayer, which vanquishes the adversary.'

101. A woman should give no sign in public of arrogance or disdain or affected manners either by voice, word, gesture or walk. All will be simple and plain, tempered and seasoned with modesty and propriety. In all places gravity and severity in speech, in countenance and in every gesture become the married woman. Towards younger men of licentious habits she should show even a fierce and haughty exterior, and most of all towards women of uncertain reputation lest by her ingratiating behavior and kindness she seem to approve of their morals. She should give evidence in her facial expression of her opinion of them. Livy writes that Hispala, a well-known Roman courtesan, summoned by Sulpicia, almost fainted at the thought of meeting such a dignified woman. So married women should preserve their sense of dignity so that loose women will be ashamed even to look at them. A woman should not think that because she is married she can hear or say whatever she pleases. When she was unmarried she could have the excuse of ignorance if she heard or said anything obscene without blushing. Now as a married woman with carnal experience of a man she will not be exempt from the charge of licentiousness and disgrace if that sort of thing should arise.

102. Et quoniam leves quarundam animi tenuissima honorculi aura facile impelluntur, admonendae sunt ut graviores sint quam quae tam exiguo spiritu queant circumagi, prudentiores quam quae ignorent ut ridicula et despicienda res sit hic quem nos honorem nominamus. Quid ad rem facit Cornelia voceris an domina Cornelia? Domina an dominula vel semidomina? Hae sunt enim in Gallia differentiae. O inanem animum si tam exiguo voculae flatu movetur! Stulta, an non vides te non protinus dominam esse quod voceris? Quid qui reginas et augustas nominant feminas, an faciunt protinus quia sic appellant? Angelus Gabriel Reginam et Dominam suam Mariae tantum nomine compellat, et tu indigne accipis tuo ipsius nomine a viro meliore te nuncupari? Quanta ignoratio est eorum quae cupis! Dominam vero nemo potest vocare nisi quam adamat. Nam ea demum est illius domina et tyranna, cui servit is turpiter ac misere. Quod si honorata non est cui non praeponitur domina, omnes in populo Romano in tota Italia, Graecia, Africa inhonoratae vixerunt ac proinde miserae. Nulla enim tum mulier domina vocabatur, utique nec vir dominus. Age vero, quantum interesse putas sedeas ambulesve prima an postrema? Apud nonnullas gentes honoratissimi sunt primi, apud alias postremi, apud alias medii. Ergo hoc totum opinionibus constat, non natura rerum. Quod si opinioni satisfaciendum sit, cum es prima, puta te apud illos agere qui primis deferunt honorem; cum media, apud illos qui mediis; cum extrema, qui extremis. Sic semper videberis aestimationi tuae honestissima. Contra, ne honore nimium efferaris cum honoratissimo sita es loco, cogita te in illis esse quibus est iste locus infimus.

103. Iam cedi de via quid aliud est quam fortiorem imbecilliori indulgere, ut rectum claudo vel firmum et valentem invalido vel expeditum implicato vel celerem tardo? Et putas aliam esse causam cur viri tam blande feminas compellent, tam leniter alloquantur, tanto in pretio habere ac veneratione etiam prae se ferant quam quod imbecillum sexum et in quem levissimae quaeque offensiones penetrant ac imprimuntur altissime robustior sexus delicate contrectat ut vitra tenuia et proinde fragilia? Non ergo vestra virtus parit vobis honorem, sed aliena comitas; nec honoramini quia honorem meritae, sed quia honoris avidae. Nam cum vident vos tanto affectu id cupere et eiusmodi capi, exiguam rem benigne vobis gratificantur.

---

102. (Angelus ... compellat) *Vulg. Luc. 1, 30*

3 circumagi Γ agi **H** / ut Γ quam **H** // **5–6** Domina ... differentiae Γ *deest in* **H** // **6–7** O inanem ... movetur Γ O tenerum animum si una inflectitur vocula **H** // **7** protinus Γ ideo **H** // **8–9** faciunt protinus Γ etiam faciunt **H** // **13** turpiter ac misere Γ misere et abiecte **H** // **15** tum **WW²B** tu **V** // **19** constat Γ consistit **H** // **22** aestimationi Γ opinioni **H** // **28** leniter Γ suaviter **H** // **29** prae se ferant Γ videantur **H** / quem Γ quo **H** // **32** comitas Γ humanitas **H**

102. And since some shallow-minded women are easily influenced by the slightest breeze of a paltry honor, they must be admonished to be more serious-minded than to be swayed by such light gusts of wind and prudent enough to know what a ridiculous and despicable thing worldly esteem is. What difference does it make whether you are called Cornelia or Lady Cornelia, Madame or Mademoiselle or Demidame? For these distinctions are observed in France. What an empty mind if it can be affected by the faint sound of a word! Foolish woman, don't you see that you are not a lady simply because you are called by that title? Do those who call women queens and empresses immediately make them so by giving them this name? The Angel Gabriel called his queen and mistress by the simple name of Mary, and do you deem it unworthy to be called by your proper name by your husband, who is superior to you? How ignorant you are of your true desires. No one can call a woman mistress except it be the one he loves, for she in the end is his mistress and tyrant, to whom he is a base and ignoble slave. But if no woman is worthy of honor unless she has the word 'Lady' prefixed to her name, then all those Roman women in all of Italy, Greece, and Africa lived in dishonor and misery, for no woman was called 'Lady' then, and no man was called 'Sir.' Come now, how much difference do you think there is whether you have the first place or the last either in sitting or walking? Among some peoples to be first is the place of honor, among others it is to be last, among others still, to be in the middle. This is all based on men's opinion, not on nature. Therefore if you wish to satisfy opinion, when you are in the first place, think that you are among those who give pre-eminence to the first place; when in the middle, as if you were among those who honor that position and similarly if you are in the last place. In that way you will always have the place of honor in your own opinion. And conversely, so that you will not be too exalted when you are given the place of honor, imagine that you are among those who regard it as the lowest.

103. As for people giving place to you in the street, is it not the stronger yielding to the weaker, the sturdy-limbed to the lame, the strong to the infirm, the unencumbered to the one laden down, the swift to the slow? And do you think there is any other reason why men address women so charmingly and hold them in such esteem and even veneration but that the stronger sex handles the weaker with delicacy like thin and fragile glass, and because the slightest offenses wound them and leave a deep mark? Therefore it is not your virtue that wins you honor, but the politeness of others, nor are you honored because you deserve honor, but because you are greedy for honor. When they see that you wish it so avidly and are won over by it, it is a small thing for them to gratify your wishes. They call you 'Lady',

Vocant dominas, arrident, colloquuntur blande, verba quantulo constant?
Cedunt via; leve est tantilli itineris dispendium et interim respirant. Locant
priores; bene sedebunt sub vobis. Dant partem in domo instructiorem, vestes
molliores, aurum, argentum, gemmas; idem faciunt et pueris, ne plorent, nec
5 vos sapientiores pueris existimant nec estis quamdiu illis movemini. Denique
vobis relinquunt quae male vos urunt adempta, illis contempsisse magnifi-
cum ac gloriosum est, tum ut ea excolatis et custodiatis quae ipsis non vacat.
Et quia vos norunt tales, nemo honoratiores putat quod honoremini a viris,
sed illos potius educatos et comes qui honores concedunt eis quas sciant hon-
10 oris imagine aegre carituras.

   104. Vir sum, sed quatenus vos patria quadam caritate instituendas suscepi, nihil quod ad eruditionem vestram pertinere credam vel celabo vel dis-
simulabo. Etiam mysteria nostra detegam nescio qua virorum gratia. Itaque
volo uti ne ignoretis rideri vos et inani illa honorum specie deludi a nobis,
15 ac quo estis honorum cupidiores, hoc nobis maiori esse et ludibrio et fabulae. Largimur vobis ampliter ineptias illas quas vos honores vocatis, sed
non mercede nulla, nam vos vicissim nobis de stultitia affectuum et iudi-
ciorum vestrorum non parvas nobis praebetis voluptates. Nescitis profecto
ubi solidus honor est situs: mereri honorem decet, non expetere; et sequi
20 is debet, non captari. Argumentum vobis erit honorem vos mereri, cum
contemni non aegre patiemini. Et est hic natura atque ingenio sic perverso
ut (quod de crocodilo physici scribunt) fugientes persequatur, persequentes
fugiat, asper blandientibus, blandiens asperis. 'Nulla expeditior ad gloriam
via,' inquit Socrates, 'quam per virtutem; quae sola gloriam nec quaerit et
25 invenit.' Catonem Uticensem Sallustius scribit maluisse bonum esse quam
videri; ideo quo minus gloriam quaerebat, eo magis assequebatur. Ergo certissima ad verissimos honores via est virtus; quae ut inhonorata esse nequit,
ita nec contemni se indignatur. Nam ut plane quid sit honor intelligatis, est
is veneratio quasique testimonium excellentis virtutis. Virtus autem se ipsa
30 contenta est, honorem non requirit; et eo minus quo est excellentior. Nos
tribuimus cum recto et debito volumus officio defungi. Vulgo illud fertur
honorem deberi feminis; quod feminae, non iniquae adversum sese iudices,
facile agnoscunt, libenter amplectuntur; imperite hoc atque inscite, ut alia
populus permulta. Nam si constat praestantiorem in omni virtutum genere
35 esse virilem sexum, huic debetur honos a femineo, non vice versa.

---

104. (Nulla ... invenit) *Sen. epist. 79, 13* // (Catonem ... videri) *Sall. Catil. 54, 6*

1 quantulo Γ quanti **H** // **2** leve Γ facile **H** // **7** tum ... vacat Γ *deest in* **H** / et custodiatis
WW² *deest in* **BV** // **9** educatos et comes Γ civiles et moderatos **H** // **11–12** instituendas
suscepi Γ suscepi instituendas **H** // **14** inani illa **H** inani Γ // **16** vocatis Γ dicitis **H** // **21**
patiemini Γ feretis **H** // **28**–p.128,**10** Nam ut plane ... aeger a valido Γ *deest in* **H**

they smile at you, talk to you persuasively. What does a word cost? They make way for you in the street. This too costs them just a little going out of their way, and in the meantime they catch their breath. They place you first at table, for they do not mind sitting below you. They give you the better appointed part of the house, softer garments, gold, silver, precious stones. They do the same thing for children so that they will not cry, and think you no wiser than children, as indeed you are not if you are influenced by such things. They leave you those things which if taken away cause you great pain, while for them it is a matter of pride and boastfulness to show their disdain for them and to have you cultivate and keep things for which they have no time. And since they know what you are like, no one will think that you are more respected because you are respected by men, but will rather think that they are well-bred and polite to show respect to those who they know will take it ill if they are without a semblance of honor.

104. I am a man but since I have taken it upon myself to educate you through paternal affection, I will not hide or dissimulate anything that pertains to your education. I will even reveal our secrets, although I do not know if men will appreciate my doing so. So I want you to know that you are laughed at and deluded by us with that empty appearance of honor, and the more desirous you are of honors the more you are an object of derision and slanderous talk. We generously lavish on you those absurdities that you call honors, but not without compensation, for you in turn provide us no small pleasure through the foolishness of your emotions and fancies. You do not know at all where true honor is to be found. Honor must be merited, not sought after, and it must come in due course, not be courted. The proof that you deserve honor is when you are not offended at being treated with contempt. It is of such a perverse nature that, as the natural historians write of the crocodile, it pursues those that flee it and flees those who pursue it, fierce to those who are kind to it and gentle with those who are cruel to it. 'There is no quicker way to fame,' said Socrates, 'than through virtue, which is the only thing that does not seek glory, yet finds it.' Sallust writes that Cato the Younger preferred to be good rather than appear good. Therefore the less he sought after glory, the more he attained it. The surest road to true honors is virtue, which, just as it cannot be without honor, so it does not resent being despised. If you wish to know the true definition of honor, it is the respect for and testimony, so to speak, of outstanding virtue. Virtue is content with itself; it does not seek out honor and the more outstanding it is, the less it does so. We bestow honor when we wish to carry out a duty. There is a popular saying that honor is owed to women, and women, who are not unfair judges in their own regard, readily acknowledge and gladly welcome it. But this is an ignorant and uninformed statement, as is often the case with the common people. For if it is agreed that the male sex is superior in every kind of virtue, honor is owed to them by women and not vice versa.

105. Deus quoque, auctor omnium et institutor, cum virum feminae praeficit, honestiorem declarat virum et huic esse honorem deferendum; nisi forte ita sumus absurde perversi, ut reges ac principes debere subditis suis honorem existimemus, et non contra, potius subditum principi. Non esset profecto si rex agricolae aut famulo caput nudaret et loco cederet, non inquam esset honos, sed ineptia vel fatuitas aut res ludicra. Ita non est honos qui a viro feminae exhibetur, sed lusus quidam et res deridicula. Quanto esset verior sententia non sic: honorandae feminae, sed hunc in modum elata: cedendum imbecillitati muliebri, ferendae aut tolerandae feminae tamquam sexus infirmior a robustiore, ut caecus a vidente, aeger a valido! Assentationes, adultationes, blanditias quae putat honores esse vel laudes, digna est cui honores laudesque non aliae contingant. Et tamen sunt aliquae tam dementes quae cum adulari se sciant, laudari tamen credant. Quid ignoratis, miserae, quantum laudibus assentatio distet? An vos esse laudes putatis eas quas nec ille ex animi sui sententia profert et vos scitis tum falsas esse, tum illum ex animo non loqui, sed vel ridendi vel fallendi gratia simulare? Nemini de vestris bonis plus credideritis quam vobismetipsis. Quae se exploravit femina plane perspicit nihil in se habere quod laudem mereatur praeter animum qui se laude omni indignum censet. Si quid boni adest, Dei munus est, illi acceptum referatur, illi laus, illi gratiarum actio; sin quid mali, nostri sceleris est, ut probrum et reprehensio iure ad nos pertineat, laus ad alium. Et quamvis honorem contemnendum suadeam, nolim tamen pro nihilo haberi dedecus pudicitiae; proximus est ad impudicitiam gradus. 'Quae potest non timere suspicionem adulterii potest non timere adulterium,' inquit Porcius Latro. Cum vero haec sit in humanis honoribus, in decore, in laudationibus vilitas, abiectae mentis est ita se demittere ut humana cuiquam invideat.

106. Quod si honores laudesque invidere turpe est, multo magis pecuniam aut vestes aut possessiones; praestat enim decus hisce omnibus. Nec formam invideri convenit nec valetudinem nec fecunditatem. Munera haec Dei sunt, ut alia omnia quae contingunt mortalibus (sicut nos dicimus) bona, ut appareat iam non ei qui illa recepit invidere nos, sed distributorem beneficiorum suorum, Deum, culpare ac reprehendere. Taceo quod haec non magis habenti invidenda sunt quam magna impedimenta longum et difficile

---

105. (Quae ... adulterium) *Sen. contr. 7, 9*

14 laudibus Γ a laudibus **H** / distet Γ differat **H** ∥ **15** sui Γ *deest in* **H** / profert Γ dicit **H** ∥ **16** illum Γ illa **H** ∥ **18** exploravit femina Γ exploravit et novit **H** / perspicit Γ videt **H** / habere Γ esse **H** ∥ **21** probrum et Γ *deest in* **H** ∥ **22–25** Et quamvis ... Porcius Latro Γ *deest in* **H** ∥ **25–26** in decore, in laudationibus Γ *deest in* **H** ∥ **26** abiectae Γ vilissimae **H** ∥ **28** laudesque Γ *deest in* **H** ∥ **28–29** magis pecuniam Γ minus pecuniam decet **H** ∥ **29** decus Γ honor **H** ∥ **32** appareat iam Γ videamur **H** ∥ **32** nos Γ *deest in* **H** ∥ **34**-p.130,1 impedimenta ... ingressis Γ iter ingressis impedimenta **H**

105. God also, the author and originator of all things, in setting man over woman, indicates that man is more worthy of honor, and it must be rendered to him, unless we have become so absurdly perverse as to think that kings and princes owe honor to their subjects rather than the subject to his lord. If a king were to uncover his head before a farmer and yield place to him, that would not be honor, but pure foolishness and mockery. So it is not honor that a man shows a woman, but a farce and a travesty. How much more accurate that maxim would be if instead of saying that women are to be held in honor, it should be changed to say that we must make concessions to the weakness of women; women must be put up with and tolerated as the weaker sex by the stronger, the blind person by one who has sight, the sick by the healthy. The woman who thinks that flattery, adulation and blandishments are honors deserves no other honors and praise. And yet there are some women who are so out of their mind that although they know they are being flattered, they still think they are being praised. Poor wretches, don't you know how greatly flattery differs from praise? Do you consider it praise when he who gives the praise does not express his true feelings, yet all the while you know that it is false and that he is not speaking sincerely, but merely for the sake of ridicule and deception? You should believe no one more than yourselves concerning your own worth. A woman who has examined herself sees clearly that there is nothing in her that deserves praise except a mind that deems itself unworthy of all praise. If there is any good in her, it is the gift of God, it is owed to him, to him is due all praise, all thanksgiving. If there is any evil, it is owed to our wickedness. All reprehension and remonstrance rightfully belongs to us, all praise to another. Although I am recommending that honor should be spurned, I do not wish that dishonor done to chastity should be considered a matter of no importance. It is very close to unchastity. 'She who does not fear the suspicion of adultery, does not fear adultery itself,' said Porcius Latro. Since there is such worthlessness in human honors, dignity and praise, it is the quality of a lowly mind to abase itself to such an extent that it envies anyone for any human thing.

106. But if it is a vile thing to envy honor and praise, it is much worse to envy money or clothes or possessions, for this is to confer honor on these things. It is not fitting either to envy beauty or health or fecundity. These are gifts of God, as we said of all good things that fall to the lot of mortals. It would seem as if we do not envy the one who has received these gifts, but that we blame and reproach God, who distributes these blessings. I won't mention that the posessor is not more to be envied for these than people about to set out on a long and difficult journey should be envied

---

105. Porcius Latro: a native of Spain and friend of Seneca the Elder, a writer on Roman declamation. He was one of the greatest speakers of the Augustan period.

iter ingressis. Quid enim aliud haec sunt fortunae bona quam molestae sarci-
nae in vita et, quod pessimum omnium est, quae animum ad caelestia ten-
dentem nutu et pondere suo ad terram detrudant? Si absit livor, facile et illud vitium devitabit quod ex livore nasci fere solet, ut litigent, iurgentur, con-
5   vicientur, alienae domi curiosae sint inspectentque ac scrutentur quid agant,
quid dicant, quomodo et unde vivant. Haec numquam honesta mulier faciet, sed impudens et digna proscindi satura, nisi illud forte cures ut indigenti
subvenias. Tibi enim derelictus est pauper, orphano tu eris adiutrix. Felix si
haec est mens, de qua in psalmo dicitur: 'Beatus qui intelligit super egenum
10   et pauperem; in die mala liberabit eum Dominus. Dominus conservet eum
et vivificet eum et beatum faciat eum in terra et non tradat eum in animam
inimicorum eius. Dominus opem ferat illi super lectum doloris eius; universum stratum eius versasti in infirmitate eius.'

CAP. IX.   QUOMODO AGENDUM DOMI

15   **107.** Duobus illis, pudicitiae et amori coniugis summo, si peritia regendae
domus accedat, iucundiora fiunt et feliciora connubia. Sine hoc tertio res
familiaris, sine illis prioribus matrimonium non constat, sed saeva et perpetua est crux. Paulus prudentiae et castitati mulierum curam rei familiaris
adiungit; de quo loco Divus Ioannes Chrysostomus sic inquit: 'Animadver-
20   tite, obsecro, indicibilem Pauli diligentiam. Is qui intactum nihil relinquit
quo nos a tempestatibus mundanorum negotiorum abducat, domesticae rei
magnam prae se fert curam; videlicet ea rite constituta magnus patet locus in quo caelestis gratia conquiescat. Alioqui pariter concidunt universa.
Mulier quae domum studiose curat, ut eodem studio pudicitiam conservet
25   necesse est, nam huic curae et administrationi deserviens non facile deliciis,
conviviis et intempestivis aut vanis lusionibus occupabitur.' Tantum Ioannes
Constantinopolitanus.
     108. Lacaena in bello capta, rogata a victore quid sciret facere, 'Domum,'
inquit, 'regere.' Viros Aristoteles ait in re domestica quaestores debere esse,
30   feminas custodes quaesitorum. Quas in hoc videtur finxisse natura meticu-
losas, ne parta profunderent, addita semper cura et anxietate ne desit. Quod

---

106. (Beatus ... eius) *Vulg. psalm. 40, 1–3*
     107. (Animadvertite ... occupabitur) *Ioh. Chrys. in epist. Tit. 2, 5 hom. 4, PG 62, 686*
     108. (Lacaena ... regere) *Plut. mor. 242C //* (Viros ... quaesitorum) *Aristot. pol. 3, 4
(1277b) //*

---

2 in vita Γ *deest in* **H** // **3** detrudant Γ deiciant **H** / livor Γ invidia **H** // **3–4** et ... devitabit
Γ illud pelletur vitium **H** // **4** livore Γ invidentia **H** // **7** forte cures Γ forsan agas **H** //
16 iucundiora Γ laetiora **H** // **18–27** Paulus ... Constantinopolitanus Γ *deest in* **H**

for their heavy baggage. For what else are these blessings of fortune than troublesome burdens in life? And, worst of all, by their weight they force the mind down to earth as it strives after heavenly things. If envy is absent, then it will be easy to avoid other vices that usually come of envy, such as quarreling, scolding, reviling, curiosity about what goes on in another household, prying into what they do, what they say, how they live and by what means. A good woman will never do such things, but only a shameless one, deserving of scathing rebuke, unless you wish to come to the aid of the indigent. The poor have been left in your care and you will give help to the orphan. Blessed are you if yours is the mind of which the Psalmist says: 'Blessed is he who gives thought to the poor and the needy. In the day of evil the Lord will deliver him. May the Lord preserve him and give him life, and make him blessed upon earth and not hand him over to the will of his enemies. May the Lord bring him succor on his bed of sorrow; you have changed his bed-covering in his illness.'

CHAPTER 9. HOW SHE SHOULD BEHAVE AT HOME

107. If to the two virtues of chastity and great love for one's husband there is added skill in governing a household, then marriages become happier and more harmonious. Without the third there is no family prosperity, without the other two there is no marriage, but harsh, unending torment. Paul joins to prudence and chastity in women the care of the household, and commenting on this passage St. John Chrysostom has this to say: 'Notice, I pray you, the unspeakable diligence of Paul. He who leaves nothing untouched of all that could remove us from the tempests of worldly occupations gives great attention to domestic affairs. Where those matters are duly regulated, there is ample room for divine grace to find a peaceful welcome. If not, everything collapses at once. The woman who zealously takes care of her home must necessarily guard her chastity with equal zeal, for when she is devoted to the management of these tasks she will not easily occupy herself with luxurious habits, banquets and untimely and vain pastimes.'

108. A Spartan woman captured in war was asked by her conqueror what she knew how to do. She answered, 'I know how to keep house.' Aristotle with regard to the managing of a household said that men should be the earners and women the custodians of the earnings. Nature seems to have made them meticulous in this regard, not to waste what has been acquired and to be ever anxious and concerned that it not be lacking. But if a woman

si mulier larga sit, numquam vir tantum poterit cogere quantum haec brevi dissipabit. Ita res tota familiaris dilapsa ilico consistere non posset. Non decet ergo honestam matrem familias profusam esse. Nec pudicitiae multum parcunt quae pecuniae non parcunt, ut de Sempronia Sallustius refert, 'Cui cariora semper omnia quam decus aut pecunia fuere, pecuniae an famae minus parceret haud facile discerneres.' Non quod placeat eam iniuste parta velle mordicus retinere aut vetare ne vir in sanctos usus pecuniam distribuat et qui nummus semel eius arcam ingressus est, tamquam in labyrintho aut turri Danaes exitum non inveniat; quod aliquae faciunt, ignarae quatenus servandum et continendum sit.

109. Idcirco Essaei mulieres secum in illam sacratiorem vitam non inferebant quod negarent idoneas esse communitati rerum. Nam quod semel apud se vidit femina pati non potest gratis alio transire! Itaque parsimoniae ac frugalitati familiam assuefaciet. Nam hae feminarum potius partes sunt quam virorum, sed ita ut sciat aliud esse parsimoniam ac avaritiam, multum inter frugalitatem et sordes interesse, non idem esse sobrie vivere et esurire. Dabit operam ne quid omnino desit familiae in cibario et vestiario. Qua de re audienda est Aristotelis sententia: 'Tria,' inquit, 'cum sint (opus, cibus et castigatio), cibus sine castigatione et opere petulantem reddit; opus vero et castigatio sine cibo violenta res est et infirmum facit servum. Restat igitur ut opus faciendum mater familias ministris dispenset et cibum sufficientem quae est servi merces.'

110. Administret omnia ex voluntate et iussu mariti aut eo certe modo quem sciat illum neutiquam improbaturum; non aspera in familiam nec dura, sed mitis et benevola, ut matrem magis experiantur quam dominam, sicut Hieronymus inquit. A quibus mansuetudine potius quam severitate exigat reverentiam, ad quam brevissima est per virtutem via. Nihil addunt auctoritati et venerationi rixae, iurgia, convicia, clamores, plagae; detrahunt citius. Consilio autem, ratione, gravitate morum, verborum, sententiarum quidvis perficias celerius ac commodius quam impetu et violentia. Magis veremur prudentes quam iracundos; plus cogit quietum imperium quam

---

108. (Cui ... discerneres) *Sall. Catil. 25, 3*
109. (Essaei ... rerum) *Plin. nat. 5, 73* // (Tria ... merces) *Aristot. oec. 1, 5 (1344a)*
110. (matrem ... dominam) *Hier. epist. 148, 25, PL 22, 1216*

2 dissipabit Γ prodiget **H** / dilapsa ilico Γ brevi dilapsa **H** // **6** placeat Γ *deest in* **H** // **7** velle Γ velim **H** // **9** aliquae Γ quaedam **H** // **11** sacratiorem Γ sanctiorem **H** // **11–12** inferebant Γ ducebant **H** // **17** omnino Γ *deest in* **H** / in ... vestiario Γ non modo in cibo sed nec in vestitu **H** // **21** dispenset Γ tribuat **H** // **24** neutiquam Γ non **H** // **25** mitis Γ comis **H** // **27** addunt Γ adducit **H** // **28** clamores Γ *deest in* **H** // **30** ac commodius Γ *deest in* **H** // **31** veremur prudentes Γ prudentes veremur **H**

is prodigal, a man will never be able to earn enough without her dissipating it in a short time. In that way the family possessions would quickly go to ruin and would not last. Therefore a good mistress of the household will not be extravagant. Those who are free with money will be equally liberal with their chastity, as Sallust relates of Sempronia: 'Everything else was dearer to her than honor or money so that it was hard to distinguish whether she regarded money or her good name less.' I do not say that I approve that she hold on tenaciously and unreasonably to what has been acquired or forbid her husband from using the money for good works, or that once the money has entered her strongbox it will never find its way out, as from the Cretan labyrinth or the tower of Danaë. Some women are guilty of this, ignorant of how much they should save or hold on to.

109. For that reason the Essenes did not admit women into their sacred way of life because they said they were not suited to a sharing of goods in common. When once a woman has seen something in her possession she does not allow it to pass on to another free of charge. So a woman will accustom her family to parsimony and frugality, for this is the role of women rather than of men, but in such a way that she knows the difference between parsimony and avarice, frugality and squalor, and that living frugally is not the same as going hungry. She will see to it that nothing be lacking to the family in food or clothing. In this regard we should hearken to the opinion of Aristotle: 'There are three things—work, food, and punishment. Food without work and punishment makes them insolent. Work and punishment without food is cruel and makes the servant weak. It follows therefore that the mistress of the household shall apportion the work to be done by the servants and will provide sufficient food, which is the servant's reward.'

110. She will administer everything according to the will and command of her husband, or certainly in a way that she knows he will not disapprove. She will not be harsh with the servants or stern, but mild-mannered and benevolent, so that they will look upon her more as a mother than a mistress, as Jerome said. She will require respect of them through mildness rather than severity, and the shortest road to this is through virtue. Quarrels, chiding, abuse, clamor and blows do not add to authority and respect, but rather detract from them. You can achieve whatever you wish more quickly and more opportunely by discretion, reason, seriousness of purpose, words and advice than through hostility and violence. We respect prudent persons more than angry ones. A quiet command is more persuasive than a

---

108. Danaë: She was shut up in a tower by her father but Zeus came to her in a shower of gold. From their union the hero Perseus was born.

109. Essenes: Members of a religious sect that flourished in Palestine from the 2nd cent. B.C. to the end of the 1st cent. A.D. They were strict observers of the Law of Moses and lived ascetic lives of seclusion.

vehemens; imperiosior concitatione quies. Quod cum dico, non inertes esse matronas aut segnes, sed reverendas moneo, ne sic quiescant ut dormiant; ne sic praecipiant ut contemnantur. Vigilent, intentae sint, severae sine saevitia, acres sine amaritudine, diligentes sine violentia. Neminem oderint ex familia, praesertim si non malus est. Quod si diu domestico eius ministerio usi simus, non alio habeatur loco quam fratris aut filii. Feles et canes aliquamdiu domi alitos diligimus, quanto is affectus verius erga hominem praestandus est!

111. In ancillis et asseclis et pedisequis et iis denique omnibus quae vel necessitate coactae vel mercede adductae inserviunt, magna et imprudentiae et improbitatis flagitia ex inscientia nascuntur non aliter atque in turba universa operariorum atque imperitorum hominum. Itaque docendae et admonendae sunt, ut meminerint praecepti non cuiuslibet de vulgo hominis, sed Pauli, ut naviter et mansuete et benigne atque etiam hilariter obeant munus suum, non obloquentes, non responsantes, non obmurmurantes, sed ne tristes quidem vel asperae, ne gratiam laboris et apud homines et apud Deum amittant. Tum puras contineant manus a furtis et rapacitate, in quo gratiores gerunt animos bestiae omnes quam multi hominum. Quae enim fera adeo est immanis ut alimentorum atque educationis beneficium sic remuneretur ut de commodis illius detrahat, a quo tot commoda percepit? Quamquam non solet id fieri nisi ab animis deiectis et plane dignis servitute; quibus quae praeditae sunt, gula sunt voraces ac lurcatrices, rapaces manibus, et conqueruntur non esse sibi aperta omnia. Garrulitate futtili ac periculosa et indignantur arceri ab arcanis; importune petaces nec expleri possunt absque respectu ullo non ex quanto cumulo accipiant, sed quid suae cupidatati satisfaciat. Malam impudentemque sub parentum vilitate ac sordibus educationem in familias honestas transferunt et criminantur deinde dominas impatientiae. Intentae suis utilitatibus dominas oderunt et amorem ab eis exigunt. Quin iniuria sese affici credunt si non accipiant quod nec meruerunt. Inter haec vitia, cum haec omnia ex sententia non cedunt, virulente domum illam obtrectant, ubi integre et sancte habitae sunt nec licentia est flagitiis praebita.

112. Ergo sciant quae sic se gerunt et se esse homines ac sacra illa intinctas aqua sistendasque aliquando ante tribunal Christi, qui non secus rationem ministerii ac officii sui ab illis reposcet quam regiminis a magnis

111. (naviter ... munus suum) *Vulg. Eph. 6, 6–7*

2 moneo Γ hortor **H** // **5–6** domestico ... simus Γ domi ministrarit **H** // **9–12** In ancillis ... Itaque docendae et Γ *deest in* **H** // **12–14** admonendae sunt ... Pauli Γ admonendae etiam sunt quae ministrant, meminerint dicti Pauli **H** // **14–15** atque ... suum Γ hilariter etiam et cum suavitate oboediant munus suum **H** // **15** non responsantes Γ *deest in* **H** // **16** vel asperae Γ *deest in* **H** // **18** gerunt animos Γ sunt **H** // **21–22** dignis servitute Γ servitute dignis **H** // **22**–p.136,**9** quibus quae praeditae ... ex quibus ipsae sustentantur Γ *deest in* **H**

vehement one. Calm has more authority than agitation. I do not mean that matrons should be sluggish or inert, but I advise them to inspire respect and not be so tranquil that they appear to be asleep. They should not give orders in such a way that they are despised. Let them be alert and attentive, severe without being cruel, strict without harshness, exacting without being too rigorous. They are not to hate anyone among the servants, especially if he is not bad. If a servant has had long service with you, he should be regarded more like a brother or a son. We love dogs and cats that we have nurtured for many years. How much more deserving of affection is a human being!

111. Among maidservants, domestic servants, female attendants and in general, all those who act as servants, constrained by necessity or induced by financial rewards, ignorance is the cause of many acts of imprudence and dishonesty, as often happens among the masses of unskilled workers. And so they must be instructed and advised to remember the precept not of any ordinary mortal, but of Saint Paul that they accomplish their tasks with alacrity and tranquility, in a friendly and even joyful spirit, without criticism or defiance or murmuring, not sullen or ill-tempered, lest their work lose favor both with God and with men. Let them keep their hands unsullied by theft or rapacity, in which respect brute beasts show more gratitude than many men. What wild beast is so savage that it would repay the kindness of nourishment and rearing by causing harm to the one from whom it received so many benefits? But this is usually done only by men of lowly spirit, well deserving of servitude; those possessed of such qualities are slaves of their gullet, voracious, gluttonous, light-fingered, and they grumble that everything is not open to them. They engage in idle and dangerous talk and are offended if they are not privy to every secret; they beg shamelessly and are never satisfied; they do not consider the ample wages they receive but think only of satisfying their own boundless cupidity. They bring the wicked and impudent upbringing received in the mean circumstances of their paternal home into honorable households and then accuse their mistresses of impatience. Intent on their own advantages they hate their mistresses and yet demand love from them. They think they are ill-treated if they do not receive what they have not merited. In addition to these vices, if everything does not go according to their wishes, they denounce that house violently, where they were given exemplary treatment but were not given the opportunity to cultivate their vices.

112. Therefore let those who act in this way know that they are human beings who have been dipped in that sacred water and will one day stand before the tribunal of Christ, who will demand of them an account of their ministry and duties just as he does of the rule of great princes. In every

principibus. Animus enim et mens a Christo spectatur in quocumque homine, non magnitudo aut qualitas condicionis vel fortunae, quippe faciem
hominum Deus non respicit, qui iudicibus suis praecipit ut personam pauperis in iudicio ne accipiant nec ideo secundum illum pronuntient quod sit
5   pauper. Et sicut gratus est Deo pauper mitis, iustus, Christo similis, ita exo-
sus atque abominabilis qui vitia paupertati adiunxit.

113. Quocirca concupiscentias suas cohibeant et aliena non minore cura
ac fide tractent quam propria, persuasae aliena non esse ex quibus ipsae sustentantur. Dominos et dominas non secus diligant et colant ac patres ma-
10   tresque, quippe altor educatorque non alio est quam patris loco. Id nomen
ipsum ostendit, quo eri et erae, patres et matres familias nuncupantur, tum
Romano more libertini patronorum nomina usurpabant tamquam parentum. Quae domi audierint ac viderint arcana esse putent omnia nec posse
sine ingenti scelere enuntiari, non solum interea dum in illis aedibus degunt,
15   sed nec postquam migrarint. Quorsum enim et parietes et fores pertinent si
istae omnia patefaciunt? An non praestaret viperam domi alere quam eiusmodi futtiles, ex quarum loquacitate et saepenumero vel sinistris interpre-
tationibus, natis ex hebetudine vel mendaciis, ex odio atque ira, magnae
calamitates conflantur innoxiis et honestis hominibus? Quomodo illae aut
20   quando tantam iacturam sarcient et tantum delictum luent?

114. M. Livio Druso architectus quidam aedes se aedificaturum recipie-
bat in quas ex nulla domo alia esset prospectus. 'At potius,' inquit ille, 'aed-
ifica mihi domum, si potes, in qua quicquid agam universus populus Ro-
manus possit aspicere.' Fidenter quidem Drusus. Et sane sic est: bonis om-
25   nibus ita vivendum in privato quemadmodum vivere vellent in publico et sic
intra domesticos parietes agendum ut si subito nos alieni conspiciant, nulla
sit erubescendi causa. Verum enimvero ea est per totum humanum genus
et corporum et animorum imbecillitas ut multa ex usu sit celari. Multa tol-
erantur domi quae foras elata inepta et ridicula iudicentur; praesertim quod
30   unusquisque nostrum quam veniam sibi poscit non vult alii tribuere; tanta
est in nobis iniquitas. Et quae ipse serio facit quotidie, in alio si semel deprehenderit, deridet atque etiam calumniatur.

115. Ex hisce delationibus quae simultates atque inimicitiae in civitate
tota oriantur nemo non saepe experitur, dum omnes et aliena curiose scru-
35   tari avemus et nostra vel sciri vel maligne vel sinistre iudicari aegerrime

---

112. (faciem ... accipiant) *Vulg. Deut. 1, 17*
114. (M. Livio Druso) *Plut. mor. 800F; Vell. 14, 1*

9 diligant et colant **Γ** diligent et colent **H** // **11** eri et erae **Γ** *deest in* **H** // **13**–p.138,17
Quae ... filiabus **Γ** *deest in* **H** // **20** sarcient **BV** sarcirent **WW**[2]

man it is the soul and the mind that Christ examines, not greatness or social position or fortune, since God does not look at a man's face and he bids his judges not to regard the person of the poor man in their judgement or to judge him on the grounds of his being poor. And as the poor man who is meek, just and like unto Christ is pleasing to God, so he who has joined vices to poverty is hated and abominable.

113. Therefore maidservants must check their own evil impulses and treat things that belong to others with no less care and loyalty than they do their own, persuaded that what gives them sustenance is not something alien to them. They should love their masters and mistresses no differently than their fathers and mothers, since one who nourishes and rears you is like a father. The name itself declares it: masters and mistresses are called fathers and mothers of the household. Moreover, according to Roman custom freed slaves used the names of their masters, as if they were their parents. Whatever they hear or see in the house they should consider as secrets that cannot be revealed without incurring the gravest guilt. This should be observed not only while they are still dwelling there but even after they have moved away. Of what use are walls and doors if the servants divulge everything? Would it not be better to raise a viper in the house than such unreliable people, whose loquacity and often malicious interpretations, which arise from stupidity or lying, hate and anger, are the source of calamities for innocent and upright persons? How or when will they ever make amends for such damages or expiate such a crime?

114. An architect promised Marcus Livius Drusus that he would build him a house into which no other house would have a view. 'Rather build me a house,' he said, 'in which the whole Roman people can see whatever I do.' Drusus spoke with great assurance. And in truth so it is: all good men should live in private just as they would wish to live in public, and we should conduct ourselves within the walls of our house in such a way that if others were suddenly to see us, there would be no cause for shame. But such is the weakness of body and soul that besets the human race that many things are kept concealed through custom. Many things are tolerated at home which when exposed to public view are judged to be foolish and ridiculous. This is especially true of things for which we all demand pardon for ourselves but are not willing to grant it to others. Such is our unfairness, and while a person may do certain things in sober earnest every day, if he catches someone else at them but once, he makes fun of him and even calumniates him.

115. Everyone knows by experience what rivalries and enmities take rise throughout the city from these revelations, since we are all eager and curious to pry into other people's affairs but become vexed if our own affairs are

114. Marcus Livius Drusus: eldest of a circle of ambitious nobles around the orator L. Licinius Crassus; political reformer; tribune of the people, 124–91 B.C.

ferimus. Turbatur per haec civium tranquillitas. Procedit malevolentia in rabiem, unde rixae et pugnae et inter potentes factiones, inter minores vero delaturae et calumniae de capite, de fortunis, de existimatione. Verbum erat vetus: 'Nocens metuit poenam, innocens casum.' Non placet hoc; illud ve-
5 rius: 'Nocens metuit poenam, innocens calumniam.' Et tantorum malorum causa est famularum garrulitas, quae irata effundit non quantum viderit, sed quantum suppeditat animus cupidine ultionis ardens. Erae si pactae mercedi assem detrahant iniquissimae erunt nec ulla eis esse potest venia apud Deum. Quanta quiritatio! Qui clamores! Quae exsecrationes! Nam istis pro
10 ludo est sic miscere ac turbare res quietas et familias bene constitutas vel evertere vel affligere. Quod sic vivant, in culpa est tarditas atque imperitia, quae nulli umquam bono esse potuit. Numquam illis venit in mentem spectari actiones omnes nostras, tum verba et cogitatus, a iudice illo aeterno, qui retribuit unicuique secundum opera ipsius.

15 **116.** Matres familias quod celari expediat ne committant quibusvis famulabus, sed fidei spectatae. Ipsae vicissim famulae taciturnitate ac fide eas se praestent, quibus non aliter possint quaevis concredi quam ipsis filiabus. Nihil dicant neu agant quod domina aut liberis accipi queat in exemplum aut incitamentum peccandi. Gravius plerumque delinquitur exemplo quam
20 facto. Si ita vixerint, condicionem non commodiorem solum sibi reddent, sed honestiorem quoque, gratam Deo, gratam hominibus et ad meliorem fortunam certissimum gradum; alioqui in miseria illa servitutis consumentur, invisae omnibus et despectae. Haec potissimum sciant et teneant famulae; tum legant interdum aliquid quod mentem et mores possit excolere.
25 Quod si legere non norunt, auscultent legentes attente; intersint contionibus cum vacabit, occupatis vero, dum interquiescunt, erae aut filiae quae vel audierint vel legerint referant, unde prudentiores ac meliores evadant. De famulabus satis dictum; redeamus ad matronas.

117. Fidelius et gratius obsequium est quod ab amore impetratur quam
30 quod a metu exprimitur. Metum abesse placet, reverentiam non placet. Ne sis famulis viris nimium blanda nec comis nec facilis nec festiva nec multum cum eis versare; nec tecum vel colludere quisquam eorum audeat vel iocari. Sis eis sane cara, sed non tam cara quam verenda. Non vis timeri ut domina, at venerationem exige ut mater. Famulare genus licentiae avidum
35 est, quam ipsi sibi ostensam arripiunt et augent. Non perinde exacte viro

115. (Nocens ... casum) *Publil. N 629*

18 dicant neu agant Γ seu dicant seu agant **H** // **18–19** quod domina ... peccandi Γ quod a matre aut filiabus familias aut etiam aliis famulabus accipi in exemplum peccati possit **H** // **19** delinquitur Γ peccatur **H** // **20–28** Si ita vixerint ... De famulabus satis dictum Γ *deest in* **H** // **28** redeamus ad matronas Γ Sed ad matres familiae redeamus **H** // **31** blanda nec comis Γ blanda mater familias **H** // **32** vel colludere Γ aut colludere **H** // **32–33** vel iocari Γ aut iocari **H** // **33** verenda Γ reverenda **H** / timeri Γ metui **H** // **35** perinde Γ tam **H**

known or adversely construed. The tranquility of the city is disturbed because of these reports. Malevolence breeds wrath and thence come quarrels
and fights and factions among the powerful, and among the lower classes
accusations and calumnies about a person's life, fortune and reputation.
There was an old saying: 'The guilty one fears punishment, the innocent
fears chance.' It would be truer to say 'The guilty one fears punishment,
the innocent fears calumny.' The cause for all these evils is the garrulity of
female servants, who in their resentment unbosom their feelings freely, reporting not what they saw, but what their vengeful spirit suggests to them.
If their mistresses withhold one farthing from their stipulated wages, they
are monsters of injustice and will never find pardon with God. How much
public protest! What turmoil! What execrations! They think it a game to
confound and embroil the peaceful state of things and to overturn or injure
families of good standing. The reason why they live this way is their mental
torpor and ignorance, which never did anyone any good. It never occurs to
them that all our actions, words and thoughts are seen by that eternal judge,
who gives retribution to everyone according to his works.

116. Mistresses of the household should entrust matters that must be concealed only to servants of proven loyalty. Maidservants should show themselves of such reticence and loyalty as to be trusted no less than daughters.
They should not say or do anything that could be taken by their mistress
or their children as an example or incentive to do wrong. Often one sins
more by example than by deed. If they live in this way, not only will they
render their existence more agreeable, but their life will be more honorable,
pleasing both to God and to men, and a sure step towards a better fortune.
If not, they will consume their lives in the misery of servitude, hated and despised by all. This is the principal lesson female servants should learn. Then
they should read now and then something that will improve their mind and
their morals. If they cannot read, they can listen attentively to others who
read to them. When they have time they should assist at sermons; when they
are occupied, in their moments of rest their mistress or her daughters may
tell them things they have heard or read so that they may come away more
sensible and morally better. I have said enough about maidservants. Let us
return to married women.

117. A service obtained by love is more loyal and more satisfying than
one extracted by fear. It is good that fear be absent, but not respect. Do
not be too kind or obliging or indulgent or sociable with male servants and
do not associate with them too much. Let none of them dare joke or banter with you. Be loved by them, but not so much loved as revered. You
do not wish to be feared as a mistress, but demand the veneration due to
a mother. The servant class hungers after freedom and if it is offered to
them they seize upon it and add to it. I would not direct the male head

praeceperim caveat ne sibi familiam fecerit nimis familiarem quam mulieri, cui nolim multum esse cum famulis commercii. Nec cum eis pleraque trans- igat; ne arguat ipsa; ne castiget viros; marito id muneris relinquat. Sit tota cum famulabus suis et pedisequis quarum sint mores integri et pudicitia ex- plorata. Ipsa plurimum simul exemplo adiuvabit, simul monitis, praeceptis, adhortationibus, tum diligenti cura, ne quid eam lateat quomodo famulae vivant et vitiis remedia opponat ac velut morbis antidota.

118. Si qua parum sincere habere integritatem deprehensa est aut credita nec obiurgationibus et castigatione proficitur, pellatur domo. Facile proxima quaeque venenum corrumpit et credit suspicax vulgus famulas dominarum esse similes. Quam illud est apud Hieronymum frequens dominas ex ancil- lis aestimari! Nec mirum cum Graeco proverbio etiam catellae dominarum mores dicantur referre. Et illi apud Terentium adolescentes de sordibus et negligentia cultus ancillae pudicitiam colligunt dominae. Homerus sapien- tem Ulyssem scribit cum domum redisset, eas occidisse ancillas quae cum procis concubuerant, quod hae non solum probrum domo, sed periculum quoque pudicitiae Penelopes attulissent. Rex David post Absalonem filium suum devictum eas concubinas suas quas Absalon ex consilio Achitophe- lis incestu polluerat in perpetuam custodiam a se seposuit, unde numquam postea eductae sunt. Ipsa matrona iis artibus se exercebit quas altero li- bro exposuimus et in officio continebit famulas ut casta Lucretia, quam lu- cubrantem cum ancillis et pensa partientem regii iuvenes deprehenderunt. Quod eo diligentius exsequetur et accuratius si qua familiae pars labore hoc alenda est.

119. Salomon in laudibus sanctae feminae quaesiisse illam ait lanam et linum et operatam consilio ac diligentia manuum suarum. Theano Meta- pontina rogata quae esset optima matrona versu Homeri respondit: 'Telam quae tractat lectum curatque mariti.' Ex ea industria (pergit dicere sapi- ens Rex) 'Facta est quasi navis institoris, de longe portans panem suum,' ac ne somno indulgere nimium ostendat, addit: 'De nocte surrexit deditque

---

118. (dominas . . . aestimari) *Hier. com. Is. 8, 24* // (catellae . . . referre) *Paroem. Diogenianus 5, 93; Plat. rep. 563C* // (Terentium) *Ter. Haut. 292–299* // (Rex . . . eductae sunt) *Vulg. II reg. 20, 3* // (altero libro) *inst. fem. Christ. 1, 15–17* // (Lucretia . . . deprehenderunt) *Liv. 1, 57, 9* **119.** (Salomon . . . suarum) *Vulg. prov. 31, 13* // (Theano . . . mariti) *Hier. adv. Iovin. 1, 42, PL 23, 273* // (Telam . . . mariti) *Hom. Il. 1, 31* // (Facta est . . . suum) *Vulg. prov. 31, 14* // (De nocte . . . demensum) *Vulg. prov. 31, 15*

---

1 nimis **HWW²** minus **BV** // **4** et pedisequis Γ *deest in* **H** // **6** adhortationibus Γ *deest in* **H** // **12** aestimari Γ iudicari **H** // **14** pudicitiam Γ argumentum pudicitiae **H** // **17–20** Rex . . . eductae sunt Γ *deest in* **H** // **21** exposuimus Γ diximus **H** // **23** exsequetur et accu- ratius Γ et laboriosius aget **H** // **26** ac diligentia Γ *deest in* **H** // **30**–p.142,1 De nocte . . . demensum Γ Et de nocte surrexit deditque praedam domesticis suis; nec tantum opus, sed refectionem operae et cibos ancillis suis **H**

of the household to observe the same lack of familiarity that I prescribe for the women, whom I do not wish to associate too freely with the servants. She should not generally have transactions with them or reprimand them or punish them herself, leaving this duty to her husband. Let her spend time with those of her maidservants and waiting-women who are of upright character and proven chastity. At the same time she will help them by example, admonitions, precepts, incentives and vigilant care so that no aspect of their life is hidden from her and so that she may apply remedies to vice just as antidotes are prescribed for diseases.

118. If one is discovered whose moral integrity is less than acceptable or is believed to be so, and if she does not profit by scolding and correction, she must be dismissed from the house. Poison easily contaminates everything around it and the suspicious crowd believes that servants are like their mistresses. How often do we encounter the saying in Jerome that mistresses are judged by their servants. This is not surprising since according to the Greek proverb 'Even lap-dogs are said to mirror the character of their mistresses.' And those young men in Terence's comedy judge the chastity of the mistress from the squalor and unkemptness of her handmaid. Homer writes that the wise Ulysses on his return home killed those maidservants who had lain with the suitors, because not only had they brought disgrace to the house, but they had endangered the chastity of Penelope. After the defeat of his son Absalom King David sequestered indefinitely those of his concubines whom Absalom had defiled at the instigation of Achitophel, and they were never released from this confinement. The mistress of the household will occupy herself in those skills that we mentioned in the previous book and will keep her servants at their duties, like the chaste Lucretia, whom the king's son and his companions found working with her handmaids and apportioning them their tasks. She will accomplish this duty the more diligently and carefully if part of the household must be supported by this labor.

119. Solomon in his praise of holy women said 'She seeks wool and flax, and works with the diligence and skill of her hands.' When Theano of Metapontum was asked who was the best matron, she answered with a verse of Homer: 'She who plys the loom and attends to her husband's bed.' Through such industry, the wise king continues, 'She has become like a merchant's ship, bringing her bread from afar.' And to show that she did not indulge too much time in sleep he says 'She rose up at night and gave food

---

118. Terence's comedy: In the *Self-Tormentor* the two young men, Clitipho and Clinia, learn from the slave Syrus that Bacchis, Clitipho's mistress, lives a modest life at home in the company of a shabby and ill-kempt little maid, a sign that their mistress is beyond reproach.

119. Theano: Believed to have been the wife or daughter of Pythagoras.

domesticis suis cibum demensum.' Hinc recipiens se cum famulabus, quid cuique faciendum esset praecepit. Sedulae mulieris est cibum quidem toti familiae parare, operam vero solis feminis indicere. Viris indicat, ut videbitur, maritus. De lucubratione mulieris versus sunt apud Vergilium sane quam lepidi atque elegantes:

> Inde ubi prima quies medio iam noctis abactae
> Curriculo expulerat somnum, cum femina primum,
> Cui tolerare colo vitam tenuique Minerva,
> Impositum, cinerem et sopitos suscitat ignes,
> Noctem addens operi famulasque ad lumina longo
> Exercet penso, castum ut servare cubile
> Coniugis et possit parvos educere natos.

Postea vero quam est familiae satisfactum, ex iis quae supersunt largitur ad eleemosynam. 'Manum,' inquit, 'suam aperuit inopi, et palmas suas extendit ad pauperem.'

120. Non debet sancta mulier sic divitiis congerendis incumbere quin pauperibus distribuat et inopibus subveniat, nec tenuiter, sed plena manu, cogitans ad faenus se illa dare in hoc saeculo et in altero multo plura et potiora recepturam. Addit vero: 'Non timebit domui suae a frigoribus nivis.' Nec timebit etiam si pauperibus non solum expressum nummmum inter digitos porrexerit, sed si manum aperuerit et palmam extenderit, quasi copiose elargita nec timebit, quoniam diligentia sua et lanificio nihil domi suae in necessitatibus deest. 'Et omnes domestici eius vestiti sunt duplicibus.' Nihil enim est in re familiari conducibilius quam bene pasci et bene vestiri, non ad voluptatem, sed ad necessitatem; non delicate, sed utiliter. Male tamen continetur virtus quae adversis ex propinquo exemplis sollicitatur. Ideo matrona ipsa primum omnium victu suo parsimoniam doceat, sic facillime curam illius ministris ingeret. Alioqui iniquum existimabunt famuli ac famulae id te exigere quod ipsa non praestes semperque ad custodiam tuorum praeceptorum invitos atque obmurmurantes pertrahes. Tu ipsa igitur semper sicca esto, semper sobria, nec causa tantum famulitii tui quantum tui ipsius. Quam foeda res est ebrietas et ingluvies, maximae oppugnatrices et pudoris et pudicitiae, hostes nominis honesti! Nemo ebriosam et voracem feminam non ceu infaustam et inauspicatam avem abominatur. Omnes inter immodicos cibos periclitari pudicitiam sciunt, cum nullum est capitis et lateris discrimen.

119. (Inde ... natos) *Verg. Aen. 8, 407–413* // (Manum ... pauperem) *Vulg. prov. 31, 20*
120. (Non ... nivis) *Vulg. prov. 31, 21* // (Et omnes ... duplicibus) *Vulg. prov. 31, 21*

1–12 Hinc recipiens ... educere natos Γ *deest in* **H** // **13–14** Postea ... eleemosynam Γ Id cum abunde satis actum est ex iis quae supersunt facit eleemosynam **H** // **23** necessitatibus Γ necessitatibus sive in hiemis usum **H** // **30** atque Γ et **H** // **35**–p.144,1 cum nullum est ... subdit his Salomon Γ *deest in* **H**

in due measure to her servants.' From there she met with her servants and instructed them on what was to be done. It is the job of a diligent wife to prepare the food for the entire household and apportion tasks only for the female servants. The husband will assign work to the male servants, as we shall see. Concerning the night vigils of the woman there are some charming and elegant verses of Virgil:

> When night had run the middle of its course
> And driven sleep away, when first to rise
> The faithful wife, whose task it is to ply
> The distaff and pursue her humble spinning,
> Stirs the ashes of the slumbering fire,
> Adding night to the labors of the day
> And sets her servants to their long day's work
> To keep the nuptial bed inviolate
> And bring her progeny to manhood.

After taking care of the household she dedicates what is left over to almsgiving. 'She has opened her hand to the needy and extended her hands to the poor.'

120. The holy woman should not so devote her energies to the accumulation of wealth that she does not distribute to the poor and come to the aid of the indigent, and that not sparingly but without stint, convinced that she gives this on loan in this world and that she will receive more and better in the next. He adds: 'She will not be afraid of the colds of snow for her household.' She will not be afraid even if in addition to offering a coin to the poor, squeezed from her fingers, she opens and reaches out her hand with generosity. She will not fear since by her diligence and wool-making nothing is lacking to her house in the time of need. 'And all her servants are clothed in double garments.' There is nothing more expedient in domestic affairs than to be fed and clothed well, not for the sake of pleasure, but as needed, not luxuriously, but practically. It is difficult to maintain virtue that is harassed by bad example existing close by. Therefore the mistress of the household will teach frugality first of all by her own life, and thus will more easily inculcate it into her servants. Otherwise they will think that you are requiring of them what you yourself do not exemplify, and you will have to suffer their reluctance and grumbling in the fulfilment of your commands. Therefore you must always be abstemious and sober not solely for the sake of your domestic staff but for your own sake. What a foul thing are drunkenness and gluttony, mortal enemies of modesty and chastity, and inimical to a good name! There is no one who does not abhor a drunken and gluttonous woman as a bird of ill omen. Everyone knows that chastity is in peril when eating is immoderate and there is no longer any distinction between head and groin.

121. Subdit his Salomon: nec relinquit domi suae aliquid sibi incognitum quin subinde inspiciat omniaque cognita sibi et prompta faciat, ne cum usus poscat aut ignoretur quicquam aut nimis sit quaerendum. Tum quis status, quae condicio rei familiaris, quantum expendi, quantum retineri, quomodo pasci, quomodo vestiri conveniat. Ait enim: 'Consideravit semitas domus suae.' Ipsa videlicet in angulo quopiam domus nens aut suens aut texens aliquid denique similis operis obiens in quo liberior est cogitatio, mittet animum suum per cubicula, per arcas, per vestiaria, per quicquid est domi, ut consideret quid desit, quid superfluat, quid emendum, vendendum, sarciendum. Multum haec diligentia rem familiarem tuetur ac sustentat. Aderit puellis operi intentis, sive dum coquunt, sive dum nent, sive dum texunt, sive dum suunt, sive dum supellectilem verrunt. Exactius haec omnia fiunt praesente domina et frugalius. 'Frons occipitio prior est,' ait Cato. Quodque illi prudenter dixerunt, 'Nihil magis vel equum saginare vel arvum uberare quam domini oculum,' ad matrem familias remque domesticam transferri potest: nihil esse quod aut conservet diutius rem domesticam aut integrius, mundius, elegantius quam gnavae et diligentis matronae oculum. Haec agens et labori perpetuo incumbens panem otiosa non comedit et paret Deo, qui non vult nos sine sudore faciei nostrae vesci pane nostro. Exemplum etiam et praeceptum Pauli sequitur, qui inter eos quibus mysterium Domini annuntiabat, tamen otiosus non edebat panem, sed in labore ac fatigatione dies et noctes, quantum ei a divino ministerio vacabat, manus occupabat opificio suo, ne quem gravaret, illud crebro admonens, dignum non esse ut edat qui recusat laborem.

122. Neminem patietur mulier domum ingredi sine mariti iussu, ut ab Aristotele praeceptum est. Multo enim clausior erit domus cum vir peregre aliquo erit profectus; quo tempore, quemadmodum Plautus inquit, bonas mulieres aequum est facere ut absentes viros perinde habeant quasi praesentes. Sed quatenus totius domus cura illa interior mulieri incumbit, tenebit remedia vulgaribus et paene quotidianis morbis eaque in cellula habebit parata quibus marito, parvis liberis et familiae, cum res feret, subveniat,

---

121. (Consideravit ... suae) *Vulg. prov. 31, 27* ∥ (Frons ... est) *Cato agr. 4, 1* ∥ (Nihil ... oculum) *Aristot. oec. 1, 6 (1345b)* ∥ (panem ... comedit) *Vulg. prov. 31, 27* ∥ (in labore ... laborem) *Vulg. II Thess. 3, 10*
122. (Neminem ... iussu) *Aristot. oec. 3, 1* ∥ (bonas ... praesentes) *Plaut. Stich. 99*

3 poscat **Γ** venerit **H** / sit quaerendum **Γ** quaerendum sit **H** ∥ **6–10** Ipsa ... sarciendum **Γ** *deest in* **H** ∥ **10** tuetur ac sustentat **Γ** promovet **H** ∥ **11** operi intentis **Γ** ministrantibus **H** ∥ **13–14** Frons ... Cato **Γ** *deest in* **H** ∥ **14** illi prudenter **Γ** prudentes illi **H** ∥ **16** transferri **Γ** aptari **H** ∥ **17** mundius **Γ** *deest in* **H** ∥ **18** Haec ... incumbens **Γ** Et cum haec egerit operi semper intenta **H** ∥ **20** etiam et **H** etiam **Γ** ∥ **22–23** manus occupabat **Γ** intentus erat **H** ∥ **24** recusat laborem **Γ** laborem recusat **H** ∥ **26–27** peregre ... tempore **Γ** abierit et tamen **H** ∥ **31** res feret **Γ** usus poscet **H**

121. Solomon goes on to say that there is nothing in her house that she does not know, but she regularly looks into everything and knows where everything is, so that when the need arises she will not be at a loss or waste time in looking for some object. She should know the financial status of the household, how much should be spent, how much saved, how to provide for the feeding and clothing of those in her care. Solomon said, 'She has examined every nook and cranny of her house.' That is to say that in whatever corner of the house she finds herself, whether she be spinning, sewing, weaving or employed in some other task in which she can give free rein to her thoughts, she will review in her mind the bedrooms, closets, wardrobes, and every part of the house to discover what is lacking, what is superfluous, what has to be bought, sold or repaired. This kind of attentiveness will protect and maintain family possessions. She will supervise her maidservants at their work, whether they are cooking, spinning, weaving, sewing or sweeping the floor. All these things are done more accurately and more thriftily when the mistress is present. 'The master's face is better than his back' said Cato. And that wise saying, 'Nothing fattens the horse or fertilizes the field so much as the eye of the master' can well be applied to the mistress of the household and the management of domestic affairs. There is nothing that preserves family possessions longer, more intact, cleaner or more orderly than the prudent and watchful eye of the mistress. Doing these things and busying herself with her own work at all times 'She does not eat her bread idly' and obeys God who does not wish that we eat our bread without the sweat of our brow. She also follows the example and precept of St. Paul, who in the midst of those to whom he announced the mystery of the Lord, did not eat his bread in idleness, but in labor and fatigue day and night. For as long as he had time from his divine ministry, he used his hands in the performance of work, so that he would not be a burden to anyone, frequently giving the advice that he who refuses to work does not deserve to eat.

122. A woman will not allow anyone to enter the house without the orders of her husband, as it was enjoined by Aristotle. The house will be kept much more closed when her husband goes away on a long trip, at which time, as Plautus said, it is right that good women should think of their absent husbands as present. And since the care of the inhabitants of the house falls upon the woman, she will keep remedies on hand for common and almost daily maladies and will have them ready in a larder so that she may attend to her husband, small children and the servants when required and will not

---

121. eye of the master: In Spanish the proverb is: 'Ojo del amo engorda el caballo.'

ne arcessere subinde medicum necesse habeat et omnia ex pharmacopolio
emere. Neque vero mulierem velim arti se medicae dedere aut sibi nimis
hac in re fidere. Frequentibus et paene quotidianis morbis suadeo medelas
ut norit, veluti tussi, distillationibus, scabiei, torminibus, solutae alvo vel con-
5   strictae, lumbricis, dolori capitis aut oculorum, febriculae, luxationi, adustioni, levi scissurae et similibus quae singulis prope diebus levissimis de causis contingunt. Adde his victus quotidiani rationem, maximum ad integram
valetudinem momentum, quae sumenda, quae vitanda, quando, quatenus.
Atque eam quidem peritiam discet potius ex usu aliarum prudentium ma-
10   tronarum quam ex consiliis cuiusquam propinqui medici, ex libello aliquo
facili ea de re conscripto quam ex magnis et accuratis medicorum voluminibus.

    123. Sancta mater familias, explicita iam domesticis et familiaribus curis,
eligat sibi quotidie si potest; sin minus festis diebus secretum domi locum a
15   frequentia et strepitu sepositum. Ibi remotis paulisper solicitudinibus domus
et composito animo, reputet ad contemptum res istas mundanas: et quod
leves atque instabiles sunt et quod fragiles ac cito periturae et quod brevitas vitae nostrae it tanta celeritate ut non agi, sed rapi, non abire videatur,
sed fugere. Hinc sustollat se lectione aliqua divina in cogitationem contem-
20   plationemque rerum caelestium. Tum confessa Deo peccata sua, veniam ab
illo et pacem supplex petat oretque pro se primum, hinc Deo iam facta gra-
tior, pro marito, tum pro liberis, deinde reliqua familia, ut Dominus Iesus
meliorem omnibus mentem inspiret. Paulus, divinorum mandatorum nun-
tius, nascentem Corinthi Ecclesiam Dei docens, sic inquit: 'Si quis frater
25   uxorem habet infidelem et haec consentit habitare cum illo, ne dimittat illam; et si qua mulier fidelis habet virum infidelem et hic consentit habitare
cum illa, ne abeat a viro. Sanctificatus est enim vir infidelis per mulierem
fidelem et sanctificata est mulier infidelis per virum fidelem. Unde enim scis,
mulier, si virum salvum facies, aut unde scis, vir, si mulierem salvam facies?'
30   Quod partim ad preces attinet ('Multum enim valet iusti oratio assidua,' ut
inquit Iacobus), partim ad exemplum vitae, quod Petrus apostolus explicat
dicens: 'Similiter et mulieres subditae sint viris suis, ut et si qui non credunt
verbo, per mulierum conversationem sine verbo lucrifiant, considerantes in

---

123. (Si quis ... facies) *Vulg. I Cor. 7, 12–14; 7, 16* // (Multum ... assidua) *Vulg. Iac. 5,
16* // (Similiter ... vestram) *Vulg. I Pet. 3, 1–2* //

1 habeat Γ sit **H** // **2** emere Γ emi **H** // **3** et paene quotidianis Γ *deest in* **H** // **4** distillationibus Γ pituitae **H** / scabiei Γ *deest in* **H** // **5–6** luxationi, adustioni **WW²** *deest in* **H** *om.*
BV // **6** levi scissurae Γ *deest in* **H** // **7** contingunt Γ suboriuntur **H** / Adde his Γ Tum
et **H** // **10** quam Γ aut **H** // **13** iam Γ *deest in* **H** // **15** sepositum Γ separatum **H** // **16**
reputet ad contemptum Γ cogitet ac contemnat **H** // **17–18** brevitas Γ tanta brevitas **H** //
18 it Γ in **H** // **18–19** videatur, sed fugere Γ sed fugere videatur **H** // **29** aut ... facies
Γ *deest in* **H** // **33** mulierum **HWW²B** mulierem **V**

have to send for the doctor often and buy everything from the apothecary. I should not wish that a woman dedicate herself to the art of medicine or have too much confidence in it. I advise her to be familiar with the remedies for frequent and everyday illnesses, like coughs, catarrhs, itching, colic, loose bowels or constipation, intestinal worms, headache or aching eyes, slight fevers, dislocations, burns, slight cuts and similar ailments that occur almost daily for trivial reasons. Add to this the regulation of the daily diet, of greatest importance for the maintenance of good health, what should be consumed, what avoided, when and in what amount. She can learn this skill from the experience of other prudent matrons rather than from the advice of some near-by physician, or some simple handbook on that subject rather than from big, detailed medical tomes.

123. The virtuous woman, when she is free of domestic cares, will choose for herself daily, if possible, but if not, on feast days, a secluded part of the house, apart from the noise and bustling. There, laying aside for a while the worries of the house and recollecting her thoughts, she will meditate on the contempt of these worldly things, since they are frivolous and instable, insubstantial and quick to perish, and on how the brevity of our lives goes by with such speed that it seems not to pass but to be carried along, not to go by, but to flee. Then with the help of some divine reading she will raise herself to the thoughts and contemplation of divine things. Finally, having confessed her sins to God, she will suppliantly beg for pardon and peace from Him and will pray first for herself, then having found more favor with God, for her husband, her children and finally her whole household, so that the Lord Jesus will inspire a better mind in all of them. Paul, the messenger of the divine commands, teaching the nascent Church in Corinth, said: 'If any brother in Christ has a wife who is an unbeliever, and she consents to live with him, he should not divorce her. And if any woman has a husband who is an unbeliever, and he consents to live with her, she should not leave him. For the unbelieving husband is sanctified through the believing wife and the unbelieving wife is sanctified through the believing husband.' Wife, how do you know whether you will save your husband, or husband, how do you know whether you will save your wife? It is accomplished partly by prayer ('The assiduous prayer of the just man has much efficacy' says St. James), and partly by example of life, which the Apostle Peter explains, saying: 'Likewise let wives be subject to their husbands, so that if there are some who do not believe in the word, they may be won without a word through

timore sancto conversationem vestram.' Multas legimus feminas Christianas
quarum opera ad sanctam pietatem mariti sunt adducti, ut a Domitia Flavius Clemens e Domitiani Caesaris propinquis, a Clotilde Clodoveus, Fran-
ciae Rex, a Ingulde Hermogillus Gothorum Rex, ab aliis alii quam plurimi.

5   CAP. X.   DE LIBERIS ET QUAE CIRCA ILLOS CURA

124. Principio, si non paris, id non solum moderato perfer animo et aequo,
sed aliquatenus etiam gaude, quod incredibilis molestiae ac taedii facta sis
expers. Non est hic explicandi locus quae miseriae subeundae sint praeg-
nanti dum gestat uterum, qui dolores, quantum periculum cum enititur. Iam
10   nutriendi et educandi quae fastidia, quanta sollicitudo ne improbi et flagitiosi evadant liberi, ne quid eis adversi accidat! Quam aeternus metus quo
eunt, quid agunt, malum ne faciant neu accipiant! Equidem rationem ex-
pedire nequeo istius cupiditatis filiorum. Vis mater fieri? Quorsum? An ut
mundum augeas? Quasi vero infrequens futurus sit, nisi ipsa unum atque
15   alterum animalculum pepereris et addideris messibus Siculis et Aegyptiis
unam spiculam, ad summum duas, et ceu Deus nesciat, si velit, ex lapidibus
istis filios excitare Abrahae. Ne sis in Dei domo sollicita unde replebitur; ipse
suae domui prospiciet.
     125. At sterilitatis probrum exhorres. Illud vero cum lege Mosaica eva-
20   nuit iam ad fulgorem gratiae Christi. Nunc in lege vivis in qua etiam virginitatem connubio praeferri merito vides. Quid quod per Isaiam Dominus
pollicetur sterilibus sanctis multo ampliorem atque honestiorem locum in
sua civitate quam si numerosam reliquissent sobolem? Itaque vituperanda
est illa in Flandria quae cum nupta prope ad quinquagesimum annum sine
25   fetu vixisset, defuncto viro nupsit alteri, id solum praetendens ut experiretur

123. (Domitia ... propinquis) *Suet. Dom. 16* // (Clotilde) *Greg. Turon. hist. Franc. 2, 29–31*
// (Ingulde) *Paul. diac. hist. Lang. 3, 10; Greg. Magn. dial. 3, 31*
     124. (ex lapidibus ... Abrahae) *Vulg. Matth. 3, 9; Luc. 3, 8*
     125. (Dominus ... civitate) *Vulg. Is. 54, 1* //

1 Multas Γ Quam multas **H** // **4** Ingulde **H** Iugulde Γ // **9** dolores Γ dolor **H** // **10–11**
improbi ... evadant Γ mali sint **H** // **13–14** Quorsum ... augeas Γ Ad quid, ut repleas
mundum? **H** // **14** infrequens futurus sit Γ plenus futurus non sit **H** // **16** spiculam Γ
spicam **H** // **18** prospiciet Γ prospiciet nec sinet esse vacuam et infrequentem **H** // **19**
probrum Γ crimen **H** // **19–24** Illud vero ... Itaque vituperanda est illa Γ Christiana,
scito illud praeteriisse iam: 'Maledicta mulier sterilis in Israel.' Nunc in lege vivis in qua etiam
virginitatem connubio praeferri merito vides et audis a Domino tuo: 'Vae praegnantibus et
iis quae pepererint illis diebus;' 'Beatae steriles et ventres qui non genuerunt et ubera quae
non lactaverunt.' Qui sis (*legendum* scis) an te unam ex illis beatis esse voluerit? Quanto illa
turpius **H** // **24–25** sine fetu Γ sine fetu ullo **H** // **25** nupsit alteri Γ alteri nupsit **H** / id
solum praetendens Γ praetendens tantum **H**

the behavior of their wives, seeing your behavior in holy fear.' We read of many Christian women who by their works led their husbands to the practice of religion, like Flavius Clemens, a close relative of the Emperor Domitian, by Domitia; Clovis, King of France, by Clotild; and Hermenegild, King of the Goths, by Ingund, and many others by other women.

CHAPTER 10.   ON CHILDREN AND THE CARE THAT
MUST BE TAKEN OF THEM

124. In the first place, if you bear no children, suffer it with resignation and an even mind, and to a certain degree, even with joy because you have been exempted from an incredible burden and fatigue. This is not the place to give an account of the miseries the pregnant woman must undergo during the period of gestation, what pain and what danger when she brings forth, and later in nourishing and bringing up her children what troubles and anxiety that they may turn out wicked and unprincipled, or that some misfortune may befall them! What unending fear about where they are going, what they are doing, that they may do evil or suffer some evil! For my part, I cannot understand the reason for this ardent desire for children. Do you want to be a mother? For what reason? To increase the world's population? As if it would be sparsely populated unless you brought forth one or more little creatures and added one ear of wheat or at most two to the harvests of Sicily and Egypt. As if God did not know how to raise up children to Abraham from these stones, if he so wished. Do not be worried about the house of God being filled. He will see to his house.

125. But you dread the stigma of sterility. That vanished with the law of Moses in the radiance of the grace of Christ. Now you live under a law in which you see that virginity is deservedly preferred to marriage. What of the fact that through Isaias the Lord promises to saintly sterile women a much larger and more honorable place in his city than if they had left numerous progeny? And so that woman in Flanders should be criticized who was married until her fiftieth year without any offspring, and when her husband died, married another man with this sole purpose, to find out whose

---

123. Domitia: Usually known as Flavia Domitilla, she was the wife of Flavius Clemens, cousin of the emperor Domitian. She was banished to the island of Ponza near Naples in 96 AD because of her Christian faith.

    Clotild: She implored her husband for many years to become a Christian but he did so only after he won a battle over the Alamanni after calling upon the name of Christ.

    Hermenegild: Made King of the Visigoths in 580, Hermenegild was brought up as an Arian but was converted to orthodox Christianity by his wife Ingund, daughter of Sigebert I.

in utro, quod liberos non haberent, fuisset culpa, in se an in viro. Digna
profecto cupiditas muliere vetula, sed delira. Quamquam nescio an alia erat
secundarum nuptiarum causa. Ipsa illam obtendebat quae ad stultam multitudinem honestior videbatur. Nec illi laetum admodum fuit connubium,
5   nam filium peperit qualem nulla habere vellet. At videre cupis liberos ex te
natos. Num alii erunt quam ceteri?Habes pueros civitatis, immo baptizatos
omnes, quos materno affectu complectaris et credas ex te genitos. Hoc humanitas suadet, religio praecipit. Quid quod maritus tibi, si sit probus, instar
est multorum filiorum, ut Helcana dixit Annae suae: 'De filiis es sollicita et
10 in marito non acquiescis, qui unus plus te amat quam decem filii amarent
abs te geniti?' Profecto feminae non modo gravidae, sed vacuae quoque, immoderatis illis et absurdis appetitibus infestamini, quae picationes dicuntur.
'Quae liberorum miseris tam dira libido?' ut inquit ille. Si sollicitudines et
aerumnae, quas matribus filii pariunt, in tabella vobis depingerentur, nulla
15 esset sic avida filiorum mulier, quae non mortis instar filios expavesceret;
et quae haberet, etiam suos plus odisset quam immanes feras aut serpentes
venenosos.

126. Quod gaudium, quid laetabile est in filiis? Cum sunt pueri, merum
odium; in grandiusculis, sempiternus metus quo inclinabunt; si mali, aeter-
20 nus maeror; si boni, perpetua sollicitudo ne moriantur, ne quid eis accidat,
ne abeant, ne mutentur. Quid opus est Octaviam, Augusti sororem, huc
adducam? Utinam non essent adeo crebra exempla illarum quae ex laetis-
simis matribus subito afflictae in perpetuo luctu contabuerunt et exstinctae
sunt. Quid quod si multos habeas, maior anxietas et unius vitia gaudium
25 quod de reliquis suscipiebas non diluunt modo, sed delent. Et dixi de maribus. In feminis custodiendis quae carnificina anxietatis, in collocandis quae
moles curarum? His accedit quod parentes raro vident filios bonos. Vera
enim bonitas sapientia comitata non nisi in graviore iam et prope exacta
aetate contingit. 'Cum incipimus sapere, tum morimur,' dixit quidam. Et

125. (De ... geniti) *Vulg. I reg. 1, 8* // (Quae ... libido) *Verg. Aen. 6, 721*
126. (Cum ... morimur) *Sen. epist. 23, 10* //

1 liberos non haberent Γ non peperisset **H** // **1–2** Digna ... delira Γ Digna mulier quae
ferret maximo cum fastidio ac labore uterum et parturiens summo cum cruciatu animam
eiceret **H** // **4–5** Nec illi laetum ... vellet Γ *deest in* **H** // **5** liberos Γ filios **H** // **6** Num
Γ An **H** / ceteri Γ ceteri pueri **H** // **8–11** Quid ... geniti Γ *deest in* **H** // **11** quoque Γ
deest in **H** // **11–12** immoderatis ... dicuntur Γ immoderatos illos et absurdos appetitus
habetis **H** // **13** miseris **HWW²B** miserae **V** / ut inquit ille Γ *deest in* **H** // **15** sic Γ tam **H**
/ mortis instar Γ ut mortem ita **H** // **18** quid laetabile Γ quae iucunditas **H** / in **H** *om.* Γ
// **19** odium **HWW²B** otium **V** // **24** vitia Γ scelera **H** // **25** suscipiebas **H** suspiciebas Γ
/ non ... sed Γ *deest in* **H** // **28** iam ... exacta Γ *deest in* **H** // **29** Cum ... quidam Γ
deest in **H**

fault it was, hers or her husband's, that they had no children. This desire was worthy of an old woman, but one who had lost her senses. And yet I don't know if there was any other reason for a second marriage. She gave that as her reason, since it seemed more honorable to the ignorant crowd. But the marriage did not bring her much happiness, for she bore a son the like of which no woman would wish to have. But you wish to see children born of you. Will they be any different from the rest? You have children of the city, all of them baptized, whom you may embrace with maternal affection and think they were born of you. The law of mankind recommends this, religion commands it. And besides, your husband, if he is a good man, is the equivalent of many children, as Elkanah said to his wife, Hannah: 'You are concerned about having children and you do not find tranquility in your husband, who loves you more than ten children that might be born to you.' Indeed, women, whether you be pregnant or empty, you are victims of those immoderate and absurd appetites that are called 'cravings'. 'What terrible desire for children has invaded these unhappy souls' as the poet said. If the troubles and afflictions that children cause for their mothers were painted for you on a panel, there would be no woman so eager for children who would not fear them like death, or one who already had them who would not hate them like ferocious animals or venomous serpents.

126. What joy, what reason for rejoicing is there in children? While they are small, it is nothing but tediousness; when they are a little older, there is continual fear of what direction they will take; if they turn out bad, everlasting grief; if good, you are constantly preoccupied that they may die, that something will happen to them, that they may go away or change. What need is there to adduce the example of Octavia, the sister of Augustus? Would that there were not so many examples of those women, who from the happiest of mothers were suddenly stricken with affliction, wasted away in unceasing grief and died. Then, if you have many children, there is greater anxiety and the vices of one not only diminish but destroy the joy you received from the others. I have been speaking of male children. In watching over daughters what torture and anxiety! What a host of cares in finding matches for them! Furthermore, parents rarely see their children behaving properly, for true goodness, accompanied by wisdom, comes only at a more mature age and almost at the end of one's life. 'When we begin

125. 'cravings': Vives uses the medieval Latin word *picationes*. The medical term *picae* is still used for the nutritional cravings that sometimes occur during pregnancy.

126. Octavia: The classical example of a misfortunate woman. After the death of her husband, her son Marcellus, destined to succeed Augustus, died at the age of nineteen. She never ceased her mourning, retired from the world and forbade any mention of her son in her presence, according to Seneca. She later suffered the repudiation of her second husband, Marc Antony, but brought up all his surviving children by Fulvia and Cleopatra.

Plato beatum illum esse ait cui vel in senectute datur recte et sapere et vitam
instituere. At ea filiorum aetate iam parentes in pulverem abierunt. Quid
quod paucissimi omnino filii gratiam parentibus vel referunt vel habent pro
tot aerumnis? Immo negligunt eos a quibus tanta sunt cura enutriti; oderunt
5 eos a quibus sunt tenerius dilecti quam ipsi a sese. Habiti sunt a parentibus
blande atque indulgenter, ipsi eos graviter et aspere accipiunt.

127. O ingrata mulier, quae non agnoscis quantum a Deo acceperis beneficium quod vel non pepereris vel filios ante maerorem amiseris! Ut scitissime Euripides dixerit carentem liberis infortunio felicem esse. Sed haec
10 potuissent a nobis plurimis verbis extendi, nisi quod hoc utique loco minime
essent necessaria. Quae ergo non paris, vide ne in maritum reicias sterilitatis tuae culpam; in te forsan est vitium, quae es vel natura vel Dei voluntate sterilitatis damnata. Inter maximos philosophos constare video feminas fetus non gignere suo saepius quam virorum vitio. Paucos viros steriles
15 genuit natura, feminas plurimas; sapientissimo consilio, quod in virili infe-
cunditate maius est damnum quam in feminea. Plus enim ex viro proventus est in generando quam ex femina. Quod si in te infecunditas est, mulier,
frustra insanis; quantumcumque scelerum animo concipias numquam fetum
concipies utero. Quid quod Dei privatis consiliis, aequissimis illis quidem,
20 sed nobis ignoratis, plerumque nulla ex coniugio provenit soboles? Nam
Dei munus est ut bonos liberos, ita liberos omnino provenire; idcirco ad
alia remedia accurrere quam ad Deum supervacaneum est. A Deo petenda
est proles et bona proles, nam si proles contingat mala, praestaret viperam
peperisse vel lupum.

25 **128.** Sic ergo roga filium, ut Anna Helcanae uxor, quae precibus et lacrimis et sanctitate vitae impetravit non filium modo, sed prophetam et iudicem in Israel. Sic ut altera Anna Ioachim, quae tota Deo confisa Mariam
orbis Reginam saluti hominum edidit. Sic ut Elizabetha Zachariae, quae
etiam sterilis Ioannem illum Domini nuntium genuit, qui multos filios genuit
30 Christo, quo maior nullus ex muliere natus est. Dominus Sarae sterilitatem

---

126. (beatum ... instituere) *Plat. rep. 331A*
127. (carentem ... esse) *Eur. Med. 1092*
128. (Anna ... Israel) *Vulg. I reg. 1, 11* // (Elizabeta ... natus est) *Vulg. Luc. 7, 28* //
(Dominus ... Isaac) *Vulg. gen. 17, 5* //

1 ait Γ dixit **H** // 2 instituere Γ agere **H** // 2–6 Quid quod paucissimi ... aspere accipiunt Γ *deest in* **H** // 8–9 scitissime Γ non immerito **H** // 10 utique loco Γ tempore **H** // 15
quod Γ quo **H** / virili Γ viri **H** // 16 maius est damnum Γ maior iactura **H** // 17–18 frustra insanis Γ insanis scelesta. Nullus te umquam implebit vir **H** // 18–19 quantumque ...
utero Γ itaque conceptis multis animo nefariis facinoribus ne unum quidem fetum concipere
utero poteris **H** // 22 Deum supervacaneum Γ preces supervacaneum et impium **H** // 25
roga Γ posce **H** // 27 Israel Γ Israel, Samuele **H**

to be wise, we die,' said a certain sage. And Plato said: 'Happy is the man to whom it is given to achieve wisdom and to order his life aright even in old age.' But when children have reached that age, their parents have returned to dust. What of the fact that very few children show or even feel gratitude to their parents for all their troubles? On the contrary they neglect those by whom they were brought up with so much care. They hate those from whom they received more tender love than they had for themselves. They were treated kindly and indulgently by their parents and they show harshness and surliness in return.

127. O ungrateful woman, that you do not recognize how great a benefit you have received from God in not having borne children or having lost them before they brought you grief. How appositely Euripides put it: 'She who lacks children is happy in her misfortune.' I could have expounded on this subject more copiously, except it is not necessary at this point. If you do not bear children, be careful that you do not cast the blame on your husband. Perhaps the defect lies in you because you were condemned to sterility either by nature or by the will of God. I see in the writings of the greatest philosophers a consensus that women fail to bear offspring more through their own deficiency than through that of their husbands. Nature produced few sterile men, but many women, according to a wise plan of creation, because male sterility is a greater loss than female, since the power of propagation lies more in the man than in the woman. But if you are cursed with infecundity, my dear woman, it is useless to behave like a madwoman. Whatever wicked deeds you may conceive in your mind, you will never conceive offspring in your womb. Oftentimes through the secret designs of God, just in themselves but unknown to us, there is no offspring in a marriage. For it is a gift of God that good children or any children at all are forthcoming. Therefore it is a waste of time to have recourse to any other remedies than to God. We must ask for offspring, and good offspring, from God, for if you produce bad offspring, it would be better to have given birth to a viper or a wolf.

128. Therefore, ask for a son as did Hannah, the wife of Elkanah, who by her prayers, tears and sanctity of life was granted not only a son, but a prophet and judge of Israel. Or imitate the other Anna, wife of Joachim, who, placing her whole trust in God, gave birth to Mary, Queen of the world, for the salvation of mankind. Or Elizabeth, wife of Zachary, who though sterile gave birth to John, precursor of the Lord, who brought forth many children for Christ, the greatest man ever born to woman. To Sarah,

---

128. Anna: The parents of the Blessed Virgin are never mentioned in the Sacred Scriptures but the names of Anna and Joachim and various events in the early life of Mary are recorded in the apocryphal gospel, *Protoevangelium Iacobi*, widely circulated in the early centuries of Christianity.

suam non inique ferenti eo tempore quo sterilitas magno probro habebatur
filium in senectute dedit, Isaac, imaginem Christi Domini. Et hic ipse Isaac
pro Rebecca coniuge sua sterili Dominum oravit, a quo impetravit geminos duorum ingentium populorum auctores. Uxori Manne sterili, modestae
ac pudicae feminae, Angelus Domini Samsonem ex ea nasciturum nunti-
avit, iudicem et liberatorem Israelis. Tales accipiunt quae sic petunt. Verba
Angeli ad Samsonis matrem sunt haec: 'Sterilis es et absque liberis, sed concipies et paries filium. Cave ergo ne bibas vinum ac siceram nec immundum
quicquam comedas, quia concipies et paries filium cuius non tanget caput
novacula. Erit enim Nazaraeus Dei ab infantia sua et ex matris utero, et ipse
incipiet liberare Israel de manu Philistinorum.'

129. Haec admonent me ut ipse praegnantes admoneam, interea dum
uterum gestant ne indulgeant crapulae ne inebrientur. Multi quae a matribus acta sunt dum gestabantur vitae totius moribus rettulere. Et quatenus
imaginationis vires magnae ac validae sunt in humano corpore, matres dum
uterum gestant dent operam ne quam admittant vehementem cogitationem
deformis rei, turpis, obscenae. Pericula item devitent in quibus foeda aliqua
visu species possit occurrere. Quod si eas occasiones adeant, praecogitent
quicquid possit oculis offerri, ne ex inopinata novitate noceat si quid subito
aspexerint, unde contrahat noxam fetus.

130. Iam susceptis liberis, quae adhibenda in his educandis cura maius esset disserere quam ut capi proposito posset opere, si fusius essent singula ex-
promenda. Qua de re a veteribus et a recentioribus conscripta sunt plurima
etiam dicatis in id ipsum libris. Ego vero pauca attingam quae muneris videantur esse prudentis matronae. Ante omnia mater thesauros suos universos in liberis sitos esse ducet. Opulenta quaedam Campana cum Romam
venisset exceptaque esset hospitio a Cornelia Gracchi, mundum omnem
suum muliebrem Corneliae explicuit, qui erat sane dives metallis, vestibus,
gemmis. Eum ubi laudasset Cornelia, rogavit Campana ut et vicissim illa
cimeliarchium suum aperire haudquaquam gravaretur. Abierant Gracchuli
ad ludum litterarium. Respondit se sub vesperum facturam. Pueris reversis,

128. (Isaac ... auctores) *Vulg. gen. 25, 21–22* // (Sterilis ... Philistinorum) *Vulg. iud. 13,*
3–5
    130. (Opulenta ... thesauri) *Val. Max. 4, 4*

2–4 hic ipse ... geminos Γ *deest in* **H** // **4** Manne **HWW²B** Manue **V** // **6** petunt Γ petunt.
Nam ex sceleribus concepti quid possunt esse nisi mera scelera **H** // **13** indulgeant crapulae
Γ crapulae indulgeant **H** // **14–20** Et quatenus ... contrahat noxam fetus Γ *deest in* **H** //
24 vero Γ *deest in* **H** // **27–28** mundum ... muliebrem Γ thesauros suos **H** // **28** erat sane
dives Γ erant sane divites **H** // **29** gemmis Γ et gemmis **H** / Eum ubi Γ Quos cum **H** / vicissim illa Γ illa vicissim **H** // **30** cimeliarchium suum Γ suos **H** / haudquaquam Γ non **H** //
30–31 Abierant ... litterarium Γ Non erant filii domi, nam ierant ad ludum litterarium **H**

who endured her sterility with even mind at a time when sterility was regarded as a great disgrace, the Lord gave a son in her old age, Isaac, the
image of Christ. And this same Isaac prayed to the Lord for his barren wife
Rebecca and obtained from him two champions of two mighty peoples. To
the sterile wife of Manoah, a modest and chaste woman, the angel of the
Lord announced that Samson would be born, judge and liberator of Israel.
That is what is given to those who ask in this way. The words of the angel to
the mother of Samson are these: 'You are barren and without children, but
you will conceive and bear a son. Beware that you drink no wine or strong
drink and eat nothing unclean for you will conceive and bear a son whose
head no razor will touch. For he shall be a Nazarite of God from birth and
from his mother's womb and he shall begin to liberate Israel from the hand
of the Philistines.'

129. These words remind me to warn those that are pregnant that as
long as they are carrying their child they do not indulge in excessive drinking and drunkenness. Many children have inherited for a whole life time
the vices their mothers engaged in during the period of gestation. And since
the power of the imagination is incalculable in the human body, pregnant
mothers should take care not to entertain violent thoughts of anything mon-
strous, foul or obscene. Let them avoid any dangerous occasions in which
some ugly sight may come before their eyes. And if they are exposed to such
dangers, let them think beforehand of what they may encounter so that no
harm may befall the child in their womb from some unexpected sight.

130. Once the children have been born, the discussion of the care that
must be devoted to their upbringing would go beyond the limits that I proposed for myself in this work, if I were to examine each aspect singly in
any detail. On this subject many things have been written by ancient and
modern writers in entire books dedicated to that study. I shall touch upon
a few things that seem to me to be the duty of a wise matron. Above all,
a mother shall consider that all her treasure lies in her children. A certain
wealthy woman from Campania came to Rome and was welcomed into the
home of Cornelia, the wife of Gracchus, and she spread out all her feminine adornments, for she was rich in precious metals, wardrobe and jew-
elry. When Cornelia had congratulated her on her splendor, the Campanian
woman asked if Cornelia would mind showing her her precious jewels. The
two young Gracchi had gone off to school. She answered that she would
do so in the evening. When the children returned, she said: 'These are my

'Hi mihi unici thesauri,' inquit. Cum Ionica Lacaenae de textura gloriaretur
operosa et sumptuosa, haec respondit, 'Atqui mihi quattuor filii omni virtute
praediti textura et pretium et opes sunt.' Quocirca in hoc thesauro conser-
vando atque excolendo nullus recusandus est labor. Omnia facilia reddet
caritas et levia.

131. Nutriet, si poterit, suo lacte et parebit naturae voci, quae tributis
mammis et copioso puerperis lacte clamare videtur ac iubere, 'Nutriat
quae peperit, ut cetera agunt animalia.' Quin sapiens et benigna rerum
omnium parens quem sanguinem in corpusculum fetus in utero vertebat,
eum post partum ad pectus, tamquam copiosi cuiusdam et salubris fontis
craterem transmittit in lac candefactum, ut sit unde partus sustentetur, nec
deserit tenerum ex utero emissum quin eodem pastu alat quo finxerat.
Haud parva sane mercede a natura ipsa nutrienti pro opera tributa et
tamquam relata gratia quod fetum ipsius nutriat, ut saniora sint corpora
illarum quae hoc faciunt, cum eae quae nutriendi laborem recusant inter
lacteum humorem exsiccandum multum adeant periculi. Accedit his quod
utilius est fetui maternum lac quam nutricis; tum quia ex quibus constamus,
ex eisdem congruentissime alimur nihilque est convenientius infanti quam
ea ipsa substantia ex qua est fictus; tum quia nutrix non raro alumnum
suum admovet pectori invita et subirata; mater contra alacris semper ac
laeta vel ipso pueri sui conspectu; si quid erat in animo nubili, exhilarata,
gaudens ridensque eo magis quo avidius illum haurire contemplatur. Quod
si coepit iam ridere aut balbutire, incredibili alacritate ac laetitia perfunditur,
unde quantum salubritatis lac trahat credi non posset, hoc non in humano
tantum genere, sed per animantes omnes generale est naturae beneficium.
De canibus (ut unum pro omnibus exemplum ponam) sic scribit Columella:
'Nec umquam eos quorum generosam volumus indolem conservare patiemur
alienae nutricis uberibus educari, quoniam semper et lac et spiritus maternus
longe magis ingenii atque incrementa corporis auget.' Sunt tamen quas iustae
causae excusant. Itaque nolumus videri sine exceptione praecepisse et hac
de re locutus sum volumine superiore.

132. Si litteras mater sciat, ipsa parvulos pueros eas doceat, ut eadem
utantur matre, nutrice, et magistra magisque ament et promptius discant,
adiuvante amore in eam quae docet. Puellas praeter litteras artibus etiam

130. (Cum Ionica ... sunt) *Plut. mor. 241D*
131. (Sapiens ... finxerat) *Gell. 12, 1, 13* // (Nec ... auget) *Colum. 7, 12, 12* //
(volumine superiore) *inst. fem. Christ. 1, 8–9*

1 de Γ *deest in* **H** // **2** respondit ... mihi Γ inquit mihi vero **H** // **6** naturae voci Γ voci
naturae **H** // **10** pectus Γ mammas **H** // **10–11** tamquam ... craterem Γ *deest in* **H** //
11 partus Γ ille **H** // **12** finxerat Γ finxit **H** // **13–30** Haud parva ... sine exceptione
praecepisse Γ *deest in* **H** // **31** locutus sum volumine Γ dixi libro **H** // **32** Si Γ Deinde
si **H** // **34** eam quae Γ eum qui **H**

only treasures.' When an Ionian woman was boasting to a Spartan woman about a woven fabric, richly and artfully made, the latter replied 'But I have four sons endowed with every virtue and they are my fabric and prize and wealth.' Therefore in preserving and caring for this treasure no effort should be spared. Love will render everything easy and light.

131. She will nurse them with her own milk if she can and hearken to the voice of nature, which gave her breasts and a supply of milk for the newly-born and seems to cry out: 'Let her nurse what she has borne as other living things do.' The wise and generous parent of all things that supplied blood for the formation of the foetus in the womb transfers it after birth into the white milk of the breasts, which are like a reservoir of abundant and whole-some nourishment for the sustenance of the child. She does not forsake the tender offspring that has issued from her womb but nourishes it with the same food with which she created it. Nature returns no small thanks to the nurturer for her contribution and compensates her by giving her a more healthy body for cooperating in the work of nature, while those who refuse this hardship of nursing run great risks in drying up their milk. Moreover, a mother's milk is more beneficial to the child than that of a wet-nurse. Since it is most fitting that we are nourished from the same source from which we are made, there is nothing more adapted to the infant than that same substance from which it is formed. Besides, it is not uncommon that the wet-nurse suckles the child reluctantly and with some feeling of annoyance whereas the mother is always willing and happy and the very sight of her child dispels any clouds of sadness and with gladness and cheerfulness she smiles happily to see her child sucking eagerly at her breast. And if it begins to laugh or lisp, she is filled with incredible enthusiasm and happiness. It is unbelievable what advantages to health are procured from a mother's milk, not only in the human race but in the realm of all living things. Concerning dogs, to give one example of many, Columella writes: 'We will never allow pups to be nourished by another mother, if we wish them to retain their su-perior breeding, since a mother's milk and spirit foster their physical growth and their temperament.' There are some, however, who have good reason to be exempted. I do not wish to make prescriptions without exception and I have spoken of this matter in the previous volume.

132. If the mother knows literature, she should teach her children when they are small so that they have the same person as mother, nurse and teacher and love her more and learn more readily with the help of the love they have for their teacher. As for her daughters, in addition to letters she

---

131. Columella: a writer born in Cadiz, Spain, fl. 50 AD. His work, *De re rustica*, is the most comprehensive treatise on agriculture that remains to us from ancient Rome.

instituet muliebribus, lanam et linum tractare, nere, texere, suere, rem domesticam colere et administrare. Non erit piae matri molestum vel litteris
interdum dare operam vel lectioni sapientum et sanctorum librorum, si non
sua, certe liberorum gratia, ut erudiat, ut meliores reddat. Eurydice iam
natu grandior litteris se et praeceptis morum tradidit, tantum ut haec in
filios transfunderet, quod et fecit. Infans enim primam audit matrem, primam balbutiem ad illius sermonem conatur effingere, ut illa aetas nihil aliud
quam imitatur et in hoc solum dextera est. Primos sensus primamque mentis
informationem ex iis sumit quae de matre vel audit vel videt. Itaque plus est
in matre ad effingendos puerorum mores positum quam quis putet. Illa vel
optimum facere potest vel pessimum. Ut optimum faciat, paucula praecepta
in brevia conferemus. Det operam ne saltem filiorum causa rustice loquatur,
ne idem sermo in teneris puerorum animis infixus simul adolescat cum aetate et ubi invaluerit, dediscere vix possint. Nullum sermonem melius aut
tenacius discunt pueri, nullum expressius quam maternum. Illum cum vitiis
ipsis aut virtutibus, si quid horum habet, reddunt.

133. In Valentiam meam a Iacobo Aragoniae Rege ex Agarenorum impuritate vindicatam (quo nomine fausta est nobis semper illius viri memoria), in
eam ergo his pulsis immigrare iussi sunt frequentes viri Aragonii et mulieres
Ilerdenses a quibus incoleretur. Ex utrisque nati filii sermonem matrum
tenuerunt, eumque iam per plures quam ducentos et quinquaginta annos
loquimur. Tiberii et Caii Gracchi eloquentissimi sunt habiti, at horum linguam mater Cornelia formavit, cuius prisco saeculo lectae sunt epistolae
eloquentiae plenissimae. Istrina, Scytharum Regina, Aripithis uxor, ipsa
Sylem filium Graecis litteris instituit. Nutrices vetat Plato inanes aut aniles
fabulas pueris suis narrare. Idem praecipiendum matribus; hinc enim fit ut
quidam ex prima illa educatione in grandiorem aetatem vel teneros vel frac-
tos et pueriles animos referant, ut nihil grave ac prudens audire et sustinere
queant, sed tantum libros ineptissimarum fabularum sectentur, qui nec
veri quicquam narrant nec verisimile. Habebunt igitur ad manum parentes

---

132. (Eurydice ... fecit) *Plut. mor. 14B*
133. (Tiberii ... plenissimae) *Cic. Brut. 211* // (Istrina ... instituit) *Hdt. 4, 78* //
(Nutrices ... narrare) *Plat. rep. 377C*

14–15 aut tenacius Γ *deest in* **H** // **15** Illum Γ *deest in* **H** // **17–18** impuritate vindicatam Γ
manibus extortam **H** // **18–19** quo nomine ... in eam ergo Γ *deest in* **H** // **19** immigrare Γ
migrare **H** // **21** eumque **HWW²** eum quem **BV** // **24** Aripithis **H** Ariphitis Γ Ariapithes
Hdt. // **25** Nutrices vetat Γ Praecipit nutricibus **H** // **25–26** inanes ... narrare Γ ne
inanes aut aniles fabulas pueris suis narrent **H** // **26** praecipiendum matribus Γ matribus
dicendum **H** // **28** et pueriles Γ *deest in* **H** / ut nihil Γ nihil ut **H** // **29** sed Γ *deest in* **H**
/ ineptissimarum Γ ineptissimos **H** / sectentur Γ sectantur **H**

will instruct them in the skills proper to their sex: how to work wool and flax, to spin, to weave, to sew, and the care and administration of domestic affairs. A pious mother will not think it a burden to consecrate some moments of leisure to literature or to the reading of wise and holy books, if not for her own sake, at least for the sake of her children, so that she may teach them and make them better. When Eurydice reached a certain age, she devoted herself to literature and moral teachings solely so that she might pass this on to her children, which she did. The infant hears its mother first, and tries to imitate her speech in its first stammerings, since that age can do nothing but imitate and is skillful only in this. Its first sense perceptions and first information of the mind it takes from what it hears or sees from the mother. Therefore much more depends on the mother in the formation of the children's character than one would think. She can make them either very good or very bad. I will give a few precepts in brief on how to make them good. Let her take care not to speak in an uncouth manner, at least for the sake of her children, lest that type of speech remain fixed in the tender minds of children and increase with age, and be hard to unlearn once it has taken root. Children learn no speech better or more retentively than that learned from their mother. They reproduce it with whatever defects and virtues it may have.

133. When James, King of Aragon, had freed my city of Valencia from the defilement of the Moors (for which his memory will be forever blessed), he had many men from Aragon and women from Lérida immigrate to this city to repopulate it. The children born from these matches retained the language of their mothers, which is what we have been speaking for two hundred and fifty years. Tiberius and Gaius Gracchus were regarded as very eloquent speakers and their language was formed by their mother Cornelia, whose letters, filled with eloquence, were read in earlier times. The Istrian woman, Queen of the Scythians, wife of Ariapithes, personally taught her son Scyles Greek. Plato forbids nurses from telling idle old wive's tales to their charges. The same should be prescribed for mothers, for it is from this source that some children from this early upbringing still retain childish and capricious minds in later years and cannot bear to hear serious and sensible discourse, preferring books of foolish tales that do not contain a particle of truth or anything that resembles it. Parents therefore will have on hand

---

132. Eurydice: Not the mythical Eurydice, wife of Orpheus, but a woman of Illyria married to Pollianus, to whom Plutarch dedicates his *Coniugalia praecepta* (*Advice to Bride and Groom*), one of Vives' chief sources.

133. James: Jaime I, King of Aragon, liberated the city of Valencia from the Moors on 9 October 1238.

Moors: Vives uses the term Arageni, a medieval Latin word that signifies descendants of Hagar and Ishmael.

letters: Cicero expresssed his admiration for them in his rhetorical treatise, *Brutus*.

iucundas quasdam historiolas et honestas fabulas, quae ad commendationem
virtutum, ad vitiorum odium tendant. Illas primum audiet puer et cum nondum quid vitium sit, quid virtus intelliget, has tamen amare incipiet, illa
odisse. Simul cum his affectionibus adolescet ac se similem conabitur effin-
5   gere eorum quos mater recte fecisse confirmabit, dissimilem eorum quos
prave. Addet mater laudes virtutum, detestationes vitiorum, utrasque crebro repetat et inculcet rudibus animis. Habeat familiaria sancta quaedam
dicta et vitae formulas, quae frequenter audita puerorum memoriae vel aliud agentium inhaerescant.

10   **134.** Accurrunt ad matrem pueri, de omnibus eam consulunt, omnia ex
ea percontantur, quaecumque responderit credunt, mirantur, habent pro
compertissimis. O matres, quanta occasio vel optimos reddendi filios vel pes-
simos! Hinc infundendae sunt rectissimae opiniones et purae Christianae.
Opes, potentiam, honorem, gloriam, nobilitatem, formam res esse vanas,
15   stultas, contemnendas; iustitiam vero, pietatem, fortitudinem, continentiam,
eruditionem, clementiam, misericordiam, caritatem generis humani: haec
demum pulchra, haec admiranda, haec sectanda, haec fidelia et solida esse
bona. Non magnifaciendum in quo illa superiora insint, sed in quo haec altera. Quicquid ab aliquo factum narrabitur sapienter, ingeniose, honeste,
20   prosequatur laudibus; quicquid nequiter, vafre, subdole, impudenter, improbe, nefarie, magna reprehensione. Cum puerum complectetur, cum de-
osculabitur ac volet bene precari, non haec precetur: 'Utinam tibi contingant maiores opes quam Croeso aut Crasso aut Cosmo Medici aut Fuggeris; maiores honores quam Pompeio aut Caesari; utinam felicior sis Au-
25   gusto et Alexandro'; sed sic: 'Utinam tibi det Christus ut sis iustus, ut con-
tinens, ut fortunae contemptor, ut pius, ut sectator sui, imitator Pauli, inte-
grior Catonibus, melior Socrate aut Seneca, iustior Aristide, doctior Platone
aut Aristotele, eloquentior Demosthene vel M. Tullio.'

1 historiolas **Γ** historias **H** // **4** affectionibus **Γ** affectibus **H** // **6** prave **Γ** male **H** // **8**
formulas **Γ** praecepta **H** // **11–12** habent pro compertissimis **Γ** oracula putant **H** // **17**
fidelia **Γ** vera **H** // **18** superiora insint **Γ** priora sunt **H** // **18–19** altera **Γ** *deest in* **H** //
19 factum narrabitur **Γ** narrabitur factum **H** // **20** quicquid **Γ** quicquid ab aliquo **H** //
23–24 aut Cosmo ... Fuggeris **Γ** *deest in* **H** // **24** maiores **Γ** utinam maiores **H** / aut **Γ**
quam **H** // **25** et Alexandro **Γ** *deest in* **H** // **27** iustior Aristide **Γ** *deest in* **H**

pleasant stories and edifying tales which lead to the commendation of virtue and the deploring of vice. The child will hear these stories first of all and before understanding what vice and virtue are, he will still come to love the latter and hate the former. He will grow up with these mental attitudes and will try to emulate those examples that his mother will approve for his imitation and will try to be unlike those examples that she denounces as immoral. The mother will heap praise upon virtue and express her hatred of vice, doing this repeatedly so that it will sink into their impressionable minds. She should have a stock of pious sayings and rules of life, which from frequent repetition will be inculcated into the child's memory, even if he is occupied with something else.

134. Children run to their mother, ask her advice about everything, ask her all sorts of questions, and whatever she answers they believe, admire and consider as the gospel truth. Mothers, how many opportunities you have to make your children good or bad! At this age high moral principles and pure Christian ideals must be infused —to despise the vain foolishness of wealth, power, worldly honors, fame, nobility, and beauty; to hold as beautiful and worthy of admiration and imitation and as the only true and substantial good justice, piety, fortitude, temperance, learning, clemency, mercy and love of humankind. No praise should be given to those who possess those former qualities, but only to those who are conspicuous for the latter. Whenever mention is made of someone having acted wisely, intelligently or honorably, let her be prodigal in her praise. Whatever is done wickedly, cunningly, deceitfully, insolently, dishonestly or impiously will receive her severe reprehension. When she embraces the child, kisses him and prays for him, let her not pray in this wise: 'May greater riches come to you than those of Croesus or Crassus or Cosimo de' Medici or Fugger, greater honors than were given to Pompey or Caesar. May you be more fortunate than Augustus and Alexander.' But pray thus: 'May Christ grant that you be just, temperate, contemptuous of fortune, pious, a follower of his, an imitator of St. Paul, more upright than the two Cato's, better than Socrates or Seneca, more just than Aristides, more learned than Plato or Aristotle, more eloquent than Demosthenes or Cicero.'

---

134. Croesus: King of Lydia in Asia Minor (560–546 B.C.). his conquests and gold mines brought him proverbial wealth.

Crassus: Marcus Licinius Crassus, nicknamed Dives (the Wealthy),a member of the first triumvirate together with Caesar and Pompey. He also was proverbial for his riches.

Cosimo de' Medici: (1384–1464), founder of the Medici family that ruled Florence from 1434 to 1537. He was one of the richest men of his time.

Fugger: Probably Jakob Fugger, called 'the Rich' (1459–1525), scion of a rich family of bankers and merchants that established itself at Augsburg around 1368. The family reached the peak of their fortunes under the Emperor Charles V.

Aristides: An Athenian, surnamed the Just, great rival of Themistocles; drew up the laws of the Delian Confederacy.

135. Haec putabit maxima, haec expetenda, haec quaeret, haec concupiscet quae sibi velut optima precari audiet eos quibus est carissimus. Numquam vel dictum a puero vel factum nequiter, impudenter, improbe, procaciter, petulanter excipiat mea matrona risu et osculis. Eiusmodi assuescent pueri quae viderint probari et grata esse parentibus; haec iuvenes et viri non deponent assueta. Castiget eum et ostendat illa non agenda nec sibi placere. Contra, amplexibus et osculis prosequatur si quam aliquando melioris indolis significationem ediderit. Sunt in nobis igniculi quidam seu semina virtutum a natura indita, ut Stoici philosophi observarunt; nostri synteresin Graeco verbo nominant, quasi conservationem et scintillam iustitiae illius, qua primus auctor generis humani donatus erat a Deo. Ille igniculus adolescere modo liceret, ut illi sentiunt, ad magnam nos virtutem perduceret, sed obruitur depravatis iudiciis atque opinionibus, et dum lucere incipit ac in flammam se attollere, non modo nullo adiutus alimento, sed adversis quoque flatibus et imbre oppressus, exstinguitur. Parentes, nutrices, nutricii, magistri eruditionis, consanguinei, necessarii, familiares, magnus erroris magister populus: hi omnes semina illa virtutum radicitus conantur exstirpare et emicantem igniculum stultitia suarum opinionum tamquam ruina opprimere.

136. Universi divitiis plurimum deferunt, nobilitati assurgunt, honores adorant, potentiam quaerunt, formam laudant, gloriam admirantur, voluptatem sequuntur, paupertatem conculcant, nullum rentur maledictum gravius quam inopiam, simplicitatem animi derident, religionem habent suspectam, eruditionem invisam, probitatem omnem aut dementiam nominant aut fraudem. Illa optant cum bene precantur, haec si quis nominet, velut infausta exhorrent atque ominosa. Ita fit ut iaceant haec atque spernantur, nemo se his dedat; illa in pretio, illa in honore sint, omnes ad ea currant. Unde tanta improborum et stultorum copia, boni ac sapientes usque adeo rari, cum tamen natura illa melior hominum propensior suapte sponte in virtutes sit quam in vitia. Sancta matrona his corruptis opinionibus integrioribus aliis et Christiana dignis occurret in suoque puero bonorum praeceptorum ac consiliorum instillatione igniculum illum quem diximus fovebit, semina irrigabit, ut in magnam lucem ille, haec in frugem ingente

---

135. (igniculi … indita) *Cic. fin. 5, 18* // (Stultitia … eam) *Vulg. prov. 22, 15*

1–2 haec concupiscet Γ et cupiet **H** // **4** osculis **H** oculis Γ // **9** observarunt Γ dicunt **H** // **11** donatus erat Γ conditus **H** // **12** ut illi sentiunt Γ *deest in* **H** / magnam nos virtutem Γ summam nos virtutem vitamque beatam **H** // **14** in flammam Γ *deest in* **H** // **15** et imbre Γ *deest in* **H** / oppressus Γ impulsus **H** // **17** magister populus Γ populus magister **H** // **18–19** stultitia … ruina Γ *deest in* **H** // **20** divitiis plurimum Γ plurimum divitiis **H** // **22–23** nullum … inopiam Γ *deest in* **H** // **24–25** aut dementiam … fraudem Γ stultitiam vocant **H** // **26** iaceant … spernantur Γ haec iacent, haec spernantur **H**

135. He will consider the petitions made in his behalf by those to whom he is most dear to be his most important goals; these he will seek after and strongly desire. The wise mother will never give an approving look or smile at something said or done by the child that was naughty, impudent, wicked, wilful or unruly. When children become used to seeing that these actions are approved by their parents and are pleasing to them, they will not put them aside when they are young or even as mature men. She must punish him and show him that they are not to be done and that she is not pleased with them. On the other hand she should reward him with embraces and kisses if he gives any sign of better tendencies. There are certain little fires within us which are, as it were, the seeds of virtue implanted by nature, as the Stoic philosophers observed. Christians call it by the Greek word *synteresis*, a kind of survival or spark of that justice bestowed by God on the first parent of our race. If that little fire were permitted to grow, according to the Stoics, it would lead us to great virtue. But it is overwhelmed by depraved judgements and opinions and when it begins to glow and burst into flames, not only is it not aided by any fuel but it is smothered by adverse winds and rain and extinguished. Parents, nurses, guardians, masters of learning, relatives, close friends, acquaintances, the common people, great teacher of error, all of these try to pluck out these seeds of virtues by the root and stifle this flickering fire with the stupidity of their opinions, as if beneath a collapsed building.

136. All without exception give great importance to riches, pay homage to nobility, adore honors, seek power, praise beauty, admire distinction, follow after pleasure, trod on poverty, esteem no curse to be greater than neediness, deride simplicity of heart, hold religion suspect, learning in abhorrence, and call any form of virtue madness or fraud. Those former things are the object of their prayers and if anyone makes mention of the latter more virtuous qualities, they shrink from them as if they were unlucky or of evil omen. As a result virtues are neglected and despised and no one cultivates them, while worldly ideals are held in honor and esteem and all aspire to them. For this reason there is such a great supply of stupid and dishonest men and a dearth of good and wise men, although the nobler nature of man is more inclined to virtue than to vice. The dutiful mother will counteract these corrupt opinions with other more high-minded ones worthy of a Christian woman and will nurture in her child that little fire we just spoke of by instilling good precepts and advice and will water the seed so that the fire will grow into a great light and the seed into a fruitful crop. She will not

135. *synteresis*: A word first used by Saint Jerome in his commentary on Ezechiel (1,10) to mean the spark of conscience that is represented by the eagle, one of the four living creatures. The term is usually spelled *synderesis* in Christian theology, imitating the Byzantine Greek pronunciation of the word. Scholastic philosophers, notably Thomas Aquinas, distinguish between *synderesis* as a habit of mind and *conscientia* as a single act of judgement.

optimamque consurgat. Nec franget nervos et corporis et ingenii et virtutis molli educatione ac indulgentia; ne cibis obruat, ne somno nimio et deliciis dedere se pueros patiatur. Retardant haec mentis celeritatem. Et sunt quaedam matres quibus numquam satis edunt, bibunt, dormiunt, vestiuntur, cu-
5 rantur filii. Traducant diligentiam hanc ad mentis curam, quae efficit ut et mens et corpus valida et robusta sint. Raro memini vidisse me magnos et praestantes sive eruditione et ingenio sive virtute viros qui essent indulgenter a parentibus educati.

137. Quid quod nec corpora robur iustum accipiunt debilitata deliciis?
10 Ita, dum servare filios credunt matres, perdunt et, dum laborant ut sanius ac integrius vivant, stultae valetudinem debilitant et minuunt vitam. Ament sane filios ut amari par est, plurimum scilicet. Quis enim naturae legem vel abrogare conetur vel improbare et cuius immanitatis est non amare quem pepereris? Sed amorem celent, ne ex hoc licentiam arripiant pro libidine
15 agendi. Nec impediat amor quominus et a pueris vitia per verbera, fletus, lacrimas arceamus et corpus ac ingenium firmiora reddantur severitate victus atque educationis. De virga et castigatione apud Sapientem virum haec sunt consilia, quibus parere unumquemque nostrum convenit: 'Stultitia colligata est in corde pueri et virga disciplinae fugabit eam.' 'Noli subtrahere
20 a puero disciplinam. Si enim percusseris eum virga, non morietur. Tu virga percuties eum et animam eius de inferno liberabis.' 'Virga atque correctio tribuit sapientiam; puer autem qui dimittitur voluntati suae confundit matrem suam.' Videlicet caro peccati proclivis in malum a sua origine factum est nequissimum mancipium, quod nisi plagis emendari non potest. Ideo
25 Dominus quem corripit et castigat amare se profitetur. In quo decet cordatos parentes imitatores esse divinae indulgentiae. Neque enim is amat filium qui correctione et castigatione eius abstinet. Sicut idem Sapiens inquit: 'Qui parcit virgae odit filium suum; qui autem diligit illum instanter erudit.'

138. Matres, hoc velim ne ignoretis: maximam partem malorum homi-
30 num vobis esse acceptam referendam, ut intelligatis qualem vobis debeant filii gratiam. Vos stultitia vestra pravas opiniones ingeritis, vos alitis, vos peccatis, flagitiis, sceleribus eorum etiam arridetis. Vos vadentes ad summas virtutes, abhorrentes ab opibus mundi et diaboli pompa, lacrimis vestris et acerbis reprehensionibus ad diaboli laqueos revocatis, quoniam mavultis eos

---

137. (Stultitia ... eam) *Vulg. prov. 22, 15* // (Noli ... liberabis) *Vulg. prov. 23, 13–14* // (Virga ... suam) *Vulg. prov. 29, 15* // (caro peccati) *Vulg. Rom. 8, 3* // (Dominus ... profitetur) *Vulg. Hebr. 12, 6* // (Qui ... erudit) *Vulg. prov. 13, 24*

2–6 ne cibis obruat ... et robusta sint Γ *deest in* H // **7** sive eruditione Γ sine eruditione H / sive virtute Γ sine virtute H // **11** minuunt vitam Γ vitam minuunt H // **13** conetur Γ nitetur H // **14** pro libidine Γ quidlibet H // **16** firmiora Γ valentiora H // **30** intelligatis Γ videatis H // **31–32** peccatis, flagitiis Γ *deest in* H // **32** vadentes Γ tendentes H

enervate the child's physical and mental powers by a pampered and indulgent upbringing, nor will she dull his energies with excessive nourishment or allow him to spend too much time in sleep and pleasant pastimes. These things retard the alertness of the mind. There are some mothers who in their zealous care think their children never have enough to eat or drink, or have enough hours of sleep or sufficient clothing. Let them transfer this solicitude to the care of the mind, which provides for the health and vigor of mind and body. I have little remembrance of seeing great men who excelled either in learning and intelligence or in virtue, who were brought up indulgently by their parents.

137. Need I say that bodies weakened by delicate living do not attain to their proper strength? While these mothers think they are looking after the welfare of their children, they are ruining them and in their efforts to have them live a healthier and sounder life, in their stupidity they impair their health and shorten their days. Let them love their children, by all means, as they ought to be loved, more than all else. Who would try to abrogate or object to the law of nature, and who is so cruel as not to love those to whom she has given birth? But let them hide their love so that their children will not take advantage of it to do as they please. Do not let love hinder you from keeping your children free of vice through blows, tears and weeping. Through severity of diet and upbringing both mind and body are made stronger. Concerning the rod and punishment these counsels are found in the Book of Wisdom, which each of us ought to obey: 'Folly is bound up in the heart of a child, but the rod of discipline will drive it from him. Do not withhold discipline from a child; if you beat him with a rod, he will not die. You shall beat him with a rod and save his soul from hell. The rod and reproof give wisdom, but a child left to his own will bring shame to his mother.' Indeed, the sinful flesh, inclined to evil from its origins, has become a wicked servant that can be corrected only by blows. Therefore the Lord declares that he loves the one whom he corrects and reproves. In this it behooves parents of good sense to imitate God's manner of indulgence. He who refrains from the correction and punishment of his son does not love him. As the wise man said, 'He who spares the rod hates his son, but he who loves him disciplines him diligently.'

138. Mothers, I do not wish you to be unaware that it is your responsibility, for the most part, that evil men exist, which will make you conscious of what kind of gratitude your sons owe you. Through your stupidity you fill them with wrong notions and continue to foster them; you even smile at their sins, crimes and wrongdoings. When they are striving after the most noble virtues, shunning the world's riches and the pomps of the devil, you summon them back to the devil's snares through your tears and bitter reproofs since you prefer to see them rich and honored rather than good.

videre divites et honoratos quam bonos. Agrippina, Neronis Caesaris mater, cum super filio consuluisset divinaculos, 'Imperabit,' responderunt illi, 'sed matrem occidet.' 'Occidat,' inquit,' dum imperet.' Utrumque contigit: et imperavit et occidit, sed cum nec occidi Agrippina vellet, et filio paratum
5 esse a se imperium paeniteret. Vos denique indulgentia vestra nec per laborem vultis eos virtutem discere et per delicias gaudetis vitiis obrui. Idcirco fletis et lugetis plurimae (nam non de omnibus loquor) et meritas etiam in hac vita datis dementiae vestrae poenas, cum filios esse doletis quales ipsae fecistis. Nec ab eis redamamini qui inamabiles se omnibus esse propter
10 amorem vestrum sentiant. Nota est adolescentis illius fabula qui cum ad supplicium duceretur, colloquium matris exposcit oreque ad matris aurem admoto tamquam aliquid secreto dicturus, auriculam eius morsu amputavit. Increpantibus qui aderant quod non fur modo, sed impius in parentem esset, respondit hoc esse praemium educationis. 'Nam si illa me,' inquit, 'cum
15 puer libellum sodalis in schola surripui, quod fuit primum meum furtum, castigasset, non ad haec essem facinora progressus. At illa indulsit et osculo furem excepit.'

139. Fuit Brugis cum haec ederem mulier, quae duos filios indulgentissime ac proinde corruptissime adversa patris voluntate educarat. Illa clanculum
20 suppeditare pecuniam unde luderent, potarent, scortarentur. Alterum vidit suspensum, alterum capite truncatum. Quocirca vulgari verbo sapienter admonemur praestare ut ploret puer quam senex. Quid de illo matrum furore dicam quae filios deformes, distortos, imperitos, hebetes, inertes, ebriosos, insolentes, stolidos plus amant plerumque quam formosos, rectos,
25 eruditos, acutos, sollertes, sobrios, modestos, quietos, prudentes? Quid istuc est, errorne mentium humanarum an meritum pro peccatis nostris supplicium, ut amemus quod minime amandum est? Mutae animantes formosissimis vel catulis vel pullis blandiuntur atque adeo indicium hoc in eis est generositatis filiorum, cum cari sunt matri. Venatores illum fore optimum
30 canem praesciunt cuius feta maximam gerit curam, pro quo ante alios est sollicita, quem primum refert in cubile. In hominum genere illum fere scias esse vilissimum et despicatissimum quem mater amat tenerrime.

140. Vultis vere ab eis amari ea praesertim aetate qua sciunt iam quid sit vere et sancte amare? Efficite ne vos admodum ament, cum quid sit amor
35 adhuc ignorant et parentibus placentam aut favum aut saccharum praefe-

138. (imperabit … imperet) *Tac. ann. 14, 9*
139. (Venatores … cubile) *Plin. nat. 8, 151*

1 et honoratos Γ *deest in* H // 2 consuluisset divinaculos Γ divinaculos consuluisset H // 5 esse Γ *deest in* H // 12 tamquam … dicturus Γ *deest in* H // 18–22 Fuit Brugis … puer quam senex Γ *deest in* H // 24 insolentes Γ immodestos H // 26 errorne Γ error H // 28 indicium Γ argumentum H // 30 praesciunt Γ sciunt H // 32 amat tenerrime Γ tenerrime amat H // 33 iam Γ *deest in* H

When Agrippina, the mother of Nero, consulted soothsayers concerning her son, they answered: 'He will be emperor, but he will kill his mother.' 'Let him kill me,' she said, 'as long as he is emperor.' Both prophecies were fulfilled: he was emperor and he killed her, but by then Agrippina did not wish to be killed and she regretted that she had been instrumental in making him emperor. You wish your sons to learn virtue through your indulgent upbringing rather than through toil and you are happy to see them overcome by vice in the midst of worldly comforts. Therefore many of you mourn and weep (for I speak not of all) and you pay the deserved penalty for your madness in this life, pained to see how you have formed them. And you are not loved by them in return since they feel that they are unlovable to everyone because of your love for them. Everyone knows the story of the young man, who when he was being led to torture, asked to speak to his mother and moving his mouth to her ear as if he were going to whisper something to her in secret, bit it off. When the bystanders reproached him for this act, that not only was he a thief but impious towards his mother, he replied that this was the reward for his upbringing. He said: 'If she had punished me when as a boy I stole my companion's book, which was my first theft, I would not have reached this criminal state. But she was lenient and welcomed the thief with a kiss.'

139. While I was writing this treatise there was a woman in Bruges who had brought up her two sons with extreme leniency and as a result in a depraved manner against the wishes of their father. She secretly supplied them with money to gamble, drink and go whoring. She saw one of them hanged, the other decapitated. The wise old saying tells us: 'Better children weep than old men.' What can I say of the madness of those mothers who often show more love for children that are ugly, deformed, ignorant, dull-witted, lazy, drunk, insolent and stupid than for those who are handsome, upright, learned, sharp-witted, clever, sober, well-behaved, quiet and prudent? How is this to be interpreted, as an aberration of the human mind or a merited punishment for our sins that we love what is least to be loved? Mute animals fawn on the most beautiful of their young, and when the mother shows them particular affections, it is a sign of their noble stock. Hunters know beforehand that the best dog is the one which the mother cares for most among her offspring, the one to which she shows most attention and which she first carries back to her whelping-box. But among mankind, as a rule, the one to whom the mother shows most affection is the most worthless and contemptible of all.

140. Do you wish to be truly loved by your children at an age when they know what true and holy love is? Then be sure not to have them love you when they do not yet know what love is, and prefer cakes, honey or sugar to

runt. Nullum filium mater tenerius amavit quam mea me. Nullus umquam minus se matri sensit carum; numquam fere mihi arrisit, numquam indulsit et tamen cum domo tribus aut quattuor diebus, ea ubi essem inscia, abfuissem, paene in gravissimum incidit morbum; reversus, desideratum me

5 ab ea non intellexi. Ita neminem magis fugiebam, magis aversabar quam matrem puer; nullum mortalem magis in oculis tuli adolescens. Cuius mihi nunc memoria sacratissima est et quoties occurrit, quam corpore non possum animo et cogitatione dulcissima complector. Sodalem habui Lutetiae doctum in primis virum, qui inter cetera faventis numinis beneficia et il-

10 lud reponebat quod indulgentissimam matrem amisisset. 'Quae si viveret,' inquit, 'ego nec Lutetiam eruditionis gratia venissem et domi inter aleas, scorta, delicias, voluptates, uti coeperam, consenuissem.' Qui potuisset ille matrem amare quam mortuam esse gaudebat? Sapiens mater non filio delicias potius optabit quam virtutem, non opes magis quam eruditionem, quam

15 bonum nomen, non vitam indecoram citius quam honestam mortem.

141. Lacaenae mulieres filios malebant pro patria honeste cadere quam vitam servare fugiendo. Ita plurimas memoriae traditum est ipsas suis manibus ignavos filios interemisse, illo addito elogio: 'Nec meus hic fuerat, nec Lacedaemonius.' Sophia, cum tres haberet speciosissimas filias, tribus virtu-

20 tum nominibus insignitas, Spem, Fidem et Caritatem, iugulatas pro Christi gloria laetissima spectavit et non procul ab urbe Roma ipsa suis manibus sepelivit Hadriani Caesaris principatu. Non tam ergo artes quaestuarias docebunt parentes liberos quam sanctas, nec proponent imitandos eos qui opes maximas brevi tempore fabricati sunt, sed qui ad summas virtutes per-

25 venere. Merito reprehenduntur Megarenses, qui filios suos sordidam frugalitatem et avaritiam docebant, habituri pro liberis frugi servos. Antiqua haec Megarensium reprehensio in quam multos hodie Europae populos merito posset conferri, Florentiam et Genuam Italiae, Burgos Hispaniae, Londinum Britanniae, Rotomagum Galliae! Ita fit quod contingere passim videmus ut

30 moniti toties rem quaerere, rem facere, rem augere, rem quocumque modo parare, facinora suscipiant capitalia et nefaria; cuius culpae non exiguam partem parentes sustinent, suasores, auctores, impulsores. Et quod omnium iustissimum est: cum alia deest ad divitias via, parentes ipsos filii expilant.

---

141. (Lacaenae ... Lacedaemonius) *Plut. mor. 241A; 242A* // (Megarenses ... docebant) *Diog. Laert. 6, 41* //

1 tenerius Γ magis **H** // **2** matri sensit carum Γ a matre sensit diligi **H** // **4–5** desideratum ... intellexi Γ nec desideratum me ab ea cognovi **H** // **8** Sodalem Γ Amicum **H** // **10** reponebat Γ numerabat **H** // **21** spectavit Γ vidit **H** // **24** opes ... tempore Γ maximas opes brevi **H** // **26-29** Antiqua ... Galliae Γ *deest in* **H** // **29** Ita fit quod Γ Ita etiam efficiebant quod et nunc **H** // **31–32** exiguam ... impulsores Γ exigua pars parentibus imputanda est suasoribus, auctoribus, impulsoribus **H** // **33** deest Γ deerat **H** / expilant Γ expilabant **H**

their parents. No mother loved her son more dearly than my mother loved me. But no son felt less loved by his mother than I. She practically never smiled at me, was never lenient towards me, and yet when I was away from home for three or four days and she did not know where I was, she almost fell into a grave illness. When I returned I did not know how much she had missed me. There was no one I avoided more or shunned more as a child than my mother, but as a young man no one was more constantly in my thoughts than she. Her memory is most sacred to me even now and whenever she comes to mind, I embrace her if not physically, in mind and in thought. I had as a schoolmate in Paris a very learned man, who counted among the numerous blessings he had received from God the fact that he had lost a very indulgent mother, saying: 'If she were still living I would not have come to Paris to study and I would have grown old at home devoting my life to gambling, whores, entertainments and pleasures, as I had begun.' How could he have loved his mother if he was happy that she was dead? The prudent mother will not prefer comforts for her son rather than virtue, wealth rather than learning and a good name, an inglorious life rather than an honorable death.

141. Spartan women preferred that their children should die honorably for their country rather than save their lives in flight. Wherefore it is recorded that many of them slew their cowardly children with their own hands, adding this as a funeral inscription, 'He was never my son, nor a true Spartan.' In the reign of Hadrian Saint Sophia had three daughters, whom she named after the three theological virtues Faith, Hope and Charity. She looked on with spiritual joy when they were strangled for the greater glory of Christ, and buried them with her own hand, not far from Rome. Parents will not teach their children the arts of making financial profit, but the arts of sanctity. They will not propose as models those who have accumulated great wealth in a short time but those who have attained to the highest virtue. The Megarians are deservedly reprehended for teaching their children sordid frugality and avarice, for they converted them into thrifty slaves rather than children. This ancient reproach of the Megarians might well be leveled at many peoples of Europe today: Florence and Genoa in Italy, Burgos in Spain, London in England, Rouen in France. Thus we see the common occurrence that those who have been continually urged to acquire wealth, make profit, increase their possessions, and procure riches at any cost resort to grievous crimes, punishable by death, and no small part of the blame is to be attributed to their parents, the instigators and promoters of these actions. And what is most fitting of all is that when other paths to riches are not available,

141. Sophia: Saint Sophia was a legendary Roman matron who was converted to Christianity during the reign of Hadrian. The tombs of her daughters are to be found on the Appian Way and in the catacombs of Calixtus.

Quod si saepta vident ad nummos omnia, incipiunt odisse patres et ex odio
mortem optare, quaerere tollendi rationem et plurimos a propriis liberis veneno sublatos perhibent, quibus longum est senis mortem exspectare. Ergo
qui parentes filios docuerunt pecuniam rebus omnibus esse anteponendam,
5   ipsi vim praecepti illius in se experiuntur; ipsis parentibus pecuniam liberi
praeferunt. Exprobrant saepe parentibus filii vitia sua, tamquam illorum vel
exemplo vel negligentia sint corrupti. Iuvenis ille luxuriosus, luxurioso patre natus, apud declamatores sic loquitur: 'Meam luxuriam patri imputabo.
Non sub severa fui disciplina, non sub bene institutae domus lege, quae pos-
10   set adolescentis formare mores et a vitiis aetatis abducere.'
142. At cum continenda est prima liberorum aetas et severitate sanctae
disciplinae cohibenda ne in vitia per licentiam excurrat unde aegre revocetur,
nec auferenda de pueri dorso virga, tum praecipue filiae nulla sunt indulgentia
tractandae. Corrumpit indulgentia filios, at filias perdit funditus. Licentia
15   viri fimus deteriores, feminae scelestae, quoniam solutum in voluptates
et affectus ingenium ni frenis cohibeatur, ruit praeceps in mille facinora.
De quo est sapiens admonitio Iesu, filii Sirach: 'Filiae tibi sunt; serva
corpus illarum et non ostendas hilarem faciem tuam ad illas.' Et filiae
quidem quemadmodum sint educandae superiore libro demonstravi. Ea
20   leget mater quod multa insunt etiam quae maritas instituant et matrum
est curare ut ea filiae exsequantur quae praecipimus. Posteaquam parentes
quantum fieri potest providerint ne quid verbis turpe, foedum, obscenum,
perniciosum, nefarium animo pueri insideat, factis magis atque exemplis
providebunt ne quid videat puer quod effingere sine turpitudine non possit.
25   Et est alioqui aetas illa, ut dixi, plane simica, quae nihil profert suum;
utique nec habet, omnia imitatur. Quid quod aliena forsitan exempla
deleverint parentes ab animis puerilibus auctoritate et amore sui, adde etiam
bene monendo; quod vero ipsi fecerint, reprehendere non poterunt, nec si
reprehendant, movebitur tantum puer iis quae audit quam quae videt. Recte
30   Iuvenalis plus habere ponderis parentum exempla apud filios quam multorum

---

141. (meam luxuriam ... abducere) *Sen. contr.* 2, 6, 2
142. (Filiae ... illas) *Vet. Lat. Sirach 7, 26* // (superiore libro demonstravi) *inst. fem.*
Christ. 1, 10–12 //

1 Quod ... vident Γ Et si saepta viderent **H** / incipiunt Γ coeperant **H** // 3 perhibent Γ
scimus **H** / est Γ erat **H** // 3–6 Ergo ... praeferunt Γ *deest in* **H** // 7–8 luxurioso patre
natus Γ luxuriosi patris filius **H** // 12 revocetur Γ revocetur et sicut vir sapientissimus
consulit **H** // 15 solutum Γ soluta **H** // 16 et Γ *deest in* **H** / ingenium Γ animans **H**
// 17–18 De quo est ... tuam ad illas Γ *deest in* **H** // 19 demonstravi Γ dixi **H** // 20
quod Γ tum quod **H** / maritas Γ coniugatas **H** / et Γ tum quod **H** // 21 Posteaquam
Γ Et cum dictis **H** // 22 verbis Γ *deest in* **H** // 23 insideat Γ insidat **H** // 25 profert
Γ agit **H** // 26 utique nec habet Γ *deest in* **H** // 26 Quid ... forsitan Γ Ac forsan
aliena **H** // 27 ab Γ *deest in* **H** // 29 Recte Γ Nec male **H** // 30 ponderis parentum
exempla Γ virtutis exempla parentum **H**

children despoil their own parents. When they see that all avenues to wealth are closed to them, they begin to hate their parents and this hatred makes them desire their death and find a way to get rid of them. In fact they tell that many parents were poisoned by their own children, who were tired of waiting for them to die. And so those parents who taught their children that the accumulation of riches was to be put before all else end up experiencing themselves the effect of their own teaching. Children prefer money to their parents and often blame their parents for their own vices as if they were corrupted by their example and negligence. The prodigal young man born of a prodigal father makes this lament in the textbooks of elocution: 'I shall blame my prodigality on my father. I was not brought up with stern discipline, under the regime of a well-governed household which could form a young man's character and withdraw him from the vices of that time of life.'

142. But while those first years must be subjected to severe discipline lest the child fall into vices from which he will not easily recover later on, and there should be no sparing of the rod with boys, young girls especially should not be treated with too much leniency. Indulgence corrupts boys, but is the utter ruin of girls. We men become worse through permissiveness but women become wicked, since once their nature is set free for pleasures and passions, it will plunge headlong into a multitude of vices unless it is reined in. Jesus, son of Sirach, gives this admonition: 'If you have daughters, look after their physical welfare, but do not show them a cheerful countenance.' Concerning a daughter's education I have given instruction in the previous book. A mother should read it because there are many things there that are instructive for married women and it is a mother's duty to ensure that daughters put what I have taught into practice. As far as possible parents should see to it that no lowly, foul, obscene, dangerous or wicked word be planted in a child's mind, and they shall do this more by example than by word so that the child will not see anything whose imitation would be to its detriment. And besides, as I have said, that age is one of apish imitation and produces nothing of its own. Certainly it has nothing of its own, but imitates everything. Parents perhaps may be able to extirpate from young minds examples taken from others by their authority and love, and one may add also, by good advice. But they will not be able to reprimand them for things of which they themselves are culpable, and even if they tried to do so, the child is moved more by what it sees than by what it hears. Juvenal is right in proclaiming that the example of parents has more weight with

---

142. **Jesus, son of Sirach**: A scribe and teacher in Jerusalem who wrote the *Book of Sirach*, also known as *Ecclesiasticus*, accepted as a canonical book in the Catholic Bible.

172 J. L. VIVES

doctorum monita et praecepta. Ita unico malefacto gravius nocebunt quam
multis sancte consultis profuerant. Ideoque in Satira decima quarta sapienter
suadet his verbis:

> Nihil dictu foedum visuque haec limina tangat
> Intra quae puer est. Procul hinc, procul inde puellae
> Lenonum et cantus pernoctantis parasiti.
> Maxima debetur puero reverentia, si quid
> Turpe paras, nec tu pueri contempseris annos,
> Sed peccaturo obsistat tibi filius infans.

143. Numidiam Quadratillam sugillat Caecilius Plinius quod pantomimos
effusius fovebat quam principi feminae conveniret. In eo tamen prudentiam
anus laudat, quod Quadratum nepotem suum adolescentem spectare nec
domi nec in theatro pantomimos suos permiserit, cumque vel illos auditura
esset vel animum calculorum lusu laxatura, solita nepoti esset iubere abiret
atque studeret. Idem auctor Hispullae, uxoris suae amitae, maximas agit per
epistolam gratias quod uxorem suam apud ipsam educatam suasibus atque
exemplis ad rectum honestumque finxerit nihilque in illa domo viderit nisi
sanctum et imitandum. Ac nimirum erga filias maior debet adhiberi vigilantia
ne quid vel pudorem vel pudicitiam vel modestiam maculet, quo haec in
femina exactiora perquiruntur quam in viro. Et feminae animalium omnium
ingeniosius imitantur quodque est utrique sexui commune promptius ac
perfectius vitia. Nec contineri possunt si auctoritas in exemplum accedat,
ut si matrem aut quam vulgo probari vident effecturae sint.

144. Hinc in civitatibus quarum principes sunt improbae, rarae sunt ple-
beiae probae. Et quae a malis educantur non frequenter sunt aliusmodi. Nec
certissimum non est vetus verbum similem matris filiam. Neque tamen adeo
est matris similis filia atque educatricis, unde nothae pleraeque quae apud
sanctas ex patribus avias adoleverunt, a matribus degenerantes, vitam vir-
tutemque aviarum educatricium expresserunt. Censor M. Cato C. Manlium
senatu movit quod uxorem praesente filia deosculatus esset. Nescit rudis aetas cur quidque fiat, at eosdem actus reddit velut speculum acceptas for-
mas, non eisdem finibus. Quod intelligens prudentissimus iuxta et sanctis-
simus senex Eleazarus, cum ex edicto Antiochi iuberetur carnes suillas edere

---

142. (Nihil ... infans) *Iuv. 14, 44–49*
143. (Numidiam ... studeret) *Plin. epist. 7, 24* // (Hispulae ... imitandum) *Plin. epist. 4, 19*
144. (Censor ... esset) *Plut. mor. 139E* //

3 suadet his verbis Γ sic suadet **H** // **14** iubere Γ praecipere **H** // **16–17** suasibus ... finxerit Γ optimis praeceptis instituerit **H** // **18** imitandum Γ honestum **H** // **23** vident effecturae sint Γ videt effictura sit **H** // **25** probae Γ bonae **H** / aliusmodi Γ aliae **H** // **27** nothae **HWW²B** notae **V** // **29** expresserunt Γ sequuntur **H**

children than the advice and precepts of many learned men. Consequently, they will do more serious harm by a single misdeed than they profited them with many holy counsels. In the fourteenth satire he gives this wise advice:

> Let no vile word or sight befoul
> The house where dwells a child.
> Far from his door all ladies of the night,
> And the chant of the prowling parasite.
> The greatest reverence is owed the child,
> If you plan some wickedness, do not
> Despise his tender years, but rather
> May a guileless child forestall your sinful act.

143. Pliny censures Numidia Quadratilla for showing more enthusiasm for pantomimes than was befitting a woman of high standing. At the same time he praises the wisdom of the old woman for not allowing her young grandson Quadratus to watch pantomimes either at her house or in the theatre. When she was going to see them or felt like relaxing in a game of draughts, she would order her nephew to go somewhere to study. The same author gives warm thanks to Hispulla, his wife's aunt, because in bringing up his wife she gave her an upright and honorable training through her own word and example and ensured that she saw nothing in that house but what was blameless and worthy of imitation. And surely greater vigilance must be exercised in the case of daughters so that nothing will stain their chastity, honesty and modesty, which are more strictly required of a woman than of a man. The female of all species is more clever at imitation, and in the aptitude for vice, which is common to both sexes, they show more quickness and ability. If authority is added to example, there is no stopping them, as when they are to imitate their mother or some woman whom the common crowd approves.

144. It thus comes about that in cities where women of gentle upbringing are bad, then it is rare to find any lowly born women to be good. And those who are brought up by evil women rarely turn out otherwise. There is great truth in the old proverb: 'The daughter is like the mother.' But the daughter is not so much like the mother as she is like the one who brought her up, so that there are many bastard daughters who grew up with their paternal grandmothers, who were virtuous women, and deviating from their mother's character, took on the virtuous way of life of their grandmothers. Cato the Censor removed Gaius Manlius from the Senate because he kissed his wife in the presence of his daughter. The age of innocence does not know why things are done, but reproduces the same actions, as a mirror reflects images, but not for the same ends. The wise and saintly Eleazar understood this. He was ordered by a decree from Antioch to eat pork and

recusantique gentiles amici suaderent ut saltem edere se simularet, ut illo praetextu dimitteretur tamquam regiae voluntati obtemperasset, mori se respondit malle quam aliquid agere quod in exemplum rei pessimae accipi a iuvenibus posset. Hisque verbis usus est: '"Non enim aetati nostrae dignum
5 est fingere ut multi adolescentes, arbitrantes Eleazarum nonaginta annorum transiisse ad vitam alienigenarum et ipsi propter meam simulationem et propter modicum corruptibilis vitae tempus decipiantur, et per hoc maculam atque exsecrationem meae senectuti conquiram. Nam etsi praesenti tempore suppliciis hominum eripiar, sed manum omnipotentis nec vivus
10 nec defunctus effugiam. Quamobrem fortiter vita excedendo senectute quidem dignus apparebo, adolescentibus autem exemplum forte relinquam, si prompto animo ac fortiter pro gravissimis ac sanctissimis legibus honesta morte perfungar." His dictis confestim ad supplicium trahebatur. Ii autem qui eum ducebant et paulo ante fuerant mitiores, in iram conversi sunt prop-
15 ter sermones ab eo dictos, quos illi per arrogantiam prolatos arbitrabantur. Sed cum plagis perimeretur, ingemuit et dixit: "Domine, qui habes sanctam scientiam, manifeste tu scis quod cum a morte possem liberari, duros corporis sustineo dolores, secundum animam vero propter timorem tuum libenter patior." Et iste quidem hoc modo vita decessit non solum iuvenibus sed
20 universae genti memoriam mortis suae ad exemplum virtutis et fortudinis derelinquens.'

145. Instituendi sunt igitur etiam exemplo parentum filii nec eis ostendendum quod facile in vitium transeat, ne ipsi facilius transferant simul imperitia meliorum simul hominum natura in peiora proclivi. Punivit Dominus
25 Heli iudicem et pontificem Israelis, non quod filiis suis Ophni et Phinees malo ipse fuisset exemplo, sed quod pravos et flagitiosos non castigasset. Itaque casu e sella interiit translatumque est sacerdotium in aliam familiam. Quanto gravius vindicabit in eos parentes qui ipsi vel exhortatione vel exemplo suo liberos suos scelerate vivere docuerunt!

30 **146.** Quod si supplicium de peccatis adultorum filiorum pervasit ad patrem quatenus non quantum posset inhibuerat, quid fiet iis qui teneros ad libidines, voluptates, cupiditates, facinora vel dictis impulerunt vel factis? Contra de muliere quae filios virtuti assuefecit, doctor gentium ait: 'Mulier seducta in praevaricatione fuit, sed salva erit per filiorum generationem si
35 permanserit in fide et caritate et sanctificatione cum pudicitia.' Liberi si vita decedant, existimandum aliud hoc non esse quam depositum reddi.

---

144. (Non ... derelinquens) *Vet. Lat. 2 Macc. 6, 24–31*
145. (Punivit ... castigasset) *Vulg. I reg. 2, 34; 3, 13* // (Casu ... interiit) *Vulg. I reg. 4, 18*
146. (Mulier ... pudicitia) *Vulg. I Tim. 2, 1–15* //

31 inhibuerat Γ inhibuit **H** // **35**–p.178,17 Liberi si vita ... aeternum possideant Γ *deest in* **H**

his Gentile friends tried to persuade him at least to pretend to eat it, so that in appearance he would be considered to have obeyed the king. His answer was that he would rather die than do something that might be taken as a bad example by youth. These are his words:

> "It is not fitting at our time of life to make pretence; many young men would suppose that at the age of ninety years Eleazar had gone over to the foreigners' way of life, and might themselves be led astray because of my playing this part for the sake of a few paltry years of this corruptible life, and through this action I would bring disgrace and execration upon my old age. Even if I were to be delivered from the punishments of men for the present moment, I could not escape the hand of the Almighty, dead or alive. Therefore, by departing this life courageously, I shall prove myself worthy of old age, and perhaps I shall leave an example to young men if I die an honorable death with a ready and courageous spirit in defense of venerable and holy laws." With these words he was immediately dragged off to the torture. Those who escorted him, who had previously been more well-disposed toward him, were turned to rage because of these words, which they thought were spoken out of arrogance. But as his life was ebbing out under the force of their blows, he uttered a groan and said: "Lord, in your holy wisdom you know clearly that although I could have escaped death, I endure these harsh physical pains. Yet in my soul I suffer them gladly because of the awe I feel towards you." And so he died, and by his death he left a noble example and memorial of virtue and courage not only for the young but for all people.

145. Therefore children should be instructed through the example of their parents and they must not be shown anything that might easily be turned into vice. Otherwise they will more easily adapt themselves to that course of action because of ignorance of what is better or through man's nature, which is inclined toward the worse. The Lord punished Eli, judge and priest of Israel, not because he himself had been a bad example to his sons, Hophni and Phinehas, but because he did not punish them for their wickedness and depravity. So he died by falling from a chair and the priesthood was transferred to another family. How much more severely will he punish those parents who by their own encouragement and example have taught their children to lead a wicked life!

146. But if punishment for the sins of grown children was visited upon the parent because he did not discipline them to the best of his ability, what will be done to those who by word and deed incited their children at a tender age to lust, pleasure, cupidity and wicked behaviour? By contrast, the teacher of the Gentiles, speaking of a woman who accustomed her children to virtue, says: 'The woman was seduced by deception but she will be saved through bearing children if she will persevere in faith, charity and holiness with modesty.' If children die, we must consider this to be nothing more than the restitution of a trust. How much has been written by Plato,

De consolatione mortis quam copiose scriptum est a Platone, Cicerone,
Xenocrate, Seneca! Quam sententia illa celebris reputantibus vitae huius
in tanta brevitate tam longas aerumnas: 'Optimum non nasci, proximum
citissime aboleri.' Quam comprobarunt sapientiae assectatores profectam
(uti rentur) a Sileno quodam, qui temporibus vixerit Croesi et Cyri cum
septem Graeciae sapientibus, sed prolatam a Salomone, multo vetustiore
illis omnibus et subindicatam a Iob Husita, qui ante Moysem regulus fuit in
Arabia. Unde et gentes quaedam velut Thraces et Gallorum Druidae, tum
vitae huius taedio, tum spe quadam melioris post venturae, laetitia cantuque
eos prosequebantur qui fato defungerentur. Sed illa certissima et fidelissima
consolatio quae ex veritate sumitur, nempe consideratione futurae vitae.
Mors ex se malum non est, tantum de modo ac ratione sua censetur. Felices
quibus exitus ab hac vita in amicitia Christi contigit, infelices quibus secus! Illi
enim ad ingentem beatitudinem transmittuntur, hi ad extremos cruciatus et
miseriam. Proinde hoc est abs te curandum ut sic filios componas ac effingas
ut quandocumque iubeat eos imperator e vita tamquam e statione excedere,
gratiosi imperatori exeant, animo atque industria illi sua approbata.

147. Hoc cum ita sit, quanto gaudio excipienda est mors infantium, qui
citra sensum laborum ac sollicitudinum aevi huius, ambitionis, invidiae, arrogantiae, necessitatis antequam invadat agmen illud morborum, corpore
integro, tenuissimo quodam mortis gustu, horribilem carcerem laetissima
beatitate commutant. Quae maior optari illis posset felicitas quam ut in
odiosissima et fastidiorum ac periculorum referta vita subito celeri quodam
volatu ad diversorium transferantur? Aut quod cum aliis diutina et operosa
contingat militia, illi praemium idem tanto minore opera consequantur? Nec
grandioribus alia debet votis optari, nisi ut meritis et misericordia illius qui

---

146. (Optimum ... aboleri) *Erasm. ad. LB II, 503A* // (Iob Husita) *Vulg. Iob 3, 3*

24 Aut quod **WW²B** Utque **V**

Cicero, Xenocrates and Seneca concerning the consolation of death! How celebrated is that saying elaborated by those who reflected on the multitude of woes that encumber this brief life of ours: 'Best not to be born, and next best to die quickly.' This saying was endorsed by those who pursued wisdom; it is said to have originated with a certain Silenus, who lived at the time of Croesus and Cyrus with the seven sages of Greece, but was really first pronounced by Solomon, who lived much before all of them and was alluded to by Job from the land of Uz, who was a petty king of Arabia before the time of Moses. Whence it is that certain peoples, like the Thracians and the Druids among the Gauls, both from the tedium of this life and the hope of a better life to come, escorted with joy and singing those who met their end. But the most certain and most faithful consolation is that which is based on truth, namely, the consideration of a future life. Death is not an evil in itself; it is judged only on the manner of and circumstances of its occurrence. Happy those whose exit from this life occurred when they enjoyed the friendship of Christ! Unhappy those for whom it was otherwise! The former are transposed to immense happiness, the latter to the extremes of suffering and misery. Therefore you must take care that you so instruct and form your children that whenever the supreme commander commands them to leave this life, as they would a sentry's post, they leave in his good favor, with his approbation of their industry and good will.

147. Since this is so, with what great joy the death of infants should be welcomed, who without experiencing the toils and preoccupations of this life—ambition, envy, arrogance and necessity—before the onslaught of sickness, with body intact, with only the slightest sensation of death, exchange this horrible prison for a blissful beatitude. What greater happiness can be wished for them than that in this loathsome pilgrimage filled with dangers and cares they are suddenly transferred as if in rapid flight to their dwelling-place? Or that while others must undergo a long and exhausting campaign, they should obtain the same reward with so much less effort? We should pray for no greater blessing for them than that through the merits and mercy

146. Xenocrates: a Greek philosopher born in 400 B.C., a disciple of Plato.

Silenus: According to one legend King Midas (of the golden touch) is said to have captured the wild nature spirit, Silenus, and asked him the secret of life. Silenus replied that the best thing for mankind was never to be born, otherwise leave the world as soon as possible. The story is told in the pseudo-Plutarch *Consolatio ad Apollonium*. For this wise response he was sometimes associated with the seven sages.

Arabia: Job is now thought to have come from the land of Edom, southeast of Palestine. Scholars have detected some Arabic coloring in the language of the *Book of Job*.

Thracians: Thrace was a vast territory to the northeast of Greece occupying most of modern Bulgaria. The Thracians were a tribal people, usually depicted as cruel and rapacious by ancient writers.

Druids: priests among the Gauls and Britons. Their practices were described by Julius Caesar in his *Commentaries on the Gallic War*, Book VI, chapters 13 and 14.

nos a noxis emundavit vindicavitque a diaboli servitute, expurgatis delictis, puri laetique auferantur e tenebris vitae huius, antequam malitia immutet cor eorum, et revolent ad patriam illam in qua sita est beatitudo sempiterna. Ad quae regna vellent parentes ex se genitos evehi cum his comparanda?
5 Utique non ad alia, si non magis ab affectibus suis, quam liberorum utili- tatibus traherentur. Atqui decet ipsos filiis eam felicitatem propter inania sua gaudia, seu verius gaudiorum somnia, non invidere nec simulare se il- lorum dolere vicem, cum suam plangant. Quos tamen conveniret hilares et laetos esse ut qui cives illi progenuissent civitati·cuius Deus princeps est, an-
10 geli cives, deque ea sint optime meriti tali sobole progenita et sic educata. Hoc pacto ac merito futurum, ut arbitror, Paulus docet, 'Ut mulier salva fiat.' Ergo consultius erit ac pium magis hoc nomine gaudere quam maerore confici, quod repetitum est id quod non donatum fuerat, sed accommoda- tum, nec querelis et luctu nostro iudicium reposcentis Dei damnare. Sed pro
15 usura quantulicumque temporis habenda gratia, nec imitandi ingrati illi qui immemores percepti fructus iniuriam interpretantur, nisi beneficium quod gratis datur arbitratu suo aeternum possideant.

CAP. XI.   DE BIS NUPTIS ET NOVERCIS

148. Quae prioribus maritis elatis aliis denupserunt hoc super ea quae scrip-
20 simus sunt admonendae. Videant ne immodica superiorum virorum com- memoratione praesentes offendant. Solet hoc ingeniis hominum usu evenire, ut meliora semper videantur praesentibus praeterita, propterea quod nulla est tanta felicitas quae non multum trahat secum incommodi et amaritudi- nis admistum. Hoc cum adest, urget nos acriter; cum abiit, non magnum sui
25 sensum relinquit. Ita fit ut minus videamur transactis malis affecti esse quam afficiamur praesentibus. Vergit etiam in pronum aetas, quae in dies impor- tandis incommodis fit peior et sustinendis importatis imbecillior. Tum recor- datio vigentioris aetatis et velut comparatio cum ingravescente taedium af- fert praesentium, desiderium praeteritorum. Sed Salomoni non placet cogi-
30 tationem illam sapientis animum subire ut existimet superiores annos prae- sentibus potiores esse. Nec prudenti feminae ita videbitur, nec putabit mor- tuum maritum hoc vivente meliorem ac commodiorem fuisse. Saepe enim

147. (Ut ... fiat) *Vulg. I Cor. 7, 16*
148. (Salomoni ... esse) *Vet. Lat. Sirach 7, 11*

21 evenire **Γ** contingere **H** // 23 trahat secum **Γ** habeat **H** // **29–30** Salomoni ... cogi- tationem illam **Γ** Solomon non sinit illam cogitationem **H** // 31 potiores esse **Γ** esse me- liores **H** // **32** vivente **Γ** *deest in* **H** / fuisse **Γ** esse **H**

of him who cleansed us of our sins and rescued us from the servitude of the devil they be purged of their offenses and transported pure and jubilant from the darkness of this life before wickedness vitiate their hearts, and that they may fly back to that homeland in which everlasting bliss is to be found. To what comparable realm would parents wish their offspring to be borne away? Certainly to no other place unless they are more influenced by their own interests than those of their children. It is not right that they should resent their children's happiness because of their own empty joys or illusions of joy, or pretend that they are bewailing their children's fate when in reality they are lamenting their own. On the contrary they should be joyous and cheerful for having produced citizens of that city of which God is the ruler and the angels the citizen body, and of which they themselves are worthy for having generated and brought up such offspring. It is in this way and because of this merit, I think, that Paul teaches that the woman will be saved. Therefore it will be more well-advised and more pious to rejoice for this reason rather than be consumed with grief that what was not given but merely lent is now reclaimed. We must not by our mourning and laments condemn the judgement of God, who demands what is rightfully his, but should be thankful for the use of it that we have enjoyed for however brief a time. We must not imitate those who, forgetful of the advantage they have enjoyed, deem it an injustice if they cannot possess forever to their heart's content a benefit that is freely given.

CHAPTER 11.   ON THE TWICE-MARRIED AND STEPMOTHERS

148. For those who have married again after the death of their first husband I shall give the following additional recommendations. Let them be careful not to offend their present husband by making too frequent reference to their previous husband. It is the usual experience of mankind that the past always seems better than the present because no happiness exists that does not bring with it a great deal of disadvantages and admixture of bitterness. When this is present, it brings intense pain; when it is absent, it does not leave a significant trace of itself. It thus comes about that we are less affected by past evils than we are by present ills. Age moves forward at such a relentless pace that with each passing day the accumulation of woes becomes worse and our ability to support them more enfeebled. Then the remembrance of a more vigorous time of life and a comparison of it with that which weighs on us brings weariness with our present state and longing for the past. But Solomon does not wish that it should pass through the mind of the wise man that former years were better than the present. Nor will it seem so to the prudent woman, and she will not think that her dead husband was better or more agreeable than her present spouse. For they often deceive

falluntur, cum, si quid eas in praesenti offendit viro, tunc tantum in altero quae placuerunt recordantur, idque faciunt odiosius si in quo vivens
parum satisfacit, id magis ex animi sententia defunctus praestabat. Ibi sine
reputatione rerum aliarum ad eam solam referunt inter maritos compara-
tionem. Hinc maestitia, hinc perpetuae querelae et molestae marito voces.
Et dum mortuum complorant ac desiderare se queribundae testantur, neu-
trum retinent.

149. Novercae vulgo male audiunt tamquam iniquae in privignos sint.
Cuius rei non pauca exempla memorantur; et totum hoc genus epigrammate Graeco incessitur quod privignus quidam, cum novercae coleret sepulcrum, a delapsa ex eo columella sit interemptus. Etiam atque etiam ex-
hortandae sunt feminae, dent operam ut affectus et animi perturbationes
habeant in sua potestate. Hic fons atque origo et malorum omnium et bonorum. Affectiones si dominari in te sinas, magnum calamitatum et miseri-
arum agmen semel importabunt, quod reicere postea vix queas; sin tu illis domineris, sanctissime vives ac beatissime. Istud assequemur si in animi
tranquillitate et quiete sedulo meditati erimus quemadmodum nos geremus
ingruentibus concitationum et tempestatum causis. Non sunt ergo iniustae
et asperae novercae nisi quarum tyranni sunt affectus, quae ipsae animi
aegritudinibus non imperant, sed serviunt. Nam quae mente, ratione, iudicio ducitur, reputabit se idem cum marito esse, idcirco utriuslibet liberos
communes esse oportere. Nam si amicitia omnia reddit communia adeo ut
complures amici amicorum liberos non secus ac proprios ament, colant, adiuvent, quanto id plenius exactiusque debet coniugium praestare, cumulus
non amicitiarum modo, sed propinquitatum et cognationum omnium? Mariti patrueles, consobrini, fratres, parentes pro talibus habentur et sic nom-
inantur ab uxore; quanto id magis praestandum est filiis?

150. Tum miserebitur mulier tenerae ac infirmae aetatis et recordatione
suorum, si habet, diliget alienos, reputans communem humanae gentis sor-
tem; repperturos suos in se talem qualem ipsa alienis se praebuerit, seu fato
defungatur, seu vivat. Denique bona mulier privignis erit quod tam crebro ab eis audit, mater. Quae namque est ab omni humanitatis et man-
suetudinis sensu adeo remota quam non mitiget et flectat illa vox, 'Mater,'
a quocumque profecta sit, sed in primis a pueris, qui assentari nesciunt?

---

149. (epigrammate Graeco) *Anth. Pal. 9, 67*

3 Ibi Γ Tum **H** // **5** maestitia Γ taedium **H** / perpetuae Γ *deest in* **H** // **6** queribundae testantur Γ conqueruntur **H** // **9** non pauca Γ nonnulla **H** // **9–11** et totum ... interemptus Γ *deest in* **H** // **14** Affectiones Γ Affectus **H** / calamitatum Γ malorum **H** // **15** importabunt Γ invehent **H** // **18** concitationum et tempestatum Γ concitationis et tempes-
tatis **H** // **20** aegritudinibus Γ perturbationibus **H** // **22** oportere Γ *deest in* **H** // **23–24**
adiuvent Γ *deest in* **H** // **24** cumulus Γ summum **H** // **25–27** Mariti ... filiis Γ *deest in* **H**
// **29** diliget Γ amabit **H** / reputans Γ cogitans **H** // **34** assentari Γ absentari **H**

themselves if, when they are annoyed by some trait in their present husband, they remember only the pleasant things of their former spouse. They make this comparison all the more invidious if they find their present husband lacking in some quality in which their dead husband gave them more satisfaction. Without taking other things into account they base everything on this one comparison. This breeds sadness, unending complaints, and words that are grievous to the husband, and while they lament their dead husband and give tearful testimony of their longing for him, they lose both.

149. In general stepmothers have a bad reputation as being prejudiced against their stepchildren. This is attested to by many examples, and their whole race is attacked in a Greek epigram, which recounts that while a certain stepson was paying homage at his stepmother's tomb, a pillar collapsed and took his life. Again and again women are exhorted to make every effort to keep their emotions and passions under control. This is the source and origin of all good and of all evil. If you allow your feelings to dominate you, they will let in a great throng of calamities and miseries which you will not be able to cast out, but if you gain control over them, you will live holily and happily. We will achieve this if in peace and tranquility of mind we meditate on how we are to conduct ourselves when we are assailed by these agitations and disturbances. Stepmothers, therefore, are not unjust and harsh except those who are tyrannized by their emotions, who do not exercise control over their feelings but rather are slaves to them. A woman who is guided by reason and judgement will think of herself as one person with her husband, and will consider the children of each of them as common to both. For if friendship makes us hold all things in common so much so that many people love, cherish and assist the children of their friends just as they do their own, how much more scrupulously should this be observed in matrimony, which is the culmination not only of friendships, but of all kinships and relationships? The cousins, cousins-german, brothers and parents of a husband are regarded and addressed as such by a wife. How much more should this be true with respect to children!

150. A woman will take pity on their tender and defenseless age, and remembering her own children, if she has any, will love those of others, mindful of the common lot of all mankind, and that her own children will find that others will treat them as she treated others, whether she is dead or alive. In a word, a good woman will be a mother to her stepchildren, as she will often hear herself called. What woman is so devoid of any feeling of human kindness that she would not be moved and softened by the name of mother, whoever pronounced it, but especially in the mouths of children who do not know how to flatter, who call on them in the simplicity of their

Qui simplici animo sic compellant non alio affectu quam veram matrem ex qua nati sunt vocarent? Quam dulce est amicitiae nomen! Quot iras mollit, quot odia discutit! Matris nomine quid potest inveniri efficacius, nempe incredibili caritate plenum et constipatum? An non iratissima mitescis cum te matrem nominari audis? Immanior es quavis fera si te nomen illud non remollit. Nulla est adeo truculenta et incicur belua cui, si eiusdem generis animalculum abblandiatur, non illi protinus mitescat. Te liberi mariti tui emollire blandientes nequeunt; tu mater appellata hostem exhibes; tu concepta plerumque sine causa odia in aetatem imbecillem atque innoxiam exerces; tibi, cum Christianos omnes benevolentia et caritate fas sit esse fratres, odiosi sunt domo et affinitate coniuncti, fratres tuorum liberorum; non te manes matris illorum terrent, persequuntur, exagitant? Cognoscite, novercae, quae tales estis, impotentes iras vestras ex solis vecordiae ac vehementiae vestrae somniis natas!

151. Vitrici cur non sic oderunt privignos? Nullus fere est vitricus qui non tamquam filium privignum amet. Mentiar nisi magna etiam regna a vitricis relicta privignis legamus, non secus quam si ex ipsis nati essent. Augustus Tiberio, Claudius Neroni Romanum imperium reliquit, etiam cum ille nepotem et pronepotes haberet, hic filium; non quod se non genuisse illos ignorent, sed quia ratione et sano iudicio assequuntur nullas esse inter vitricos et privignos odiorum causas nisi ipsi moribus suis fecerint. Quid enim privigni in vitricos commeriti sunt quod non ipsis parentibus sint procreati? Hoc praestare non hominum est, sed Dei. At non blandiuntur, non semper lusitant vitrici cum privignis ut matres vellent. Hoc argumento nec patres naturales amant filios. Quid dixi hos non amare? Nonnullae sunt tam

2 nati sunt vocarent **H** nati sunt Γ // 2–3 Quot iras mollit, quot odia **HV** Quod iras mollit, quod odia **WW²B** // 3 nomine . . . inveniri Γ nomen quanto decet esse **H** // 6 Nulla . . . belua Γ Nulla bestia tam fera et truculenta est **H** // 7 abblandiatur Γ blandiatur **H** / mitescat Γ mansuescat **H** // 11 et Γ *deest in* **H** // 17 legamus Γ scimus **H** // 25 filios Γ *deest in* **H**

hearts with the same feeling as they would their true mother, who gave them birth? How sweet is the name of friendship! How many feelings of anger it assuages! How much hatred it dispels! What can be found more effective than the name of mother, a name overflowing with incredible affection? Is it not true that even when you are enraged, you are appeased when you hear yourself called mother? You are fiercer than any beast if that name does not soften your feelings. There is no wild animal so ferocious and untamed that if a tiny creature of its own kind fawns upon it, it does not immediately become gentle. Yet children of your husband cannot soften your spirit with their demonstrations of affection. You are called mother and you respond with hostility. You turn preconceived hatred often without cause upon a defenseless and innocent age. Whereas it is the divine will that all should be brothers in good will and charity, you hate those joined to you by family ties, the brothers of your own children. Does not the spirit of their dead mother frighten, persecute and harass you? Be aware, you stepmothers who live up to the name, that your uncontrolled wrath took rise solely from dreams proceeding from your own mad frenzy.

151. Why is it that stepfathers do not hate their stepchildren? Rare is the stepfather who does not love his stepson as his own son. I would be lying if my words were not confirmed by the annals of history that relate that great kingdoms were left to their stepsons by their stepfathers no differently than if they had been born to them. Augustus left the Roman empire to Tiberius, Claudius to Nero, even though the former had a grandson and great-grandson and the latter a son. It is not that they did not know that they were not their natural sons but they understood by reason and judgement that there was no cause for hatred between stepfathers and stepsons, unless they had created it themselves through their own behavior. What blame can stepfathers lay on stepchildren for not having been born their natural offspring? This is not in the power of men but of God. But stepfathers do not coddle their stepsons or play with them as their mothers would wish. By that argument natural fathers do not love their children either. Did I say that stepfathers do not love their stepchildren? Some mothers are so

---

151. Augustus: The *princeps* made Tiberius his successor only when he was forced to do so. Two of his grandsons by his daughter Julia, Gaius and Lucius Caesar, had died within two years of each other. The third, Agrippa Postumus, was of a violent nature and had to be banished. His great-grandson, Gaius (later to be called Caligula) was a two-year old infant when Augustus died.

Claudius: In neglecting to mention the intrigues that led to Nero's accession to power, Vives distorts the historical facts. Urged on by her lover, Antonius Pallas, his wife, Agrippina, schemed to have her son Domitius adopted by the Emperor thus becoming Tiberius Claudius Nero Caesar. She also contrived to have Nero marry Claudius' daughter, Octavia. Claudius' own son, Britannicus, only three years younger than Nero, was pushed aside. To insure Nero's succession Agrippina had Claudius poisoned according to both Tacitus and Suetonius.

vesanae matres ut communes liberos diligi a maritis vix credant, quod non totos dies et totas noctes cum illis ineptiant. Non potest sic ineptire virilis sexus ut muliebris. Magnitudo illa virilis animi amorem facile continet ac contegit. Dominatur illi, non servit. Sed vos novercae, quin semper privig-
5   nos osculamini, pectitis, excolitis tamquam vestros? Tantae scilicet in animis vestris ex affectionum nubilis densantur tenebrae! Quod amatis dignissimum iudicatis quod ament omnes; nemo vobis videtur satis amare. Quod oditis dignissimum odio ducitis et aliis semper amari nimis. Nec desunt quae privignos capitaliter cum oderint, amare tamen se iurent. Insanae, sive id ipsae
10   credant, sive alios sperent credituros; insaniores, si imposturam se Deo facturas confidant. Et postulas ut te audiat Christus, vocatus a te Pater, quae privignos averseris, vocata ab illis mater? Non credit Ioannes Apostolus invisibilem Deum ab eo diligi qui fratrem odit quem videt.

CAP. XII.   QUOMODO SE GERET CUM CONSANGUINEIS ET AFFINIBUS

15   **152.** Sororem Nigidius Figulus dictam esse tradit quod seorsum eat, quoniam in aliam transit domum et familiam. Quod cum ita sit, mulier nupta officiosior esse incipiet in affines quam in consanguineos. Sic decet propter multa; tum quod in illam gentem velut transplantata est cui filios generatura est, quam fecunditate sua numerosiorem factura; tum quod propinquorum et
20   consanguineorum benevolentiam iam paravit, affinium deinceps quaerendus amor. Adde his quod et filii, si genuerit, cariores sint gentilibus et propinquis suis, adiuti non modo mutua illorum in patrem, sed matrem quoque caritate. Denique multas adfert et in coniugio et in viduitate commoditates si diligare ab affinibus, multa incommoda si sis odiosa. Illud quoque spectarunt qui
25   a consanguineis ad alienos traduxere connubia, quo latius se hominum inter ipsos caritas et amicitia diffunderet quasique propagaret. Convenit

151. (Non credit ... videt) *Vulg. I Ioh. 4, 20*
152. (Sororem ... consanguineos) *Gell. 13, 10, 3*

4 servit Γ paret **H** // **11** quae Γ cum tu **H** // **13** videt Γ intuetur **H** // **15** Sororem ... tradit Γ Homo eruditisssimus Nigidius Figulus sororis etymon reddidit **H** // **21** Adde his quod et Γ Hinc quo **H** / et propinquis Γ *deest in* **H** // **23–24** Denique ... affinibus Γ Denique multas adfert commoditates si ab affinibus amere **H** // **25** connubia Γ coniugia **H** // **26** quasique Γ et **H**

mentally deranged that they think their husbands have little love for the children born to them because they do not play foolish games with them night and day. The male sex cannot play childish games as women can. The nobility of the man's spirit restrains and conceals love; he commands it, and is not its slave. But you stepmothers, why do you not kiss your stepchildren always, comb their hair, teach them good manners, as if they were your own? Such thick darkness settles upon your minds from the clouds of your passions! You think that what you love deserves everyone's love, and no one shows enough love as far as you are concerned. Whatever you hate you think is worthy of everyone's hatred and loved too much by others. There are not lacking those stepmothers who while hating their stepchildren with a deadly hatred swear that they love them. They are mad if they themselves believe it or hope that others will believe it. They are even more insane if they presume that they can deceive God. And you ask that Christ, whom you call father, will hear you when you detest your stepchildren, by whom you are called mother? The Apostle John does not believe that God, who is invisible, is loved by one who hates his brother, whom he sees.

CHAPTER 12.   HOW SHE WILL BEHAVE WITH HER RELATIVES
AND IN-LAWS

152. Nigidius Figulus writes that the word *soror* (sister) comes from *seorsum* (apart) because she goes to live apart, passing into another house and family. For this reason a married woman will begin to be more dutiful towards her in-laws than towards her own blood relations. This is proper for many reasons: because she has been transplanted, as it were, into that family, for whom she will generate children and which she will make more numerous through her fertility; then for the reason that she has already procured the benevolence of her own kinsman and must now seek the love of her husband's relatives. In addition, so that her children, if she has any, will be more beloved of their father's family and kinsman, supported by their love not only towards their father but also towards their mother. Finally, it is of great advantage both in marriage and in widowhood if you are loved by your husband's relatives and it is a great disadvantage if you are hated by them. This was the aim of those who first transferred marriage from within the family to external relationships so that love and friendship would be more widely diffused and propagated. Therefore it is expedient

152. Nigidius Figulus: scholar, grammarian, friend of Cicero, died in exile in 45 B.C. In the passage of Aulus Gellius in which this etymology is given the writer is not Nigidius Figulus, but another grammarian, Antistius Labeo. Nigidius is mentioned a few lines later in this source, which perhaps explains Vives' erroneous attribution.

ergo affinium amorem diligenter parare aut partum iam conservare, ac confovere.

153. Socrus ferunt novercalibus in nurus odiis, vicissim has non nimis ardere illarum amore ac pietate. Terentius ex communi hominum consuetudine ac sensu 'Omnes,' inquit, 'socrus oderunt nurus.' Facete illa quae etiam socrus imaginem e saccaro confectam amaram esse dixit. Plutarchus Chaeroneus, et ex hoc auctore Hieronymus contra Iovinianum narrant in Lepti Africae veterem fuisse morem ut nova nupta postridie nuptiarum ollam a socru utendam rogaret, illa porro habere sese negaret, ut statim a nuptiis, cognitis in socru novercalibus moribus, minus in posterum offenderetur si quid intercideret asperius. Mihi vero causam inimicitiae huius reputanti plerumque stultus utriusque zelus videretur esse.

154. Positus est vir velut in medio inter matrem et uxorem, utraque alteram quasi paelicem insectatur. Mater aegre fert totum filii amorem a se in nurum traduci; uxor non patitur aliam amari praeter se. Hinc simultates et odia et rixae ut inter duos canes si quis altero spectante alterum demulceat. Pythagorici olim accedentibus amicis non minui amicitiam arbitrabantur, sed augeri et roborari. Sic nec mater debet existimare se minus matrem fore si matrimonio iungatur filius, nec uxor se minus uxorem si habeat socrum. Quin potius decet alteram alteri conciliare virum si quid offensiunculae inciderit. Stulta socrus, an non vis amari a filio coniugem, amicam, sociam individuam? Tulisses igitur te marito caram non esse? Quid miserius potes optare filio quam ut cum invisa atque infensa habitet? Stulta nurus, non vis a filio amari matrem? Tu ergo matrem non amas? Amaberis tu a marito ut socia, ut dulcis coniunx; amabitur mater a marito ut cui maritus vitam et nutrimenta et educationem debeat ac pro his magnam pietatem. Nurus quando se ac maritum idem esse non ignorat, mariti matrem suam esse existimabit nec illam minus amabit nec minus reverebitur quam veram matrem, sed officiosius colet, quo illam sibi artius demereatur et conciliet.

155. Non feret moleste amari a viro matrem, immo proba et sancta femina, si maritum animadverterit non satis erga matrem morigerum, adhortabitur et rogabit ut matri eum se praestet quem esse decet filium. Augusti

153. (Omnes ... nurus) *Ter. Hec. 201* // (Plutarchus ... asperius) *Hier. adv. Iovin. 1, 48*, *PL 23, 292*
154. (Pythagorici ... roborari) *Cic. off. 1, 56*

3 nimis **H** minus **Γ** // **5** ac sensu **Γ** atque opinione **H** // **6** confectam **Γ** factam **H** // **7** narrant **Γ** narrat **H** // **11** intercideret asperius **Γ** accideret quod nollet **H** // **12** videretur **HWW²B** videtur **V** // **15** traduci **Γ** elabi **H** / amari praeter se **Γ** praeter se amari **H** // **19** matrimonio iungatur **Γ** ducat **H** // **22** caram **Γ** carum **H** // **23** invisa atque **Γ** *deest in* **H** // **27** quando **Γ** cum **H** / non ignorat **Γ** sciat **H** // **31** animadverterit **Γ** viderit **H** // **32** filium **Γ** filium. Nulla erit tam iniqua socrus quae non aequior illi nurui fiat quam pudicam et mariti amantem cognorit Agrippina, Iuliae filia **H**

to gain fully the love of one's in-laws and once gained to preserve and cherish it.

153. They say that mothers-in-law have a stepmother's hatred for their daughters-in-law and that daughters-in-law in turn have no great love or respect for their mothers-in-law. Terence voiced the common sentiment in this regard; 'All mothers-in-law hate their daughters-in-law.' One woman said wittily that even a likeness of a mother-in-law made of sugar is bitter. Plutarch of Chaeronea and after him Jerome in his polemic against Jovinian says there was an ancient custom in Leptis Magna in Africa according to which the new bride on the day after the wedding would ask her mother-in-law to lend her a pot and she would say that she had none, so that immediately after the wedding the bride would be made aware of the mother-in-law's stepmotherly character and would be less offended if in the future something more acrimonious should occur between them. When I reflect on the reason for this enmity, the jealousy of both parties seems foolish to me.

154. A man is placed in the middle between mother and wife and each of them persecutes the other as if she were a mistress. The mother is discontent because all the son's love is transferred to the daughter-in-law. The wife cannot suffer that any other woman be loved besides herself. As a consequence rivalries, hatred and quarrels arise as between two dogs when someone strokes one of them in the presence of the other. The Pythagoreans were of the opinion that friendship is not diminished by the addition of friends but increased and strengthened. So a mother should not think she is less a mother when her son marries nor a wife think herself less a wife if she has a mother-in-law, but rather the one should reconcile the man to the other if some little difference arises. Foolish mother-in-law, do you not wish your son to love his wife, friend and inseparable companion? Would you have tolerated not being loved by your husband? What greater unhappiness can you wish for your son than that he live with a hateful and hostile woman? Foolish daughter-in-law, do you not wish that a son love his mother? Do you not love your mother? You will be loved by your husband as a companion and a sweet wife while your husband will love his mother as one to whom he owes his life and sustenance and upbringing and, consequently, a debt of filial piety. Since the daughter-in-law is not unaware that she and her husband are one, she will consider her husband's mother her own and will love and respect her no less than her true mother and indeed will be more dutiful towards her so that she will please her the more and win her favor.

155. A good and virtuous woman will not take it ill if her husband loves his mother but rather if she notices that he is not attentive enough towards his mother, she will urge and entreat him to conduct himself as a true son

neptis, quae Germanico nepoti Liviae ex Druso filio denupserat, Liviae et
velut nurus et velut privigna erat invisa, aspera ipsa alioqui et vehemens,
sed tanta pudicitia et tam raro in coniugem amore, ut indomitum illum
Liviae animum duabus illis virtutibus in bonum verteret. Nurus non alio af-
5   fectu alant in necessitate socrus et sustentent ac si ex eis natae essent. Ruth
Moabitis patriam et cognationem totam propter socrum sprevit, ne miseram
et afflictam anum in tam confuso maerore desereret. Itaque illam simul con-
solabatur verbis, simul refovebat labore vicemque omni modo explebat filiae. Nec mercede pietas illa caruit, nam consiliis socrus instructa Ruth mar-
10   itum invenit Booz hominem locupletem et Obeth peperit et proavia Davidis
Regis fuit et ex eius stirpe Christus Dominus natus est.

    156. Video aliam quoque odii huius esse causam. Graves et molestae sunt
nonnumquam nuribus socrus de reprehensione, velut censoriae quaedam et
morum magistrae; vicissim his illae de domus regimine, utrubique utraeque
15   immoderatae. Nam nec castigationes et admonitiones convenit esse asperas
atque importunas, sed observanda sunt tempora nec perinde acidis utendum verbis atque efficacibus. Nec omnino convenit matrem familiae nihil
domi agere, otiosam securamque velut hospitem sedere. Contra porro iuvenibus non tantum utilia sunt senum monita, sed etiam necessaria. Quae
20   qui refugit, ne ille haud bonae indolis signum exhibet! Scias eum multa
in se habere quae reprehendantur qui est admonenti infestus. In sententiis Regis sapientis sic legimus: 'Ei qui corripientem dura cervice contemnit,
repentinus superveniet interitus, et eum sanitas non sequetur.' Numquam
non prodest obiurgatio, etiam inimici, etiam falsa, quae saltem huc prospi-
25   ciat ut cautiores reddat, ne quando committamus in quod merito eiusmodi
obiurgatio competat. Ad haec in cura rei familiaris conducibile cum primis
est iuvenem inexercitatam, inexpertam immo vel exercitatissimam seniori
auscultare. Vetulus canis non de nihilo latrat. Prudentior fies si ad tuam
prudentiam senilem adiunxeris. Quocirca cedat aliquid de iure suo utraque
30   alteri, ut ad concordiam redigantur. Socrus in tempore admoneat, adhortetur, dehortetur et, si opus sit, obiurget, omnia ex vero amore et recto affectu, non odii acerbitate; nurus vicissim attento, prompto, alacri animo audiat unde fiat melior et capessat probitatis leges a senili prudentia profectas.
Socrus nurum instituat in re domestica, sed sic tamquam futuram dominam

---

156. (Ei ... sequetur) *Vulg. prov. 29, 1*

1 denupserat **Γ** denupsit **H** // 4 illis **Γ** *deest in* **H** // 8 omni modo explebat **Γ** omnino
repraesentabat **H** // 10 Obeth **Γ** Isai **H** / proavia **Γ** avia **H** // 12–p.190,3 Video alium
quoque ... parentum ac fratrum **Γ** *deest in* **H**

should. Agrippina, the granddaughter of Augustus, who had married Germanicus, Livia's grandson through her son Drusus, was hated by Livia both as daughter-in-law and as step-daughter. She herself was of a harsh and violent nature but of such chastity and so loving toward her husband that by these two virtues she turned the indomitable pride of Livia into feelings of benevolence. Daughters-in-law should support and sustain their mothers-in-law in their time of need with the same devotion true daughters would show. Ruth, the Moabite, rejected her native land and all her kin for the sake of her mother-in-law, not wishing to desert the wretched and afflicted old woman in her sea of troubles. She comforted her with words, cheered her by her labor and fulfilled the role of daughter in every way. Nor did that piety go unrewarded, for aided by the counsel of her mother-in-law, Ruth found a husband, Booz, a rich man, and bore Obeth and was the great-grandmother of King David, from whose lineage Christ the Lord was born.

156. I perceive another cause for this hatred. Often mothers-in-law are oppressive and bothersome to daughters-in-law because of their criticism; they become censorious and assume the role of teachers of morals while in turn daughters-in-law interfere with the running of the household, and in either case there is a lack of moderation. Remonstrances and admonitions should not be harsh and inappropriate but the right moment must be chosen and the words used must not be acrimonious, but helpful, nor is it fitting that the older matron should do nothing in the house, sitting there idle and carefree like a guest. On the contrary the advice of older people is not only useful to the young but necessary as well. One who avoids this gives proof of defect of character. You can be assured that one who is recalcitrant to advice has many things that are worthy of reprehension. Among the sayings of the wise king we read: 'He who obstinately despises reproof will suddenly meet his doom, and healing will not save him.' Criticism is never unprofitable, even when it comes from an enemy, even when it is false, as long as it serves to make us more careful not to do anything that would justly deserve rebuke. Moreover, in the case of the household it is especially expedient that a young woman without practice and experience, and even after she has had much practice, should listen to one older than she. An old dog does not bark without reason. You will be the wiser if you add an older person's wisdom to your own. Therefore let each one yield some of her rights to the other so that they may achieve harmony. The mother-in-law should admonish, encourage, discourage and, if necessary, reprimand at the appropriate time, always out of true love and affection without any trace of bitterness or hatred. The daughter-in-law in turn should listen with an attentive, alert and eager spirit in order to improve herself and apprehend the rules of virtue that come from age and experience. The mother-in-law will instruct the daughter-in-law in domestic affairs but in such a way as to be a good counsellor and guide for a future mistress of a household. The daughter-in-law

proba consultrix et directrix. Nurus pareat ut domini sui matri seu potius ut suae, quandoquidem per matrimonii vinculum coniunctae sunt omnes necessitudines, tanto artius primae illae parentum ac fratrum.

CAP. XIII.   QUOMODO CUM FILIO AUT FILIA CONIUGATA
CUM GENERO ET NURU

157. Ut in ceteris rebus omnibus decet uxorem mariti se iudicio ac voluntati accommodare, ita cum opus erit liberos coniugare. Hoc cum Aristoteles in libro secundo de Re familiari docet, tum ratio ipsa praescribit ut summa in filios auctoritas sit penes patrem. Sic Romanis legibus filii non in matris, sed in patris potestate erant quamdiu viveret, etiam coniugati et grandiores natu, nisi emanciparentur. Quantam in veros filios convenit esse apud patres potestatem cum in Christum voluerit Deus aliquam esse apud Iosephum! Angelus Domini cum per quietem Iosepho nuntiat quod in utero Mariae esset non virili esse conceptum semine, sed vi ac opere Divini Spiritus, 'Pariet,' inquit, 'Maria filium et vocabis nomen eius Iesum.' Non dixit, 'Pariet tibi filium,' quod veris patribus dici solet, nam mulieres viris pariunt liberos. Et tamen addit, 'Vocabis,' ut significaret ius atque auctoritatem eius qui pater existimatur, cum Virgini dixerit, 'Vocabitur nomen eius Iesus.'

158. Velim in collocanda filia annum eius cum minimum decimum septimum exspectari. Sic Plato, Aristoteles, Hesiodus suadent; sic natura ipsa, quae magnas ad libidinem flammas prima pubertate ingenuit. Sinendum ut eae restinguantur sua sponte, quo in posterum sint ad Venerem minus proclives. Accedit ea aetate robur gestando utero, fetui alimentum et incrementa maiora. Nuptiae si sunt sacramentum, si castum et purum opus, cui adesse Deum scimus velut auspicem, Ecclesiam videmus facem praeferre tamquam pronubantem, quorsum attinent tot flagitiorum et nequitiae instrumenta, convivia virorum ac feminarum, coetus a vino et crapula saltantium, vellicantium, palpantium, nugantium, omnibus ad accendendam libidinem compositis, tanto cultu, tanta pompa? Nec deest sedulus conciliator ac proxeneta pessime contrahentium diabolus.

159. In die tanti mysterii, cum nihil non mundum sanctumque dici et agi fas sit, dapes libidinem sollicitant, formae etiam arte adiutae. Accendit

---

157. (Ut ... coniugare) *Aristot. oec. 3, 1* **//** (Romanis legibus) *Inst. Iust. 1, 9* **//** (Pariet ... Iesum) *Vulg. Matth. 1, 21*
158. (Plato) *Plat. leg. 785B* **//** (Aristoteles) *Aristot. pol. 7, 16 (1335a)* **//** (Hesiodus) *Hes. erg. 698*

---

7 coniugare Γ coniugibus adiungere **H** **//** 8 praescribit Γ iubet **H** **//** 10 viveret **H** viverent Γ **//** 11 convenit Γ decet **H** **//** 14 Divini Spiritus Γ Spiritus Sancti **H** **//** 19–p.192,9 Velim in collocanda ... peractae fuerint nuptiae Γ *deest in* **H**

will obey her as the mother of her lord and master, or rather as her own mother, since through the bond of matrimony all relationships are made one, especially those fundamental ones of parents and brothers and sisters.

CHAPTER 13.   HOW SHE IS TO BEHAVE WITH HER MARRIED SON OR DAUGHTER, WITH HER SON-IN-LAW AND DAUGHTER-IN-LAW

157. As she should adapt herself to her husband's will and judgement in all other things, so also in the matter of the marriage of their children. It is prescribed by Aristotle in the second book of his *Economics* and by reason itself that the greatest authority over the children should reside with the father. So in Roman law children were under the power of the father, not the mother, as long as he lived, even after they were married and grown up, unless they were released from his power. How much power fathers should have over their own sons if God willed that even Joseph should have some power over Christ. When the Angel of the Lord announced to Joseph in a dream that that which was in Mary's womb was not conceived of a man's seed but by the power and working of the Holy Spirit, he said 'Mary will bring forth a son and you will call him by the name of Jesus.' He did not say 'She will bear you a son,' which is what is usually said to true fathers, for women bring forth children for men, and yet he added 'You will call,' to signify the right and authority of the one thought to be his father, while he said to the Virgin: 'His name shall be called Jesus.'

158. In marrying a daughter I would advise that she be at least seventeen years old. That is the opinion of Plato, Aristotle and Hesiod. Nature too concurs in this since it engenders great feelings of sexual desire at the beginning of puberty. We must allow these feelings to be allayed spontaneously so that they will be less given to carnal lust in the future. At that age they have strength to carry children in the womb, provide nourishment for the fetus and further its development. If marriage is a sacrament, a chaste and pure action, at which we know that God is present to give his good auspices, and we see the church bearing the torch in the role of the *pronuba*, what is the meaning of all these occasions of sin and wrong-doing? Promiscuous banquets of men and women, groups of people dancing under the influence of wine and drunkenness, tickling, touching, talking nonsense, all calculated to inflame lustful desires, with everyone vaunting their best finery. Nor is there lacking that tireless intermediary and broker of pernicious unions, the devil.

159. On a day of such mystery when nothing but what is pure and holy should be said and done, the celebrations encourage lust, aided by the cunning of beauty. The wine excites you, the occasion is inviting, the lavish

157. second book: Not in the second, but in the third book (cf. app. crit.).

vinum, invitat occasio, superbiam attollit cultus, ferociam aetas. Designationes et stulti quidam honores aliis arrogantiam movent, aliis odium, aliis invidiam. Nec unus sufficit nuptiis dies, proaulia celebranda sunt et epaulia, bona interdum patrimonii parte in convivium et sportulas et congiaria effusa atque iis elargita quibus profutura non est nec habituri sunt gratiam, immo reposcent. Et haec omnia dantur mulierum vanitati, dum gulae aut superbiae aut deliciis, denique ventosae vanitati suae indulgent et vel oblectare sese gestiunt per solutissimam laetitiam vel ostentare opes, etiam quas non habent. At ubi liberorum peractae fuerint nuptiae, nurum non insectabitur prudens mulier nec eius odio putabit se amorem impetrare, non illius modo, sed ne filii quidem, si amet illam. Si bene moneat, si instituat, si coram illa ea dicat et faciat quae ipsa nurus in exemplum tum castitatis tum frugalitatis possit accipere, si non serat inter coniuges inimicitias, sed alicunde subortas tollat illosque inter se totis viribus laboret reconciliare, denique in nurum materno se esse pectore patefaciat ac declaret, facile perficiet ut sibi filium demereatur et a nuru magnum sibi amorem acquirat magnamque reverentiam. Ille quanto ardentius amabit eam ex qua genitus est et per quam uxore utitur tum castiore, tum frugaliore et secum magis concordi, ut non obligatum modo sentiat se matris beneficio, sed institutricis uxoris suae auctorisque non parvae partis felicitatis suae.

160. Nurus haud aliter in socrum erit ac in matrem affecta, per quam ipsa peritior fit ac melior maritoque suaviore gaudet atque amantiore sui. Contraria omnia in aspera socru contingunt. Filiam nuptam mater non contendet tam suam esse quam cum adhuc caelebs erat. Cogitet in alienam iam domum tamquam in coloniam missam ad propagandam illic sobolem; monebit meliorum aut monita iam in caelibatu in mentem reducet nuptae; non aget cum ea quae putarit genero displicere; non ducet ad templa; non domo proferet ac ne loquetur quidem si id credat adversa generi voluntate fieri. Ne dicas mihi, indignabunda mulier, 'Filiae meae loqui non potero?' Filia quidem tua est, sed iam non tua, femina. Quicquid in eam habebas iuris, genero cessisti. Tu potius, si ex te genitam amas et vis eam beatam videre, hoc est, concorditer viventem cum marito, sis ei consultrix semper atque auctor ut viro per omnia morem gerat, ne tecum quidem loquatur illo invito. Adulter

10 putabit Γ putet **H** // 15 se ... declaret Γ sit affectu **H** // 16 demereatur Γ magis demereatur **H** / acquirat Γ paret **H** // 17 genitus est **H** genitus Γ // 21 aliter Γ secus **H** // 22 peritior ... melior Γ peritior et melior est **H** // 23–24 non contendet Γ nolet **H** // 24 adhuc caelebs erat Γ virgo esset **H** // 25 sobolem Γ gentem **H** // 26 meliorum **HWW²B** meliora **V** // 28 adversa generi Γ generi adversa **H** // 29 dicas Γ dicat **H** / indignabunda Γ stulta **H** // 31 ex te genitam amas Γ amas filiam **H** // 33 illo invito Γ nisi ille sinat **H**

surroundings puff up pride, the time of life stirs up violent feelings. Assignments at table and certain inane honors move some to arrogance, others to hatred, others to envy. One day is not enough for the nuptials; preliminary ceremonies must be celebrated and post-nuptials, while in the meantime a good part of the family patrimony is squandered on the banquet, the take-home gifts and other donations, and, what is more, bestowed upon those to whom it will be of no benefit and who will return no gratitude, but rather will demand it as their right. And all of this is a concession to female vanity, to indulge their palate, their pride, their desire for amusement and their fickle vanity. They are eager either to amuse themselves in uninhibited pleasure or show off their wealth, even that which they do not possess. But when the wedding is over, the prudent woman will not maltreat her daughter-in-law, nor think that by her dislike she will win over her love or even that of her son, if he loves her. If on the other hand she gives her good advice, if she instructs her, if she says and does things in her presence that the daughter-in-law will accept as examples of chastity and frugality, if she does not sow discord between the two spouses but eliminates those that have sprung up from some other source and strives with every effort to effect harmony between them and manifests her motherly love for her daughter-in-law, then she will easily earn her son's affection and the great love and respect of her daughter-in-law. How much more fervently her son will love her through whose instrumentality he has a more chaste and frugal wife and one more like-minded, so that he will not only feel indebted to her as the author of his being, but as the teacher of his wife and the one responsible for no small part of his happiness.

160. The daughter-in-law will act no differently towards her mother-in-law than she would towards her own mother since through her she has learned more skills, improves herself and enjoys the greater love and favor of her husband. The exact opposite occurs in the case of a harsh mother-in-law. A mother will not claim the same rights to her married daughter as when she was single. She will consider that she has gone off to another household, as to a foreign colony, to raise up offspring there. She will give her better advice or recall to the mind of the married girl recommendations she had given her before she was married. She will not discuss things with her that she thinks may offend her husband. She will not take her to church, will not take her from her house and will not even speak to her if she thinks this would be contrary to the will of her son-in-law. And do not say to me resentfully, 'Can I not speak to my own daughter?' She is your daughter, yes, but not your wife. What jurisdiction you have over her you transferred to your son-in-law. Rather, if you love your daughter and desire to see her happy, that is, living in harmony with her husband, be her counsellor and advise her to be obedient to her husband in all things and not even talk to you if he does not wish it. Whoever wishes more control over another

est quisquis in alienam uxorem plus sibi vult licere quam maritus permittat; fur est qui rem alienam attingit domino invito. Generum non aliter amabit ac filium, reverebitur tamen plus quam filium. Neque enim licere sibi socrus arbitrabitur in generum quae in filium, nisi quod nec minus ei bene cupiet
5 nec aliter consulet atque adhortabitur, sed sic tamen ut suadere magis ac rogare videatur quam vel praecipere vel imperare. Et quando ille iam indissolubili nodo iunctus est filiae, qualiscumque sit, non tolerandus solum, sed probandus. Laudandus etiam apud filiam, ne qua discordiae occasio inter illos obrepat, id est, postremae miseriae seminarium. Felicius vivet uxor
10 si mariti mala omnino ignoret quam si cum eorum consolatione luctetur. Quid quod socrus quae generos apud filias accusant, ipsae suum damnant iudicium quae tales elegerunt?

CAP. XIV.   DE MATRE FAMILIAS PROVECTIORIS AETATIS

161. Matronae natu grandiori continget illud quod ibi, Aegyptiae volucri.
15 Narrant quibus rerum naturas perquirere curae fuit, ut annosior iam aromatis proximae Arabiae quicquid in corpore est vitiosi humoris repurget halitumque ore emittat suavissimum. Defuncta mulier et libidine et muneribus pariendi atque educandi caelestia potius quam terrena sapiet ac spirabit. Nihil sive loquetur sive aget quod non sanctissimum sit et exemplum iunioribus
20 ad imitandum. 'Tum incipiet notum esse eius nomen,' ut Gorgias dicebat, 'cum sit ignota facies.' Tum superior vita sanctissime acta incipiet proferri; tum vere proba mulier ad virum parendo imperabit et assequetur ut magna sit auctoritate apud maritum, quae semper sub mariti auctoritate vixerit. Themistoclis uxor Archippa parendo diligentissime coniugi suo Themisto-
25 cli tanto sibi illum amore conciliavit ac devinxit, ut vicissim ipse prudentissimus vir ac in primis strenuus imperator uxori paene in omnibus obsequeretur. Unde gradatio illa Graecorum per iocum a multis iactata: 'Quicquid puer hic vult (Cleophantus is erat, matri unice carus), Graeci volunt; nam quod hic vult, mater vult; quod vero mater, idem Themistocles; porro

161. (Ibi ... suavissimum) *Cic. nat. deor. 1, 81* // (Tum ... facies) *Plut. mor. 242F* // (Archippa) *Plut. Them. 32* // (Quicquid ... omnes) *Plut. mor. 185D* //

2 aliter Γ secus **H** // 3 socrus Γ mulier **H** // 5 magis Γ potius **H** // 6–12 Et quando ille ... elegerunt Γ *deest in* **H** // 7 nodo **BV** modo **WW²** // 18 caelestia ... spirabit Γ incipiet caelestia potius quam terrena sapere ac spirare **H** // 20 ad imitandum Γ quod imitentur **H** // 23 sub mariti auctoritate vixerit Γ in mariti auctoritate vixit **H** // 24–25 coniugi suo Themistocli Γ viro **H** // 25 ac devinxit Γ *deest in* **H** // 26 imperator Γ vir **H** // 27 a multis Γ plerumque **H** // 28 matri **HWW²** marito **BV** // 29 mater vult **H** mater Γ

man's wife than a husband would permit is an adulterer. Whoever touches the property of another without the owner's permission is a thief. She will love her son-in-law as she loves her own son and will have more respect for him than for her son. A mother-in-law will not presume to have the same power over a son-in-law as she does over her son, except that she will desire his welfare in equal measure and will advise and encourage him equally, but more in the way of persuasion and suggestion than giving orders. Since he is joined by an indissoluble bond to your daughter, whoever he is, he must not only be tolerated but approved. You must praise him before your daughter to prevent any semblance of discord from creeping in, for it is the seedbed of the greatest unhappiness. A wife will live more happily if she is completely ignorant of her husband's defects rather than trying to resign herself to them. What shall we say, then, of mothers-in-law who accuse their sons-in-law in front of their daughters, do they not condemn their own judgement in having chosen them, such as they are?

CHAPTER 14.   ON A MARRIED WOMAN OF ADVANCED YEARS

161. Married women advanced in years will inherit the fate of the ibis, the famous bird of Egypt. Those who have concerned themselves with the study of natural history tell us that when it comes to the end of its days it purges its body with an aroma from nearby Arabia of all foul humors and emits a passing sweet breath from its mouth. When a woman is free of all carnal desire and has fulfilled her duties of bearing and bringing up children, she will emanate an odor that is more heavenly than earthly, and shall say and do nothing but what is of great sanctity and may serve as an example to those younger than she. 'Then her name will begin to be known' as Gorgias said, 'when her face is unknown.' Then the holy actions of her past life will come to light. Then the truly good woman through obedience to her husband will hold sway and she who always lived in obedience to her husband will command great authority over him. Archippa, wife of Themistocles, through her unswerving obedience to her husband so won over his love and loyalty that this very wise man and spirited leader obeyed his wife in practically everything. This gave rise to a chain of command the Greek used to refer to humorously: 'Whatever this boy (Cleophantus, who was the darling of his mother) wants, the Greeks want. For whatever he wants, the mother wants; whatever his mother wants, Themistocles wants, and

---

161. ibis: A bird worshipped by the Egyptians, the avatar of the god Thoth. It was celebrated for its purity and its flesh was regarded as incorruptible.

Gorgias: (c.485–c.380 B.C.), one of the most influential of the ancient sophists. One of Plato's dialogues is named after him.

quod Themistocles, id Athenienses; quod Athenienses, hoc Graeci omnes.'
Dominus Abrahae praecipit Sarae uti dicto sit audiens, quoniam iam illa
senex erat et libidinis emortuae, idcirco nihil iuvenile aut impultrice libidine
pudendum consultura.

5   **162.** Neque vero quacumque sit aetate velut solutam se legibus credat
et nactam rerum omnium licentiam. Semper subici viro debet, sub eius pa-
trocinio et tutela degere et pudore ornari. Sed in hoc tempus aetatis ubi per-
venerit, locatis liberis, soluta curis terrenis, spectans quidem terram corpore
terrae reddendo, animo vero caelum ut illuc immigraturo, sensus omnes,
10   animum, mentem universam ad Dominum eriget totaque in profectionem
accincta et incumbens nihil meditabitur quod ad instans iter non accom-
modetur. Caveat modo ne ex religione in superstitionem per ignorantiam
delabatur, quod vitium aetatem illam solet infestare. Multum quidem sit
sanctis actionibus intenta, sed plus tamen fidat clementiae et benignitati
15   Dei. Ne confidat sibi, tamquam operibus suis eo perventurae quo instituit
potius quam Christi beneficio ac munere. Cumque vigeat adhuc plus animus quam corpus, detrahat corporis laboribus, addat animi. Plus oret et
attentius, saepius de Deo cogitet ardentiusque, rarius ieiunet, minus se cir-
cumeundo templa defatiget. Nihil opus est fraudet suum sibi genium aut se-
20   nile corpus extenuet. Prosit aliis bene monendo, prosit exemplo vitae suae,
reditura ad illam commodi parte haud sane exigua.

161. (Dominus ... emortuae) *Vulg. gen. 21, 12*
162. (Multum ... intenta) *Vulg. Iac. 5, 16*

2 uti ... audiens Γ dicto audientem esse **H** / quoniam iam **H** quoniam Γ // **3** impultrice
omnes edd.; Nonius 150, 29 (varia lectio = impulstrix) // **5–7** Neque vero ... Sed in hoc tempus aetatis Γ In hunc locum **H** // **8** terram corpore Γ corpore terram **H** // **9** caelum Γ
caelos **H** // **10** profectionem Γ profectione **H** // **13** quod ... infestare Γ *deest in* **H** // **15**
perventurae Γ perventuram **H** // **21** exigua Γ parva **H**

whatever Themistocles wants, so do the Athenians, and whatever the Athenians want, all Greeks want.' The Lord bade Abraham to listen to what Sarah told him, since she was now an old woman free of all carnal desires and would not counsel him anything that was childish or shameful, under the instigation of lust.

162. But of whatever age she is let her not think that she is exempt from the law and has license to do whatever she wishes. She must always be subject to her husband, spend her days under his protection and guardianship and adorn herself with chastity. But when she arrives at this age, with her children all married, freed from earthly cares, turning the eyes of her body to the earth to which she must render her body, and with the eyes of her soul looking to heaven, where she is to go to take up residence, she will raise all her senses, her mind and soul to the Lord, and girding herself for that departure, she will meditate on nothing that is not suited to that impending journey. Let her take care, however, not to slip from true religious feelings into superstition, through ignorance, a vice that often affects that age. Let her be intent on pious actions but trust more to the mercy and kindness of God. Let her not be too confident in herself, as if by her works she can arrive at her fixed goal rather than by the goodness and gift of Christ. And since the soul still retains more vigor than the body, let her omit physical labors and increase those of the soul. She will pray more frequently and with more attention. She will think more often and with more fervor of God. She will fast less often and will tire herself less in visiting churches. There is no necessity to deny her inner spirit or wear out her aged body. Let her profit others by her good advice, let her do good by the example of her life, as she will receive no small reward in return.

J. L. VIVES

DE INSTITUTIONE
FEMINAE CHRISTIANAE

LIBER TERTIUS

IOANNIS LODOVICI VIVIS VALENTINI
DE INSTITUTIONE FEMINAE CHRISTIANAE

LIBER TERTIUS
QUI EST DE VIDUIS

CAP. I.   DE LUCTU VIDUARUM

1. Sancta mulier mortuo marito maxima se accepisse damna sciat: sublatum esse pectus illud caritatis et amoris mutui plenum; non modo dimidium
animi sui periisse sibi (sic enim docti quidam homines quos validissime de-
amarent nominarunt), sed ipsam totam sibi ereptam et exstinctam. Hinc honestae lacrimae, hinc iustus dolor et planctus non improbandus; maximum
argumentum impudici animi et saevi non plorare maritum exstinctum. Duo
sunt feminarum genera quae in lugendis maritis contrariis modis aeque peccant: et quae nimis lugent et quae parum. Vidi in hac Gallia Belgica et in
Britannia mulieres maritorum morte non acrius perculsas quam si leviter no-
tus aliquis interiisset; manifestum indicium frigidae caritatis coniugalis, quo
nihil sceleratius dici potest vel detestandum magis. Respondent, cum reprehenduntur, sic ferre genium regionis; quod obtendere solent qui vitia sua
in vim siderum aut caeli solive naturam referunt. Ingenium regionis peccata
non ingerit (alioqui non delinquentes essent puniendi, sed regio) nec ab aere
vel caelo accipimus scelera, sed ex moribus. Sub omni caelo et bene vivitur
et male, nec ora est in terris ulla tam infelix quae non etiam bonos ferat,
nec ulla sic beata quae careat malis. Vidi rursum et quidem plurimas quae
maritorum salutem vel vita sua libentissime redemissent. Non est quod ingenio loci imputentur vitia. Frigidius est caelum in suprema Thracia, at de
illis Pomponius Mela sic scribit: 'Ne feminis quidem segnis est animus; super mortuorum virorum corpora interfici simulque sepeliri votum eximium
habent. Et quia plures simul singulis nuptae sunt, cuius id sit decus apud

1. (docti ... nominarunt) *Hor. carm. 1, 3, 8* // (Ne feminis ... vincere) *Mela 2, 19*

1 LODOVICI **H** LUDOVICI **Γ** / VALENTINI **HWW²** *deest in* **VB** // **8** validissime **Γ**
vehementer **H** // **14** et in Britannia **Γ** *deest in* **H** / acrius **Γ** acerbius **H** // **16** detestandum
Γ impium **H** // **18** siderum **Γ** sideris **H** // **19** ingerit **Γ** infert **H** // **21** infelix **Γ** misera **H**
// **22** malis. Vidi rursum **Γ** Dixi vidisse hic me quae mariti morte non moverentur. Vidi
etiam **H** // **23** vel **Γ** *deest in* **H** // **24** vitia **Γ** sua vitia **H** / suprema Thracia **Γ** Getica **H**
// **25** sic scribit **Γ** sic refert **H**

JUAN LUIS VIVES
ON THE EDUCATION OF THE CHRISTIAN WOMAN

BOOK THREE
ON WIDOWS

CHAPTER 1.   ON THE MOURNING OF WIDOWS

1. The holy woman should know that when her husband has died she has
suffered a most grievous loss: a loving heart, full of warmth and affection,
has been taken from her; not only has half her soul perished (for that is
how certain learned men referred to those whom they loved intensely) but
her whole self has been wrested forcefully from her and annihilated. This
is cause for honest tears, justifiable sorrow and unreproachable grief. The
greatest proof of a shameless and cruel mind is not to weep over a husband
who has died. There are two types of women equally guilty, though in opposite ways, in the matter of mourning a lost husband—those who mourn too
much and those who mourn too little. I have seen here in the Low Countries
and in Britain women who were no more stricken by their husband's death
than if some casual acquaintance had died; this is sure indication of a cold
conjugal love, than which there is nothing more wicked and more detestable.
When they are reproved for this, their answer is that it is the character of
the region in which they live, a common excuse of those who blame the influence of the stars or the weather or the soil for their vices. The character
of a region does not produce moral failings. If it were so, then wrongdoers
should not be punished, but their place of origin. We do not acquire vices
from the air or the sky but from our manner of life. One can lead a good
or a bad life in any climate. There is no region on earth so cursed that it
does not produce good men nor one so blessed that it is without evil men.
Then again I have seen many women who would gladly have paid for their
husbands' health with their own lives. One cannot ascribe vices to the nature of a certain locality. The climate of northern Thrace is bitterly cold
but Pomponius Mela writes this of its inhabitants: 'There is no lack of spirit
in the women either; their fondest wish is to be killed and buried together
with their dead spouses and since many women are married to the same
husband at the same time, they hotly contend for this privilege before those

---

1. Pomponius Mela: Born at Tingentera, near the modern Gibraltar, wrote a geogra-
phy entitled *De Chorographia* during the reign of the Emperor Claudius.

iudicaturos magno certamine affectant; moribus datur estque maxime laetum cum in hoc contenditur vincere.'

2. Ad eundem modum consuesse Indicas mulieres certare gravissimi auctores tradidere. Apud Germanos veteres, a quibus Belgae prope universi ducunt originem, 'Tantum virgines nubunt et cum spe votoque uxoris semel transigitur. Sic unum accipiunt quomodo unum corpus unamque vitam, nec ulla cogitatio ultra, ne longior cupiditas, ne tamquam maritum, sed tamquam matrimonium ament,' ut intelligas mutatos cum deliciis atque opulentia mores et divitiarum ardorem pios caritatis ardores exstinxisse. Tota lex Christi nihil aliud sonat quam caritatem, amorem, ardorem. 'Ad ignem terris immittendum veni,' dicit Dominus, 'et quid laboro magis quam ut accendatur?' Sed ubi Christo pauperi adiunximus pecuniosum diabolum et sobriae pietati luxuriam ac temulentiam, castae severitati impudicas delicias, Christianismo gentilitatem, Deo diabolum, talem societatem aspernatus Christus munera sua abstulit, diaboli reliquit. At firmitas forsan tanta est in animis earum ut ipsae se quam primum sapientia consolentur et ictae prostrataeque subito erigant. Laudarem in viro, et quidem sapiente; at in sexu imbecilli suspecta est tam importuna sapientia.

3. Maximos et sapientissimos viros doluisse mortem levium amicorum scimus, etiam ubertim illacrimatos. Solon, Atheniensium legum lator et unus ex septem sapientibus, lacrimis et planctibus celebrari exsequias suas iubet, ut indicarent amici quanto ipsius desiderio tenerentur. Occisa Romae Lucretia, cum Iunius Brutus, mortis et pudicitiae illius a regis filio laesae ultor, reges Roma exegisset bellumque ea de causa esset a regibus motum, in primo eius conflictu Brutus occubuit. Hunc matronae vindicem pudicitiae annum luxerunt. Si illae alienum virum quod alienam pudicitiam vindicasset tantopere mortuum doluerunt, quanto aequius est te tuae pudicitiae non modo vindicem, sed tutorem, tui corporis propugnatorem, tuorum filiorum patrem, familiae, domus, bonorum omnium columen, dominum, defensorem?

4. Vis dicam? Fleres, si non illinc discederes locupletior quam intraras; nunc pecuniae laetitia sensum omnem doloris lenit ac demulcet. Fleres mortuum, si amasses viventem; nunc ereptum non doles quod carus non

---

2. (Ad eundem modum ... auctores tradidere) *Plut. mor. 499C; Hier. adv. Iovin. 1, 44, PL 23, 274* ∥ (Tantum ... ament) *Tac. Germ. 19* ∥ (Ad ignem ... accendatur) *Vulg. Luc. 12, 49*

3. (Solon ... tenerentur) *Plut. Sol. 21* ∥ (Occisa ... luxerunt) *Liv. 2, 7, 4*

5 ducunt originem Γ originem ducunt **H** ∥ **6** unum accipiunt **HWW²B** unum accipiunt maritum **V** / nec **HWW²B** ne **V** ∥ **12** pecuniosum Γ divitem **H** ∥ **17** et quidem sapiente Γ *deest in* **H** ∥ **32** lenit ac demulcet Γ opprimit **H** ∥ **33** carus Γ carum **H**

assigned to give judgment. The decision is based on moral conduct and it is a great cause of joy to win in these contests.'

2. Grave writers have recorded that Indian women used to vie with one another in this same manner. Among the ancient Germans, from whom almost all Belgians are descended, 'Only virgins marry and their hope and aspiration to be a wife is satisfied but once in a lifetime. They take one husband as one body and one life and have no further thought or desire than to love not so much their husbands as matrimony itself.' You can see from this how customs change with the introduction of pleasures and riches and how the ardent desire for wealth has extinguished the holy aspirations of love. The whole law of Christ gives expression to nothing else but charity, love, fervor. 'I have come to set fire to the earth,' says the Lord, 'and what greater wish have I but that it be kindled.' But when we have joined the affluence of the devil to the poverty of Christ, and luxury and drunkenness to abstemious piety, shameless self-indulgence to chaste austerity, paganism to Christianity, the devil to God, then Christ, spurning that kind of partnership, took away his gifts and left those of the devil. But perhaps nowadays these women have such strength of character that they will find comfort as soon as possible in their own wisdom and, though beaten and prostrate, will raise themselves up immediately. I should find this praiseworthy in a man, that is to say, a wise man, but in the weaker sex this unexpected wisdom is suspect.

3. We know that great and wise men mourned the death of friends whom they scarcely knew and even shed copious tears over them. Solon, the Athenian lawgiver, one of the seven ancient sages, ordered his funeral to be solemnized with tears and lamentations so that his friends could manifest the great longing they felt for him. When Lucretia was killed in Rome, Junius Brutus, avenging her death and the violation of her chastity by the king's son, drove the kings from Rome. In retaliation the kings started a war and Brutus was killed in the first armed clash. The matrons of Rome mourned the death of this defender of chastity for a year. If they showed such grief at the death of another woman's husband because he had defended another woman's chastity, how much more reasonable is it that you mourn not only the avenger, but the protector of your chastity, the defender of your body, the father of your children, the support, master and defender of your family, home and all your possessions?

4. Shall I put it more clearly? You would weep if you did not come away from that union richer than when you entered into it; now the joy that money brings soothes and alleviates your feelings of sorrow. You would mourn him when he is dead if you had loved him when he was alive; you

---

2. Indian women: The practice of suttee is mentioned by the writer Diodorus Siculus, who lived during the time of Augustus, and also by Plutarch.

erat. Sunt quae maritos ablatos gaudeant tamquam triste excusserint iugum
et ceu nodo ac dominatu solutae nactaeque libertatem prope exsultent. O
mentium caecitatem! Non est libera navis quae rectore caret, sed deserta;
nec liber est sine magistro puer, sed vagus, sine ratione et lege. Sic mulier
5   marito orbata vere est quod audit vidua, id est, destituta et desolata. Tum
plane ventis temere agitatur ut navis gubernatore carens, et sine mente atque
consilio fertur ut puer adempto paedagogo. Dicet aliqua, 'Talis erat maritus
ut praestaret sine illo agere quam cum illo.' Nulla id umquam proba dixit
nec mala tacuit. Si tibi tam carus fuisset vir quam leges connubiorum a Deo
10   ipso latae iubent—ut alterum te esse reputares—non secus aegre ferres illum eripi quam te. Malae mulieri si maritus flagitiorum omnium licentiam
non largitur, intolerabilis est. Sanctae matronae nullus est tam molestus coniunx quem mortuum malit quam viventem. Sed hisce de rebus disputare
quid attinet? Satis superiore volumine abundeque declaratum a nobis est
15   nec probae dignam esse nomine nec uxoris, quae non toto pectore virum
amat ut se ipsa.

    5. O provida natura, seu potius sapientissimus bonorum morum magister
Deus! Nulla est virtus cuius non aliquam finxerit tam observatricem animantem ut optimo iure contemptores virtutis illius coarguat. Quam pudorem in-
20   cutiunt! Ut suggillant apiculae inertes homines; desides, formiculae! Canum
fidelitas infideles homines peiores se testatur esse; columbae et oves ut frau-
des et astutiam damnant! Fides vero et caritas coniugii columborum ac tur-
turum moribus exprimitur hominibus quasique exprobratur; quae aves (ut
Aristoteles prodidit) uno mare contentae vivunt nec alterum recipiunt. Tur-
25   tur vero, compare amisso, nec liquidam bibit nec in frondenti ramo sedet nec aliis sui generis colludentibus ac lascivientibus se admiscet. Hos
castos amores sanctosque significat Salomon cum sponsam ad se invitans:
'Vox,' inquit, 'turturis audita est in terra nostra.' Et sponsam ipsam modo
columbae assimilat, modo turturi. Audiant morosae et querulae uxores Pli-
30   nium de columbis haec narrantem: 'Pudicitia illis prima et adulteria ignota; coniugii fidem non violant communemque servant domum. Nisi caelebs aut vidua domum non relinquit et imperiosos mares subinde etiam
iniquos ferunt. Quippe suspicio est adulterii, quamvis natura non sit, tunc
plenum querela guttur saevique rostro ictus.' Sic ille. Idcirco Dominus

---

5. (Quae aves ... admiscet) *Aristot. hist. an. 9, 7 (613a)* // (Vox ... nostra) *Vulg. cant. 2, 12*
// (Pudicitia ... ictus) *Plin. nat. 10, 104* // (Dominus ... puerperae) *Vulg. Luc. 2, 24* //

2–3 O mentium caecitatem Γ stultae **H** // **5** vere est **HWW²B** vere **V** // **17** sapientissimus Γ acutissimus **H** // **18** est virtus Γ virtus est **H** // **19** illius **H** illis Γ // **19–20** contemptores ... inertes homines Γ contemptores arguat virtutis illius. Quam reprehendunt
apiculae inertes homines **H** // **22** colomborum Γ palumbium **H** // **23** exprimitur ... exprobratur Γ ostenditur **H** // **29** assimilat Γ confert **H** // **29**–p.206,**12** Audiant morosae
... utrisque coniugum.' Sic ille Γ *deest in* **H**

do not mourn him now that he is gone because you never had any affection for him. There are some women who rejoice at their husband's death as if they had shaken off some cruel yoke, as if liberated from the fetters of a despot, almost exulting in a new-found freedom. What blindness of heart! A ship without a rudder is not free, but abandoned, and a child without a teacher is not free, but directionless, without rule or law. So a woman bereft of her husband is in the true meaning of the word, widowed, that is, destitute and deserted. She is at the mercy of the winds like a ship without a rudder, and is carried along hither and thither without plan or purpose, like a child deprived of its tutor. Certain women may say: 'My husband was the kind of person that it was easier to live without than with.' No good woman ever said such a thing and no bad woman ever failed to say it. If your husband had been as dear to you as the laws of marriage that come from God dictate, bidding you to think of him as another self, you would suffer his death as if it were your own. To a bad woman, if her husband does not grant her the freedom to indulge in all kinds of misbehavior, he is intolerable. For a virtuous woman no husband is so troublesome that she would prefer him dead rather than alive. But what is the use of discussing these matters? I have made it abundantly clear in the previous book that a woman who does not love her husband with all her heart as she does herself is worthy neither of the name of good woman nor that of wife.

5. O provident nature! or rather, O God, most wise teacher of a good life! There is no virtue for which he has not created an exemplar in some living thing to refute justifiably those who scorn that virtue. What shame and humiliation bees inspire in the slothful! And ants in those who are indolent! The fidelity of dogs is proof that unfaithful men are inferior to them; and are not doves and sheep a living condemnation of fraud and cunning? Doves and turtle-doves are an example to us of the loyalty and affection of marriage and are almost a reproach to us. As Aristotle recounts, these birds are content to live with one male, and do not accept another. When it has lost its mate the turtle-dove does not drink water or perch on the leafy boughs or join in the pleasures and frolicking of the other birds of its species. It is this chaste and holy love to which Solomon refers when he invites the spouse to come to him in these words: 'The voice of the turtle-dove is heard in our land.' And he compares the spouse now to a dove, now to a turtle-dove. Difficult and quarrelsome wives should listen to what Pliny says of doves: 'Chastity is uppermost with them and adultery unknown. They do not violate their mutual fidelity and they watch over their home together. Unless she is without a mate or has lost her mate, she does not leave the house and she puts up with domineering and even abusive males. If they suspect adultery, although this is not in their nature, then they complain loudly and peck fiercely with their beaks.' For that reason the Lord wishes that doves or

offerri vult turtures aut columbas in purgatione mulieris puerperae, ut significetur infantem qui in conspectu Domini sistitur ex pudico et caro coniugio natum esse, cuius symbolum est in illis aviculis, immo et exemplum iis hominibus qui sic ab humana degenerarunt mente, ut rectum et sanctum
5 a bestiolis edocendi sint. Non gravabor et illud ex Aeliano addere: 'Cornices', inquit, 'caritate inter se quadam et fide coniunguntur. Mirum enim in modum sese amant ubi primum societatem coierunt neque illae temere ac promiscue miscentur, narrantque naturae illarum periti ex pari mortua una alteram nulli in posterum adiungi, sed viduae ac maeste aetatem degere.
10 Proditum quoque est in nuptiis antiquorum post hymnum Hymenaeo dictum cornicem invocari solitam, symbolum concordiae utrisque coniugum.' Sic ille.

6. Verum mulieres illae non peccant minus quae modum fletibus et luctui nesciunt ponere. Nam et recenti plaga immoderatis eiulatibus omnia com-
15 plent atque confundunt, capillos lacerant, tundunt pectus, genas dilaniant, caput ad parietem arietant, humi sese applodunt et luctum quam longissime protrahunt, velut in Sicilia, Graecia, Asia, Romae, ut etiam legibus Duodecim Tabularum senatusque decretis modus fuerit et moderatio luctui adhibenda. Idcirco his gentibus scribens Apostolus consolandos eos habuit,
20 dicens: 'Nolo vos, fratres, ignorare de iis qui dormierunt, ne contristemini ut ceteri qui spem non habent. Si enim credimus quod Iesus mortuus est et revixit, sic et Deus illos qui dormierunt per Iesum ducet cum eo.' Vidua lugeat maritum mortuum et quidem vero affectu. Non vociferetur, non se applosione manuum aut concussione membrorum vel corporis afflictet. Sic
25 doleat ut meminerit modestiae ac moderationis, ut aegritudinem non tam ipsa ostentet quam alii facile intelligant. Hinc ubi primus ille doloris assultus conquierit, incipiat de consolatione cogitare. Nolo afferre explicatas a philosophis longis voluminibus consolandi rationes. Feminam Christianam doceo; ex Christiana philosophia, ad quam reliqua omnis humana sapientia
30 mera stultitia est, petendam medicinam censeo. Revocemus in memoriam quod modo ex Apostolo posui: illos qui per Iesum dormierunt adducendos a Deo cum ipso Iesu ad aeternam beatitudinem; itaque bona spe debere nos esse.

---

5. (Cornices ... coniugum) *Ail. nat. 3, 9*
6. (legibus) *Cic. leg. 2, 59; Sen. contr. 4, 11; Sen. epist. 63, 13* // (Duodecim Tabularum) *Cic. leg. 2, 59* // (Nolo vos ... eo) *Vulg. I Thess. 4, 12–13* // (illos ... beatitudinem) *Vulg. I Thess. 4, 13* // (itaque ... esse) *Vulg. I Thess. 4, 17*

13 mulieres illae Γ illae mulieres **H** // **18** luctui Γ luctibus **H** // **30–31** Revocemus ... posui Γ Meminerimus dicti Apostoli **H** // **32** ad aeternam beatitudinem Γ *deest in* **H**

turtle-doves be offered in the purification of a woman who has borne a child to signify that the infant that is placed in the sight of the Lord was born of a chaste and loving marriage. These little birds are a symbol and example to those persons who have so deviated from the norms of human conduct that they must be taught what is right and holy by tiny creatures. I can add a quotation from Aelian on this matter: 'Crows' he said, 'are united to each other by a certain love and fidelity. They love each other in an extraordinary way when they first become mates, nor do they indulge in random promiscuity. Experts in the study of these birds relate that when one of them dies the other does not join itself to another mate, but lives out the rest of its existence in sad solitude. It is recorded that in ancient weddings after the hymn to Hymen this bird was invoked as a symbol of the concord between the two spouses.'

6. But those women who cannot put an end to their tears and mourning are no less guilty. They fill the air with unceasing laments over their recent loss and throw all into confusion tearing their hair, beating their breast, lacerating their cheeks, striking their heads against the wall, dashing themselves upon the ground, and prolonging their grief to great lengths, as in Sicily, Greece, Asia Minor, and in Rome, to such an extent that in the laws of the Twelve Tables and in decrees of the Senate a limit had to be set to the expression of mourning. Accordingly, when the Apostle wrote to these people he had to console them, saying 'I do not wish, brethren, that you be ignorant concerning those who have fallen asleep, so that you may not be saddened, as others do who have no hope. For if we believe that Jesus died and rose again, even so God will bring with him those who have fallen asleep in Jesus.' Let a widow mourn her dead husband with true affection, but not cry out or afflict herself by beating her hands together or with blows to her limbs or her body. In her grief she should observe modesty and moderation and not make such show of her distress that others will see it. When the first shock of sorrow subsides, she should begin to take thought of consolation. I do not wish to cite the reasons for consolation as explained by philosophers in lengthy tomes. I am teaching the Christian woman and believe that the remedy is to be found in Christian philosophy, in comparison to which all other human wisdom is mere folly. Let us call to mind what I just quoted from the Apostle, that those who have fallen asleep in Jesus will be led to eternal beatitude with the same Jesus. And so we should be of good hope.

---

5. Aelian: Claudius Aelianus (c.170–235), a Roman author and teacher of rhetoric who wrote in Greek, famous for his *On the Nature of Animals*, cited here.

Hymen: Greek god of marriage.

6. The Twelve Tables: The earliest written form of Roman law, adopted c. 450 B.C., which remained the foundation of Roman civil law until Justinian's codification about 530 A.D.

7. Cogitabit ergo prudens mulier hac lege natos mortales omnes, hac lege vivere ut naturae tamquam creditori debitum reddant quandocumque reposcet; alios quidem paulo citius, alios paulo serius, sed tamen omnes communi teneri sorte ut nascendi ita vivendi ac moriendi; animas nostras immortales esse; hanc vitam esse profectionem in aliam aeternam et felicissimam iis qui sancte ac pie temporariam hanc transegerint, quod facillimum praestat religio Christiana non meritis nostris, sed bonitate et iustitia illius qui nos a vinculis mortis sua morte exsolvit, deleto per sanguinem suum edicto illo Patris quo universum genus hominum capitis damnabatur, nisi ille subvenisset; mortem ingressum ex navigatione in portum; qui moriuntur antecedere nos brevi secuturos solutosque corporibus agitaturos in caelis aevum, quoad rursus corporibus eisdem suo quisque, non tamen pressi ac gravati ut nunc, sed induti tantum et leviter amicti, commutata mortalitate in immortalitatem, vita fruemur et beata et sempiterna. Hisce verbis iubet nos Paulus consolari invicem. Haec est germane et solide Christiana consolatio cum non diremptos amicos amici superstites cogitabunt, sed praemissos tantum in eum locum ubi paucis diebus post laetissime congressuri sint, si modo dederint operam ut quo illos profectos et credunt et sperant ipsi quoque exercitamentis virtutum perveniant. Hoc decet Christianos sacerdotes recentibus viduis praecipere, his consolationibus aegros animos refovere; non quod quidam faciunt, in funebri epulo praebibere viduae et iubere bono esse animo; non defuturum qui illam ducat, se iam animo maritum illi prospexisse. Sed quae possunt alia bene madidi inter epulas et pocula eructare?

CAP. II. DE FUNERE MARITI

8. Ut alia permulta sic et istud ex gentilitate in Ecclesia remansit, celebrari funera magna pompa. Illi enim animas intumulatorum corporum graves apud inferos perferre poenas superstitiose credebant et pompa exsequiarum gloriam tum illi, tum posteris eius acquiri autumabant. Sed nec inter eos defuere qui haec vana esse non dissimularint. Vergilius persona Anchisae, sapientissimi (ut videri vult) viri, facilem sepulcri iacturam esse ait. Et Lucanus:

---

7. (induti ... immortalitatem) *Vulg. I Cor. 15, 53*
8. (facilem sepulcri iacturam) *Verg. Aen. 2, 646* //

2–3 reposcet Γ reposcat **H** // 7 et iustitia Γ *deest in* **H** // 8 sua morte Γ morte sua **H** // 8–10 deleto per sanguinem ... nisi ille subvenisset Γ *deest in* **H** // 13–14 commutata ... immortalitatem Γ *deest in* **H** // 20 praecipere Γ inculcare **H** // 21 epulo Γ convivio **H** // 29 acquiri Γ parari **H** // 30 esse non dissimularint Γ crederent **H**

7. The wise woman will therefore reflect that all mortals were born and live under this law, that they must render their debt to nature as to a creditor whenever it shall demand it back. Some sooner, some later, we are all bound by a common lot of being born, living and dying. Our souls are immortal and this life is a point of departure for that other eternal and blissful existence for those who have spent this temporary life in a holy and pious manner. This is made very easy by the Christian religion not through our merits but through the goodness and justice of him who loosed us from the bonds of death by his death, nullifying by his blood the decree of the Father by which the whole human race was condemned to death unless he had come to its rescue. Death is the entrance into the port from a voyage at sea. Those who die precede us, who are soon to follow. Liberated from our bodies, we will lead a life in heaven until we will again be clothed with those same bodies, not weighed down and oppressed as now, but as if clad in light garments, exchanging mortality for immortality, we will enjoy everlasting happiness. With these words Paul bids us to console one another. This is genuine and lasting Christian consolation, when those who survive the death of their friends will not think that they have been taken away but that they have been sent ahead to that place where they shall soon be happily reunited with them, if they but apply themselves by the exercise of virtue to arrive where they believe and hope their friends have arrived. This is what Christian priests should preach to those who have recently become widows. With such consolations they should restore their sinking spirits, not as some others do, who toast the widow at the funeral banquet and bid her be of good cheer, assuring her that she will not lack suitors and that they already have someone in mind as her future spouse. But what else do you expect those who have drunk and eaten their fill at a banquet to disgorge?

CHAPTER II.   ON THE HUSBAND'S FUNERAL

8. As in so many other things, so in the great pomp attending funeral celebrations vestiges of paganism have remained in the Church. The pagans superstitiously believed that the souls of those whose bodies were unburied would suffer great torment in the underworld, and they thought that by the pomp of the funeral procession they could acquire glory for the dead man and his posterity. But even among them there were not lacking those who did not conceal their belief that such practices were of no avail. Virgil in the person of Anchises, a wise man, as Virgil depicts him, said the loss of a burial was a small thing. And Lucan said:

> placido natura receptat
> cuncta sinu;

> caelo tegitur qui non habet urnam.

Tum sapientiae assectatores—Diogenes, Theodorus, Seneca, Cicero, sed in primis Socrates— magnis docebant argumentis non referre ubi cadaver pu-
5 tresceret. M. Aemilius Lepidus, qui princeps Senatus sextis iam censoribus erat lectus, paulo antequam exspiraret, praecepit filiis lecto se strato sine lin-teis, sine purpura efferrent; in reliquum funus ne plus quam aeris denos con-sumerent; gloria nobilitari maximorum virorum funera solere, non sumpti-bus. Valerius Publicola et Agrippa Menenius, alter regum expulsor et vindex
10 libertatis, alter publicae pacis interpres ac sequester, tum alii excellentis-simi plerique viri sepulturae honorem adeo contempserunt ut in imperio et maximis opibus versati ne unde quidem funeris choragium conduci posset viventes prospexerint, facturi haud dubie si tantum ipsi credidissent esse in sepultura bonum quantum populus.
15 **9.** Venio ad nostros. Religionis Christianae martyres non putarunt sua interesse ubi exanime iaceret corpus, modo animae esset optime prospec-tum; Christum cum animas reddet corporibus, facile domi suae, quam ipse exploratissimam cunctam habet, etiam tenuissimos corporum cineres inven-turum. Augustinus libro de Civitate Dei primo: 'Omnia,' inquit, 'ista, id
20 est, curatio funeris, condicio sepulturae, pompa exsequiarum, magis sunt vivorum solacia quam subsidia mortuorum. Si enim aliquid prodest impio sepultura pretiosa, oberit pio vilis aut nulla.' Atqui longe aliter videmus rem

---

8. (placido ... sinu) *Lucan. 7, 810–811* // (caelo ... urnam) *Lucan. 7, 819* // (Diogenes) *Diog. Laert. 6, 79* // (Theodorus) *Cic. Tusc. 1, 102; Diog. Laert. 2, 97–103; Val. Max. 6, 2, ext. 3* // (Seneca) *Sen. dial. 9, 14, 3* // (Cicero) *Cic. Tusc. 1, 102; nat. deor. 1, 2* // (Socrates) *Plat. Phaid. 115C* // (Lepidus ... sumptibus) *Liv. perioch. 48, 11–16* // (Valerius Publicola) *Liv. 2, 16, 7; Val. Max. 4, 4, 2* // (Agrippa Menenius) *Liv. 2, 33, 22*
    9. (Omnia ... nulla) *Aug. civ. 1, 16–19* //

6 paulo Γ *deest in* **H**

Nature receives all into her great lap;

The sky covers those who have no grave.

Moreover the great advocates of wisdom—Diogenes, Theodorus, Seneca, Cicero, but especially Socrates—taught with convincing arguments that it makes no difference where the corpse rotted. M. Aemilius Lepidus, who was elected leader of the Senate on six occasions, instructed his children a short time before he died to carry out his body on a bier not spread with sheets or purple and that they should not spend more than ten sesterces on the rest of the funeral. He said that the funerals of great men were ennobled by their fame, not by lavish expenses. Valerius Publicola and Menenius Agrippa, one the expeller of the kings and champion of liberty, the other the spokesman and arbiter of public peace, and many other outstanding men so disdained the honor of burial that though invested with great power and rich in resources, never took thought in their lifetimes about the preparations for their interment. Surely they would have done so if they had believed that burial was so important, as the common people did. I come now to our own times.

9. The martyrs of the Christian religion did not think it was important where their lifeless body lay as long as they had made ample provision for their soul. They were confident that when Christ would restore their souls to their bodies, he would easily find even the finest ashes of their bodies in his home, which he knows from top to bottom. Augustine in the first book of the *City of God* says: 'All these things, viz., the care of the body, burial arrangements, the pomp of the funeral procession, are more a consolation to the living than any advantage to the dead. If an expensive funeral is of any benefit to the impious, then a cheap funeral or none at all will do harm to the

8. Diogenes: Called the Cynic (c.412—c.423 B.C.), flouted all human conventions by his life and teachings. To show his disregard for death he left instructions to either cast him out without burial to be devoured by wild beasts, or to place him in a ditch and throw a handful of earth over him or to throw him into the Ilissus.

Theodorus: Of Cyrene, born c.340 B.C., called 'the Atheist.' He was forced to leave Athens because of his religious and moral views. Cicero and others tell the story of him that when he was threatened with crucifixion by Lysimachus, King of Thrace, he replied that it made no difference whether he rotted on the ground or in the air.

M. Aemilius Lepidus: Ancestor of the triumvir. He became pontifex maximus in 180 B.C., censor in the following year and was *princeps senatus* from his censorship until his death in 152 B.C.

Valerius Publicola: Livy tells us that as consul together with Junius Brutus in 509 B.C. he overthrew Tarquinius Superbus, last king of Rome. In spite of his great renown he was so poor that his resources were not sufficient to pay for his funeral. He was buried at public expense.

Menenius Agrippa: Consul in 503 B.C., he convinced the *plebs* of the futility of secession from Rome, using the parable about the limbs and the belly. He, too, died so poor that his estate could not bear the expenses of his funeral and he was buried by the common people, who each contributed a few pence for the purpose.

se habere neque enim apparatus exsequiarum cruciatum divitis Azoti apud
Evangelium lenivit nec ignominiae Lazaro fuit humi abiectum esse illius cadaver. Ille in inferno male actae vitae pendit supplicia, Lazarus in sinu Abrahae reficitur et mercedem accipit vitae innocenter et pie traductae. Neque
5   tamen haec eo tendunt ut sepulturae prorsus tollantur. Nam et sancti patres
— Abraham, Isaac, Iacob, Ioseph—de sepulturis suis morientes nonnulla
mandarunt et Tobias ab angelo Domini commendatur quod mortuos contumulaverit. Verum enimvero funebrem totum apparatum mortui utilitatem
spectare decet, non viventium. Mortuo autem cum solo Deo res est, qui in
10   defunctis vitae superioris approbat merita ut puram castamque illorum qui
vivunt mentem. Non fastus illi gratus, non opum placet ostentatio, sed sancta
fides ac fiducia in ipsum, tum caritas in genus humanum. Eleemosynam si fe-
ceris accipies et misericordiam consequere misericors. Para et tibi et mortuis
tuis amicos de iniquo mammona, ut in altera vita reperiatis qui vos excipi-
15   ant in aeterna tabernacula. Dominus in Evangelio propter opera caritatis
vel exhibita paradisum reddit vel negata negat. Tum de ratione eleemosy-
nae praecipit, ne fortunas tuas vicinis aut potentibus impartiaris, qui cum
opus sit rependant et velut beneficium faenereris, quae munera merito quidam de saeculo hamata nominavit, ceterum tenuibus et mendicis largire, qui
20   referre gratiam pari munerum genere non valeant, ita demum uberrimam
a Deo mercedem recepturus.

     10. Quanto igitur praestat vestire pauperes extraneos quam divites con-
sanguineos, reficere esurientes profanos quam opulentos sacerdotes et quod
in ceram magnasque sepulcrorum et operosas moles impenditur tenuibus
25   sive viduis sive pupillis et inopi hominum generi erogare! Quanto certius
hinc faenus et uberius! In die fletus tui memineris eorum qui necessitatibus
pressi semper flent. Illorum lacrimae tuis succedent, illorum laetitia te exhi-
larabit, illos reperiet mortuus tuus advocatos patronosque aeterno illi iudici
gratissimos, qui causam suam agant, qui capite periclitanti tam anxie adsint
30   quam in suorum ipsorum periculo. Satis apparet ex his quae dixi quid de

---

9. (cruciatum ... traductae) *Vulg. Luc. 16, 20–25* // (Abraham) *Vulg. gen. 25, 9* // (Isaac)
Vulg. gen. 35, 29 // (Iacob) *Vulg. gen. 49, 29* // (Ioseph) *Vulg. gen. 24, 25* // (Tobias ...
contumulaverit) *Vulg. Tob. 12, 12* // (Eleemosynam ... misericors) *Vulg. Tob. 4, 7–8* //
(Para ... tabernacula) *Vulg. Luc. 16, 9* // (fortunas ... impartiaris) *Vulg. Luc. 14, 13* //
(quae ... nominavit) *Plin. nat. 9, 30*

5 prorsus Γ *deest in* **H** // **10** approbat merita Γ laetatur meritis **H** // **10–11** ut puram ...
illorum qui vivunt mentem Γ ut pura castaque mente **H** // **11** non opum placet ostentatio
Γ aut opum ostentatio **H** // **18–19** quae ... nominavit Γ *deest in* **H** // **21** recepturus Γ
accepturus **H** // **29** periclitanti *omnes edd.* (= periclitante)

pious.' And yet we see that such is not the case. The funeral preparations did not alleviate the torment of the profligate rich man in the Gospel nor was it a disgrace to Lazarus that his body was left unburied upon the ground. The former suffers torment in hell for the evil life he led while Lazarus is restored in the bosom of Abraham and receives the reward of a pious and innocent life. This is not to say that the practices of burial should be done away with altogether, for the holy fathers Abraham, Isaac, Jacob and Joseph gave instructions about their burial as they were dying, and Tobias is commended by the angel of the Lord because he had buried the dead. But the provisions for burial should be directed to the good of the dead, not the living. The dead man has to deal with God alone, who recognizes in those who have died the merits gained in their former existence, as he does the pure and chaste mind of those who are living. He is not pleased by pageantry and ostentation but by holy faith and trust in him, and love for one's fellow man. If you give alms, you will receive them, and being merciful, you will obtain mercy. Make friends for yourself and for your deceased at the expense of the mammon of iniquity so that in the next life you may find those who will welcome you into eternal dwellings. The Lord in the Gospel promises paradise to those who perform works of charity and denies it to those who do not. On the method of giving alms he instructs you not to share your fortunes with your neighbors or with the powerful, who will repay you if the need arises. This would be like lending money at interest, which a certain secular writer justly called 'gifts with hooks attached.' Rather give generously to the poor and needy, who cannot return your favor in equal measure, and thus you will receive in the end a rich reward from God.

10. How much better it is to clothe poor strangers than rich relatives, to feed hungry strangers rather than wealthy priests, and to distribute to poor widows and orphans the great expenditures devoted to candles and magnificent tombs! How much more certain and more copious the interest to be gained in this investment! In the time of your mourning remember those under the yoke of necessity who are always in tears. Their tears will accompany yours; their joy will cheer you. Your deceased will find in them advocates and patrons to plead his cause who enjoy much favor before that eternal judge, and be as present to him in his day of peril as they were in their own. From what I have said it is sufficiently apparent what I think of

---

9. Profligate rich man: Vives here uses the word Azotus, which, if taken as a proper noun, would signify a person from the city of Ashdod in southern Palestine. This interpretation seems rather unlikely. Perhaps Vives confused the story of Dives and Lazarus with the parable of the prodigal son in the preceding chapter of Luke's Gospel, where the Greek word ἀσώτως, with the meaning of 'lavishly' or 'prodigally,' is used. Vives may also have been thinking of the definition of *asotus* given in Cicero, *De finibus* 2, 23.

Mammon: The word *mammonas* used in the Greek New Testament and in the Vulgate is a transcription of an Aramaic word meaning wealth regarded as an object of worship.

viduis illis sentiam quae ut splendide maritos efferant, creditores fraudant
vel legatis non satisfaciunt, cum haec cura oportuerit esse prima. Nihil hic
necesse est disseram quam astringant homines debita, tum sanctitatem tes-
tamentorum quanti conveniat momenti esse. Solidus duraturusque honor
5   funeris in hominum animis situs est, non in pompa iustorum nec tumulo
marmore vel aere aut metallo pretiosiore substructo. Boni viri quamvis hu-
mili sepulturae bene precantur omnes. Magnifica malorum mausolea exse-
crantur, hoc acerbius et odiosius si sciant de inique parata pecunia erecta
esse. Quid dicam si propria vel per vim erepta vel dolo detenta? Tunc nullus
10 dirarum finis et iustarum imprecationum. Mortui debita in illum transeunt
qui hereditate eius crevit; alienum aes quod maritus contraxit naturae, immo
divinis legibus, tam debet uxor quam vir. Quae solvendo est nec dissolvit,
fur est et in mariti voluntatem et in coniugii caritatem ac foedera et in leges
Dei contumeliosa est nec ab humanis legibus libera.

15   CAP. III.   DE MEMORIA MARITI

11. Meminerit vidua et hoc habeat semper ante oculos animas nostras non
una cum corporibus interire, sed exui corporis sarcina et exsolvi vinculis istis corporeae molis mortemque discessum esse ac dissociationem corporis et
animi, animas vero non ita in aliam immigrare vitam ut rebus nostris om-
20 nibus penitus renuntient. Auditae sunt nonnumquam a viventibus et multa
de nostris actibus eventisque cognoscunt vel ex sorte suae beatitatis vel in-
terpretibus angelis qui inter nos et illas crebro commeant. Quocirca oportet
piam viduam existimare non sibi prorsus maritum sublatum esse, sed tum
vita animi, quae vera et expressa vita est, tum etiam sua de illo perenni
25 recordatione vivere. Vivunt enim apud nos vel absentes amici vel corporibus
liberi, si viva illorum imago pectoribus nostris impressa assiduis nostris cogitationibus quotidie renovetur recensque semper vivat in nobis et vigeat. In-
terierunt omnino si leto, hoc est, oblivioni traditi sint. Valeriam Messalinam,
Sulpicii coniugem, interrogabant fratres sui post mariti mortem, cum et ae-
30 tate esset adhuc integra et valido corpore et forma eleganti, nubere iterum
an vellet. 'Minime vero,' inquit illa, 'nam Sulpicius mihi semper vivet.' Hoc

11. (Minime ... vivet) *Hier. adv. Iovin. 1, 46, PL 23, 276*

2 cura Γ *deest in* **H** // 4–5 honor funeris Γ funeris honor **H** // 8 acerbius et Γ *deest in* **H**
/ erecta Γ condita **H** // 9–14 Quid dicam ... ab humanis legibus libera Γ *deest in* **H** //
20 nonnumquam Γ plerumque **H** // 21 vel ... beatitatis vel Γ *deest in* **H** // 22 oportet Γ
decet **H** // 23 sublatum esse Γ periisse **H** // 24–25 perenni recordatione Γ cogitatione **H**
// 29 interrogabant Γ rogabant **H**

those widows who in order to give a splendid funeral to their husband defraud creditors or do not fulfill testamentary legacies, when this should be their first care. I need not discourse here about how men are bound by debts and how important is the sacrosanctity of testaments. The real and enduring honor of funerals resides in men's hearts, not in the pomp of funeral ceremonies, nor in tombs of marble or of bronze or more precious metals. All pray at the tomb, no matter how humble, of a good man; they curse the magnificent mausoleums of the wicked, with all the more bitterness and hatred if they know it was built with ill-gotten money. And what if it was their own money extorted by violence or retained by fraudulent means? Then there would be no end of curses and just imprecations. The debts of the deceased are passed on to the one who was aggrandized by his inheritance. Personal debts that the husband contracted are by divine and natural law incumbent on wife and husband. The woman who is solvent and does not discharge her debts is a thief. She does injustice to the will of her husband, to the love and covenants of marriage and to the laws of God, and is not yet free of her legal obligations.

CHAPTER III. ON THE MEMORY OF ONE'S HUSBAND

11. The widow should remember and have it ever before her eyes that our souls do not perish with the body but are released from the burden of the body and freed from the fetters of this bodily weight. Death is a parting and a physical separation of body and soul, but the soul does not migrate into another life in such a way that it completely renounces all earthly things. They are sometimes heard by the living and they know many of our actions and events either through the privilege of their beatitude or through the intermediacy of angels, who frequently communicate between them and us. Therefore the pious widow should consider that her husband has not been altogether taken away from her, but that he is still alive with the life of the soul, which is the true and real life, and also in her constant remembrance of him. Friends who are absent from us or free of their bodies still live with us if their image is impressed on our mind and is daily renewed and continually present in our thoughts, living and thriving within us. They have completely died when they have been consigned to death, that is, oblivion. Valeria Messalina, the wife of Sulpicius, was asked by her brothers after her husband's death whether she wished to marry again since she was still youthful, healthy of body and a woman of refined beauty. She answered, 'Indeed not, for Sulpicius will always be alive for me.' These were the sen-

---

11. Valeria Messalina: Sister of Valerius Messala Corvinus, married Servius Sulpicius Rufus, a famous Roman lawyer. Some of his legal opinions are preserved in Justinian's *Digest*.

gentilis et de immortalitate animorum incerta; quid Christiana? Ergo memoriam mariti non velut mortui, sed absentis colet vidua maiore veneratione
ac pietate quam fletu. Magnum illi ius iurandum erit per coniugis manes; sic
agat, sic vivat quomodo marito, iam non viro, sed spiritui cuidam simplici
5   puroque et tamquam numini placitura sciet. Illum sibi observatorem et cus-
todem apponat non actionum exteriorum modo, ut antea circumsaeptum
corpore, sed nunc eo exoneratum liberumque ac merum spiritum, conscientiae quoque suae. Sic familiam tractet, sic administret domum, sic educet
liberos ut gaudeat coniunx et bene secum actum sentiat quod talem post
10   se reliquerit uxorem. Ne ita se gerat ut de flagitiosa et scelesta femina irati
manes poenas sumant.

12. Cyrus Maior moriens apud Xenophontem filiis mandat ut ob immortalitatem animi sui cultumque et reverentiam deorum aeternorum memoriam sui pie inviolateque conservent. Sit vero finis aliquis lacrimarum et fle-
15   tus, ne sic nos videamur lugere mortuos nostros ut exstinctos penitus, sed
tamquam absentes. Si tam venerabilem sanctamque esse viduae convenit
mariti memoriam, qua poena dignae illae censebuntur quae maritorum manes maledictis et acerba insectatione prosequuntur? Quae aperte testantur
numquam illos fuisse sibi caros dum viverent, utique nec futuros quibus
20   postea nupserint. Nemo est enim a vitiis immunis et qui non aliquid habeat
quod displiceat. Quisquis eas audit non omnino stupidus, quid cogitare aliud
de eis potest quam non futuras apud secundos alias quam fuerint primis?
Nam de priore amicitia experimentum sumitur ad sequentem. Insanae non
vident et condicionem sibi per eiusmodi maledicentiam difficiliorem inventu
25   reddi, et si rursum matrimonio iungantur, adduci maritos in suspicionem
non minus se illis fore odio quam superiores fuerint. Nam si illos amassent,
numquam potuissent animum inducere ad eum modum de illis et sentire et
loqui quorum desiderio conveniebat et amorem et pietatem esse auctam.

CAP. IV.   DE CONTINENTIA ET HONESTATE VIDUAE

30   **13.** In tradendis vidualis vitae legibus unde melius exordiar quam a Pauli
dictis, qui ad Corinthios scribens, 'Caelibes,' ait, 'curare quae sunt Domini,
quemadmodum illi placeant; coniuges vero quae sunt mundi, quemadmodum

---

12. (Cyrus ... conservent) *Xen. Kyr. 8, 7, 22*
13. (Caelibes ... faciant) *Vulg. I Cor. 7, 34*

5 sciet Γ non ignorat **H** ∥ **6–8** non actionum exteriorum ... conscientiae Γ non actionum
modo, sed conscientiae **H** ∥ **14** conservent Γ servarent **H** ∥ **15** penitus Γ prorsus **H** ∥
16–28 Si tam venerabilem ... pietatem esse auctam Γ *deest in* **H** ∥ **30** tradendis Γ dandis **H**
/ legibus Γ praeceptis **H** ∥ **31** dictis, qui Γ illius, inquam, Pauli, qui se omnia factum
omnibus scribit, ut omnes Christo lucri faceret et in laudibus suis sollicitudinem ponit
omnium ecclesiarum. Is ergo **H**

timents of a pagan woman who had no certainty about the immortality of
the soul. What then is to be expected of a Christian woman? Therefore a
widow shall cultivate the memory of her husband, not as if he were dead,
but absent, with more veneration and piety than weeping. It will be a great
oath for her to swear by her husband's departed spirit. Let her so live and
act in the knowledge that she will please her husband, no longer a man, but
a pure and simple spirit, almost a divine presence. Let her place him as an
observer and guardian not only of her external actions, as he was when confined by the body, but now relieved of this burden, a free and pure spirit,
he will become the guardian of her conscience as well. Let her so deal with
her family, so administer the household, so bring up her children that her
spouse will rejoice and feel that he has been fortunate to have left such a
wife behind him. Let her not conduct herself in such a way that his angry
spirit will take vengeance on a wicked, unprincipled woman.

12. In Xenophon we read that Cyrus the Great as he was dying ordered
his sons to preserve his memory piously and inviolably for the sake of the
immortality of his soul and for the honor and reverence due to the gods. Let
there be an end to tears and weeping lest we seem to be mourning our dead
ones as if they were completely annihilated rather than merely absent to us.
If it is fitting that a widow preserve such a revered and holy memory of her
husband, what punishment will they deserve who pursue their husband's
dead spirit with curses and bitter abuse, and who declare openly that they
never loved them while they were alive and would never love any others
whom they might marry in the future? No one is exempt from faults or
some unpleasant qualities. Whoever hears them, unless he is completely out
of his mind, cannot but think that they will behave in the same way with
a second husband as they did with the first. From a previous friendship we
gain experience for the next one. These demented women do not see that
such evil talk will make it all the more difficult to find a prospective partner,
and if they do marry again, their husbands will be led to suspect that they
will be no less hated than were their predecessors. For if they had really
loved their husbands, they would never have been able to bring themselves
to feel and speak of them in such a way, when in fact their love and piety
should have increased by their longing for them.

CHAPTER IV.   ON THE CHASTITY AND MORAL RECTITUDE
OF A WIDOW

13. In treating of the laws of widowhood where could I better begin than
with the words of Paul who, writing to the Corinthians, said, 'Unmarried
women are occupied with things that pertain to the Lord, how they may

satis coniugi faciant.' Ita maritatam convenit totam de mariti moribus ac
arbitrio pendere, solutam vero marito ad coniugem se sanctarum omnium
feminarum vertere, Christum Iesum. Iam ergo abeat ornatus ille et cultus corporis qui, cum maritus viveret, videri poterat illius oculis tributus,
nunc marito mortuo totus apparatus, tota vita ad illius voluntatem attemperanda qui marito successit, mortali immortalis, homini Deus. Huic vero
sola comenda et excolenda mens est, quam sibi unicam despondet Christus,
in qua acquiescit et deliciatur. At componunt se nupturae. Quae de virginibus diximus huic congruunt loco. Et multo minus decet ornari viduam,
quae non modo ipsa quaerere condicionem non debet, sed ne oblatam quidem vel arripere vel accipere. Invita et reluctans et inevitabili necessitate
compulsa venit ad alteras nuptias proba mulier. Adde quod in virgine toleratur cultus, fastiditur in vidua. Quis enim non aversetur, quae post primum virum adhuc nupturiat ac profiteatur se alterum expetere et repudiato sponso Christo nubit diabolo, deinde homini, simul vidua et coniunx
et adultera? Quanto facilius meliusque condicionem illae reperiunt quae
viduitatem habitu corporis, cultu, et moribus exprimunt. Capiuntur enim
etiam obsceni ac flagitiosi honestate virtusque vel malitiae grata est. Ita ex
iis quae vident coniecturam faciunt si illas ducerent et contingeret sibi prioribus fato defungi, cuiusmodi essent viduas relicturi. Nullus est maritus qui
non et suam mortem ab uxore doleri velit et se desiderari.

14. Sed cum de coniugatis illa tum philosophorum dicta tum apostolorum praecepta habeamus, quid ipsos de viduis sentire par est. De quibus
Paulus ad Timotheum scribit: 'Vere vidua et desolata speravit in Deo et in-
sistit precibus noctes et dies; quae vero deliciatur vivens mortua est. Haec
praecipe, ut irreprehensibiles sint.' Vivere creduntur iis qui et ambulare illas
et edere et bibere et loqui et ceteris vitae muneribus fungi extrinsecus cer-
nunt. Si quis tamen immittere in penitissima viscera obtutum posset seu
potius in arcana mentis, videret peccatricem animam remotam a Deo, vita
sua exstinctam iacere. Hoc Paulus, hoc Ambrosius, hoc Hieronymus, hoc
Augustinus, hoc sancti omnes una eademque sententia clamant: lacrimas,
luctum, solitudinem, ieiunia, ornamenta esse sanctae viduae. Porro, quae
convivia, quos lusus frequentatura vidua esset, quas choreas Paulus ipse
satis explicavit cum insistere illam dixit orationibus die ac nocte. Sic oportet

---

14. (Vere ... sint) *Vulg. I Tim. 5, 5–6* //

1 moribus ac Γ *deest in* H // **4** videri ... tributus Γ poterat illius oculis datus videri H //
5–6 attemperanda Γ attemperanda est H // **11–12** et inevitabili ... compulsa Γ *deest in* H
// **12** venit Γ trahitur H // **12–13** toleratur cultus Γ cultus toleratur H // **13** fastiditur in
vidua Γ in vidua fastiditur H // **14** adhuc nupturiat ac Γ *deest in* H // **14–15** repudiato Γ
abiecto H // **15** coniunx Γ coniugata H // **18** obsceni ac Γ *deest in* H / virtusque ... Ita
Γ *deest in* H // **20** defungi Γ fungi H // **29** mentis Γ pectoris et mentis H // **34** explicavit
Γ indicavit H

please him; married women are concerned with the things of the world, how to please their spouse.' Therefore it behooves the married woman to be totally dependent on the dispositions and wishes of her husband, but when she no longer has a husband, she should turn to the holy spouse of all women, Jesus Christ. All that adornment and personal care should now be gone, which while the husband was living might have been seen as a desire to please him, but now that he is gone all display and all of her life should be adjusted to the will of him who succeeded her husband, an immortal in the place of a mortal, God in the place of man. For him it is the mind alone that must be adorned and embellished for it is this that Christ espouses for himself alone and in which he finds delight and satisfaction. 'But those who intend to marry look after their appearance' someone may say. What I said of virgins is applicable here. A widow should adorn herself much less, since she should not be seeking a match and should not readily accept it when it is offered. A good woman approaches a second marriage unwillingly and reluctantly, compelled by unavoidable necessity. Besides, in a virgin personal adornment is tolerated, in a widow, it is repugnant. Who would not feel aversion for a woman who after having one husband still yearns to re-marry and proclaims openly that she is looking for another, and in repudiation of her spouse, Christ, marries first the devil, then a man, thus becoming widow, wife and adulteress all at once? How much more easily those women who express their widowhood in their bearing, dress and demeanor find a new match. Even depraved and dishonorable men are attracted by good morals, and virtue is pleasing even to malice. From what they see they conjecture if they were to marry them and had the ill-fortune to die first, what kind of widow they would leave behind them. There is no husband who does not wish his death to be mourned by his wife and that he be missed.

14. But since we have the sayings of the philosophers and the teachings of the Apostles on married women, it is reasonable to hear what their feelings are about widows. Of them Paul writes to Timothy: 'She who is a real widow, left alone, has put her hope in God and perseveres in prayer night and day, whereas she who is self-indulgent is dead even though she lives. Give these commands so that they may be above reproach.' Those who see them walking, eating, drinking and talking and performing the other external functions of life think they are alive. But if one could fix his gaze on their inmost organs or rather peer into the secrets of their mind, he would see a sinful soul estranged from God lying there lifeless. Ambrose, Jerome, Augustine, and all the saints reiterate this same thought: that tears, mourning, solitude, fasts are the adornments of the pious widow. Paul himself made it sufficiently clear what banquets, diversions and dances a widow should frequent when he said that she should persevere in prayer day and night. When

sublato iam mortali marito cum immortali versari otiosius et liberius, confabulari crebrius et suavius. Apertius eloquar: oportet viduam tum attentius orare tum frequentius, ieiunare longius, sacrificio sacrisque contionibus multam adesse, legere studiosius et se in comtemplationem efferre eorum quae vitam moresque meliores reddant.

15. Anna, Phanuelis filia de tribu Aser, quae annos septem a virginitate sua cum viro marito exegerat, post octoginta quattuor viduitatis annos a Christo Domino in templo reperta est, unde non discedebat, ieiuniis et precibus diebus atque noctibus sedula et intenta. Plures et maiores in vidua quam in coniugata virtutes exigimus. Haec enim accommodare se mortalis viri arbitrio debet cui nupta vivit et divisa est inter virum et Deum; illa vero immortalem accepit coniugem Christum. Unde fas est ut praestantiora iam sint omnia et tanto marito congruentia. Nec divisa est, sed cuncta illi uni vacare, ut debet, ita et potest. Verba pudiciora sint et modestiora siquidem speculum solet esse oratio animi et morum uniuscuiusque. Vetus dictum est: 'Qualis vita, talis oratio.' Nocent etiam cogitationibus spurca verba. 'Corrumpunt mores bonos collocutiones malae,' quod ex Menandro Paulus Apostolus ait.

16. Non modo viduae verba eiusmodi velim esse quae incorrupte casteque quae sit opus enuntient, sed quae vel mores audientium instituant eruditione, emendent exemplo, quatenus est quoddam orationis genus ab homine profectum qui magnam prudentiam magnae probitati adiunxit; quod cum ad exprimendos tantum animi conceptus tendere videatur, obiter tamen eruditionem instillat et excolit mores. Neque vero quod viduata coniuge humani matrimonii legibus soluta est ideo nihil sibi crediderit non licere. Saepenumero ostendunt viduae quales in connubio fuerint et retegunt licentia viduitatis quod celabant mariti metu, ut aviculae caveis liberatae ilico ad ingenium redeunt. Huiusmodi viduas devitari Apostolus praecipit, quae condemnationem prae se ferunt, quod primam fidem irritam fecerunt. Multae enim vitia utcumque in coniugio dissimulata impetu effundunt, adempto viri obice quo cohibebantur. Tum demum intelligitur qualis sit vel natura vel moribus femina, cum tantum licere potest quantum libeat. Nam sicut Hieronymus inquit: 'Illa vere pudica dicenda est cui licuit peccare, si voluit.' Cui enim sola defuit occasio, huic omnia adfuerunt ad impudicitiam.' Nunc oportet circumspectius agere feminam quando vitia omnia ipsi imputantur,

---

15. (Anna ... intenta) *Vulg. Luc. 2, 36–38* // (Corrumpunt ... malae) *Vulg. I Cor. 15, 33; Men. Sent. 803 (ed. Jaekel, p.79)*
16. (Illa ... voluit) *Hier. adv. Iovin. 1, 47, PL 23, 277*

9 sedula et Γ *deest in* **H** // **11** et divisa ... Deum Γ *deest in* **H** // **13–14** Nec ... potest Γ *deest in* **H** // **15** dictum est Γ est verbum **H** // **17** quod Γ ut **H** // **23** et excolit mores Γ et virtutem **H** // **27–28** Huiusmodi ... fecerunt Γ *deest in* **H** // **28–29** Multae enim Γ Sic multae **H** // **31** libeat Γ libet **H** // **32** voluit *Hier.* **H** noluit Γ

her mortal husband has been taken away, the widow should have more time to pass at leisure with her immortal spouse, to speak to him more frequently and more intimately. To make myself clear, the widow should pray more frequently and with greater devotion, fast longer, attend mass and sacred functions, read more diligently, and turn her thoughts to those things that improve life and morals.

15. Anna, the daughter of Phanuel of the tribe of Aser, who had lived seven years with her husband, was found by Christ the Lord in the temple after eighty-four years of widowhood. She never departed from there, diligently intent on prayer and fasting day and night. We require more and greater virtues of a widow than we do of a married woman. The latter must adapt herself to the will of a mortal man to whom she is married, and she is divided between God and man. The former has received Christ as her immortal spouse, and therefore everything must be of a higher order befitting such a spouse. She is not divided but she can and must devote herself entirely to him. Her words must be more chaste and more modest inasmuch as speech is the mirror of the soul and character of every person. The old saying has it: 'As is your life, so is your speech.' Filthy words are detrimental to our thoughts. 'Evil conversations corrupt good morals,' Saint Paul says, quoting Menander.

16. I wish not only that a widow's words express her meaning chastely and honestly but that they instruct and correct those who hear them by their learning and example, for there is a certain type of speech that men utter which joins great wisdom with great goodness. Though it seems only to express the concepts of the mind, it also instills learning at the same time and reforms morals. A woman widowed of her husband should not think that she is exempt from the laws of human marriage and may do whatever she pleases. Often widows show what they were like when married and in the freedom of widowhood reveal what they concealed from fear of their husband, as birds freed from the cage immediately return to their true nature. The Apostle teaches that such widows should be avoided, since they publicize their own guilt, rendering their first vows void. Many women give free vent in a sudden outpour to the vices dissembled during their marriage, now that the obstacle posed by their husband has been removed. A woman can be seen for what she is by nature and in character when she is free to do whatever she pleases. As Jerome said: 'The truly chaste woman is the one who could have sinned if she wished. But the one to whom only the opportunity was lacking is always prepared for unchastity.' As a widow a woman must act more circumspectly since all vices are imputed to her, just as all

ut virtutum laus penes eam solam manet, quippe maritus dum viveret, utro-
rumque magnam partem in se derivabat.

17. In viduitate Christus maritus facile aderit volenti sancte vivere illique
acceptum referendum est si quid boni exit; nobis vero, si secus. Et quem-
5   admodum in proba uxore deliciae omnes collocatae sunt viro, sic credi vix
possit ut cara, ut iucunda est Christo quae vere viduam praestat, hoc est, cui
in hac vita desolatae tota spes ac fiducia, deliciae cunctae et voluptates sunt
in Christo. Huiusmodi praecipit Paulus etiam ab episcopis haberi in pretio.
Multa enim per earum preces impetrat Ecclesia a Christo. Talis meruit in-
10 ter primas cernere in templo Christum et de illo iis qui aderant vaticinari.
Talis et laudatur testimonio Dei et commendatur nobis iussis illius. Nam
per Isaiam ait: 'Iudicate pupillum et iustificate viduam.' Rursus in psalmo,
de Christo Domino: 'Pupillum et viduam suscipiet.' Et in Exodo: 'Viduae
et pupillo non nocebitis; si laeseritis eos, vociferabuntur ad me et ego au-
15 diam clamorem eorum et indignabitur furor meus percutiamque vos gladio
et erunt uxores vestrae viduae, filii vestri pupilli.'

CAP. V.   QUOMODO AGENDUM DOMI

18. Etsi frequentem in templo, assiduam in orationibus voluerunt sancti esse
viduam, humanarum tamen rerum curae non exemerunt. Doctor ecclesia-
20 rum de viduis loquens ad Timotheum: 'Si qua vidua filios aut nepotes habet, discat primum propriam domum pie tractare et vicem reddere pro-
genitoribus.' Haec doceat vidua, haec discant filii, haec nepotes modeste se
gerere et pie parentibus obsequi. Plerumque id videmus evenire ut sub vidua
educati minus iis quibus oportet pareant, corrupti nimia viduae indulgen-
25 tia, ita ut in proverbium apud aliquas gentes et potissimum nostram abierit:
'Alumnus viduae,' de male educatis adolescentibus, de iuventute corrupta,
praeferoci et perditis vitae rationibus. Consulerem feminae viduae ut curam
educationis liberorum probo alicui et gravi mandaret viro. Nam ipsa amore

---

17. (Paulus ... pretio) *Vulg. I Tim. 5, 5* // (Talis ... vaticinari) *Vulg. Luc. 2, 36–38*
// (Iudicate ... viduam) *Vulg. Is. 1, 17* // (Pupillum ... suscipiet) *Vulg. psalm. 146, 9* //
(Viduae ... pupilli) *Vulg. ex. 22, 22–24*
    18. (Si qua ... progenitoribus) *Vulg. I Tim. 5, 4* //

2 derivabat Γ trahebat **H** // 4 exit Γ agimus **H** // 5 collocatae Γ sitae **H** // 7–8 voluptates
sunt in Christo Γ voluptates in Christo **H** // 9 impetrat Ecclesia Γ impetratur Ecclesiae **H**
// 11–12 Nam per Isaiam ... in psalmo Γ In psalmo centesimo tricesimo Dominus ait: 'Viduam eius benedicens benedicam' et per Ezaiam: 'Iudicate pupillum et iustificate viduam.'
Rursus in alio psalmo **H** // 19 exemerunt Γ subtraxerunt **H** // 19–20 Doctor ecclesiarum Γ Apostolus Paulus **H** // 26 Alumnus viduae Γ Viduae alumnus **H** / adolescentibus
Γ iuvenibus **H** // 26–27 iuventute ... rationibus Γ praeferocibus et perditis **H**

praise of virtue remains solely with her, for while her husband was alive, a great part of the responsibility for both vice and virtue was attributed to him.

17. In widowhood Christ the spouse will give his help to one who wishes to live a holy life and to him must be attributed any good that is produced and to us any evil. And just as a man places all his joy in a good wife, so it can hardly be imagined how dear and agreeable to Christ is the woman who shows herself a true widow, that is, one who, left alone in this life, puts all her hope and confidence, all her joys and pleasures in Christ. Of such a woman Paul teaches that she is held in much esteem even by bishops, for the Church obtains many things from Christ through their prayers. Such a woman merited to be among the first to see Christ in the temple and to make prophecies about him to those who were present. Such a woman is praised by the testimony of God and is commended to us by his command, for he said through Isaiah: 'Seek justice for the orphan, and defend the widow.' Again in the psalm, concerning Christ the Lord: 'He will shelter the orphan and the widow.' And in Exodus: 'You shall not harm a widow or an orphan. If you do harm to them, they will cry out to me, and I shall hear their cry. And my wrath will be kindled and I shall strike you with the sword, and your wives shall become widows and your children orphans.'

CHAPTER V.   HOW THEY SHOULD CONDUCT THEMSELVES AT HOME

18. Although saintly men have wished that the widow visit the church frequently and be assiduous in prayer, they did not exempt her from practical concerns. The Doctor of the Church speaking to Timothy about widows said: 'If a widow has children or grandchildren, let her first teach them their religious duty to their own family and to make some return to their parents.' The widow should teach these lessons and her children and grandchildren should learn to behave modestly and show loyalty to their parents. We often see it happen that those brought up by a widow are less obedient than they should be to those to whom they owe obedience, spoiled by the excessive indulgence of the widow, so that the expression 'A widow's child' has become a proverb among many peoples, especially our own. It is used of young men who are badly brought up, of corrupt, insolent youths who lead a morally depraved life. I should counsel a widow to place the care of the upbringing of her children in some virtuous and sensible man, for out of

18. A widow's child: This proverb is cited in Francesc Eiximenis, *Lo llibre de les dones* ed. Frank Naccarato, rev. Curt Wittlin (Barcelona, 1981), I, ch. C, p. 153: 'Mas les viudes solen mal nudrir lus infans, en tant que infant mal nudrit es apellat nodrit de viuda comunament.' For Eiximenis cf. *De inst.* vol. I, p. xxv.

caeca nimium se putat severe tractare filios, etiam quando maxime indulget.
Non quin fuerint sapientissimae aliquot viduae quae filios prudentissime et
optime educarint, velut Cornelia, quae Gracchos, et Veturia, quae Mar-
cium Coriolanum, ut hic quicquid praeclare gereret in re publica sive domi
5   sive foris, hoc stimulo pungeretur atque excitaretur ut se matri atque edu-
catrici suae approbaret.

    19. Quemadmodum instituendi sint liberi dixi volumine superiore. Illinc
petat vidua quae ad curam hanc facere existimet. De familia idem Apostolus inquit: 'Si quis (et consequenter si qua vidua) suis et maxime familia-
10   ribus non prospicit, fidem abnegavit et est infideli peior.' Ceterum ne ipsa,
praesertim si sit adhuc aetate non mala, admiscendam se habeat turbae fa-
mulorum, audiat quid Divus Hieronymus suadeat Salvinae: 'Tenera,' inquit, 'res in feminis fama pudicitiae est et quasi flos pulcherrimus cito ad
levem marcescit auram levique flatu corrumpitur, maxime ubi et aetas con-
15   sentit ad vitium et maritalis deest auctoritas, cuius umbra tutamen uxoris
est. Quid facit vidua inter familiae multitudinem, inter ministrorum greges?
Quos nolo contemnat ut famulos, sed ut viros erubescat. Certe si ambi-
tiosa domus haec officia flagitat, praeficiat his senem honestis moribus, cuius
honor dominae dignitas sit. Scio multas clausis ad publicum foribus non
20   caruisse infamia servulorum, quos suspectos faciebat aut cultus immodera-
tus aut crassi corporis nitor aut aetas apta libidini aut ex conscientia amoris
occulti securus animi tumor, qui etiam bene dissimulatus frequenter erumpit
in publicum et conservos quasi servos despicit.' Haec sunt Hieronymi verba.

    20. Quibus hoc addo, ut et famulitium minuat vidua, virorum praeser-
25   tim, et sibi grandiorem natu feminam adiungat probam prudentemque sub
qua vivat, quam de rebus quae ad muliebrem curam pertinent consulat. Si
ipsa gravis annis iam sit, senem asciscat consanguineum vel affinem cui fidat.
Denique consilio semper utatur viri quem sciat prudentia valere et rebus suis

---

18. (Veturia ... Coriolanum) *Val. Max. 5, 4, 1*
19. (Si quis ... peior) *Vulg. I Tim. 5, 8* // (Tenera ... despicit) *Hier. epist. 79, 8, PL 22,*
730

9 Si quis ... vidua **Γ** Si qua vidua **H** // **12** suadeat Salvinae **Γ** Salvinae suadeat **H** // **16**
vidua **HWW²** *deest in* **BV** // **26** quae ... pertinent **Γ** mulierum **H**

blind love she thinks she is treating her children too severely even when she is far too lenient with them. Not that there were not some very wise widows who brought up their children very well and wisely, such as Cornelia with the Gracchi and Veturia with Marcius Coriolanus, who in all his glorious deeds for the republic, at home or abroad, was goaded and inspired by the incentive to win the approval of his mother and the one who brought him up.

19. I have spoken in the previous book of how children should be instructed. The widow may seek there what she should do in this regard. Concerning the family the Apostle said: 'If anyone (and consequently any widow) does not take care of his own, especially those of his family, he has renounced the faith and is worse than an unbeliever.' But she should not, especially if she is still of a comely age, mix too freely with the members of her household, hearkening to the words of St. Jerome to Salvina:

> The reputation of chastity is a delicate matter with women, and like a beautiful flower it quickly withers at the slightest breeze and is damaged by the slightest breath of wind. This is especially true when the woman is at an age prone to vice and the husband's authority is absent, whose shadow is a wife's protection. What business has she among the crowd of the household and the flocks of servants? I do not wish that she look down upon them as servants but that she feel shame in their presence as men. In any event, if her pretentious house requires these services, let her put an elderly man of good morals in charge of them, one who bases his honor on the esteem of his mistress. I know that many women, even though the doors of their house were closed to the public, have suffered from the bad reputation of their male servants, who aroused suspicion either by the immoderate care they took of themselves or the sleekness of their plump bodies or their age prone to lust or a carefree haughtiness that comes from the knowledge of a secret love. Even if well concealed this frequently bursts out into the open and he despises his fellow servants as if they were his slaves.

20. I add to these recommendations that a widow should decrease her domestic staff, especially the men, and should hire an older woman, one who is upright and prudent, under whose regime she will live and whom she will consult in things pertaining to womanly responsibilities. If she herself is already well advanced in years, then let her take to herself an old kinsman of the family in whom to confide. Finally, let her always avail herself of the advice of someone whom she knows to be a man of good sense, who will

18. Marcius Coriolanus: He received this cognomen for his capture of the Volscian town of Corioli, but later turned against Rome and at the head of a Volscian army besieged Rome c.490 B.C. It was only at the entreaty of his mother, Veturia, and his wife, Volumnia, that he returned to Rome.

19. Salvina: A lady at the imperial court, whose husband Nebridius, prefect of Gaul, had died. Jerome wrote her a rather stern and outspoken letter, in which he warns her of the dangers of widowhood and counsels her to watch over her son and daughter.

bene cupere et perspecta esse fide. Prisci Romani feminas in virorum potestate semper voluerunt esse, tum patrum, tum maritorum, tum fratrum, tum
propinquorum. Habitabit libentius cum socru aut affinibus quam cum matre
aut propinquis, simul propter mariti memoriam, cui tributum videri potest
quod plus illius gentem et sanguinem diligit quam suum, simul quod in eam
familiam translata est cui liberos vel peperit vel certe erat paritura. Ad haec,
severior quam inter consanguineos creditur esse inter affines pudicitiae disciplina, ubi caritas putatur minor et hinc indulgentia prope nulla et com-
pressior licentia. Sed sancta mulier non adeo his movebitur, quamquam his
quoque, ut mariti memoria ac pietate. Sic Antonia minor, Octaviae et Marci
Antonii triumviri filia, Drusi uxor, cum socru Livia consenuit. Sic Ruth patriam et domum socrui Noemi posthabuit. Nisi forte apud socrum aut affines
sint lascivi aliqui et petulantes iuvenes, qui existimationi maculam, castitati
periculum afferre possint, vel affines ipsae mulieres haud prorsus honeste
audiant. Tunc enim ad consanguineos migrare consultius fuerit.

CAP. VI.   QUOMODO FORIS

21. Prodeundum erit quandoque domo. Id faciant contectae et re ipsa osten-
dentes quod nomine praeferunt. Vidua enim et Graece et Latine quasi desolata et deserta dicitur. Multum ergo inter solam et comitatam viro intererit.
Si tantam et morum severitatem et cultus ab uxore exegimus, quid facturi
existimamur in viduis? Exemplum oportet illas esse continentiae, frugalitatis,
pudicitiae. Si exemplum, qui conveniet illas comptas instructasque diaboli
armis procedere, ut cum vanitatem animi proferant tum laqueum Satanae
tendant pro exemplo Christi? Optime Sanctus Ambrosius: 'Lugubri habitu
et severa ac tristi fronte premi petulantes oculos, restingui libidines.' Tutissi-
mum erit rarius in publicum exire idque socia gravi aliqua et proba femina,
recta via quo intendas. Templa ne quaeras ubi frequentia sit et celebritas virorum, sed ubi solitudo in qua peccandi licentia sit nulla, orandi autem copia
et occasio amplissima. Cum sacerdotibus ac monachis nihil necesse habet

---

20. (Prisci ... propinquorum) *Liv. 34, 2, 11; Inst. Iust. 1, 8 sq* ∥ (Antonia ... consenuit)
Val. Max. 4, 3, 3 ∥ (Ruth ... posthabuit) *Vulg. Ruth 1, 16*
   21. (Lugubri ... libidines) *Ambr. vid. 51, PL 16, 250* ∥

4 tributum Γ datum **H** ∥ **12** forte Γ *deest in* **H** ∥ **23** ab uxore exegimus Γ in uxore pos-
tulavimus **H** ∥ **23–24** facturi ... viduis Γ futurum in viduis putatur **H** ∥ **26** procedere
Γ prodire **H** / animi Γ animi sui **H** ∥ **30** celebritas Γ celebritates **H** ∥ **32**–p.228,**1** nihil
... versari Γ quid opus est multum versetur **H**

look after her interests and is a man of proven reliability. The ancient Romans wished their women to be always under the control of men, whether they be fathers, husbands, brothers or close relatives. She should prefer to live with her mother-in-law rather than with her mother or her own relatives, both in memory of her husband, to whom it will be seen as a tribute in that she prefers his family and race to her own, and because she transferred into that family, for which she bore or at least would have borne children. In addition, respect for chastity is considered to be more severe among the relatives of the spouse than among the immediate family, since love is less strong there, and hence tolerance is almost non-existent and freedom more restricted. But a holy woman will not be motivated so much by these considerations, although these will also influence her, as by the memory of her husband and her devotion to him. So the younger Antonia, daughter of Octavia and Mark Antony the triumvir, the wife of Drusus, spent her last years with her mother-in-law, Livia. So Ruth preferred the country and home of her mother-in-law, Noemi, to her own. That is my advice unless, living with the mother-in-law or in-laws, there are some licentious and wayward young men who can harm her good name or even put her chastity in jeopardy, or if some of the female relatives have a tainted reputation. In that case it would be wiser to return to your own relatives.

CHAPTER VI.   HOW SHE SHOULD BEHAVE IN PUBLIC

21. Widows will have to go out into public occasionally. Let them do this with their heads covered and showing in their whole demeanor what they profess in name. For the word widow in Greek and Latin means 'abandoned' and 'left alone.' There is a great difference between a woman who is alone and one accompanied by a husband. If we required such severity of character and dress from a wife, what shall we expect in a widow? They must be an example of chastity, frugality and modesty. If they are to be an example, how will it be fitting that they issue forth adorned and attired with the armor of the devil, vaunting their proud spirit and laying the snares of Satan instead of the example of Christ? St. Ambrose said very well: 'Mourning garments and a severe, sad countenance inhibit lewd glances and extinguish lustful desires.' It will be safest to go out into public rarely and then with a good, respectable woman and to go directly to your destination. Do not seek out churches where there are crowds of men, but where there is solitude, in which there is no opportunity to sin but ample opportunity to pray. You need not

---

20. Antonia: Antonia Minor's husband, Nero Claudius Drusus, died at the age of thirty. His father, Tiberius Claudius Nero, was the first husband of Livia, whom Augustus later married.

multum versari. Astutus est diabolus et magno usu didicit qua quisque arte
subverti possit. Facile quod cupit efficit nactus occasionem, quoniam aliud
non habet in quod incumbat. Si quem de pietate consulere vult vidua, deli-
gat senem aliquem cui libido iam emortua sit nec tamen alia vitia renata,
5   non attentum ad rem nec qui assentari in animum inducat pecuniae spe,
solida et sobria eruditione quique tum ingenio tum experimentis prudentiam collegerit, ne aut mentem feminae plus quam opus est constringat nec
frena licentiae remittat nihilque vel antiquius habeat vel carius quam verum
piumque. Ad hunc referat vidua si quid dubitat, ignoret ceteros. Hierony-
10   mus Eustochio sic consulit: 'Si quid ignoras, si quid de Scripturis dubitas,
interroga eum quem vita commendat, excusat aetas, fama non reprobat,
qui possit dicere, "Desponsavi enim vos uni viro, virginem castam exhibere
Christo." Quod si nullus sit talis qui possit exponere, consultius est aliquid
nescire secure quam cum periculo discere.' In foro, in consessu virorum, in
15   turba nihil esse debet viduae; in quibus locis magnum est periculum iis rebus quae viduae commendatissimae sunt: pudori, pudicitiae, existimationi
et sanctitati.
     22. Decet viduam ita agere ut non modo sibi consulat sed etiam aliis.
In publico, sub oculis virorum, multis contrectantibus, paulatim efficatur
20   frons, nutat cum verecundia pudicitia, adducitur utraque in discrimen. Et
si expugnata non est, certe oppugnata dicitur. Et de expugnatione loquitur
quisque non quod verum est, sed quod libet. Iam curae mundi huius ardorem illum caelestium rerum frigefaciunt. Et quod Dominus in Evangelio suo testatur, inter sentes decidit semen, quod praesentis vitae curis solli-
25   citudinibusque suffocatur nec sinitur in optimam frugem excrescere. Ac ut
mare in quod venti incubuere etiamnum sedatis ventis transactaque tempestate agitatur, sic humanus animus, solutus pridem negotio saeculi huius,
illud adhuc animo et cogitatione volvit et post laborem anhelat nec continuo ab opere ad tranquillitatem suam redit. At commoto animo cuiusmodi
30   futurae sint preces vides: anxiae, confusae, caenum mundi istius spirantes,
ut flumine aut fonte turbato non licet puram et liquidam haurire. Quies
animi est quae nos altissime ad divina colloquia sustollit, ut Magdalenam

---

21. (Si quid ... discere) *Hier. epist. 22, 29, PL 22, 415* // (Desponsavi ... Christo) *Vulg.*
II Cor. 11, 2
22. (inter ... semen) *Vulg. Luc. 8, 14* // (Magdalenam ... intenta) *Vulg. Luc. 10, 39* //

2 possit Γ posset **H** // **3** de pietate Γ *deest in* **H** // **9** ignoret ceteros Γ ceteros ignoret **H**
// **13** Quod ... talis Γ Aut si non est **H** / consultius Γ melius **H** // **26** etiamnum ...
tempestate Γ etiam sedatis ventis et transacta tempestate **H** // **28–29** nec continuo ... redit
Γ nec concitatus ad tranquillitatem suam continuo redit **H** // **30** confusae Γ turbatae **H**
// **31** turbato Γ commoto **H** / puram et liquidam Γ nisi lutulentam **H** // **32** sustollit Γ
extollit **H**

frequent the company of priests and monks. The devil is shrewd and through long experience he has learned in what manner each one can be seduced. He easily obtains what he desires when he has found the right moment, because this is his sole occupation. If a widow wishes to consult someone about religious matters, let her choose an old man whose lust is already spent and has not been replaced by new vices, one who is not after his own advantage, and does not use flattery through hope of gain, a man of solid and serious learning, who has acquired wisdom through native intelligence and experience. Such a man will not put excessive constraints upon the woman's spirit nor will he relax the reins that curb freedom, and will deem nothing more important or worthy of more esteem than truth and piety. Let the widow have recourse to such a person if she has doubts and ignore others. Jerome gives this advice to Eustochium: 'If you be ignorant of something or have doubts about something in Scripture, ask one whose way of life commends him, whose age absolves him from blame, whose reputation does not condemn him, who can say: "I have espoused you to one man, to show yourself a chaste virgin to Christ." If you cannot find such a man to instruct you, it would be wiser to remain ignorant in safety than to learn to your own peril.' A widow does not belong in the marketplace, in male gatherings, or in crowds. In those places there is great danger for the virtues which are most honored in a widow—chastity, modesty, good reputation and holiness.

22. A widow must behave in such a way as to consult the best interests of others as well as her own. In public, exposed to men's eyes, in contact with many people, little by little she assumes a bold air; chastity and shame waver and are exposed to danger. If she is not defeated in the battle, she is surely under assault. And as far as being under the assault of the enemy is concerned, everyone speaks of it not as it really is, but as he likes. The cares of this world make cool our fervor for heavenly things, and as the Lord bears witness in the Gospel, if the seed falls among thorns and is suffocated by the cares and anxieties of this life, it cannot grow to fruition. And as the sea that has been stirred up by the winds is still in agitation after they have subsided and the storm is passed, so the human mind, freed from the affairs of this world, returns to it in feeling and thought and is still breathless after its labors and cannot return immediately to its usual tranquility. When the mind is disturbed you see what kind of supplications it will make—anxious, confused, smelling of the mud of this world—just as one cannot draw clear and limpid water from a turbid spring. Peace of mind is that which elevates us to colloquies with the divine, as it did with Mary Magdalen, who put

---

21. Eustochium: (368–418). With her mother mother Paula, a Roman noblewoman, she was given spiritual guidance by St. Jerome. She and her mother followed the saint to the East and directed several convents in Bethlehem. Jerome's letter to her is a long treatise on virginity.

illam quae nuntio rebus humanis misso sédebat iuxta Domini pedes, verbis illius intenta. Idcirco Christi elogio commendatur quod optimam elegerit partem quae numquam ab ipsa auferetur. At dicet aliqua, 'Periclitatur patrimonium; intenditur mihi lis.' De illo audi Ambrosium: 'Ne dixeris, "Sola ego
5 sum." Castitas solitudinem quaerit, pudica secretum, impudica conventum. Sed negotium habes et intercessorem adversarii vereris. Apud iudicem pro te Dominus intervenit, dicens: "Iudicate pupillo et iustificate viduam." Sed patrimonium vis tueri: maius pudoris est patrimonium, quod melius regit vidua quam nupta. Servus peccavit: ignosce; melius est enim alterius culpam
10 feras quam tuam prodas.' Sic ille.

23. Quid quod ita videmus natura nostrorum ingeniorum comparatum esse ut commendatissima sit iudicibus causa illius qui vel infirmos patronos habet vel nullos? Tunc enim in vicem patronorum succedunt iudices, cum contra patrociniis et advocatis minutissimis iudices plerumque adversentur.
15 Scilicet ut nimias opes odimus, sic exiguas tenuesque adiuvamus, ut efferentes se deicere atque deprimere conamur, demissos attollere. Quin etiam sic fere statuimus (sicuti prudens quidam vir dixit) ut in omni certamine qui potentior est, etiam si iniuriam accipit, tamen quod plus potest facere videatur. Idem de patronis putato me locutum quod de iudicibus. Quis omnibus
20 probatior erit illius viduae causa quam viderint pudore impediri ac cohiberi ne ipsa probet. Commendatior eius quae minus commendarit, verisimilior illius quam sanctitati deditam non credunt facile vel retenturam quod suum non sit vel repetituram. Ita sancta femina non litigatoris argumenta in forum affert, sed auctoritatem testimonii et magni praeiudicii gravitatem.
25 **24.** Illa vero loquax et frequens et proinde importuna necesse est obtundat et odio sit et sibi quae diximus patrocinia detrahat. Et haec quidem vel de bonis iudicibus advocatisque locutus sum vel quos ipsa malos esse nescit. Nam sunt quidam usque adeo pravi et flagitiosi ut in his iura non aequitate, sed turpi libidine regantur; in quos publicae disciplinae severitas
30 profecto animadverteret, nisi verissimum esset quod sapiens ille dixit leges aranearum telis esse simillimas: quae minuta animalcula irretiunt, a maiusculis rumpuntur. Ceterum hos, si tales esse non ignorarit proba vidua (ilico

---

22. (optimam … auferetur) *Vulg. Luc. 10, 42* // (Ne dixeris … prodas) *Ambr. vid. 57, PL 16, 251–252*
   24. (leges … rumpuntur) *Plut. Sol. 5, 2* //

---

3 numquam Γ non **H** / auferetur **BV** auferretur **HWW²** // **11–12** Quid … causa Γ Nos etiam uti ignara ne sis volumus commendatissimam esse iudicibus causam **H** // **15** Scilicet Γ Quod naturaliter **H** // **16** attollere Γ extollere **H** // **16–17** Quin etiam … vir dixit Γ Quin et natura iudiciis humanis comparatum est, sicut prudens vir inquit **H** // **28–29** Nam sunt quidam … regantur Γ Nam sunt quidam tam procaces et nequam ut patrocinia et indicia (=iudicia) libidine vendant **H** // **31–32** a maiusculis rumpuntur Γ maioribus caedunt **H**

aside worldly things and sat at the Lord's feet, intent on his words. For that reason she received Christ's praise, that she had chosen the best part and it would not be taken away from her. But some woman may object: 'My patrimony is at risk; a suit is being brought against me.' Listen to Ambrose on this point: 'Do not say "I am alone." Chastity seeks solitude; the modest woman seeks seclusion, the unchaste one seeks company. If you have a lawsuit pending and fear your adversary's attorney, the Lord intervenes with the judge, saying "Seek justice for the orphan and defend the widow." If you wish to protect your patrimony, the heritage of chastity is greater and a widow keeps it better than a married woman. If your servant erred, forgive him. It is better to bear up with another's fault than lay bare your own.'

23. What of the fact that we see that the judge is so disposed by natural inclination to favor the cause of the one who has weak advocates or none at all? In those cases the judges take the place of advocates since they often oppose the most cunning defenders and advocates. This is because we have a natural aversion to great power and wealth and help those with little resources and try to abase and humble those who exalt themselves and raise up the lowly. In fact it is the common belief (as a wise man once said) that in every contest he who is more powerful, even if he is the victim of injustice, seems to be the one who does wrong, simply because he is more powerful. What I have said of judges you may consider to apply also to advocates. To all of them the case of the widow will be a stronger one when they see that she is impeded and inhibited by her modesty from giving convincing arguments herself. The less she recommends her own cause, the more approval she receives. The cause of a woman vowed to a life of holiness is more worthy of belief since they do not believe that such a person would retain possession of or seek after what is not her own. Thus a good woman does not bring the arguments of a litigant into court but the authority of testimony and the weight of a previous favorable opinion.

24. The loquacious, importunate busybody will inevitably pester and annoy her hearers and deprive herself of the protection I mentioned. I have spoken of good judges and advocates or those whom the widowed woman does not judge to be evil. But there are some who are so corrupt and dishonorable that they render their decisions not according to fairness but motivated by shameless lust. The severity of public good order would exact punishment for these abuses except that, as a wise man said, laws are like spiderwebs that entrap tiny insects, but are broken by bigger prey. But if a virtuous widow knows them to be such (their public reputation will reveal them for

enim fama reteguntur), non modo cum certissimo fortunarum damno vitabit
et fugiet, sed cum praesentissimo vitae discrimine. Idem censeat me de quibusvis lascivis libidinosisque dixisse. Porro de circumcursatione et de aedibus alienis Pauli praeceptum est velut inhonoras esse reiciendas eas viduas
5   quae otiosae domos circumeant. Nec otiosae tantum sunt verum et garru-
lae et curiosae, effutientes quae non oportet. Sunt enim quae iam, ut sibi
quidem videntur domesticis suis negotiis perfunctae, alienis impudenter se
ingerunt et velut sapientes suadent, adhortantur, praecipiunt, reprehendunt,
cavillantur; foris mire oculatae, domi caecae.

10   CAP. VII.   DE SECUNDIS NUPTIIS

25. Secundas nuptias reici in totum ac reprobari haereticorum est. Melius
esse continere quam iterum nubere non modo consilium est Christianae
puritatis, hoc est, divinae sapientiae, sed gentilis quoque, id est, humanae.
Germanas feminas (uti recensui) tantum virgines nupsisse scribit Cornelius
15   Tacitus. Et cum aliae maritis in prima iuventa orbatae iterum uxores fieri
noluerunt, tum insignes maxime: Valeria, Messalarum soror, et Porcia Minor, Catonis filia, apud quam etiam, cum femina laudaretur optimis praedita
moribus quae secundum haberet maritum, Porcia respondit felicem et pudicam matronam numquam bis nubere; Cornelia, Gracchorum mater, Pto-
20   lemaei Aegyptii Regis nuptias ad quas post Gracchi mortem ingentibus pro-
missis alliciebatur, recusavit maluitque Cornelia Gracchi esse quam divitis
Aegypti Regina. In scaena et theatris secunda matrimonia exagitantur etiam
mimorum carminibus. 'Habent' inquit 'maledicti locum crebrae nuptiae,'
et 'Mulier quae multis nubit multis non placet.' Valerius Maximus anti-
25   qua referens instituta sic inquit: 'Quae uno contentae matrimonio fuerant
corona pudicitiae honorabantur. Existimabant enim eum praecipuae matronae sincera fide incorruptum esse animum qui post depositae virginitatis
cubile in publicum egredi nesciret, multorum matrimoniorum experientiam
quasi legitimae cuiusdam intemperantiae signum credentes.'

24. (inhonoras ... oportet) *Vulg. I Tim. 5, 13*
25. (Germanas ... Tacitus) *Tac. Germ. 19* // (Valeria ... nubere) *Hier. adv. Iovin. 1, 46,*
PL 23, 276 // (Cornelia ... Regina) *Plut. Tib. Gracch. 1, 4* // (Habent ... nuptiae) *Publil.*
H 311 // (Mulier ... placet) *Publil. M 524* // (Quae ... credentes) *Val. Max. 2, 1, 3*

2 censeat Γ putet **H** // 5 circumeant Γ circumeunt **H** // 6 effutientes Γ loquentes **H** //
6 quidem Γ *deest in* **H** // 7 perfunctae Γ defunctae **H** // 19 bis Γ praeterquam semel **H**
// 21 divitis Γ *deest in* **H** // 24–29 Valerius ... credentes Γ *deest in* **H**

what they are), she will avoid them at all cost even to the detriment of her possessions and at the risk of her own life. The same goes for all lecherous and libertine individuals. As for running about from one house to another, Paul teaches that widows who idly gad about from house to house should be ostracized as dishonorable. Not only are they idle but garrulous and inquisitive, blurting out things they should not. For there are some widows who, when they think they have performed all their own domestic tasks, insolently meddle in the affairs of others and like wise counsellors give advice, encouragement, instructions, reprimands and criticisms; they are remarkably sharp-eyed outside their home but blind when at home.

CHAPTER VII.   ON SECOND MARRIAGES

25. It is heretical to say that second marriages should be totally rejected and condemned. That it is better to abstain than marry again is not only a counsel of Christian purity, that is, of divine wisdom, but also a recommendation of pagan, that is, human wisdom. Cornelius Tacitus writes, as I have mentioned before, that among German women only virgins married. There have been women who were widowed in their early youth but refused to marry again, especially women of great renown: Valeria, the sister of the Messalae, and Porcia the Younger, daughter of Cato, of whom it is told that once when a woman of very good morals, who had a second husband, was being praised in her presence, she replied that a happy and chaste woman would never marry twice. Cornelia, the mother of the Gracchi, refused marriage to Ptolemy, King of Egypt, after the death of Gracchus, although she was wooed with great promises, preferring to remain Cornelia, wife of Gracchus, rather than queen of wealthy Egypt. In popular representations and in the theater second marriages are satirized even in the songs of mimes: 'Frequent marriages give rise to bad report'; 'The woman who marries many men is pleasing to many men.' Valerius Maximus with reference to ancient practices says: 'Those who were content with one marriage were honored with a crown of chastity, for they were of the opinion that the mind of a true noblewoman remained uncontaminated in its essential purity if after losing her virginity in the marriage bed she would no longer show herself in public. They thought that the experience of many marriages was an indication of a kind of legitimate intemperance.'

25. Valerius Maximus: He wrote a handbook of illustrative examples of memorable deeds and sayings, *Factorum ac dictorum memorabilium libri IX*, during the reign of Tiberius. It was very popular during the Middle Ages and is frequently used by Vives in this treatise.

26. Afferuntur nonnullae a viduis causae cur nubere se praetexant velle; de quibus hunc in modum Divus Hieronymus ad Furiam scribit: 'Solent adolescentulae viduae, quarum nonnullae abierunt retro post Satanam, cum luxuriatae fuerint in Christo nubentes, dicere: "Patrimoniolum meum quoti-
5   die perit; maiorum hereditas dissipatur; servus contumeliose locutus est; imperium ancilla neglexit. Quis procedet ad publicum? Quis respondebit pro agrorum tributis? Parvulos meos quis erudiet et vernulas quis educabit?" Et hanc, proh nefas, causam opponunt matrimonii, quae vel sola debuit nuptias impedire. Superducit mater filiis non nutricium, sed hostem; non parentem,
10 sed tyrannum. Inflammata libidine obliviscitur uteri sui et inter parvulos suas miserias nescientes, lugens dudum, nova nupta componitur. Quid obtendis patrimonium? Quid superbiam servulorum? Confitere turpitudinem. Nulla idcirco maritum ducit ut cum marito non dormiat. Aut si certe libido non stimulat, quae tanta insania est in morem scortorum prostituere castitatem
15 ut augeantur divitiae et propter rem vilem atque perituram pudicitia, quae et pretiosa et aeterna est, polluatur? Si habes liberos, nuptias quid requiris? Si non habes, quare expertam non metuis sterilitatem et rem incertam certo praefers pudori? Scribuntur tibi nunc sponsales tabulae ut post paululum testamentum facere compellaris. Simulabitur mariti infirmitas et quod te mori-
20 turam facere volet, ipse victurus faciet. Aut si evenerit ut ex secundo marito habeas filios, domestica oritur pugna, intestinum proelium. Non licebit tibi amare liberos nec aequis aspicere oculis quos genuisti. Clam porriges cibos, invidebit mortuo et nisi oderis filios, adhuc eorum amare videberis patrem. Quod si de priore uxore sobolem habens domum te introduxerit, etiamsi
25 clementissima fueris, omnes comoedi et mimographi et communes rhetorum loci in novercam saevissimam declamabunt. Si privignus languerit et condoluerit caput, infamaberis ut venefica. Si non dederis cibos, crudelis; si dederis, malefica diceris. Oro te, quid habent tantum boni secundae nuptiae ut haec mala valeant compensare?' Haec Hieronymus.
30 **27.** Sed de continentiae laudibus et dissuasione secundarum nuptiarum, quid ipse post Hieronymi torrentem aut Ambrosii dulcem ambrosiam queam dicere? Ex illis petat qui desiderat. Nobis illa in hunc locum afferenda

26. (Solent ... compensare) *Hier. epist. 54, 15, PL 22, 557–558* // (luxuriatae ... Christo) *Vulg. I Tim. 5, 11*

1 praetexant Γ dicant **H** // **29** Haec Γ Tantum **H**

26. Many reasons are adduced by widows, which they put forward as a pretext for their desire to remarry. This is what St. Jerome says of them, writing to Furia:

> Young widows, some of whom have turned back to follow Satan after indulging their sensual desires in their marriage under the law of Christ say: "My meager patrimony is diminishing daily, my ancestral inheritance is being dissipated, a servant spoke to me insultingly, my maid servant ignored my orders. Who will handle my public affairs? Who will be responsible for the rents of my estates? Who will see to the education of my children? Who will bring up my children and my house-slaves?" And—for shame!—they adduce, as a reason for re-marriage the very thing which of itself should have prevented their marriage. A mother does not bring home a foster-father for her children but an enemy, not a parent but a tyrant. Enflamed by her passions, she forgets the fruit of her womb and before her own children, who are ignorant of their unhappy fate, she puts aside her recent mourning and arrays herself as a new bride. Why do you use your patrimony as an excuse, or the arrogance of your servants? Confess to your moral turpitude. No woman takes a husband in order *not* to sleep with him. Or if lust is not the stimulant, what madness is it to prostitute your chastity like a whore so that you can add to your wealth, and that for a worthless and perishable thing a precious and permanent possession, your chastity, is polluted? If you have children, why do you seek to marry? If you do not have any, why do you not fear sterility, which you have already experienced, and prefer something uncertain to the certain loss of your chastity? Betrothal papers are being drawn up for you now so that later you will be compelled to make a will. Your husband will feign illness, and what he wants you to do when you are on the point of death he will do himself, confident that he will survive you. If it should happen that you have children of this second husband, then domestic strife and internal contention will result. You will not be allowed to love your own children or regard them with equal affection. You will have to bring them food in secret; he will be jealous of your dead husband and if you do not hate your own children, he will think that you still love their father. But if he has offspring by another wife when he takes you into his home, even if you have a heart of gold, you will be portrayed as the cruel step-mother, the butt of all writers of comedy and mimes and every rhetorical commonplace. If your stepson is ill or has a headache you will be defamed as a poisoner. If you do not feed him, you are cruel; if you do, you will be called a witch. I beseech you, what great blessing can there be in a second marriage to outweigh all these evils?

27. What can I add of my own concerning the praises of continence and dissuasion of a second marriage after the torrential eloquence of Jerome or the sweet ambrosia of Ambrose? She who wishes can seek it there. It is not for me to cite these passages here, since it is not my purpose to give

---

26. Furia: A friend of Jerome, to whom he wrote a long letter on the duties of a widow.

non sunt, qui non adhortationes ad aliquod vitae institutum scribimus, sed praecepta de illo quodcumque fuerit. Quamquam in hoc auctor essem castae feminae ut in sancta viduitate perseveret, eo magis si filios habet, qui videtur coniugii finis et fructus esse. Quod si in hoc degendae aetatis genere non confidit se vel libidinis stimulos superaturam vel famae loquacitatem sinistre suspicacem, audiendus erit Apostolus Paulus ad Corinthios: 'Dico et viduis et caelibibus bonum illis esse si manserint quemadmodum et ego. Sin vero non continent, connubio iungantur. Praestat enim matrimonium contrahere quam uri.' Et ad Timotheum: 'Iuniores viduas reice. Postquam enim licentiose abusae fuerint Christo, nubere volunt, habentes praeiudicium quod primam fregerint fidem. Simul et otiosae discunt domos circumire; nec otiosae tantum, sed et nugaces et curiosae, loquentes quae non oportet. Volo igitur iuniores nubere, filios gignere, domesticam rem administrare, nullam occasionem maledicti praebere adversario. Sunt enim quaedam quae iam conversae secutae sunt Satanam.'

28. Nolunt quaedam nubere, praetendentes libertatem. Si ea est libertas spiritus ut liberius te cunctam Deo dices sine cura mariti, quis id non probet? Sin vero ut absque reprehensore aut admonitore facias quicquid animo fuerit collibitum, libertas est carnis et occasio non libertatis, sed exitii. Neque est probae ac prudentis feminae indicium postulare ut nullius potestati atque auctoritati subdatur sexus rudis ac infirmus, quem semper humanae ac divinae leges virili potestati ac regimini subiecerunt. Aliae secundas nuptias non amore puritatis ac castitatis recusant, sed gloriae. Quibus non aliud a Christo dicetur quam quod fatuis virginibus: 'Nescio vos,' et quod hypocritis: 'Recepistis mercedem vestram.' Istae a maritis hominibus viduae, vanae atque infrugiferae stultitiae non tam nupserunt quam misere et laboriose serviunt. Videant tamen quae nubunt ne ilico a mariti funere aut post paulum. Id signum est viventes non amasse, de quorum morte acceptum dolorem, luctum, desiderium tam breviter deponunt. Et si quid de domo aut filiis providendum est, curent ante strepitum nuptialem et ante dominium alterius mariti. Nec parentibus, si habent, ius illud in se adimant, quin eis plurimum in quaerenda condicione atque adeo totum deferatur. Neque enim quod virum amiserunt idcirco etiam patrem, et quia mariti legibus solutae sunt, protinus et parentum quoque, quae non minus debent nunc eis viduae quam antea virgines.

27. (Dico ... uri) *Vulg. I Cor. 7, 8–10* // (Iuniores ... oportet) *Vulg. I Tim. 5, 11–15*
28. (Nescio vos) *Vulg. Matth. 25, 12* // (Recepistis mercedem vestram) *Vulg. Matth. 2, 5*

3 eo magis Γ maxime **H** // **4** esse Γ *deest in* **H** // **5–6** se vel ... audiendus erit Γ se libidinis stimulos superaturam, audiendus erit **H** // **7** et viduis et caelibibus Γ in coniugatis et viduis **H** // **8** connubio Γ coniugio **H** // **10** praeiudicium Γ iudicium **H** // **11** fregerint Γ reiecerint **H** // **16–27** Nolunt quaedam ... et laboriose serviunt Γ *deest in* **H** // **27** quae nubunt Γ *deest in* **H** // **31**–p.238,**29** Nec parentibus ... ut sibi pro arbitrio maritum deligant Γ *deest in* **H**

exhortations to a certain manner of life but rules concerning it, whatever it may be. Nevertheless, I would encourage the chaste woman to persevere in holy widowhood, all the more so if she has children, which is the goal and fruit of marriage. But if a woman is not confident that in leading this type of life she will be able to overcome the stimulations of lust or the talkativeness of evil tongues always ready to find fault, let her heed the words of the Apostle Paul to the Corinthians: 'I say to widows and to the unmarried that it is well for them to remain single as I do. But if they cannot exercise self-control, they should marry. For it is better to marry than to burn.' And to Timothy he says: 'Do not accept young widows, for when their natural desires make them unfaithful to Christ, they want to marry again, and so they incur condemnation for having violated their first pledge. Besides, they learn to become idle and go around from house to house, and they are not merely idlers, but gossips and busybodies, saying what they should not say. Therefore, I would have younger widows re-marry again, bear children, manage their households and not give the adversary any opportunity to revile us. For there are some who have already turned away to follow after Satan.'

28. Some do not wish to marry, alleging freedom as an excuse. If it is freedom of the spirit you desire in order to dedicate yourself entirely to God more freely without having to care for a husband, who would not approve of it? But if it is so that you may do whatever you please without anyone to reprehend or admonish you, then that is freedom of the flesh, and the occasion not of freedom, but of death. It is not the token of an upright and wise woman to ask that the inexperienced and weak sex be subject to no power or authority when human and divine laws have always made it subject to the power and rule of men. Some refuse second marriages not for love of purity and chastity, but for vainglory. They will hear from Christ what he said to the foolish virgins, 'I know you not,' and what he said to the hypocrites, 'You have received your reward.' These women, widowed of their husbands, have not become brides of a vain and fruitless stupidity but rather its unfortunate and toiling slaves. But as for those who remarry, let it not be immediately or shortly after their husband's death. That would be a sign that they did not love them when they were alive, since they so quickly put aside their sorrow, grief and mourning. And if they must make provision for their house or their children, let them take care of it before the turmoil of the wedding and before coming under the control of the new husband. And if they have parents, they should not deprive them of the right they have over them and they should give them great power, even total discretion, in arranging the new marriage. For the fact of losing a husband does not mean they have also lost their father, and although they are freed from the laws of their husband, this is not true in the case of their parents, to whom they owe no less now that they are widows than when they were unmarried women.

29. Sancti viri Ambrosii sententiam de hoc habemus, qui in libro de Abraham patriarcha primo sic scribit: 'Mulier si qua amisso marito adolescentula
laqueum infirmitatis suae timet incidere, si vult, nubat tantum in Domino,
ut electionem mariti parentibus deferat, ne appetentiae existimetur auctor
5   si ipsa de nuptiis suis electionem sibi vendicet. Expetita enim magis debet
videri a viro quam ipsa virum expetisse.' Sic ille. In locum parentum consanguinei atque affines seniores succedunt illarumque castiganda est impudentia quae non solum inconsultis iis quibus parentum reverentiam debent,
sed invitis quoque et interdum reclamantibus ipsae sibi maritos inveniunt.
10 Plane testificantur se non tam hoc agere ut carnis incitamentis sine scelere
eant obviam quam hunc virum ad libidinem cum eo explendam appetere,
facturae sine connubio si sine dedecore liceret. Itaque respectui hominum,
non Dei, coniugium praetenditur, ne quis sit qui reprehendere audeat vitium, cui obiectum est sacramentum. Deus tamen reprehendet et puniet
15 cuius oculis nullum obstabit velum, quin vitium ipsum intueatur nudum
apertumque; talia enim sunt omnia ante illum. Si ratio pietatis tantum in
earum valet animis et effugere volunt culpam idque unum quaeritur per
coniugium, nihil debet ipsarum referre quis sit maritus, modo a crimine
vindicet per matrimonium. Et hoc honoris illis habeant quibus caelesti ora-
20 culo iubentur obtemperare, ut cupido sit mulieris, electio parentis. Significet
mulier se velle nubere; pater declaret cui nubet. Quid quod affectu occupa-
tus animus non satis quod e re futurum est dispicit; nam ea est affectus omnis
natura, commovere, concitare, turbare omnia, obscurare veri atque honesti
lucem ut cerni non queat.
25 **30.** Sunt vero liberiores viduae aliquae non propinquorum cura; quippe
sapienter est a vetere populo Romano institutum, apud quem nulla femina
ne privatam quidem rem sinebatur agere sine auctore, in manu esse voluerunt parentum, fratrum, virorum. Sed quibusdam id ab auctoribus suis
conceditur ut sibi pro arbitrio maritum deligant. Hae viros quaerant eius-
30 modi quibus congruum sit viduas copulari: non iuvenes lascivos, ludibundos, imprudentes, indulgentes, qui nec se nec uxorem nec domum sciant
regere, sed virum mediam aetatem praetergressum, sobrium, severum, reve-
rendum, magno usu rerum, cordatum, qui totam domum prudentia sua in
officio contineat, qui sapientia sua sic omnia moderetur et temperet ut hi-
35 laritas quaedam domi sit sobria et pareatur sine contumacia et in opere familia perseveret sine molestia et pura sint omnia atque integra, quoniam
illi haec scient placere cui se uni approbari omnes pluris facient quam toti

---

29. (Mulier ... expetisse) *Ambr. Abr. 1, 91, PL 14, 454*

29–30 Hae viros quaerant eiusmodi Γ Viros quoque eiusmodi quaerant **H** ∥ **30–31** lascivos, ludibundos Γ lascivos, ardentes, ludibundos **H** ∥ **34** moderetur et temperet Γ temperet et moderetur **H** ∥ **36** perseveret Γ sit **H** ∥ **37** approbari Γ probari **H**

29. We have the opinion of Saint Ambrose on this subject, found in the first book on the patriarch Abraham: 'If a woman loses her husband while she is still young and is in fear of falling victim to her weakness, let her marry in the Lord, if she so wishes, leaving the choice of a spouse to her parents so that she will not seem to be driven by desire, if she were to arrogate this right to herself. It should be made to seem that she was sought after by the husband rather than the contrary.' In place of parents older blood relatives or relatives through marriage should be called upon. Widows who find husbands for themselves without consulting those to whom they owe the respect due to parents, or do so against their advice and objections, are worthy of rebuke. They make it quite clear that they are doing this not so much to counter the impulses of the flesh without committing sin as to satisfy their lustful desires, and would do so without marrying if it were possible without incurring disgrace. Therefore the marriage is contracted out of respect for men not for God, so that no one will dare reprehend as a vice that which has the protection of a sacrament. God, however, will reprehend and punish it, since nothing is veiled from his eyes, but rather he sees the vice naked and exposed, as all things are visible to him. If it is only through pious motives and the desire to escape guilt and for no other reason that marriage is sought, they should not be concerned about who the husband is, as long as he frees them from any fault through marriage. And they owe this honor to those whom they are ordered to obey by a divine oracle, that the desire should come from the woman but the choice from the parent. The woman signifies that she wishes to marry; the father decides whom she will marry. Besides, when the mind is seized by feelings of passion, it does not see what is beneficial to it, for the nature of all passion is to stir up, excite and confound everything, to obscure the light of what is good and true so that it is not discernible.

30. But there are some widows who are more free, who are not in the care of their relatives, contrary to the established practice of the people of ancient Rome, among whom no woman was allowed to perform even a private action without a person of authority and who wished the woman to be in the power of parents, brothers or husbands. But it is granted to certain women by their guardians to choose a husband at their own discretion. They should seek husbands proper for widows to marry, not lascivious, carefree, imprudent, complaisant young men, who are not able to govern either themselves or a wife or a household. They should look rather for a man past middle age, serious, severe, respected, experienced, judicious, who by his tact keeps the whole household attentive to their duty, and by his wisdom so regulates and directs everything that a sober good humor reigns in the house, that there is obedience without defiance, that the members of the household persevere in their task without trouble and that everything is clean and intact, since they know that they find acceptance with the one person whom they wish

civitati. Quod si velut coacta ad alteram condicionem pertrahitur vidua, par est ut nuptias occultet quarum est ipsi desiderium turpe, ne id ostentet populo in quo culpam metuit. Itaque secundae nuptiae silentio ac paene clanculum transigentur sine strepitu ac choreis et coniuges acquiescentes consanguineorum affiniumque conscientia alienos devitabunt, ut coniunctos prius audiant matrimonio quam coniungi. Nemo in foedo suo morbo medicinam sibi adhiberi poscit publice. Nemo, nisi forte insanit, assecutum se praedicat quod expetisse vituperabitur.

DE INSTITUTIONE FEMINAE CHRISTIANAE FINIS

1–8 Quod si velut coacta ... quod expetisse vituperabitur Γ *deest in* H

to please more than the whole city. But if the widow is forced into another match against her will, it would be best to conceal the wedding, the desire for which is loathsome to her, lest she reveal to the people something for which she fears censure. Therefore second marriages should be celebrated in silence, almost in secret, without fuss and dancing, and the spouses, satisfied that the wedding is known to their relatives, will avoid strangers, so that people will hear of the fact of their marriage rather than of their plans to be married. No one with a foul disease asks publicly that medicine be administered to him, and no one, unless perhaps he is insane, claims to have attained something which he will be criticized for having even desired.

END OF THE INSTRUCTION OF THE CHRISTIAN WOMAN

APPENDIX

DE CONIUGIO

1. Non est hic de coniugii vel laudibus vel vituperio disserendi locus neque sunt veteres quaestiones attingendae (velut sitne sapienti ducenda uxor) nec illae nostrorum hominum de coniugio, caelibatu et virginitate et aliae quae ab Augustino disputantur et reliquis nostrae pietatis scriptoribus. Scio non defuisse qui vehementer coniugium sint insectati nec haereticos solum—ut Manichaeos, qui abstinere in totum nuptiis iubebant; quorum error explosus atque eiectus est—sed gentiles quoque qui de toto prope sexu sententiam ex quibusdam malis tulerunt nimis vulgari more; quo de universa gente solemus pronuntiare, cognitis aliquot; sic infames fuerunt Poeni perfidia, Cilices latrociniis, Romani avaritia, Graeci levitate. Deberent honestae matronae odio habere et insectari improbas tamquam dedecus et labem totius sexus. Neque vero sic vituperare ullus ausus est muliebre genus quin rem optimam, auspicatissimam, prosperrimam fateretur esse bonam mulierem et, quemadmodum Xenophon in Oeconomicis inquit: 'maximum ad viri felicitatem momentum.' 'Nihil est usquam dulcius bona coniuge,' ait sapiens Theognes. Xystus in sententiis viri gloriam illam vocat. Euripides tragicus, qui exacerbatus duabus parum pudicis uxoribus tragoedias suas conviciis et maledictis mulierum refarsit dictusque est Graeco verbo feminarum osor, affirmare tamen non dubitat nullam esse tantam voluptatem quantam boni capiunt coniuges. Et Hesiodus, poeta feminarum inimicus, ut nihil infelicius ait viro qui in malam uxorem incidit, ita nihil felicius eo qui nactus est bonam.

2. Solomon ille, propter mulieres dementatus et ex sapientissimo insipientissimus factus, quasi exsecrans facinora sua saepenumero in feminarum reprehensionem magno rapitur impetu, sed ita tamen ut plerumque de quibus sentiat aperte eloquatur. In Proverbiis enim mulierem insipientem et audacem inopem panis effectum iri scribit et ab uxore malefica sic

---

1. (Oeconomicis) *Xen. oik. 6, 11* // (Nihil . . . coniuge) *Thgn. 1225* // (Xystus) *Sext. Pyth. 237 (Chadwick, p.39)* // (Euripides . . . osor) *Gell. 15, 20, 5* // (nullam . . . coniuges) *Eur. apud Stob. 3, 2 (Nauck, p.400)* // (Hesiodus) *Hes. erg. 702*
    2. (Proverbiis) *Vulg. prov. 5, 4*

1 *Hac in appendice caput invenies quod in* **H** *nec non in* **V** *legitur libri secundi primum; quod caput Vives ipse in editionibus posterioribus remotum voluit; itaque deest in* **WW²B**. *Capita libri secundi in hac nostra editione ut numerata inveniunter in* **WW²B** *numeravimus.* // **15** Theognes **HV** = Theognis // **18** capiunt **V** cupiunt **H** // **21** Solomon **H** Salomon **V**

APPENDIX

ON MARRIAGE

1. This is not the place to discuss the praise or blame of marriage or to touch on those inveterate questions, as whether a wise man should take a wife, or those topics treated by our own Christian authors concerning marriage, celibacy and virginity, and other questions disputed by Saint Augustine and the other writers of our holy religion. I know there have not been lacking those who vehemently attacked the institution of marriage, not only heretics, such as the Manichaeans, who required total abstinence from marriage, whose error was condemned and rejected, but also pagans who pronounced judgment on the entire female sex from some evil examples in accordance with that all too common practice of judging a whole nation from knowledge of only a few individuals. Thus the Carthaginians became notorious for their treachery, the Cilicians as brigands, the Romans for their avarice, the Greeks for their fickleness. Respectable matrons ought to hold in hatred and vent their hostility upon dishonorable women as a disgrace and shame upon their whole sex. Yet no one has dared to pour blame upon the female sex without having to admit that a good woman is the best of possessions, bearer of good fortune and a favorable omen. As Xenophon says in his *Oeconomicus*: 'She is the greatest cause for a man's happiness.' 'There is nothing sweeter than a good wife,' said the wise Theognis. Sextus in his *Sentences* calls her a man's glory. The tragedian Euripides, who was exasperated by two unvirtuous wives and filled his tragedies with invectives and maledictions against women and was called a woman-hater in Greek, still does not hesitate to say that there is no greater pleasure than that which two good spouses enjoy. Hesiod, a poet hostile to women, said that just as there is nothing more unfortunate for a man than to find a bad wife, so there is nothing more fortunate than to happen upon a good one.

2. Solomon, who lost his mind because of women and from a wise man became the most foolish of men, as if cursing his own misdeeds, is often carried away with great passion in his castigation of women, but in such a way that he often states clearly what kind of women he means. In *Proverbs* he writes that a foolish and bold woman will be without bread and that

On Marriage: In the first edition (**H**) the second book begins with a chapter entitled *De coniugio*, which is omitted in the revised version, and consequently did not belong to the definitive text as far as Vives was concerned; cf. the critical apparatus at the beginning of the second book. This chapter does not appear in **WW²B**, but it is reprinted by Majansius (**V**) with a few corrections (perhaps they were printing errors in **H**). The numbering of the chapters in our edition follows that of the definitive version.

1. Manichaeans: Once considered a Christian heresy, but more of a religion in its own right, Manicheism was founded by Mani or Manichaeus (216-274). It taught that life in this world is radically evil. The elect of the religion abstained from all sexual contact while the catechumens were allowed to marry but to avoid the procreation of children.

Carthaginians: In Latin the ironic phrase *Punica fides*, literally 'Punic' or 'Carthaginian' faith, was commonly used to refer to their proverbial craft and deceit.

Cilicians: Inhabitants of a region in the south-east of Asia Minor, notorious for their piracy on the high seas.

Two unvirtuous wives: Their names were Melito and Choerine according to ancient lives of the poet.

Woman-hater in Greek: i.e. 'misogynist.'

consumi virum ut lignum a teredine. At in eodem opere quam splendidum est ac gloriosum mulieris probae praeconium de qua inquit: 'Nobilis in portis vir eius quando sederit cum senioribus terrae; fortitudo et decor indumentum sanctae mulieris et ridebit in die novissimo. Os suum aperuit sapientiae et lex clementiae in lingua eius. Surrexerunt filii eius et beatissimam praedicaverunt et vir suus laudavit eam. Multae filiae congregaverunt divitias, tu supergressa es universas.' Haec et alia sapientissimus Rex quae a cordatissimis quibusque magno consensu approbari video. Nam de coniugio quid disputarint ingeniosi homines, seu declamarint potius, non laboro; tametsi docti homines ducendam uxorem praeceperunt, quod et fecerunt ipsi. Septem illi Graeciae Sapientes uxorem duxerunt in primis; deinde Pythagoras, Socrates, Aristoteles, Theophrastus, Catones, Cicero, Seneca; nimirum quod nihil magis viderent secundum naturam esse quam viri et feminae coniunctionem; qua et hominum genus, in singulis mortale, in universis fit sempiternum et id posteris reddis quod a maioribus accepisti ac velut naturae gratiam refers. Aristoteles in libris moralibus ducendam civili viro uxorem suadet, non tantum liberorum causa, sed etiam convictus: ea enim est prima et maxima coniunctio. Ita profecto se res habet.

3. Ex illa communione ac amicitia universali qua cuncti homines ceu fratres ab uno rerum omnium parente Deo derivati continentur, qua nos natura ipsa, quae prope in omnibus hominibus eadem est, inter nos caritate quadam devincit, artior est illa quae inter eos qui eisdem sacris communicant; deducitur in angustius humanis institutis ac iure civili et in cives propensiores quam in exteros sumus. Ex civilibus cariores sunt necessarii; ex istis amantur magis iuncti sanguine; iunctorum sanguine nihil est propinquius uxore, quam primus ille generis humani proauctor primum visam professus est statim os esse ex ossibus suis et carnem ex carne sua. Et cum nondum vel patres essent vel matres, tamen legem tamquam naturae verbis tulit: 'Propter hanc relinquet homo patrem et matrem et adhaerebit uxori suae et erunt duo in carnem unam.' Quis neget sacratissimam rem esse coniugium, quod Deus in Paradiso instituit puris adhuc et integris hominibus nec ulla macula inquinatis, in matre elegit, praesentia approbavit et in celebritate nuptiarum primum miraculorum suorum facere voluit ibique ostendere specimen divinitatis suae, ut declararet ad eos servandos se venisse qui et per sic coniunctos perditi erant et per sic coniunctos nascebantur? Verum hic de matrimonii laudibus non scribimus, quas facundissimi viri magnis saepe orationibus sunt persecuti; tantum sanctam feminam instituimus.

2. (Nobilis ... universas) *Vulg. prov. 31, 23–29* // (Aristoteles in libris moralibus) *Aristot. oec. 1, 3 (1343b)*

3. (os esse ... ex carne sua) *Vulg. gen. 2, 23* // (Propter hanc ... carnem unam) *Vulg. gen. 2, 24* // (primum miraculorum suorum) *Vulg. Ioh. 2, 1–11* // (ad eos servandos) *Vulg. Matth. 18, 11; Vulg. Luc. 19, 10*

15 se res habet **V** res habet **H** // **16** ceu fratres **H** seu fratres **V**

a man is so consumed by a bad wife as wood is by a ship-worm. But in the same work how splendid and marvelous is his encomium of the good woman, of whom he says: 'Noble is her husband at the city gates, as he takes his seat among the elders of the land. Fortitude and dignity are the vesture of a holy woman and she will laugh in the last day. She has opened her mouth unto wisdom and the law of kindness is upon her tongue. Her children have risen up and called her blessed and her husband has commended her. Many women have amassed riches, but you have surpassed them all.' These and other things the wise king said, which I see meet with the universal approval of all wise men. I do not strive to enter into what men of great discernment have discussed or rather declaimed; nevertheless, learned men have taught that one should marry, as they themselves did. To begin with, the Seven Sages of Greece married; after them Pythagoras, Socrates, Aristotle, Theophrastus, the two Cato's, Cicero, Seneca, no doubt because they saw that there was nothing more natural than the union of man and woman, whereby the human race, which is mortal in its individual members, is perpetuated in its totality. In this way you render to posterity what you received from your forebears and return thanks, as it were, to nature. Aristotle in his moral writings exhorts the citizen to marry not only for the sake of having children but also for living together, since that is the first and most important union that exists. And indeed this is the case.

3. Beginning with that association and friendship by which all men are joined together like brothers descended from God, the Father of all things, by which nature itself, which is much the same in all men, binds us together with a certain bond of love, that which exists among those who share the same sacraments is closer and it is made closer still through human institutions and civil law, and we are more prone to establish relations with our fellow citizens rather than with strangers. Among citizens our special friends are dearer to us, and among these, our kinsfolk are more beloved, and of those joined by blood none is closer than the wife, whom that first progenitor of the human race, upon first seeing her, immediately proclaimed she was bone of his bone and flesh of his flesh. And when there were not yet fathers or mothers he formulated a law as if it were a law of nature: 'For her sake a man shall leave father and mother and shall cling to his wife, and they shall be two in one flesh.' Who will deny that marriage is a most sacred thing, which God instituted in Paradise, when mankind was yet pure and untouched and defiled with no stain? He chose it in his mother, he approved it by his presence at the marriage feast and he wished to perform the first of his miracles on that occasion and there to give an example of his divinity to declare that he had come to save both those who were lost through such unions and those who were born to them. But we are not writing here of the praise of marriage, which men of great eloquence have often done in long discourses; we are only instructing the virtuous woman.

I. INDEX NOMINUM

II. INDEX LOCORUM

III. INDEX VERBORUM MEMORABILIUM

SELECTED WORKS OF
J. L. VIVES

General Editor:

C. MATHEEUSSEN

ISSN 0921–0717